P9-DHZ-856

ROBERT M. HUTCHINS

A CENTENNIAL PUBLICATION OF THE
UNIVERSITY OF CHICAGO PRESS

Mary Ann Dzuback

Robert M. Hutchins

Portrait of an Educator

THE UNIVERSITY OF CHICAGO PRESS
Chicago and London

Mary Ann Dzuback is assistant professor in the Department of Education at Washington University in St. Louis.

The University of Chicago Press gratefully acknowledges the contribution of the Exxon Education Foundation toward the publication of this book.

The University of Chicago Press, Chicago 60637
The University of Chicago Press, Ltd., London

Printed in the United States of America
00 99 98 97 96 95 94 93 92 91   5 4 3 2 1

ISBN 0-226-17710-6 (cloth)

Library of Congress Cataloging-in-Publication Data

Dzuback, Mary Ann.
Robert M. Hutchins : portrait of an educator / Mary Ann Dzuback.
p. cm.
Includes bibliographical references (p.) and index.
1. Hutchins, Robert Maynard, 1899– 2. University of Chicago—Presidents—Biography. 3. University of Chicago—History.
I. Title.
LD925 1929.D98 1991
370′.92—dc20
[B] 91–15156
CIP

∞The paper used in this publication meets the minimum requirements of the American National Standard for Information Sciences—Permanence of Paper for Printed Library Materials, ANSI Z39.48-1984.

For my parents, Juanata Childers Dzuback and Joseph Philip Dzuback, for my sisters, Margaret, Jayne, and April, and for my brothers, Joseph and John Childers Dzuback, educators all, with love, gratitude, and hope.

C O N T E N T S

P R E F A C E

When Robert Maynard Hutchins criticized the modern university in the 1930s, many educators cheered. Increasingly specialized academic disciplines, rigid departmental divisions, and scientistically oriented research already had begun to disturb many teachers and scholars. Hutchins' recommendations for reorganizing the university were more controversial. Restoring the classical liberal arts as the sole legitimate study for undergraduates and raising philosophy to its former position as the preeminent mode of inquiry struck many scholars as anachronistic means of solving the problems Hutchins so eloquently described. His prescriptions seemed more appropriate to Aristotle's Greece or to the scholastic universities of the Middle Ages than to the University of Chicago, where Hutchins proposed them, in the twentieth century. They also appeared unrealistic in view of the continuing expansion of knowledge, the hard-won protection of free inquiry, and the widening access to higher education among America's young people that also characterized the modern university.

Hutchins published *The Higher Learning in America* (1936) seven years into his presidency of the University of Chicago. What brought Robert Hutchins to this adversarial relationship with the intellectual life of the modern university and what emerged from that relationship in his work as an educator are concerns of this biographical study.

Edmund Morgan described John Winthrop's central problem as "the question of what responsibility a righteous man owes to society."[1] It is a question the Hutchins family passed on to each generation in America. When Robert Hutchins took it up in the twentieth century, he treated it as an educational crusade. "I have assumed," Hutchins wrote in 1956, "that the duty of an educator is to try to change things from the way they are to the way they ought to be."[2] In the process of reconstructing his life and work, one can see that he saw his duty more specifically as trying to change the ways people thought about ideas, principles, and practical problems, enabling them to act more critically and powerfully through the exercise of reason.

Hutchins' attempts to "change things" are extraordinarily enlightening for what they tell us about the politics and culture of the University of

Chicago and, more generally, modern American universities. His arguments and the conflict they aroused illustrate the role of the university in American society: as gatekeeper to opportunity, as legitimator of certain kinds of scholarly work, and as critic of and informer to society. The persistent appeal of Hutchins' reasoning is obvious in contemporary policy debates about the content and organization of higher education. Proposals making the great books of the Western world central to the curriculum continue to generate conflict in the academic community, as do suggestions that all knowledge ultimately is unified. The resistance Hutchins encountered in the 1930s and 1940s is instructive for these discussions.

Hutchins' tenure as president and chancellor of the University of Chicago is at the center of this study of his life. It is where he defined his ideas about education, developed his criticism of the organization and content of university work, and gained a wide and loyal following among academics and the public. From his efforts at the university came later crusades in the foundation world to change the public's thinking about the media, politics, world peace, law, and education.

Why study Robert Hutchins' life and work as an educator? His contemporaries included many distinctive university leaders. Lotus Delta Coffman of the University of Minnesota, James Bryant Conant of Harvard, Nicholas Murray Butler of Columbia, and James Rowland Angell of Yale established new programs, encountered faculty opposition, and survived the Depression just as Hutchins did. But Hutchins was a star among these men. His personality was magnetic. He was stunningly attractive and quick-witted, a perfect candidate for press coverage and often enchanting in encounters with groups and individuals. He was gifted with powerful oratorical skills, rooted in strong convictions about individual freedom, public responsibility, and Judeo-Christian morality.

Hutchins used this gift to criticize higher education and the development and organization of modern scholarship at a time when increasing numbers of Americans were availing themselves of opportunities to attend college and the president of the United States was recruiting his principal advisers from among them. Hutchins raised important questions about how the structure of the university inhibited the full understanding of the problems scholars studied. He reminded those who were responsible for the education of college students of their moral and intellectual duties not only as teachers but also as scholars. Time and again, he acted to protect the work of students and faculty at the University of Chicago from the intrusions of state officials, members of the public, and trustees of the university.

Hutchins' leadership, occasionally brilliant and often courageous, was also problematic. His policy recommendations presented simple, reasonable, and logical arguments but were curiously removed from the complex cultural reality of the institutions he criticized. His administrative actions on educational policy at the University of Chicago lead one to question whether he had a realistic understanding of the institution and its faculty. His work as a foundation administrator exhibited a marked inability to deal with the complications of human relationships and to establish enduring institutional structures to carry on the kinds of intellectual work he advocated.

Hutchins was an astute, charismatic, and often perceptive man. The people he alienated would also say that he was stubborn, arrogant, distant, and simplistic in his thinking, his speaking and writing, and his actions. His friends would argue that he was loyal, committed, unfailingly courteous, gentle, and kind, though few could claim him as an intimate. He exhibited enormous promise for public service when he was a student at Yale, according to his classmates. Late in his life, his colleagues continued to expect great wisdom from him. As a critical biographer concerned with the context of Hutchins' life as well as his intellectual and personal qualities, I have found fascinating the question of why such promise remained unfulfilled.

For all his brilliance, Hutchins did not develop into a seminal thinker in educational theory and in law, two intellectual pursuits that occupied his attention. He was not a university giant along the lines of a Charles William Eliot, Daniel Coit Gilman, or William Rainey Harper. Probably the time for such giants had passed. Rather, Hutchins was a strong leader who challenged the modern university they had built, inspiring a number of scholars to develop their research and teaching in unique and significant ways. His criticism of the university's structure resulted in no fundamental reorientation of the university in the United States, or of the University of Chicago. Yet his work as an educator to change people's thinking about the creation, organization, and dissemination of knowledge represents a significant moment that merits study in the history of modern higher education.

ACKNOWLEDGMENTS

THIS WORK, WHICH BEGAN as a dissertation, has been significantly revised with the assistance of more people than I can acknowledge. In the process of working on the biography, I found myself alternating between enormous respect for Hutchins and sheer mystification at his arrogance and stubborn adherence to a collection of ideas that seemed incompatible with the realities of twentieth-century higher educational institutions in a democracy such as that of the United States. The portrait that has emerged in these pages is the result of reading and rereading in manuscript collections, weighing and reweighing what I found in light of some excellent primary and secondary material on Hutchins and on the modern university, its students, and its faculty, and talking over my ideas with numerous colleagues, friends, and family.

I am grateful to the archivists and their staffs and assistants at all of the collections used, including Gerald Roberts at Berea College; Pat Douglas at the Center for the Study of Democratic Institutions, and Elizabeth Witherell at the University of California at Santa Barbara Library, Special Collections; Philip N. Cronenwell at Dartmouth College; Sharon B. Laist at the Ford Foundation; Rodney Dennis at Houghton Library, Harvard University (material from the Buchanan Papers is quoted by permission of the Houghton Library); Roland Baumann at Oberlin College; Nancy Bressler at Seeley Mudd Library, Princeton University (all materials from Princeton University Libraries are reprinted with permission); Emily J. Oakhill and Tom Rosenbaum at the Rockefeller Archive Center; and Judith Ann Schiff at Sterling Memorial Library, Yale University. The interlibrary loan staffs at Teachers College, Columbia University, and at Washington University were persistent in searching for literature I needed.

I did most of my research in Special Collections at the Joseph Regenstein Library, University of Chicago. Daniel Meyer was of inestimable assistance throughout the project, offering his wide knowledge of the collections, patiently listening to my ideas, and generously sharing some of his own. Richard Popp and Elizabeth Sage were helpful in digging up obscure facts, and the staff, particularly Linda DeCelles and Carol Mackie, responded to my requests with courtesy and good cheer over the years.

Interviews with Hutchins' friends and colleagues provided a variety of perspectives on him and his activities. Without fail, these people were kind and courteous, some following up with further interviews, letters, or conversations. I thank Mortimer Adler, who opened his files as well as his memories to my inspection; Mark Ashin; Harry S. Ashmore; Preston Cutler, whose insights were very helpful; Thomas I. Emerson; Wilbur H. Ferry, who was most generous with his time and energy; David Freeman; Francis S. Hutchins, whose memories of his family were crucial to my account; Frank K. Kelly; Edward H. Levi; Milton Mayer; Donald McDonald; Florence Mischel; John U. Nef; Elizabeth N. Paepcke, who spoke with welcome candor; Joseph Schwab; and Ralph Tyler, whose balanced perspective was important to my thinking.

Theodore S. Crane informed me about some of the Crane family discussions of Hutchins and sent me in search of useful essays. John Henry Schlegel read a portion of the manuscript and shared his perspective on Hutchins' work at Yale. Ralph W. Nicholas brought me up-to-date on the undergraduate program at the University of Chicago. Barry D. Karl provided astute insights on Hutchins at the university. Edward S. Shils allowed me to read his memoir of Hutchins before it was published. And Adam Yarmolinsky generously sent me a chapter in draft from his autobiography.

My seminar group at Teachers College, Columbia University, read and made suggestions on numerous chapters and drafts. Katherine Bordonaro, Deborah DeSimone, Stacy Hosford, Sarah Henry Lederman, Edith N. MacMullen, Beverly Rubin, Sue Ann Weinberg, and Bette Weneck were also working in biography or institutional history at that time, which made their critiques particularly helpful.

Other colleagues and friends have generously read and commented on the manuscript, often with painstaking care. I appreciate the critical readings the anonymous reviewers of the *History of Education Quarterly*, the *American Journal of Education*, and the University of Chicago Press gave to parts or all of the manuscript. Many of their suggestions have significantly improved the book.

Parts of a previously published article, "Hutchins, Adler, and the University of Chicago: A Critical Juncture," *American Journal of Education* 99 (1990): 57–76, appear in various chapters here.

Harold S. Wechsler offered a ready ear, much good advice on the college chapters, and tremendous encouragement in the final stages of the project. Leon Botstein's suggestions have been very helpful throughout the project. I shall be forever grateful to him for encouraging me to pursue my own education over the past twenty years, and to Karen, Joe, Patrick, and Beagan Wilcox for helping me to do so. This work on Hutchins has been a significant part of that education, and my experience in an experimental college no doubt contributed to my skepticism of the rationales underlying institutional structures.

The members of my dissertation committee at Columbia University offered many comments that enabled me to reframe my analysis of Hutchins' educational work. Lawrence A. Cremin, Ellen Condliffe Lagemann, Robert McCaughey, Walter P. Metzger, and Douglas M. Sloan read the early effort carefully and commented extensively. Douglas Sloan, supervisor of my dissertation, launched me on the topic of Hutchins, offered good advice about sources and leads to pursue, and wisely left me to follow through on them. He read early drafts of this manuscript and offered encouragement at crucial stages. Ellen Lagemann was a staunch supporter from the moment I entered Teachers College; a research assistantship with her first inspired my interest in the history of education. Her faith in my abilities exceeded my own at times, and her pointed comments about the Hutchins biography gave me good reasons to strive to improve it.

Lawrence Cremin read every word of the early work, commented extensively, and provided me with a research and teaching assistantship. He continued to offer strong encouragement and very critical readings as I pursued the revisions, referring me to new studies that were relevant, reminding me that the work was important enough to keep at it, and helping to remove the occasional obstacle that threatened completion. His endless respect for scholarly integrity and his high standards have shaped fundamentally my understanding of academic work. I am very fortunate to have known him as a teacher and a colleague.

The department of education at Washington University generously assisted in the completion of this project in numerous ways. John Pingree and other members of the staff typed a number of early drafts and helped me to meet various deadlines. My colleagues here, particularly chairmen Alan Tom and Bryce B. Hudgins, were consistently encouraging.

Two grants provided material support in the completion of the biography. A Spencer Foundation Small Grant enabled me to conduct further research and, with a Washington University Faculty Research Grant, to set aside enough time to write.

The enthusiastic assistance of the staff of the University of Chicago

Press, particularly John Tryneski's supervision of the publication process, Jennie Lightner's careful copyediting, and Joan Sommers' designing skill, was invaluable.

Finally, the completion of this project owes much to my family. Nicholas and Topher Best were formidable allies in my work; they provided me with ample reasons to take some time off occasionally so that I could return ready to continue. Jean Jennings opened her arms and her cabin on the Umpqua River to me a number of times; there can be few better places to rest. Peter Best read the whole manuscript with a discerning eye and offered countless editorial suggestions. His strength and patience and his love, loyalty, and humor sustained me. My parents and my sisters and brothers, to whom this book is dedicated, were my first teachers. Their great faith in me and in this book and their loving solidarity in difficult times are truly exceptional.

PART ONE *Self-Definition, 1899–1929*

Quick, brilliant, naive, idealistic, committed are all words that have been used to describe Robert Hutchins. He had a magnetic presence, a supreme self-assurance that attracted people to his ideas and programs and, from his youth, marked him as a leader. An exploration of the Protestant evangelical culture of his early life is essential to understanding his rise to educational leadership in twentieth-century American higher education. His ideas about how to lead wisely, prudently, and creatively emerged from this context. The shared language, beliefs, and commitments of the Oberlin College community during Hutchins' childhood were confirmed by the roles his minister father and grandfather assumed. They were augmented by family members whose accomplishments and contributions were recognized by their local communities. His early life was enveloped in this culture.

Hutchins' stint in the Army during World War I and his final two years at Yale were merely patina on a personality profoundly shaped by his family and Oberlin. His standards as a schoolteacher were based on his own education. His oratorical skills as secretary to the Yale Corporation were fueled by the convictions he acquired early in life. His expectations of social science research and his attempts to create an intellectually exciting and ethically acceptable educational program in Yale's law school also were rooted in this evangelical Protestant culture.

The Oberlin of the early twentieth century exemplified for Hutchins the ideal intellectual community. It was a community he would spend his entire life trying to re-create.

CHAPTER 1 *Oberlin Boyhood*

FROM NICHOLAS HUTCHINS, who arrived in America in 1670, to Robert Hutchins' daughters in the 1930s and 1940s, Protestant beliefs and values were an essential part of every Hutchins' upbringing. The Protestant cultural tradition that gave rise to Horace Bushnell's *Christian Nurture* and, later, Washington Gladden's *Applied Christianity* shaped the familial education of generations of Hutchins children.[1] Hutchins family members helped build, and participated in, the widespread Protestant evangelical networks of the nineteenth and twentieth century in the United States.[2] This Protestant culture significantly influenced Robert Hutchins' approach to the world. Mediated in great measure by his family and by the educational institutions he attended, evangelical Protestantism laid the foundations of the ways he sought, received, and transformed what he learned.

Robert Hutchins' family connections indicate the sources of his strong character and the development of the social networks that provided the opportunities he encountered in his youth and early career. Nicholas Hutchins, who settled in Groton, Massachusetts, his son John, of Plainfield, and his grandson Ezra (1715–95), of West Killingly (now Danielson), Connecticut, were all farmers of the rocky New England soil. They were devout Protestants.[3] Ezra's son Penuel (1762–1841), a farmer, was the first Hutchins of record to enter a learned profession. He received a medical diploma from Yale College. Like many men of his social class and situation, he combined his vocations as farmer and physician. Penuel sent one son, Ezra, to Brown University. Ezra was the first American Hutchins to pursue a career in law.

Another of Ezra's sons, Isaac Thompson Hutchins (1786–1884), taught school. He was a community leader, an outspoken abolitionist, and a champion of anti-Masonic struggles. A Whig with strong faith in the common school to teach literacy and in the family and the church to build character, Isaac proselytized about the importance of systematic Christian character training for young children within the family.[4] Like Bushnell in *Christian Nurture,* Isaac believed that careful parental teaching would elicit children's innate goodness. In addition, it was essential to bring more souls into the Church at a time when American society was becoming increasingly heterogeneous, urban, and industrialized.[5]

Isaac's community leadership and faith in education reflected two characteristics that marked nearly all his descendants' lives. His son Robert Grosvenor Hutchins (1838–1921) was a thoughtful and introspective youth who resisted the pull of revival fervor until he could accept all the clauses of the Articles of Faith. He refused to be swayed by the conversion of his young companions, including his future wife, Harriet Palmer James, but continued to try to live by the word.[6] An abolitionist like his father, Robert Grosvenor Hutchins concluded that the Fugitive Slave Law was immoral and inhumane. Like many of his contemporaries, he was a strong admirer of Abraham Lincoln.[7] He attended Phillips Academy in Andover, Massachusetts, and Williams College, finishing in 1861, two years behind his future colleague Washington Gladden. He graduated from Andover Theological Seminary in 1865, after serving on the Christian Commission, preaching to the soldiers at City Point during the Civil War. In 1867 he married Harriet Palmer James, whose family had emigrated from Wales in 1635. She had followed her own evangelical lights, attending Wheaton Female Seminary in Norton, Massachusetts, and completing the course in 1859.

Harriet and Robert Grosvenor Hutchins had six children, five of whom survived into adulthood. The children became part of the various evangelical networks that would augment Hutchins' fifty-year ministry, beginning in Brooklyn, New York, in the late 1860s, moving to the Midwest, including Oberlin, Ohio, a locus of nineteenth-century evangelical activity, and ending in Berea, Kentucky, in 1921. Robert Grosvenor Hutchins preached with a simple, spontaneous emotional style that would repel his grandson Robert Maynard Hutchins but drew love and respect from his congregations and inspired his son William James Hutchins to follow him into the ministry.[8] He preached at the First Congregational Church of Columbus, Ohio, for a decade, from 1872 to 1882, and was succeeded in that pulpit by Washington Gladden, whose espousal of social Christianity eventually would influence both Robert Grosvenor and William James Hutchins' preaching.

Where Washington Gladden became involved in social Christian organizations, Robert Grosvenor Hutchins continued to support conservative causes and organizations, including temperance and the Home Missionary Society. From 1880 to 1883 he was a trustee of Oberlin College.

Shortly thereafter his conception of Christian ministry broadened to include social and political problems. By the time he joined the Oberlin community as pastor of the Second Congregational Church in 1886, he had begun to preach Gladden's message of "applied Christianity," which he and his liberal colleagues saw as "the application of Christianity to personal, social, and political life."[9]

Robert Grosvenor Hutchins' children benefited from the conservative and the liberal Protestant teachings of the nineteenth century. Isaac reminded his grandchildren to read the Bible and follow its maxims, to work on their spelling and writing, and to engage constantly in the tasks of self-education and self-improvement.[10] The "applied Christianity" they learned from their father's preaching and the evangelically oriented formal education in the Oberlin community broadened their Christian commitment. Harriet James Hutchins' work among the poor provided them a pragmatic lesson in the application of Christianity to daily life. Until her death in 1890, she was a model of religiously inspired social service.[11]

William James Hutchins (1871–1958) and his sisters, Grace James and Fannie Collins, and his brothers, Robert Grosvenor and Francis Sessions, attended Oberlin Preparatory School. Grace continued at the Oberlin Conservatory of Music. Fannie, Will, and Grosvenor attended the college while Francis was sent to Williams College in the hope that its conservative discipline would curb his fondness for practical jokes.[12]

Robert Grosvenor Hutchins was an erect, bearded man with the straight shoulders, pronounced cheekbones, and steady gaze of all the Hutchins men. His son Will exhibited a similar uprightness and concern for spiritual matters. Will also showed a respect for intellectual accomplishment that significantly shaped the behavior and attitudes of his own son, Robert. As a student at Oberlin Preparatory School from 1886 to 1888 and Oberlin College from 1888 to 1890, Will Hutchins was part of "the evangelical college in transition."[13] He studied the classical course in the college and earned high grades in Latin, Greek, mathematics, chemistry, and rhetoricals. He sang bass with the Oberlin Musical Union. In keeping with Oberlin's evangelical mission, he worked for the cause of temperance reform. He also was a spiritual counselor to his fellow students. He listened to the sermons of Dwight L. Moody and other evangelists in his free time. In 1890 he went to Yale, but he returned to Oberlin in the summers to teach.[14]

At Yale, Will Hutchins attended William Rainey Harper's biblical literature lectures, joined the glee club, and made numerous friends. He graduated second in his class (1892) and won Phi Beta Kappa, an honor that his son Robert would receive nearly thirty years later. His "rhetoricals" at Oberlin and years of listening to his father's preaching proved to be good training for public speaking. He won Yale's highest honor in oratory in his senior year—the DeForest Prize, another honor his son Robert would take as a Yale student. Hutchins returned to Oberlin in 1893 and spent the next two years at the Oberlin Theological Seminary, tutoring students in Greek to help finance this study.[15] Transferring to Union Theological Seminary in New York to prepare to enter the Presbyterian ministry, he finished in 1896. Something of an iconoclast, he did not believe in original sin, imputed guilt, or the absolute historicity of Genesis or Exodus. These were all signs that his theology was modernist rather than conservative.[16]

Like many of his liberal colleagues, Hutchins had accepted Darwinian evolutionary theory and the higher criticism of the German and American theologians of the period. His doctrinal positions were problematic to conservative members of the Brooklyn Presbytery, who called him back for questioning before they would agree to his ordination. In the end, they had no doubts as to his suitability as a practicing minister. According to one member of the group, he was good, frank, noble, and intelligent.[17] He was ordained in the summer of 1896. In August he married Anna Laura Murch, a native of Cleveland whom he had met at Oberlin. His father officiated at their wedding.

Anna Murch's family also provided models and standards for the next generation of Hutchins boys. Her grandfather Nathaniel J. Murch, a sailor, brick maker, and farmer, married Mary B. Fullerton, the first white female born in Ellsworth, Maine. Anna's father, Maynard Hale Murch (1827–1908), also was a sailor. On his first voyage, at the age of eleven, he sailed nearly around the world over the course of more than a year. He learned shipbuilding in Bath, Maine, and eventually moved west to Cleveland, Ohio. After his first wife died, he married Lucy M. Stephenson (1844–1920) in 1870. He and Lucy had three children. Anna Laura and Maynard Hale Murch, Jr., survived into adulthood. Maynard, Jr., became a prominent businessman in Cleveland. Maynard, Sr., continued to build and captain ships on Lake Erie. He was known as a man of "moral courage" and great faith, who never sailed without his Bible.[18]

Anna Murch attended Cleveland Public High School, passed her Latin examination in 1890, and spent the years from 1890 to 1894 enrolled at Oberlin College. Like Will Hutchins, she took a rigorous course of study, including mathematics, sciences, French, German, rhetoricals, English, Bible, Latin, psychology, and political economy. She graduated with a bachelor of arts degree in 1896 from Mount Holyoke College, otherwise known as Mary Lyon's "Puritan convent," which, in addition to her Oberlin experience, provided her with appropriate training to be a minister's wife.[19] A gentle, shy woman, most comfortable administering quietly to people's needs, she was Will Hutchins' devoted partner, serving alongside him wherever they lived.[20]

Their first parish was the Bedford Presbyterian Church in Brooklyn, New York, only a few blocks from Robert Grosvenor Hutchins' church. As they established their own family, Will Hutchins became a widely respected minister who, from 1896 to 1907, built an increasingly large and complicated organization on the corner of Dean and Nostrand streets. William Grosvenor Hutchins was born in 1898, Robert Maynard Hutchins was born in 1899, and Francis Stephenson Hutchins was born in 1902. While her husband created a parish responsive to the needs of their congregation and neighborhood, Anna taught her sons the simple courtesies they would need as good Christians and successful men. She read Dickens and other works to them and took them weekly to the public library.[21]

William and Robert could not help but be influenced by their father's leadership. In addition to the morning and evening family prayers and Sunday school, the boys attended church twice on Sundays, which included listening to their father's sermons.[22] Under his guidance, the congregation and Bible school grew. The church initiated a range of activities for children and adults that combined evangelical goals with social service. Will Hutchins' pastoral work reflected the Social Gospel preached by Washington Gladden and such proponents of the institutional church as William S. Rainsford at St. George's, an Episcopal church across the East River.[23]

Will Hutchins' sermons demonstrated his conviction about the functions of the Church in American urban society and were influenced by Gladden's *Applied Christianity* and the theological ideas of Henry Churchill King, who became president of Oberlin College in 1902.[24] Hutchins urged his congregation to ponder the importance of assuming responsibility for one's life and of helping others despite personal inconvenience. The Sunday school, he told them, was central to a Christian nurture that ultimately could improve society. He thought social conditions could be ameliorated if people worked together, especially if they were working for God.[25] It was the responsibility of citizens, he maintained, to stop political graft in city government. He reminded the congregants of the abuses perpetrated on children throughout history, but especially as a result of urban poverty and child labor in modern industry. He described the extensive needs of the city's poor blacks, who also were God's children. He believed that conversion alone could not improve the social and economic conditions in which black citizens lived. Impoverished blacks by right were politically equal and required extensive missionary assistance to gain greater control over their lives.[26]

Hutchins' message was not lost on his sons. They acquired an acute sense of their father's moral and social commitments, which influenced their decisions to work in education rather than business or some other occupation. Education would allow them to contribute to society with few of the moral compromises other professions seemed to demand.

Will Hutchins' message and dynamic style of delivery were known to his colleagues. In 1907, Henry Churchill King, president of Oberlin College, invited him to accept a professorship of homiletics in the School of Theology at Oberlin. Hutchins struggled with his decision. He felt that his "real work" was to take every opportunity to help the truly needy as he performed his daily ministry.[27] Making his decision even more difficult, his parishioners pleaded with him to stay at the Bedford Church. After consultation with his father and with encouragement from Washington Gladden, Hutchins accepted the appointment.[28] His decision reflected the practical and moral principles that were to have a lasting influence on his children.

Hutchins was concerned that his family not be under pressure to maintain the kind of social standing his pastorate increasingly required. The smaller Oberlin salary would be balanced by the nearness of Anna's family, the more limited opportunities to spend money, the high quality of education available to his sons, and the safety of the expansive outdoors.[29] He and Anna had many personal attachments to the college and the town.

Professionally and spiritually inseparable to Hutchins, the ability to influence the training of whole generations of ministers and the opportunity to teach Bible to freshmen gave him a "larger field of present usefulness."[30] Practical considerations would not have been enough to justify the move. The appeal of a larger mission—and, not incidentally, the part he would play in it—was the decisive factor. With his social and religious commitments, his strong moral principles, and his intellectual and rhetorical talents, he could not have chosen a more appropriate place to raise his sons.

Will and Anna Hutchins lived in Oberlin from 1907 until 1920. He took the Holbrook professorship in homiletics and taught freshman Bible, a course required of all male freshmen in those years. Once again assuming a community leadership role, he undertook to invigorate the spiritual life on campus through his work on the Committee on Religious Interests.[31] He attended YMCA and YWCA meetings, leading prayer and discussion sessions. He attempted to raise President King's interest in getting "boys' club" work started on campus for the black students attending Oberlin, probably an effort to counteract racism among students influenced by Jim Crow attitudes prevalent at the time.[32]

Hutchins' work as professor of homiletics was renowned. He received many offers of positions at other institutions, including the chairmanship of the department of homiletics at Union Theological Seminary in New York, but turned them all down to stay at Oberlin.[33] He continued to preach, primarily at local churches, and often took his sons Robert and William with him. The kind of certainty that Robert would echo many years later in his arguments that the university should be the locus of moral and intellectual revolution was evident in Will Hutchins' sermons. He told students, for example, that Christianity could provide a secure vantage point from which to view the world and to pursue one's learning and career.[34] He told the Social Science Club that, despite the different religious backgrounds of Oberlin students, the Christian life was the source of "permanent values" that could be discovered through participation in prayer and service to the community, and could be reinforced by the ways that professors taught their subjects and treated their students.[35]

The strength of parental pedagogy is difficult to measure. Nevertheless, Will and Anna Hutchins' consistent teaching of consideration for others, personal responsibility, courtesy, community service, discerning right from wrong, and hard work was a powerful influence on their sons. This influence was reinforced daily in the Bedford Church and especially in the Oberlin community. As a boy of six, Robert Hutchins kept a notebook of drawings he made and words he was learning to write as a student at P.S. 138 in Brooklyn. Many of the pictures were typical children's drawings; they included representations of houses, flowers, fires, hearts, boats, even a coal bucket, each labeled with the appropriate word. The object to occur most frequently was a book with the inscription "GODS WORD" in childish rounded letters on the open pages.[36]

When their parents told them they were moving west to Ohio, the Hutchins boys were convinced they would be entering dangerous Indian territory. What they found was a small town of clapboard houses and stone and brick buildings, with a public green in the center, much like the New England towns its evangelical founders had left behind. Oberlin was surrounded by farmland, woods, and fields. The college took up most of the center of town. There were trolley tracks along College Street that went all the way into Cleveland, about twenty miles distant. When the snow melted in spring, the fields and roads turned to mud. For people who loved the outdoors, there were sports, games, hiking trips, and picnics. The Hutchins boys attended the public elementary school. They traveled in the summertime with Will and Anna to Congregational, Presbyterian, and YMCA camps. At the camps they attended prayer meetings, swam, and played tennis.

The children were immersed in the Oberlin College environment. They took many of their meals in faculty boarding houses, privy to adult discussions of campus and larger political issues. Robert and William attended Oberlin Academy, and all three boys enrolled in the college, though Francis would be the only one to graduate with a bachelor's degree from Oberlin. During his four years in the academy from 1911 to 1915, Robert studied English literature, rhetoric, and composition; Latin, algebra, and geometry; Greek and Roman history; physics; German; and four years of Bible. His grades were consistently good, a reflection of his desire to excel and his parents' encouragement of hard work and self-discipline.[37]

One could not attend Oberlin without being affected by its evangelical culture. The Martyr's Arch, erected in memory of Oberlin alumni missionaries killed in the Boxer Rebellion, marked one entrance to the campus. The college's historic commitment to the education of women and African-Americans continued to be manifest in the student enrollment. By the early 1900s women were taking part in every aspect of the Oberlin curriculum and extracurriculum and were quite active on behalf of suffrage. African-Americans, a proportionately smaller group, were also active, but to a lesser extent.[38] Oberlin's antebellum abolitionist activity and its citizens' participation in the Underground Railroad were legendary and reflected not only belief in fundamental spiritual and political equality but also action to support that belief.[39] This commitment to principles at Oberlin persisted into the twentieth century. Robert Hutchins remembered that the college's major "legacy" to Oberlin men and women was "the nonconformist conscience" and the willingness to die for one's principles.[40]

The evangelical fervor was stronger when Will Hutchins was a student, but by the 1890s "Oberlin perfectionism," the attempt to establish a

Christian community of the elect in the wilderness, had begun to fade.[41] Faculty members were incorporating the new social sciences into their teaching and writing. Oberlin was not the only college undergoing such a transition; George E. Peterson has described this pattern in his study of New England colleges.[42] After the turn of the century, intellectual rigor and concern for social issues became increasingly important as Christian pietism declined at the college.

With Henry Churchill King's presidency at Oberlin, the trustees reaffirmed Oberlin's evangelical ties and recognized the modernist thinking of Protestant theologians of the twentieth century. King encouraged the reinterpretation of Oberlin's theological tradition in light of its implications for social service. He thought that greater religious commitment and social consciousness, manifest as a sacred respect for others, would revitalize democracy.[43] Consonant with King's theme of the brotherhood of man in Christ, social service became the dominant characteristic of the activities of student organizations at Oberlin.

The ideals of progressive reformers and the ideas emerging from the social sciences coalesced at Oberlin. The decrease in specifically religious activity signaled a rise in academic expectations. Intellectual development became the curricular focus of the college. Emphasis on factual knowledge in the social sciences was at least partially justified by the usefulness of facts in the design of reform measures. The New Haven scholarship Louise Stevenson describes in her examination of the development of the social sciences at Yale in the nineteenth century was carried forward at Oberlin in the inherent assumption that social science scholarship, indeed academic work itself, would lead to Christian reform.[44] Though at Oberlin the emphasis was increasingly secular, there persisted a righteous and optimistic belief in the compatibility of democracy and Christianity that shaped the curriculum and extracurriculum.

Growing up in such a community did not guarantee that all members would conform fully to its tenets. However, living in a family that affirmed them reinforced the Hutchins boys' immersion in this system of belief. Will Hutchins was a hard model to emulate. His own father thought Will was "more Christlike than any masculine person" he had ever known.[45] Kemper Fullerton, his senior colleague at the Oberlin Theological Seminary, noted that, more than any other influence, Will Hutchins' example moved Fullerton "to live a Christ-like life."[46]

Robert Hutchins made a point of distinguishing himself from his father. His distaste for the emotional rhetoric of his grandfather's preaching quite possibly helped him resist the evangelical tone of Oberlin's messages. By the end of his freshman year in the college, he had stretched to the limits the community's tolerance for his practical jokes and wild behavior. Conceivably in reaction to the expectation that he should be especially well behaved because he was Will Hutchins' son, Robert was prone to pull pranks and turn them to his profit, once caught. Rather than imitating the "Christ-like" behavior of his father, Robert was learning and refining something akin to his Uncle Francis' sense of humor.[47]

One instance involved a devout man of the community, Thomas B. Henderson, who attended weekly prayer meetings on Thursday nights at one of Oberlin's churches. Robert and his friends apparently were fascinated with the man's Winton, because they reputedly took it out joyriding and returned it each Thursday evening by the time Henderson emerged from his prayers. One time, they reportedly drove the car to Wellington, a picturesque town about eight miles south of Oberlin, and had the misfortune to run out of gas on the way back. They pushed it off the road and returned to Oberlin on foot.[48]

When notices of a $150 reward for information on the lost vehicle appeared all over town, Robert's Oberlin propriety overwhelmed him. He convinced his friends that it would be in the best of the community's tradition of courage and forthrightness to confess to Henderson, who took a dim view of their antics and called the sheriff. After a rather heated session in his living room, Henderson decided rather than press charges to allow the boys to repent publicly. No doubt Will Hutchins spoke in Robert's favor. Still, Robert would not let well enough alone and, as they were leaving, suggested to Henderson that, since their confession had saved him from having to pay anyone the reward, he might like to share some of the $150 with them. His father and friends got him out of Henderson's house intact, and all the boys repented on their knees in President King's office.

Tall, lanky, dark-haired, with clear, even features and the Hutchins steady gaze, Robert was a popular boy on campus. He so exhausted himself in the rope pull and other freshman initiation events that his father persuaded President King to discontinue such activities for a time.[49] Robert's freshman class elected him president. In return for their support, he climbed hundreds of feet up the heating plant smokestack to paint on it the class of 1919 numerals. President King wrote Will Hutchins in June of 1916 that Robert and his friends had gone far enough with their latest prank.[50] If he had not been such a good student or so quick to mock himself with the self-deprecating humor that his friends and family found endearing, Robert might have been in greater trouble.

Apparently, the campus rules bothered him most. In 1915, he submitted this "Early Treatise on Education" to the community:

> In Oberlin, I must not smoke.
> I don't.
> Nor listen to a naughty joke.
> I don't.
> To flirt, to dance, is very wrong.
> Wild youths choose women, wine, and song.
> I don't.
> In Oberlin I must not wink at pretty girls
> Or even think about intoxicating drink.
> I don't.
> I kiss no girls, not even one.
> Why, I don't know how it is done.
> You wouldn't think I'd have much fun.
> I don't.[51]

His rebelliousness did not deter him from ultimately productive activities. He participated in the Oberlin Gospel Team, preaching to "the heathen" in Ohio towns.[52] He assumed a number of leadership roles, including secretary and later vice-president of the men's senate. He was a member of the *Oberlin Review* board and the Alpha Zeta debating society. He managed the football team and played on the tennis team. His personable, friendly, energetic nature found plenty of outlets among a remarkably egalitarian group of students from farming, teaching, and professional families.[53] The democratic atmosphere at Oberlin was so marked that even Theodore Roosevelt called it "the community of the applied square deal" during his 1912 campaign stop there.[54]

Robert was a good debater. He developed a style at Oberlin that he would rely on throughout his life. A combination of clear expression and strong examples, it was like his father's homiletic delivery. His arguments were supported by conviction and fueled by the debates and lectures of prominent progressives and socialists Oberlin invited to the campus. John Spargo, socialist author of *The Bitter Cry of Children,* Raymond Robins, a Chicago-based social reformer, Scott Nearing, socialist and economics professor at the University of Pennsylvania, Lincoln Steffens, journalist and reformer, Robert G. Macauley, editor of the *Single Tax Review,* and many others spoke in Oberlin while Hutchins was a student.[55]

In addition to bringing in such speakers, the college encouraged discussion of important issues. In response to the continuation of the European war, students and faculty voted unanimously to support a peace settlement along the lines advocated by Jane Addams and the National Peace Federation.[56] Other issues discussed included politics, labor problems, government, suffrage, and immigration. Robert, for example, helped to win a debate by taking the affirmative position on whether there should be federal or state control of the nation's mineral resources.[57]

Unlike the nineteenth-century evangelistic ethos of the college, the Oberlin of the progressive reform era tolerated a greater variety of response from students and faculty. Much of the discussion and social service that took place in the community was premised on the twin convictions that what one believed mattered and that one ought to be able to argue intelligently and rationally for a belief. Furthermore, discussion and action could result in some change. The success of the abolitionist movement testified to this faith, as did the martyrs memorialized by the Martyr's Arch.

Distinguished alumnae including Mary Eliza Church Terrell and Anna Julia Howard Cooper, who combined the causes of suffrage and civil and educational rights for African-Americans, represented the strength of conviction in keeping alive not necessarily popular, but morally and socially correct, causes. The service ideal of President King and faculty members like Will Hutchins, who supported community service with theological arguments and regular contact with students, reiterated in different ways the power of individual agency and collective action. Former Oberlin students and faculty members were testaments, too, to the role of intellectual work in suggesting and implementing social change. John R. Commons in history and George Herbert Mead in philosophy had made significant contributions to their academic disciplines and to their communities at the University of Wisconsin and the University of Chicago.

One result of this faith in human agency and collective action was that some students became invested with a greater sense of the importance of their studies. In Robert Hutchins' case, the motivation to perform well in his classes was already present. After it caught his eye at the breakfast table, he was determined from an early age to possess a Phi Beta Kappa key like his father's.[58] He was gifted with a quick intelligence and a love of reading that was encouraged by his parents. His father had a large library. His older brother William remembered that Robert spent a great deal of time in his room "reading and reading" while he (William) was left with the household chores.[59] Robert's interest and diligence were rewarded in the college. He received consistently high grades. In fact, he got C's only in physical training, which reflected his lifelong aversion to any exercise other than tennis and fishing.

His courses as a freshman and sophomore exhibit not only Oberlin's attempt to locate the study of subjects in their social, economic, and historical context but also its effort to relate them to larger social issues in the present. Robert studied English composition, elementary Greek, ancient history, advanced German, and literature, his freshman year. The required freshman Bible course was a study of "the world of Jesus." It included the politics, geography, economy, religious and ecclesiastical culture, and living conditions of ordinary people in Palestine as well as background in the history of the Gospels. He received an A- and an A for his work in freshman Bible.[60] Consistent with the Oberlin emphasis on "hard intellectual work," Robert took courses during the summer.[61] He studied such topics as tariffs, trade regulations, South American trade, and the social and economic effects of war, of socialism, of conservation, and of women's suffrage with economist Hazel Kyrk, who anchored theory in contemporary problems in economics.[62]

In his second year at Oberlin, Robert read and translated Greek, studied the elementary principles of economics, took chemistry and another history course, and pursued what appears to have been his two real loves, English and German. He read all of Tennyson's works his sophomore year. And he was permitted to enroll in Professor Eugene Mosher's course on Goethe's *Faust,* an intensive examination through the novel of the culture of Germany and its contribution to modern life and thought.

After his tour of duty in the United States Army Ambulance Corps from 1917 to 1919, he returned to Oberlin for a summer and studied the history of philosophy, which encompassed the history, methods, and problems, as well as the periods of development, of philosophical movements in the West. He also studied American history, focusing on American foreign policy and America in the world war. That summer he finished his academic career at Oberlin with an introduction to modified behavioral psychology, a course emphasizing the analysis of complex behavior and the dynamic aspects of human nature.

More than simply a list of courses, Hutchins' studies at Oberlin reveal interesting and significant aspects of his educational training at that institution. Much of the course work appears to have been interdisciplinary.

Freshman Bible included history and a variety of perspectives on the ideas presented in the Gospels. Economics examined political and social issues in addition to principles of economic systems. German literature looked at German culture and thought. Greek did not simply involve recitation; it included translation and discussion of literature. Hutchins, a tough critic of higher education by the middle 1930s, remembered this period of his formal study at Oberlin as "the best teaching" he had "seen or experienced anywhere."[63]

Robert was challenged intellectually at Oberlin. His last two years at Yale were easy compared to his work at Oberlin. Beyond what he gained implicitly in his understanding of the disciplines, particularly the humanities (by nature interdisciplinary) and the social sciences, he acquired a conception of what knowledge could do. As the social sciences and other subjects were taught at Oberlin, there was the expectation that students would use the knowledge they gained to do something of service after they left college.[64]

Before 1900, students were encouraged to translate the duty of service into missionary work, the ministry, teaching, or some such vocation. After 1900, evangelicalism was less powerful, but the commitment to use one's education to improve society remained. Hutchins' German professor, William Eugene Mosher, is a good example of this transition. He attended the academy and the college, tutored German in the college after he graduated in 1899, and studied for his Ph.D. at the University of Halle, finishing in 1904. He returned to Oberlin as an instructor in German and by 1907 was made head of the department of German languages and literature. During his time as professor of German, he sustained not only a commitment to intellectual rigor but also a concern for social issues.

Because of the nativism accompanying the United States' entry into the war in 1917, Mosher and the rest of the faculty agreed temporarily to close the German department, a move that later was seen as proof of his loyalty.[65] Mosher translated his concern for public issues into a new career when he took a leave from the inactive department. He developed expertise in public utility economy, worked for the Bureau of Municipal Research in New York City, and later became dean of the Maxwell School of Citizenship and Public Affairs at Syracuse University.[66]

In Mosher's class on Goethe, Robert Hutchins and Thornton Wilder, who entered Oberlin as a freshman in 1915, became friends. Like Hutchins, Wilder came from an evangelical Protestant background, though his father was more demanding and inflexible than Will

Hutchins.[67] Oberlin was Wilder's first major escape from paternalistic authority. He was an unconventional, exotic young man who had never quite fit in at the other schools he had attended, but he was fully accepted at Oberlin. He sang in the First Congregational Church choir, where Will Hutchins occasionally preached, and regularly visited the Hutchins home. Though Wilder's intellectual commitment was more literary than academic and was fostered as much by literary clubs as by the curriculum, his standards for hard work developed at the college. Wilder and Hutchins met again at Yale after the war. In the 1930s Hutchins invited Wilder to join the faculty at the University of Chicago. Their friendship continued throughout their lives and was rooted in the shared culture of Oberlin.

Oberlin's social service message shaped Robert's brothers' life choices. After attending Oberlin and graduating from Yale College, William Grosvenor Hutchins worked for two years in the advertising department at Condé Nast in New York but could not make himself care about the amount of advertising space he sold for the company. He turned instead to teaching. "From the first hour in the classroom he knew this was where he ought to be," but burdened with an inability to tolerate unprincipled behavior, William moved from school to school until he arrived at the Asheville School in Asheville, North Carolina. There he found a headmaster unswayed by pressure from wealthy parents and who supported Hutchins' high academic expectations and disciplinary standards. He eventually became headmaster at Asheville and remained there the rest of his life. According to his brother Francis, William was "probably the best teacher in the family."[68]

Francis Stephenson Hutchins also became a educator. He worked as a teacher in the Oberlin Shansi Memorial Schools in China and, from 1925 to 1939, served as trustees' representative, then vice-president, of the Yale-in-China Association (Yali) in Hunan Province.[69] In 1939 he returned to the United States to succeed his father as president of Berea College. Berea College had been established in 1855 by abolitionists with connections to Oberlin. Initially a one-room school for black and white children of Appalachia, it reopened after the Civil War as an academy and a college. In 1908 a Supreme Court decision forced Berea to comply with Kentucky's laws against racial integration in educational institutions. When Will Hutchins became president of the college in 1920, he brought African-American speakers, poets, artists, musicians, and ministers to the community to encourage interracial understanding. During his tenure he solicited enough support from various foundations (Rosenwald, Danforth, and

Carnegie) and individuals to reorganize the academic program consonant with Berea's mission to incorporate labor, education, and Christian morality in everyday life. When he retired to become an adviser to the Danforth Foundation, the institution he handed to his son Francis was financially stable, cohesive, and scholastically improved.[70]

After Francis Hutchins took the presidency, he expanded the reach of the institution to rural schools, provided traveling libraries, and supported the teacher-training program. He made it a practice to consult faculty members about his plans for institutional change. When Kentucky's Day Law was abolished in 1950, he attempted to bring African-American students into the college, an effort that took longer than he anticipated. He reaffirmed Berea's Christian concern for the social conditions and needs of Appalachian students and maintained the high academic expectations Oberlin had taught him to value.

Clearly, the Hutchins family and the Oberlin tradition of service helped to shape the predilections and conscious choices of Robert's brothers, William and Francis. Robert's translation of the lessons he learned was more subtle than his brothers'. William and Francis became involved in institutions that were an extension of the Oberlin ethos. Smaller and more cohesive communities that held intellectual and moral values more compatible with Oberlin's, their primary goal was education of the intellect and the character. By contrast, Robert Hutchins was to make his mark on institutions that were more diverse in their purposes and goals than early twentieth-century Oberlin had been.

In the 1920s Yale was an institution undergoing significant change. Robert participated in that transformation. At the University of Chicago in the 1930s, he would direct an institution whose faculty members sought a variety of intellectual goals and who saw no need to hold the institution to any overarching set of principles and methods. He would not be able to play Henry Churchill King to his University of Chicago community. As a group, the University of Chicago faculty would be singularly uninterested in having their president lead them on a moral mission to reform the world of higher education.

What did Hutchins take with him into adulthood from his safe and cohesive evangelical Protestant childhood and from his youthful exposure to the Oberlin community? It is impossible to determine absolutely how character traits are transmitted or acquired, what is learned and what inherited. There are certain marks of character, ways of initiating or responding to situations, and expectations for personal and public conduct that Robert Hutchins manifested in his behavior, choices, and outlook. The all-enveloping Christian nurture that Isaac Hutchins provided his children and that Robert Grosvenor Hutchins gave to his, William James Hutchins gave to his own, along with a secure sense of their self-worth.

The assumption that the Hutchinses would not only serve their communities but also lead, through newspaper columns, reform activities, pulpits, classrooms, or institutional administration, particularly affected Robert Hutchins. That moral principles would guide that leadership was taken for granted. The Hutchins (and James and Murch) family faith in the ability of education to change individuals and the larger society was echoed at Oberlin and reflected in all of Robert Hutchins' later work.

Honesty, integrity, and commitment were manifest in a variety of Hutchinses' activities, from Robert Grosvenor Hutchins' unwillingness to convert without accepting all the Articles of Faith to Will Hutchins' refusal to bow to the Brooklyn Presbytery even though it might cost him his ordination. Courage backed by strong religious faith was implicit in Maynard Hale Murch's life. A similar courage would enable Robert Hutchins to face numerous storms throughout his career as an educator. His fearless assertion of his opinions was another characteristic of the Hutchinses. Robert's Aunt Fannie fought hard to become a doctor in the late nineteenth century, when few women entered professions. Her bluntness and determination were the stuff of family stories. His Uncle Francis Sessions Hutchins' youthful rebelliousness, wry humor, and professional life provided Robert Hutchins with a broader view of the world and of what good people could be and do. That he chose to study law is suggestive of Francis' influence.

Robert Hutchins gained from his father and mother a clear understanding of right and wrong. Self-reliance, self-control, independent thinking, and fairness were qualities that Will and Anna Hutchins held in high esteem. Robert did not adopt (in his public life) the content of the evangelical message his father had preached from his pulpits, lecterns, and books.[71] He did absorb the form of the message, the manner of the sermon, the skill required to make a point in the clearest and simplest way, and the power of conviction in carrying one's message to the rest of the world, a skill that is obvious in every speech and essay he ever delivered or wrote.

Robert acquired from the Oberlin community an extension and expansion of what his family gave him, much as the larger Protestant networks, organized for abolition, temperance, and social reform, had served his great-grandfather, grandfather, and father in their attempts to define themselves in relation to God and the human community. Oberlin was one of the many Protestant evangelical educational institutions to welcome Hutchins and James and Murch family members. Phillips Academy at Andover, Williams College, Andover Theological Seminary, Wheaton Female Seminary, Mount Holyoke College, Union Theological Seminary, Yale College and University all numbered among the institutions of the nineteenth century that shaped the Hutchins sense of mission and duty.

Oberlin's idealism led Robert Hutchins to believe that, through debate and rational discussion, people could be converted to one's programs and ideas. The moral and ethical concerns that professors displayed in their teaching and daily conversation indicated that moral development was intrinsic to true intellectual development. Implicit in the intellectual organization of the curriculum and the teaching of the social sciences and humanities was the belief that all knowledge ultimately was related.

Lectures and debates and the extracurriculum suggest that there was some shared conviction, despite surface dissension, that held members of the Oberlin community together in a common endeavor. The desire, perhaps even the need, to find or re-create such a community, albeit with secular goals, would remain with Robert Hutchins all his life. It was to be a heavy burden to bear in an increasingly diverse and cosmopolitan society where businessmen would become the most powerful definers of the social goals of the 1920s and material concerns would rule the world outside the Oberlin community.

His early grounding in Oberlin's powerful moral and ethical tradition made Robert Hutchins perpetually dissatisfied not only with his own accomplishments but also with every effort he made and institution he commanded. This dissatisfaction, as well as his authoritative leadership, committed hard work, and relentless criticism, had its roots in the Protestant evangelical culture of Oberlin.

CHAPTER 2 *Coming of Age*

THE DECADE FROM 1917 TO 1927 was an apprenticeship for Hutchins, a combination of learning and practice that extended his sense of himself and of what he might do with his life. His first break with the Protestant evangelical culture of his family and Oberlin came with service in the Army in World War I, but his independence was limited by working in an Oberlin ambulance unit. His more decisive break occurred when he transferred to Yale College to finish his undergraduate study. Yale, despite its evangelical roots and required daily chapel, presented a far more cosmopolitan range of ideas, people, and social and cultural opportunities. The tension between piety and intellect that had been resolved at Oberlin was manifest at Yale as a tension between character and intellect. When James Rowland Angell was appointed Yale's first nonalumnus president in 1921, the university moved decisively in the direction of intellect.

After finishing at Yale, Hutchins followed in his family's footsteps by teaching school for a year and a half. But he did not enjoy working with adolescent boys. When he accepted the position of secretary of the Yale Corporation in 1923, he had the opportunity to learn about universities under Angell, a man with wide experience in the academic culture of the modern university. For Hutchins it was the beginning of a career in university administration that would continue for nearly thirty years.

Robert and William Hutchins joined the Oberlin unit of the United States Army Ambulance Corps (USAAC) in September of 1917 without their parents' permission. The college had voted unanimously in 1915 to support peace, but when the United States officially declared war on Germany on April 6, 1917, Oberlin was prepared to serve the cause. Henry Churchill King had argued in February of that year that United States involvement in the war was justified not by some extreme "passion of national pride, but only for the great ends of civilization itself."[1] Like many liberal progressive Protestant leaders, he saw the war as a tragic necessity to uphold the virtues of Christian democratic civilization.[2] This position moved the Oberlin community in line with the nonpacifist progressives supporting American involvement.

King tended toward pacifism, except when a state was held to have violated morality.[3] In the winter of 1916 to 1917, he had maintained his opposition to a premature peace despite extensive criticism from Oberlin alumni, faculty, and the public. As their moral leader, he devoted his sermons and speeches from 1914 to 1917 to the moral issues of the war. He was successful throughout the community and with individuals like Robert and William Hutchins.

At the federal government's request, the college established the Student Army Training Corps on campus. Over three hundred young men initially enrolled. Red Cross training for young women began in mid-April of 1917. In May the federal government requested that Oberlin supply an ambulance unit for the Army.[4] Section 587 of the USAAC satisfied the request. Shortly after the corps began selecting Oberlin men, Will Hutchins preached a sermon to the recruits describing how well Oberlin had prepared them to serve the people who would most need them and to fulfill their most important goal—to end the war.[5] He, too, left Oberlin in the summer of 1917 to serve as religious work director of the YMCA at Camp Sheridan in Alabama.

Will Hutchins was not opposed to United States participation in the war. Before he left for Alabama, he had discussed with his son William, home for the summer after his first year at Yale, the possibility of serving with the ambulance drivers. Caught up in the excitement, the opportunity to serve, and the patriotic fervor of their classmates who already had enlisted, Robert and William took the trolley to Cleveland and the train to Allentown, Pennsylvania, to sign up with section 587. They had written to their father but did not wait for his response. They simply told their mother and grandfather of their plan and left. Their mother was deeply disturbed that she had been unable to dissuade them. Their grandfather was incensed that they had disobeyed him. He thought their father should order them out of the Army, particularly as Robert was under twenty-one years of age.[6]

"Unspeakably miserable" that they had not consulted him about a major decision, Will Hutchins reminded the boys that they had a way out: lack of parental permission was an acceptable excuse for leaving the Army. When they refused, he resolved to send them nothing but "cheer and courage and hope."[7] He understood why they had gone, but he was worried about the almost certain boredom they would experience during training and waiting to be sent out, and the bad influences to which they would be exposed in a military camp. From what he had witnessed as religious director, he thought the moral and civil problems in the camps, from sexual promiscuity to rude and rough treatment of recruits, were a result of the "cosmopolitan" mixture of young college men and "low-browed villains" with whom he had lunch every day.[8] He asked Sergeant Logan Omer Osborn, an older student from Oberlin who had joined the unit, to keep an eye on both boys, a duty Osborn gladly assumed.[9]

Despite Osborn's watchful eye, Robert did become bored. He was homesick enough to request that his mother write him every day. He was impatient to go to the front, but as it happened, the unit remained in Allentown for nearly a year before being transported to Europe. There were thousands of young men training at Allentown. Through the bitterly cold winter of 1917–18, they lived in unheated, drafty horse stables, sheep pens, and makeshift barracks.[10] A special duty of the Oberlin unit was to build a camp on what had once been fairgrounds. Most of the recruits at the camp were college men from all over the country. Some units were sent out fairly quickly, but section 587 remained at Allentown.

The Oberlin unit was made up of about forty-five men. With the rest of the unit, Robert and William marched with full equipment twenty miles nearly every day through the Pennsylvania countryside. Not accustomed to Army discipline, Robert rebelled. During one of the marches, when the troops halted for lunch, he made a "caustic" remark about Army food within hearing of a group of officers playing cards. For his affront, he was awarded kitchen duty "for a long time."[11] As additional punishment, he was confined to his tent. One day his comrades reputedly piled all their dry sandwiches outside the tent to show support for his "sacrificial act."[12]

The routine was not relentless. The Oberlin boys were introduced to an Allentown family in whose home they could rest, read, or study. Robert and William took occasional weekend trips to New York to visit their Uncle Francis, who had a law firm in the city and a house on Long Island. Their homesickness was assuaged by the visits of Henry Churchill King in August of 1917 and, best of all, of their mother in the fall of 1917 and May of 1918. They spent Christmas in Allentown but were allowed to return to Oberlin in February 1918 while Robert recovered from the flu and phlebitis.[13]

Despite the routine, the daily marches, and the prolonged waiting to see some action, the boys in the Oberlin unit kept their sense of humor and bolstered each other's spirits. They nicknamed William "Code" and Robert "Morals" when their father won a $5,000 award for his *Children's Code of Morals* from the National Institute of Moral Instruction, and were disappointed that the two boys would not get the money.[14] The Oberlin boys also shared their reading material with each other. Robert and William regularly received books, newspapers, and magazines, including the *Saturday Evening Post,* the *Atlantic Monthly,* and the *New Republic,* which they devoured, and they guarded each other from moral turpitude.

Their year of waiting and training finally ended in July of 1918, when twelve hundred ambulance workers were shipped to Italy. And their families began keeping vigil at home. Francis Hutchins, too young to go to war, has recalled that it was an extraordinarily "trying time" for the Oberlin community.[15] Mail from overseas was delivered in extra trips so that families could receive it as soon as it arrived. Anna Hutchins learned to speak and read Italian in an effort to share in her sons' experience. She sent them books and magazines, tended her chickens, her bees, and her garden, comforted other families, and waited for the mail. Will Hutchins completed his tour of duty at Camp Sheridan and traveled to various campuses in the fall to speak to Student Army Training Corps groups about what to expect in the camps and to give sermons and lead prayers. In November, as a member of the YMCA deputation to India and China, he accompanied Sherwood Eddy, the lay evangelist and secretary of the YMCA, on a trip that would keep him from Oberlin until after Robert and William had returned in the spring of 1919.

The men of the Ambulance Corps were the first American Army troops to arrive in Italy. They were greeted by huge crowds tossing flowers in their path. Colorful placards were posted on the buildings in the cities and towns on the way to the front. The Red Cross helped the men assemble their ambulances and throughout their service provided hospitals, equipment, and volunteer ambulance drivers. The YMCA established offices in cities, and huts at the front, to dispense comforts, reading material, and mail from home.[16]

Will Hutchins wrote to his boys two or three times a week. Remembering Robert's summer work in the YMCA office in Cleveland and hoping for the continued good influence and comfort the YMCA personnel could offer, he told the boys to visit the YMCA offices or huts where they were stationed. He instructed them on Italian history and art and shared what he knew for his own tours in Italy. He passed on news of his current travels and of home and family, making sure the boys remained connected to the life they had left.[17] This experience was the boys' first exposure to poverty and cultural differences. Robert wrote home that he and William found the poverty and filth in Italy disgusting, particularly among the children. His father reminded them that historical conditions rather than "the qualities of the people" were responsible.[18]

With a century of struggles behind them and a depleted economy, the Italians lacked adequate equipment and supplies to continue their fight. The civilian mountain population lived in extreme poverty. The terrain made transporting food, equipment, supplies, and troops difficult. By October of 1917 the exhausted Italian soldiers had become susceptible to rampant, demoralizing pro-German propaganda spread by the Austrians, leading to the desperate retreat of some of the Italian Second Army at Caporetto. Fresh troops, consisting mostly of boys, and assistance from some British and French contingents, enabled the Italians to stabilize the lines of battle in December of 1917.

In June of 1918 the Austrians began another major attack in an attempt to move into central Italy. They broke through in places along the Piave, but the Italians held them back in the mountains, and by mid-July, around the time the Oberlin unit left Allentown, had retaken the Piave sector. Robert and William were sent to different units on arrival in Italy. Robert reached Castelcuceo in the mountain region by August 11, and the men of section 587 had their first exposure to the poverty and lack of modern sanitation of rural Italian mountain life. They found such conditions disturbing and repugnant. They also had their first contact with real fighting. Heavy activity moving the wounded alternated with days of inactivity. Robert, irrepressible even under those conditions, helped to keep up the group's spirits by composing a series of verses (probably set to music) on the pain and inconvenience of diarrhea in an Army camp.[19]

When the Italians began their counteroffensive against the Austrians in October, working from the Piave to the Grappa massif and beyond, section 587 was called to its most intensive and sustained rescue effort. From October 24 to October 30, 1918, on foot and by ambulance, the Oberlin unit evacuated 1,269 wounded under heavy fire on Mount Tomba in the Grappa region.[20] The road down the mountain was steep. Its sharp twists reminded the drivers that one wrong turn could plunge an ambulance off the side of the mountain. Robert and his fellows drove through the night in the rain, with no headlights and few rests in the midst of the battle. They found that they could make a maximum of four round trips a day.[21] The offensive was successful, and the Ambulance Corps and the Red Cross followed the Italian soldiers into the mountains as they routed the Austrians. Each man in the Oberlin unit was awarded the Croce di Guerra for bravery under fire. Hutchins, typically self-deprecating, later claimed that he had mistakenly received the medal for getting jaundice.

Hutchins found the Italian soldiers impressive in battle and in their stoic handling of pain. He had a low opinion of them as individuals, though, suspecting them of thievery and deception.[22] His tolerance for the foreign was limited, yet he seemed unshaken by what his unit found in the mountains in the wake of the Austrian retreat, by the dead and wounded in the trenches and on the roads, abandoned by the Austrian army. The Austrian-occupied villages, though cleaner in his opinion than the Italian, were poorer than any seen thus far.[23] Using his college German to communicate with the Austrian prisoners, he found them intelligent and courteous and noted that, like every soldier he had met, "they seemed ready to have the war stop at any time."[24]

The Oberlin unit continued evacuating both Italian and Austrian wounded into mid-November. Robert worked with the unit until he was hospitalized with jaundice, probably acquired from eating spoiled food. He remained in Italy until April of 1919, recovering and taking tours through Italian towns near Mantua, where he was stationed. He attended opera performances, drove into the mountains, and waited impatiently for his orders to return home. He missed his family terribly and was homesick for "the Only Place On Earth."[25]

Hutchins' experiences significantly shaped his views about the Army and about war. The endless marching, bad food, boredom, repetitive tasks, and regimentation left him skeptical about the value of military training. He opposed compulsory military training for the rest of his life. His personal experience with patriotic fervor during this period of his life had a marked effect on his perceptions of war. Karl F. Geiser, because he was a professor of German history, nearly lost his job at Oberlin. Will Hutchins argued in his favor, and Robert defended him to the Oberlin community.[26] The popular press's descriptions of war as a moral crusade, the designation of the United States as the carrier of Christian civilization to the rest of the world, the power of crude propaganda, and, most important, the resultant repression of freedom of speech, of association, and of belief bred in him a revulsion for war-promoting nativism. His opposition to United States entry into World War II in 1941 was rooted deeply in this revulsion. After the atomic bomb was dropped on Hiroshima, he devoted a significant portion of his lifework to the cause of world peace.

Robert changed noticeably in his two years away from home. He went to war a gangly, mischievous boy and returned a tall, articulate, and startlingly attractive young man. Despite his father's warnings, he came back smoking cigarettes, drinking, and swearing. His ideals tempered by his war experience, he hoped to devote the remainder of his college study to politics and government, perhaps finding in those fields a way to serve society.[27]

When he and William disembarked in New York in April of 1919, their Uncle Francis met them at the docks. Francis, who had seen the boys just before they left for Italy, noted that Robert was sorry "he did not get into more active service" and was "envious of the boys who were continuously in the trenches." He had grown "unbelievably tall" and "exceptionally good looking." Dark, strong-featured, and well proportioned, his arresting physical countenance had an undeniable impact on everyone he encountered for the rest of his life. Moreover, he "had gained in poise" and had "an exceedingly good sense of humor, and a really remarkable facility for expressing himself."[28]

Robert and William returned to Oberlin for the summer, and Robert took classes in preparation for entry into Yale in the fall. He chose to go to Yale because he was ready for a more cosmopolitan educational experience and a more challenging social environment after his war service. Will Hutchins was pleased with Robert's decision to finish at his own alma mater. Yale had been good for him. He thought it might also be good for Robert.[29]

The Yale Robert Hutchins entered was quite different from the small, socially cohesive college that Will Hutchins had known. In the 1890s the college had been the prominent body in the university, with greater numbers of faculty, students, and buildings than the graduate and professional schools. There was a coherent curriculum, with required and elective courses, and a lively extracurriculum marked by the parochial traditions of class loyalty that had developed throughout the nineteenth century. The college faculty's power was preeminent, and the president, Timothy Dwight, was a minister. Religious ideas and beliefs were still incorporated into the curriculum, explicit in ethics and philosophy courses and implicit in social science and history courses.

By 1919 Yale was a modern university with a mandate from its alumni and governing body, the Yale Corporation, to reorganize the institution.[30] This reorganization involved revising the college curriculum and distributing more power to the graduate and professional schools. As a result, the college curriculum was broadened and a common freshman year was initiated to include both college freshmen and freshmen from Yale's Sheffield Scientific School. The curricular reform overrode a plan (delayed by the war) that the college faculty had developed in 1917 to increase the proportion of required courses for freshman and sophomores. One intent of the reorganization was to widen student recruitment. Western and midwestern alumni thought Yale had failed to recruit adequately from public high schools across the country and that it had relied too exclusively on eastern preparatory schools for its student body.

Departments were expanded with the reorganization. Raising the quality of the graduate and professional schools was essential to make Yale the nationally known, prestigious university the alumni, the Yale Corporation, and the graduate faculty desired. Expansion also required a shift in power over appointing faculty members, granting degrees, budgeting expenses, and determining curriculum. The power that the departments and graduate and professional schools gained, the college faculty lost.

Throughout Robert Hutchins' two years as a student at Yale there was tension in the air, which continued into the 1920s. It was generated by a disgruntled college faculty, angry that the initiative for change had shifted, and was fed by the confusion and congestion of a campus undergoing building and expansion. And it was exacerbated by the huge postwar influx of students that jammed dormitories and classrooms.

These students were more mature and independent than those who had left Yale in 1917. They saw as excessive the strictures on their behavior that had been part of the college's effort to shape character and morals. Their standards for social conduct shocked the university. They drank in spite of Prohibition laws, their sexual behavior was less constrained, and they spoke out about their dissatisfaction in student and alumni publications. For the most part, Robert Hutchins' classmates complied with the rules and participated in the curricular as well as the extracurricular life of the university. But the students who followed them in the 1920s were vocal about, and even rioted over, their discontents.

In contrast to Oberlin's coeducational, quasi-religious, service-oriented, and unpretentious social and educational atmosphere, Yale was, for Hutchins and his classmates, a male world of camaraderie and competition. For many, religious obligations were more than satisfied by daily chapel attendance. The highly competitive Yale man used his freshman and sophomore years to gain recognition on campus for athletic, social, literary, and/or intellectual accomplishments.[31] Recognition could lead to acceptance into the secret, exclusive junior and senior societies that assured easier access to prestigious social and occupational positions upon graduation.

If one was not invited on Tap Day of the junior year into Skull and Bones, Scroll and Key, or Wolf's Head (each took fifteen men a year) for the senior year, one tried for literary honors: the editorial staff of the *Yale Daily News,* the *Yale Literary Magazine,* or the *Yale Record,* a magazine of humor. The Elizabeth Club and the Yale Dramatic Association were other avenues of access to campus extracurricular life. Another, but less prestigious, activity was debating. Finally, of course, there was athletic activity. Robert Hutchins participated in all the extracurricular activities except athletics.

Hutchins fulfilled the graduation requirements in his junior year. Pursuing his postwar interest in government and politics, he studied political theory, comparative politics, and financial history of the United States. He satisfied his English requirement by taking the popular William Lyon Phelps' Tennyson and Browning course, and his science requirement by taking general biology.[32] He might well have been drawn into the further study of politics, but Yale's political science department was minimally staffed in those years. Instead, he took two law courses in the summer of 1920 and decided to stay on at Yale to study law in his senior year. Karl Llewellyn's law and society class, which explored how law worked in the economic structure, and Charles E. Clark's work in legal procedure aroused his "sharp and quick" mind in a way no other academic work had.[33]

A viable choice for a young man contemplating a future in public affairs, law supplied a challenging alternative to politics and government for Hutchins that year. Considered a "gifted and brilliant student" by his classmates, he was elected to the Torch Honor Society of the Sheffield Scientific School, even though he was not a student there.[34] His fellows also admitted him to the Order of the Coif, the law society.

Hutchins' extracurricular activities reflected his range of interests and his wide acceptance at Yale. He worked his way through his junior and senior years, an indication to his classmates of his character and stamina. He was not too proud to labor in an ice-cream spoon factory, rake lawns, or work in the dining hall in exchange for meals. He also tutored students in German, eventually establishing a tutoring bureau with his good friend Storer B. Lunt. These experiences later led him to sympathize with the problems of working students.

Hutchins' work, combined with an Oberlin-bred skepticism of material wealth as a criterion for determining character, gave him a democratic openness that was appealing to his fellows. He developed a wide range of friendships at Yale. He was able to move easily from the company of the aristocratic and elitist Henry Luce, whose father was a missionary in China and who received support from a wealthy Chicago family, to the company of William Benton, whose mother taught school and who could not afford to attend his junior prom.[35]

Hutchins was a member of the Elizabethan Club with his friend Thornton Wilder, who was considered something of a literary eccentric on campus. Hutchins was chosen for the part of Westmoreland in the Yale Dramatic Association's *King Henry IV* and appeared in another Dramat play called *Revelation.* Walter Millis, voted most scholarly by the class of 1920, nominated Robert to the prestigious senior society Wolf's Head (after he had spent his junior year as a member of Alpha Delta Phi).[36] Millis would work with Hutchins in the 1950s and 1960s as a consultant to the Fund for the Republic's basic issues program.

Beyond his "striking youthful and handsome appearance, which made him the center of attraction as soon as he came into a room," his brilliance, and the impression he made as "essentially a democratic man," Hutchins earned the respect of his classmates and the notice of the university with his prodigious public speaking talents.[37] He did not speak with emotion or add a tremolo to his voice as his grandfather had. He used concrete examples in much the way that his father used biblical passages or anecdotes from his life to support his arguments, and he spoke, often from memory, in an even, dispassionate tone. His resonant voice and simple, clear, carefully constructed logic, with occasional "audacious" remarks and an ironic, biting humor, transported his audiences. According to law professor Charles E. Clark, he already possessed this talent when he arrived at Yale.[38]

He belonged to Delta Sigma Rho, the honorary debating fraternity, and in his senior year won a place on the intercollegiate debating team for the Triangular Debates at Bates College, Georgetown University, and Harvard. William Benton, who also was on the team, remembered that Hutchins was the anchorman in the Harvard debate. Though Harvard had conceded Yale's case, Yale still had to prove it, so Benton as the number-two person "pitched into Harvard." Hutchins, though, "went ahead with his beautifully prepared speech and proved the case beautifully." "Indifferent" to winning, Hutchins "wanted to persuade the audience about truth itself."[39]

Hutchins' concern for truth pervaded his public speaking from his junior year in college throughout his life. Recognizing his rhetorical power, the university asked him during his junior year to speak to alumni audiences from the undergraduates' point of view. His brother recalled that he spoke to one group at the New Haven Lawn Club and was sharply critical of "the tired businessmen who made up the board of trustees."[40] Anson Phelps Stokes, the secretary of the university under Arthur Twining Hadley, called Hutchins into his office to reprimand him. Hutchins stated that he had done what the university had asked. He had simply conveyed the undergraduates' perspective to the alumni.

He edited the campus page of the *Yale Alumni Weekly* in the spring of his senior year, covering topics from athletic performance to such student infractions as a snowball fight that resulted in broken windows on campus. On occasion he also used the column as a forum for bringing issues to public attention, thus beginning a lifelong career as a self-appointed critic. He argued that students thought the student government should have more power to determine disciplinary measures for such problems as class cuts and athletic infractions. He criticized the president of the university for the great remoteness he seemed to be maintaining from the undergraduate population.[41]

In the months before commencement his penchant for truth telling brought him to Stokes' attention a second time. Arthur Twining Hadley, Yale's president since 1899, was to retire and James Rowland Angell was to be inaugurated in his place at commencement on June 21, 1921. Hutchins suggested in his column that the petition seniors had circulated and signed protesting the limitation on commencement-inauguration tickets had been "buffaloed by the University authorities."[42] When Stokes objected to his terminology, Hutchins wrote to him explaining that he had "merely set down the Campus point of view" as he knew it. Whether or not it was printed was a decision he preferred to leave to the editors. Still, he had learned his mother's lessons well and apologized for adding to Stokes' "difficulties."[43]

His next notable contact with the secretary's office at the university was when it became his own in 1923, at James Rowland Angell's request.

Hutchins' interest in persuading his fellows of the truth as he understood it was manifest in his debating, in his writing for the *Alumni Weekly,* in his dealings with his fellow students, and in his oratory. As his tutoring partner Storer B. Lunt noted, he "saw through any guff and was amused." He was an extraordinarily self-confident young man. "Nothing pleased him more than to ridicule the pompous or to pull the rug out from under a fake."[44] Not always funny, his quick responses also could bite, perhaps a manifestation of his honesty and skepticism.

Charles E. Clark remembered that Hutchins was asked to give a welcome speech in behalf of the students to James Rowland Angell, who was invited to the campus in February of 1921, shortly after the Yale Corporation had chosen him to succeed Hadley to the presidency. Hutchins' speech "quite carried away the audience" with its contrast of "the dreary outlook before the choice and the warmth of spring after the announcement." His "brashness" put off former president William H. Taft, then a professor at Yale, and, according to Taft, hurt Hadley so much that he left the room. His "daring remarks" could please or "sting."[45]

Robert's father worried that his occasional imprudence "would really trouble him" in his adult life.[46] In fact, it did. The "quick and illuminating turn" he could give to an idea in a speech or the "apt, succinct, and devastating response" he could make to a question would delight interviewers, reporters, and audiences throughout his life.[47] His wit—honest as it may have been in intention—was troublesome when it was at someone's expense. He was to alienate members of his faculty, trustees, and people who did not know him well and were not impressed with his forthrightness or humor. In effect, he would defeat some of his own crusades with the same verbal skill that could raise millions of dollars and draw strong support.

In 1921 he earned three exceptional honors from Yale. The first was his classmates' vote as the most likely to succeed of the class of 1921, who thought he would make a great contribution to politics and government as a public leader.[48]

The second honor, also from his classmates, was his election as class orator. He delivered his oration just before commencement. Rather than extol the virtues of Yale or of his classmates, Robert took this opportunity to assess, with some irony, the variety of ways that Yale had prepared them for the world, from the prestige the Yale name conferred on them to the "social graces" they had acquired (and might have gotten just as easily at "some convenient country club"). Like a minister unwilling to allow his congregation too much self-congratulation over some good deed well done, he addressed their complacency with being educated at Yale and the status that entailed. He argued that the pressure for social conformity at

Yale (and other eastern colleges) overshadowed any opportunity they may have had to taste "the sweetness and glory of being rational animals" and to develop into fit leaders of America. The "flat mediocrity, the crass commercialism, the narrow politics, the irreligion of commonplace affairs" in America were an indication that the nation needed more from its colleges than they were delivering. James Rowland Angell, he thought, had it right: "The purpose of college education is to inflame young men with ideas, to stimulate their intellects, to get them to think."[49]

The DeForest Prize was the third exceptional honor he received from Yale. His father had won this most coveted oratorical award in 1892. Despite the fact that Hutchins had not given any serious thought to a career in education, nor systematically to education itself, he again discussed the importance of education in his submission to the DeForest oration competition. Henry Luce had won the prize in 1920 for a speech on the need for America to develop and maintain an active foreign policy that reflected her economic and moral strength in the world.

Just as Luce's DeForest oration expressed a theme that he would reiterate throughout his career as a publisher, so Hutchins' emphasis on education in his oration reflected his ongoing concern that wealth not be a determinant of educational opportunity. Having learned about the needs of the "isolated and forgotten" mountain people "in the backyards" of Kentucky and seven other states, Hutchins made an eloquent plea to his fellows. "Our Contemporary Ancestors," the people of Appalachia, "more destitute of education than any other representatives of our race," needed to be brought into the modern world through education. They required not only more, and more equitably financed, schools but also college-educated teachers willing to go into the mountains and make a commitment to their educational future.[50] No doubt Robert's conviction that education could help these people gain control of their lives and his appeal to the service ideal made sense to the contest judges at the university.

The baccalaureate sermon Arthur Twining Hadley delivered two days before commencement reflected this ongoing, but diminishing, Yale concern for service. True competition, he argued, was Christian competition, the participation in "a contest wherein we prove our power to serve others." He pointed to the teachers at Yale who had "worked hard for small worldly reward," whose example had prepared men at Yale "to render public service in church and civil state."[51] There is some irony in the fact that, while Yale men continued to be leaders, most of them were leaders in business, where the worldly rewards were great and public service did not necessarily follow. Their college courses had incorporated more secular, objective ways of viewing knowledge than their fathers' had, and their experience in the social world was colored by the striving for material gain of an increasingly consumer-oriented society.

Hutchins graduated with honors in Yale's 1921 contribution to America's leaders.[52] Two hundred twenty-seven men received their bachelor of arts degrees with him. Many of them, like Robert's friend Bill Benton, went into business in spite of the recession that year. Fewer went to law school. Some went on to teach. And very few entered the ministry.[53]

Like his friend Benton, who started an advertising business (Benton & Bowles), made a million dollars (in assets), and retired to live on a smaller salary and devote his life to service at the University of Chicago and in public affairs, Hutchins felt compelled to measure himself by what and how he contributed to the betterment of humanity. For him, higher education was the vehicle by which he could make his contribution. On one hand, Yale's sophisticated social environment and pressure to conform whetted his appetite for a materially comfortable life. On the other hand, these aspects of his Yale experience did not diminish the standards for measuring his own self-worth and what constituted the good life that his father and mother had taught him and that Oberlin so effectively had reinforced. He was never tempted to question that such standards existed and ought to be honored.

Hutchins considered a variety of possible jobs after his graduation from Yale. He had enjoyed his law courses and his writing for the *Yale Alumni Weekly* in his last year of school. He accepted a minor position in his Uncle Francis' law firm, Baldwin & Hutchins, for the summer and considered continuing this work into the fall and studying law at night. He also thought about doing some freelance writing for the *Alumni Weekly* and the *Yale Law Journal.* He decided that the pay would be too low at the law firm and that the income from writing would not be reliable enough to justify following those options.[54] His brother William's experience with Condé Nast most likely left him uninterested in a business career.

At one point there was a history position at the Lawrenceville School, where his friend Thornton Wilder planned to begin teaching French in the fall after his return from travel in Europe, but the job was taken by someone else. He finally settled on a position teaching history and English at the Lake Placid School. For the man most likely to succeed from the class of 1921, the Lake Placid School was not the most auspicious beginning. Located at Lake Placid, New York, during fall and spring and at Coconut

Grove, Florida, during the winter months, the school was not financially well endowed. Nor did it have a reputable standing among preparatory schools. The new headmaster, a Mr. H. L. Malcolm, was taking in the reprobate sons of the wealthy, boys who had flunked out of other schools and needed to pass their College Board examinations. Apparently, Malcolm's "financial success" depended on how many boys passed.[55]

Hutchins arrived at the decision to teach at Lake Placid rather than take a chance on the other options because he was planning to be married. He had met Maude Phelps McVeigh in the summer of 1919 at his Uncle Francis and Aunt Sadie's house on Long Island. She appears to have been the first woman who interested him romantically. With his characteristic verve and unswerving commitment, he *"loved her instantly."*[56]

Maude Phelps McVeigh was tall, dark-haired, attractive, and "sensible" and had an interest in painting and sculpture.[57] A striking young woman, she was both headstrong and vulnerable. She and her sister Frances were orphans who had been raised by their wealthy and somewhat authoritarian grandfather and their aunt, Mrs. Samuel Ludlow Thompson of Bay Shore, Long Island (their mother was Maude Phelps, and their father was Warren R. McVeigh of the New York *Sun*). According to Francis Sessions Hutchins, Maude and Frances had not had a happy childhood. Despite his Uncle Francis' fears that at twenty-one he was too young to marry and that he was being "pressed" into the marriage because of Maude's unhappiness in her aunt's home, Robert did not relent.[58] Indeed, he was willing to shelve his hopes for law school and take the Lake Placid job so that he could provide for her. His parents supported his decision and gave him their blessing.[59] His father married them on September 21, 1921, and they left for Lake Placid shortly afterward.

Hutchins remembered that the school was a last resort for many of the students, who ranged from twelve to twenty-one years of age. His major task as a teacher was to make sure they could pass the College Board examinations. Hutchins used Boynton's *School Civics* and Muzzey's *Masterpieces of American History,* moving through the book at "eight pages a day."[60] He collected College Board examinations going back to 1909, when they were first published, as study aids in his history classes.

For his English classes, he used Palgrave's *Golden Treasury* to teach poetry and to provide topics for "theme building." He thought teaching poetry "the most difficult thing" an English teacher had to do. He started by having the boys explain the meaning of each poem, examining references and figures of speech in them, and he tried to teach them about meter. Palgrave's book 4 was difficult to use but was the best source for the poems that would be on the College Board examinations.[61] He relied on his Oberlin Academy experience, past examinations, and books he had used as a student to design his classes at the school.

Student motivation was a problem. Nevertheless, he set high scholastic standards and went so far as to start a debating team at the school. But he spent most of his time disciplining the students and later characterized them as "rich juvenile delinquents."[62] His headmaster thought he "performed brilliantly."[63] Yet Hutchins hated his job. After a summer in New Haven studying in the Law School at Yale, he returned to Lake Placid for the fall term. When George Parmley Day, the treasurer of the Yale Corporation, wired him in October of 1922 to set up an interview with him in Utica, New York, Hutchins jumped at the opportunity for a change.[64]

James Rowland Angell was searching for a secretary of the university to replace Anson Phelps Stokes, who had retired. The secretary's duties included public relations, which in 1922 consisted of speaking before alumni groups. Hutchins had exhibited outstanding oratorical abilities, and his choice of work after graduation suggested an interest in education. Angell offered him the position.

Hutchins was ecstatic and informed Angell that he saw it as "the greatest opportunity which could possibly come to me." He was "deeply conscious" of his "youth and inexperience" but would accept "the most important educational post in America" with hopes that Angell's choice would be justified.[65] In order to be released from his contract with Malcolm, Hutchins agreed to find a replacement and requested Yale's assistance with the task. In December, Storer B. Lunt agreed to take his place so that Hutchins could begin in his new position in January of 1923.

Hutchins' predecessor, Anson Phelps Stokes, had become secretary to the university in 1899, shortly after his own graduation from Yale College (1896), when Arthur Twining Hadley began his presidency. Hutchins saw the job as Stokes had created it in his twenty-three-year tenure. Indeed, Stokes had become a powerful member of the administration, facilitating the reorganization, mobilizing alumni, raising money, and serving as Hadley's second-in-command. He had the ears of men in the Yale Corporation and was able to persuade them not only of the need for alumni participation at Yale but also of the need to keep alumni informed and to attend to their criticisms.

In addition, Stokes had brought into the secretary's office the records of class secretaries and of the alumni fund agents, thereby staying abreast of alumni interests. He had begun with a part-time staff of two, but by 1922 his staff had grown to forty. A measure of his accomplishments as secretary and right-hand man to Hadley was his candidacy as Hadley's successor until Angell was nominated to the position. Hutchins would assume many of Stokes' official duties, but Angell would not confer on him the power or autonomy that Hadley had given to Stokes.

The Hutchinses arrived in New Haven in December of 1922. Maude enrolled in the Yale Art School. Robert encouraged her painting and sculpture, and even agreed to model for her occasionally. She received her bachelor of fine arts degree in 1926, the same year that their daughter Mary Frances (Franja) was born, and she paid the doctor's bill from the sale of one of her pieces. Hutchins was proud of her accomplishments and talent. She won the Charles Warren Prize for one of her sculptures in the same year that he graduated from Law School.

Hutchins' secretarial duties included preparing and keeping the records of the Yale Corporation, which necessitated his attendance at that body's meetings. He supervised the election of members to the Corporation and conducted its official correspondence. The university's public and alumni relations and its publications were also his responsibility. He handled the press. He oversaw the maintenance of class secretaries' records and the clerical bureau of the university. His office made all the arrangements for university lectures, concerts, and meetings. He supervised student registration at the beginning of the term and commencement exercises at the end of the school year.[66]

One of his first public tasks was to speak at a reunion of the class of 1896. Appropriately, he paid homage to Anson Phelps Stokes, a member of the class of 1896, and drew upon President Angell's theme of the goal of education at Yale: to foster education of the highest quality. He described how hard such an endeavor was for students who "had not been born in Pierce Arrow limousines" and who had to work to support themselves. They were unable to participate equally with the sons of the wealthy in Yale's social and intellectual life. Denying that Yale had ever been a democratic college, a common boast of Yale alumni based on that fact that many Yale students had worked their way through college, he entreated the class of 1896 to continue giving generously to scholarship funds.[67]

He was expected to use his exceptional oratorical gifts to solicit money from alumni. His performance as a spokesman and his competence balancing and organizing other tasks of his office more than justified Angell's confidence in his ability to take on the position. In the 1924–25 academic year, he was an instructor in a freshman social science course, in which professors from the university lectured. He led discussions and graded papers, probably to earn extra money.[68] And he still had enough time and energy to take courses in the Law School. To prevent his studies from interfering with his job, he attended classes in the summers, late afternoons, and early mornings from 1923 to 1925, when he received his LL.B. Angell not only allowed him to study while he worked but also appointed him to an instructorship on the Law School faculty in 1925. Not until 1926 did Hutchins ask for extra help in the secretary's office to deal with the university's increasing publicity needs and to allow more time for his teaching.[69]

As secretary, Hutchins sat in on Yale Corporation meetings. He witnessed debates over limiting the freshman enrollment, part of an effort, according to Marsha Synnott and Dan Oren, to restrict the admission of Jews to Yale.[70] He was privy to discussions about budget allocations for departments and schools, appointments and promotions, alumni relations, fund raising, faculty-student-administration relations, and all the other issues and conflicts a university president must work out with the trustees, faculty, and administrators.

Angell was something of a mentor to Hutchins. Neither man ever explicitly acknowledged such a relationship except in letters in the 1930s when Hutchins addressed Angell as "Boss" and occasionally discussed university problems with him.[71] Yet he closely observed Angell for four years until 1927, when he was appointed professor and acting dean of the Law School. As Yale's law school dean and then president of the University of Chicago, Hutchins incorporated a number of Angell's ideas about higher education and university organization into his own approaches to administration. He also adopted and rejected certain characteristics of Angell's leadership style. What makes this aspect of Hutchins' apprenticeship particularly significant is how it was manifest in his presidency of the University of Chicago in the 1930s and 1940s. His great respect for Angell showed in his later use and rejection of some of Angell's ideas, style, and methods, according to how well they had worked with Yale's various constituencies in the 1920s.

James Rowland Angell was the first president of Yale who had not been a Yale student. Known at the University of Chicago as "Sunny Jim," he was a "friendly" man, "quick, engaging, and full of salty good humor."[72] He was well received at Yale by the students and many members of the graduate and professional faculty. He had a harder time with the college faculty, partly because he emphasized intellectual development over college life (or extracurricular activities) and he focused on developing Yale's national reputation through the graduate and professional schools, and partly because he was not a Yale man. A midwesterner, he completed his undergraduate degree at the University of Michigan, where his father James Burrill Angell was president.

Angell began graduate work in philosophy with John Dewey at Michigan and continued with William James at Harvard. Starting doctoral study at the universities of Halle and Berlin, he returned before finishing to take an instructorship in philosophy at the University of Minnesota in 1893. In 1894 he was recruited to the University of Chicago by John Dewey, head of the departments of pedagogy, psychology, and philosophy at the new university. He developed the psychology laboratory, taught, and assisted Dewey with his experimental school.

Over the next twenty-five years, Angell conducted research at the University of Chicago. He worked with Robert Yerkes to design intelligence tests for the Army during World War I. At Chicago he served as dean of the senior colleges, dean of the faculties, and acting president. Chairman of the National Research Council (1919–20) and president of the Carnegie Corporation (1920–21), he was knowledgeable about the scientific and social scientific research that scholars were developing in universities and about the particular problems colleges faced after the war. His awareness of scholarship and his administrative experience appealed to the Yale Corporation members, alumni, and graduate and professional faculty trying to transform Yale into a modern twentieth-century university.[73]

A characteristic Angell and Hutchins had in common, which probably provided a bond despite their thirty-year age difference, was their talent for public speaking. Angell was an eloquent, graceful speaker who, like Hutchins, used wit and humor to illustrate and persuade. He possessed an elegant command of the English language. Charles E. Clark remembered that, when both men had occasion to speak at the same function, "an unusual performance was sure to result."[74]

Angell had a variety of administrative ideas to bring forth the intellectual quality he sought for Yale College and the graduate and professional schools. Some of these ideas Hutchins would later adopt. Angell thought improvements would result if admissions requirements were raised. Honors courses for undergraduates and comprehensive examinations to replace both subjective faculty evaluations and required attendance in class were means of raising quality. He believed that too much time was wasted in high school and that young men could attend college earlier. These were ideas that Hutchins attempted to incorporate in Yale's Law School when he was dean and at the University of Chicago when he became president.

Angell actively tried to recruit faculty. When his efforts were blocked by members of the college faculty, who maintained autonomous powers of appointment and promotion until the Corporation extended the president's powers in the 1930s, he worked with the graduate and professional school deans to appoint good scholars to the faculty. He also hired faculty members through such circuitous routes as the Institute of Human Relations after it was established in 1929. Hutchins, too, would use these methods when the faculty at the University of Chicago resisted his candidates for appointment and promotion. Angell was a strong advocate of raising faculty salaries, which helped to reduce the hostility of some Yale College faculty members. Hutchins informed the trustees at the University of Chicago in 1929 that his first act as president would be to raise faculty salaries.

Angell argued for cross-fertilization of the academic fields, cooperation among the faculty of different departments, and the introduction of research projects and courses that would combine disciplinary methods and content. Hutchins used these ideas in the Law School at Yale when he organized the Institute of Human Relations with Angell, and at the University of Chicago when he established a variety of interdisciplinary committees. Just as Angell tried to keep intellectual quality in the forefront of Yale's discussion of educational purposes among students and faculty, so would Hutchins do so at Chicago.[75] Finally, Angell was a staunch protector of academic freedom at Yale. Hutchins defended academic freedom throughout his career.

Some Yale Corporation and faculty members thought Angell was overly cautious with his reforms in the first decade of his presidency. Students had rioted in the middle 1920s for curricular improvements and greater social freedom, and some college faculty members continued to resist his suggestions for appointments and curricular and extracurricular change. Yet, as George Wilson Pierson has shown in his history of Yale, Angell had both the experience and the temperament that mandated persuasion and patience over coercion and undue pressure in his faculty dealings.[76]

Angell had worked with some of the most independent and autonomous faculty members in the country at the University of Chicago. He had watched them develop curricula and work out their differences over time. His study with Dewey and James and his work in psychology had led him to believe that there might legitimately be a plurality of approaches to curriculum reform and even to ways of learning and teaching depending on subject matter and student groups. His flexible and tolerant temperament made him incapable of trespassing on faculty prerogative even after the Yale Corporation granted him the power to do so.

It is not clear exactly how Hutchins perceived Angell's administrative style. His later behavior suggests that he considered Angell's reform efforts unduly slow and reticent. His own approach with the faculty at the University of Chicago would be impetuous, arrogant, and coercive in the early years of his presidency. His ideas about curriculum would be less broad and flexible than Angell's. Quite likely, Hutchins' youth, lack of direct and sustained experience with administration, and unflinching confidence in the righteousness of his own educational ideas overrode any lessons about patience he might have learned from Angell's more experienced and thoughtful early leadership at Yale.

Yale University in the 1920s was a fitting place of apprenticeship for Hutchins to learn about the organization of education and scholarship in a modern university. Angell was a significant model. In two years in the middle 1920s, he increased the school's endowment by more than $20 million. He raised faculty salaries. He valued the undergraduate college as the heart of the university. At the same time, he promoted social science research in the graduate school. He wrestled explicitly and tellingly with how undergraduate and graduate education would relate to each other within one institution. These were all problems Hutchins would face at the University of Chicago.

It is doubtful that Angell confided in Hutchins about his difficulties in negotiating his reform plans with Yale's constituencies. His own social reticence among Yale people and the difference in their ages as well as the disparity of their positions in the administrative hierarchy make that highly unlikely. When Angell appointed Hutchins dean of the Law School, the two worked together on many of Hutchins' attempts to institute reform in legal education and research at Yale. He supported Hutchins' work and believed in his scholarly and administrative potential.

Hutchins had been enormously enthusiastic when Angell first came to Yale in 1921. He wrote in his *Yale Alumni Weekly* column that "the

CHAPTER 3 *Recognition*

IF ROBERT HUTCHINS' promise as a college student was considered impressive by his classmates, his promise as a law student, teacher, and administrator was outstanding. Months before graduating magna cum laude from the Yale Law School, he was recommended for appointment as instructor. He took the position shortly after he received his LL.B. in 1925. He was appointed acting dean and associate professor of the Law School two years later, in 1927, and professor and dean in early 1928.

This recognition was partly a result of Hutchins' youthful enthusiasm for the intellectual ferment that was linking research in law with the social sciences.[1] In addition, he was able to articulate the faculty's desires for improving the status and academic quality of the Law School in relation to Harvard and Columbia, Yale's two biggest competitors for prestige and students. Finally, he was working within an economic boom that facilitated access to foundation money. These funds made his plans for interdisciplinary research and higher scholastic standards appear feasible.

Hutchins' experience as a law student was unique. His law in society course with Karl N. Llewellyn, who taught at Yale in the summers, and his independent research with Charles E. Clark went far beyond the traditional study of cases that is standard in most law schools. Hutchins' experience was so unusual that the curriculum committee of the Law School faculty voted to require him to take "fundamental subjects given in the regular course" before they would allow him to graduate.[2] When he received his degree in 1925, his conception of what legal scholarship should be was profoundly different from that of most law school graduates. Under Clark and Llewellyn he had been required to raise questions about the validity of case study and to examine legal decisions in economic and social context.

Clark had noticed Hutchins' "apt, succinct" responses on examination papers and, when Hutchins returned as secretary to the university, assisted his law studies by requesting credits for the research Hutchins did for him in legal procedure.[3] Because he could work on his own, this arrangement allowed him to fulfill his job responsibilities and to continue his law study. Observing court operations, the factual conditions that affected procedure and decisions, and the logic of legal language, Hutchins developed a critical perspective on legal procedure and legal education.[4] He and Clark joined forces to reform the Yale Law School by taking these issues into account.

Clark's and Hutchins' research and educational ideas were rooted in their predecessors' examinations of the social and economic conditions in which law operated. Rather than rely solely on precedent, Louis D. Brandeis in the early twentieth century compiled social data in his legal briefs to support his arguments. Roscoe Pound at Harvard had coined the term "sociological jurisprudence" to describe the social context of judicial rulings. In the Storrs Lectures at Yale in 1921, Benjamin N. Cardozo, the judge Hutchins later admitted he most respected, presented skeptical arguments about the conscious and subconscious decision-making processes of judges and the changes over time in jurisprudential rulings on similar issues.[5] Academic lawyers had begun to incorporate social science theory and methods in addition to case research in their scholarship.

Not all legal scholars were reformers. Most Harvard faculty, for example, adhered to the case method of legal pedagogy developed by Christopher Columbus Langdell when he was dean of the Harvard Law School in the 1870s. The case method was based on common-law rulings. It was intended to disclose not only precedent in judicial rulings but also transcendent guiding principles of procedure and decision making. Case study was the predominant method of teaching law students in the United States by the 1920s. Harvard showed few signs of departing from the method, but other academic lawyers were experimenting with new approaches to the law curriculum.[6] Their conception of legal education and of legal research influenced Hutchins' participation in the legal realist movement.

Like Harvard, Yale had first acquired its law school on a proprietary basis in the 1820s. Whereas Harvard had adopted Langdell's method in the 1870s, Yale Law School resisted the trend, maintaining its partially proprietary status with part-time faculty who practiced law. The case method was not used until 1903, when Arthur L. Corbin joined the faculty. Over the next nine years he campaigned to raise the school's standards and to induce the faculty to agree to use Langdell's method in the three-year course. He was successful in 1912.

Corbin influenced the hiring of Thomas W. Swan as dean of the Law

School in 1916 to succeed Henry W. Rogers. Together with Wesley N. Hohfeld and Walter Wheeler Cook, who joined the faculty in 1914 and 1916, respectively, Corbin and Swan attracted eight more faculty members by 1920. Edwin Borchard, Edmund Morgan, William R. Vance, and Edward Thurston produced traditional scholarship. Ernest Lorenzen, who initially seemed to have realist ideas, and three Yale Law School graduates, Charles E. Clark, Karl N. Llewellyn, and historian of law, George Woodbine, joined Corbin and Cook in the liberal wing of the faculty. Yale's reputation for teaching and scholarship significantly improved.

The methodological and intellectual criticisms Josef Redlich and Alfred Z. Reed had published in 1914 and 1921 (in reports commissioned and financed by the Carnegie Foundation on the study and profession of law) had influenced the liberal wing of the faculty. Redlich and Reed suggested that the case method was pedagogically inadequate for teaching large classes, too limited to deal with the complex administration of law at the state and federal level in the United States, and detrimental to the scholarly and scientific development of the study of law.[7] Corbin, Hohfeld, and Cook at Yale each had developed a skeptical approach to the study of cases.[8]

Corbin, despite his introduction of the case method to help modernize the Law School, had come to the conclusion that the study of judicial decisions, within the context of the facts of each case, revealed that there were no intrinsically logical rules that emerged from the cases embodying the common law. Intrinsic logic was lacking because the law changed continually. The ideas guiding the administration of justice, in order to be effective and just at any given time, should be attentive to the ways society changed. Hohfeld's untimely death in 1918 ended his work before it was fully developed, but his ideas continued to influence scholarship and teaching at Yale. He had begun elaborating a functional approach to the interpretation of legal language in cases, arguing that meanings often were not consistent from case to case. Cook went further, advocating the application of scientific methods to the study of law to incorporate and transcend logical analysis of judicial reasoning. He argued for developing empirical methods of analyzing the ways the legal system operated.

The skepticism these men incorporated in their teaching and scholarship profoundly influenced their students, including Clark, Llewellyn, and those who joined the faculty in the 1920s: Wesley Sturges, Herschel Arant, Roscoe Turner, Leon Tulin, Leon Green, and Robert Hutchins. By 1925 losses from the faculty and a limited endowment hobbled the Law

School's growth and necessitated the hiring of Yale law graduates (including Hutchins) at lower salaries simply to sustain the gains the school had made since 1916.

The major impetus for reform moved to Columbia Law School, where Cook and a dynamic young faculty gathered in the early-to-middle 1920s. Underhill Moore, Thomas Reed Powell, Cook, Herman Oliphant, Hessel E. Yntema, and Llewellyn formed a committee to examine the curriculum and make suggestions for change. Under Oliphant's direction, the committee proposed reorganizing the curriculum along functionalist lines to promote the scholarly analysis and criticism of the law by focusing on the ways law actually functioned in society. Law courses organized around how law was practiced and administered, with rigorous attention to the social and economic facts of its operation, would better train lawyers for practice. Judges might find more scientific and efficient bases for their decisions, and courts might operate more justly and humanely.

Since the 1890s, social science theory had similarly affected professionals' approaches to the reform of school systems, the administration of social welfare, and the development of labor legislation protecting women and children and other laborers. It is understandable why such a movement would appeal to a former Oberlin student armed with convictions and ready for new intellectual challenges. Through Llewellyn, Cook, Corbin, and Clark, Hutchins learned the significance of Columbia's reforms in the middle 1920s.

One functional seminar the Columbia faculty developed focused on the relationships between legal rules, judicial decisions, and business practices. Llewellyn took part in this seminar the second year, as did William O. Douglas, a graduate of Columbia Law School. Llewellyn and others designed courses on business practices that combined case materials and social science research findings. There were hopes that the whole curriculum might be organized along functional lines, reflecting faculty research in business, economics, and other social science disciplines shedding new light on legal problems and procedures.[9]

These hopes were dashed in 1928 when Young B. Smith was appointed dean by Nicholas Murray Butler, president of Columbia. Smith was interested in the research the seminars conducted, but he did not want all the work of the Law School absorbed by this new movement. He and Butler were unwilling to endanger the training of lawyers for practice by abandoning the case method and replacing it with the realists' functional approach to the curriculum. To take such a course might weaken the school's position in the eyes of members of the American Bar Association (ABA) and the Association of American Law Schools (AALS), the organizations that determined the criteria for access to the bar.

Columbia's curriculum conflict resulted in numerous resignations from the Law School. Younger faculty members resented the appointment, without consultation, of Smith over Oliphant. The controversy suggested the political issues Hutchins and Clark faced at Yale. The power and control of appointments, curriculum policies, and financial and other support for scholarship threatened to polarize faculty members. Conflicts at Yale followed predictable patterns: a younger generation versus an older generation, academic research versus preparation for practice, intellectual exploration using emerging fields of knowledge and research methods versus case book study and memorization, and generally, reform versus conservative or traditional philosophies of education.

Not surprisingly, the roots of contention were in larger social changes since the 1890s. The growth of corporations signaled the rise of big business as a dominant force in American social, political, and economic life. Brandeis' efforts to foster public service interests in the profession by recommending that the lawyer become "counsel to the situation," attentive to the public interest rather than simply to client interest, reflected early reform lawyers' concerns.[10] Felix Frankfurter, among the academic lawyers at Harvard in the 1910s, perceived the law teacher's role as essential to making future practitioners conscious of the broad implications of legal and judicial behavior.

Many academic lawyers who criticized the influence of corporations on lawyers, judges, and legislators used their teaching to call attention to the problem by relating the law to its social context. In effect, they acted on larger social concerns and through their students extended progressive influence in the 1920s to the training of lawyers. Early, respectable skeptics Oliver Wendell Holmes, whose *Common Law* characterized experience, rather than logic, as the life of law, Pound, Brandeis, and Frankfurter set the stage for the next generation. The legal realists were distinguished from such intellectual predecessors by their attempt to develop scholarship using the most recent methods and findings of the social sciences.[11]

Because of the intellectual independence of these lawyers and the nature of their questions about the law, their work did not result in a concerted movement. The legal realists were at different law schools. Not all were committed equally to empirical research in their own work, or to the same lines of argument in their criticisms, or to uniform methods of reform. Nevertheless, they constituted a network of reformers. For Hutchins, realist ideas were intrinsically bound up in the process of becoming an academic lawyer. He moved easily into this cohort of academic lawyers in 1925.

Realists were not the only innovators of the period. Academic lawyers had played a significant role in the establishment and growth of the ABA as a major gatekeeper to the profession. They also had been instrumental in the creation of the AALS in 1900. The AALS worked on and off with the ABA assuming, or trying to assume, greater responsibility for defining the standards of legal education for university law schools. Members of the two groups joined forces in 1923 to form the American Law Institute (ALI).

The ALI, an effort to transform the law itself, was financed by the Carnegie Corporation. Unlike realists from Yale and Columbia in the 1920s, who were trying to unseat the case method of pedagogy and broaden the research base of legal scholarship, the ALI members were predominantly from Harvard. Their goal was to restate the rules of law in view of existing social needs, case precedent, and how rules of law actually operated. A combination of functionalist, social, and clarification goals was reduced by the early 1930s to the simplification of rule definition using case precedent. Rather than a changed curriculum, the ALI reinforced case study in legal education, and, as Ellen Condliffe Lagemann argues, protected the legal profession's role in interpreting and making common law.[12] In addition, the restaters succeeded in clarifying the law, one of their major goals, and in providing an important resource for lawyers and appellate judges. The Yale faculty remained skeptical of the ALI's activities and the extent of change that would result.

Hutchins attended and finished law school in this fertile atmosphere of reform. That he joined the liberal wing of legal academicians is not surprising given his Oberlin background, his aspirations to intellectual independence, and his legal education with the functionalists at Yale's law school. His association with Angell made him receptive to the intellectual possibilities social science scholarship offered to legal scholars. Teaching in the Law School further influenced him. Corbin was a strong motivator of the younger faculty members. He encouraged them to consider the facts for interpreting case rulings and to pursue factual research. His emphasis on a functionalist rather than a conceptualist approach to law formed the basis of the younger faculty members' work.[13]

In his first year as an instructor, Hutchins taught procedure and public service law. In 1926 he taught evidence, a course he had not studied. According to a former student, Thomas I. Emerson (who later joined the Yale faculty), Hutchins was an "interesting, lively" teacher who had "command" of his subject and appeared "extremely able" to handle the teaching demands.[14]

In that first year, Hutchins and Clark designed an honors program that would incorporate functionalist approaches in the curriculum and proposed an Institute of Procedure to gain institutional and financial support for empirical research. Hutchins also developed his own research agenda, using scholarship in psychology to raise questions about exceptions to the law of evidence. Many of his program ideas had originated with Clark, who had in turn enlisted Hutchins' charismatic enthusiasm for them. He had not only the functionally oriented faculty's support but also Angell's for his educational reforms and research plans.

Before he became consumed by administrative responsibilities at the University of Chicago, Angell's field of research had been functionalist psychology. He distinguished psychology in his own work by looking at the discipline as a branch of biology. He studied mind in "its relation to the physical organism and its environment," in order to develop workable methods of empirical research.[15] Rather than the content of mental experience, he examined mental operations, their physical and social context, and how they contributed to adaptive behavior. He was a strong advocate, in addition, of interdisciplinary research. When Hutchins and Clark proposed research in law as one social context in which to examine the implications of social science and psychological theories and research, Angell understandably was receptive.

Angell also saw the proposal for an honors curriculum as a means of raising academic quality at Yale. Its potential to provide intellectually rigorous interdisciplinary training for future lawyers and legal scholars was attractive. A further consideration was the promise of distinguishing the Yale Law School from Harvard's and Columbia's at a time when faculty members were apprehensive about the status of the school.

Dean Swan's hiring of new faculty in the 1920s had been curtailed by lack of funds. Arthur Corbin wrote to Angell in 1924 pleading for expanded facilities, including a library and dormitories, to keep faculty already hired and to attract students who were not residents of New Haven.[16] In the same year, the faculty had voted to limit the total number of students to four hundred, though the Law School was still nearly one hundred short of that goal.[17] The Hutchins-Clark proposal suggested using "the best third year students for more effective work" and developing "modern methods of Law School study" that would incorporate seminars using "other branches of knowledge," including the social sciences, to examine such traditional domains of law study as criminal procedure.[18]

The Institute of Procedure proposal was related to the honors plan and was expected to facilitate honors work. It also was intended to assist with some of Corbin's 1924 requests. If passed and financed, the institute could enable the Law School to hire new professors and develop the seminars and the research capabilities of the faculty. It met reformers' concerns by promising to perform a "public service by assisting in the solution" of "pressing" legal problems by pursuing "scientific" study of "procedure in its functional, comparative, and historical aspects." At the same time, the institute could attract graduate students, develop Yale's reputation in the field of procedure, and "counteract Harvard's 6 million [dollar recently raised endowment] and Columbia's [prestige in] business law."[19]

Hutchins and Clark campaigned throughout the spring of 1926 to convince the older, more conservative faculty members to accept both proposals. By May of 1926 the honors plan had been revised to limit the total Law School enrollment to three hundred and, with the research seminars and small classes, to make Yale's "the first honors or research law school in America." The plan suggested an increase in tuition to cover the cost of lower enrollment. It would allow Yale to train "men to discover the actual operation of the law rather than to memorize its rules," Hutchins explained to Karl Llewellyn.[20]

It was not the research orientation specifically that the conservative faculty members found objectionable in the proposal. Rather, Swan, Corbin, Vance, Thurston, and Lorenzen objected to the tuition increase, the restriction on enrollment and consequent loss of tuition monies, and the expanse of the program. Angell, too, objected to the expense, though he agreed in principle with the direction of the research. They all were loath to endanger the gains the Law School had made since Swan had become dean in 1916. Everyone except Corbin, who disdained such concerns, found appealing the distinctive position Yale could assume as the only law school in the country with a research-based honors program.[21]

When the *New Republic* published a laudatory article on the Harvard Law School endowment, Angell asked Hutchins to reply to the article. Hutchins, not one to miss such an opportunity, presented to the faculty a sample response that touted Yale's as the only research and honors law school in the country. Both the older and the younger faculty members were impressed. Clark, Tulin, Green, Woodbine, Turner, and Sturges were Hutchins allies. The enthusiasm of this younger group wore away Arthur Corbin's resistance.[22] Corbin's support was crucial because of his long-standing unofficial leadership of the school. By the end of 1926, the faculty agreed to experiment with a third-year honors program and to limit enrollment to one hundred per class, though it already hovered around that number.[23]

The Institute of Procedure proposal was submitted, tabled, approved "in general," modified, then accepted in March of 1926 when Hutchins and Clark were authorized to present it to Angell.[24] Considering the limitations on the Law School's resources and the conservative faculty members' initial opposition to the honors plan, the proposal for the institute received a surprising amount of support. The reason for this is Clark's and Hutchins' skillful weaving of various faculty concerns into the proposal's themes.

The project they outlined implicitly enhanced the status of academic lawyers in the legal profession and confirmed their elite positions. At the same time, it supplied the means to engage in progressive social and legal reform. By volunteering to encode the rules of trial and appellate practice, pleading, and criminal procedure (all areas not covered by the ALI's restatement), Yale's researchers would be put in the powerful position of standardizing the rules. Data would be analyzed for the "effectiveness" of procedures and rules, though how effectiveness was to be defined was not addressed. Through the institute, Yale's academic lawyers would recommend measures for lawyers, judges, and legislators for reforming the legal system by making it more efficient and responsive to public needs. They would discover and present the most effective methods and rules of code, common law, and equity pleading for use in practice. They would describe problems with the rules of evidence, and uncover those determined solely by "ancient legal technicalities" rather than empirically verified logical reasoning.[25]

Empirical verification could be derived from psychological experiments (to determine reaction and motivation) and by examining the proper context for employing the rules, from jury trials to administrative board and commission hearings. How the rules were used in practice, compared with their intended use and interpretation, would also form the basis for recommendations. In addition, research would allow academic lawyers to analyze and recommend more effective means of administering criminal law, from the processes and practices of arrest to those of indictments, trials, convictions, acquittals, and punishments.

The possibilities of enhancing academic lawyers' status and of suggesting the means of reform were great attractions of the proposal. Another was the suggestion that the Yale law faculty could improve the law profession and the public's perception of the profession. Accomplishing these twin goals through scholarship particularly appealed to the younger faculty members. The "immediate value" of clarified rule statements to lawyers and judges was immense, according to Hutchins and Clark. "Accurate information soundly analyzed," rather than specific legislative measures, would provide a public service for those elected to create new laws or strike down old laws.[26] The Yale scholars could develop techniques for conducting legal research, and they could join with experts in other academic fields to do so. The intellectual basis for theory and practice would be greatly enhanced by the institute's work.

Finally, the potential prestige the Yale Law School would gain from such work was most persuasive. Yale was singularly suited to conduct the work, they argued, because it had the first graduate law program in the country, it had the first honors course in the country, and it already possessed a unique method of teaching procedure that included analyzing the means of improving it. Other law schools lacked the interest or wherewithal to engage in research in the administration of law.

The flaws in the proposal, so glaring in hindsight, were not obvious to the faculty members, not even to Corbin. The proposal inherently assumed that the collection of facts on actual practices and operations would unambiguously disclose the effectiveness of rules and practices. There was nothing to indicate methods of collection or analysis in the proposal. Hutchins incorporated a single reference to statistical analysis, but gave no clue as to what it would involve or to the development of theoretical frameworks.

The proposal also revealed Hutchins' assumption that the analysis of data would provide objective assessments of the legal system's effectiveness and the current state of jurisprudence. His tremendous faith in the ultimate reasonableness of what the scholars would find, his faith that some inherent laws or patterns would emerge ipso facto from the data is evident throughout the proposal. Given the existing lack of sophistication in linking legal scholarship with social science research in the 1920s, his naiveté, while partially responsible for the flaws, is understandable. But his lack of understanding of the state of social science research is equally responsible for the vagueness of the proposal.

This misapprehension contributed to Hutchins' subsequent difficulties as an administrator trying to inspire and organize interdisciplinary research among members of the law faculty and the social science faculty at Yale. As John Henry Schlegel notes in his study of the legal realists, the proposal was not merely a response to the strengthening claims to intellectual authority of science or scientific methods of research, which overshadowed other substantive and methodological claims in universities by the early twentieth century. It also presaged the problems of cooperative research among academic disciplines, each of which had its own methods, assumptions, and criteria for assessing findings.[27]

Hutchins failed to understand until later that good social science research did not develop automatically out of the collection of facts. At the time the research methods of the disciplines were not sophisticated enough to allow scholars to assess the truth claims of research findings in the area of legal procedure, or to make generalizations about, for example, the psychological validity of an exception to the law of evidence. What appears to have united different disciplines for Hutchins and other functionalists was the need to view the problem from a variety of perspectives. In addition, they assumed that guides to reform would naturally result from a particular cross-disciplinary study. When scientific claims in the interest of objectivity began to preclude the reform ends of various studies, the collection of facts appeared aimless and meaningless to Hutchins and others who grew skeptical of social science research in the 1930s.[28]

Despite faculty support for the institute, Angell's approval, and the Yale Corporation's assent, Hutchins' and Clark's comprehensive plan as described in the proposal went no further. The Corporation refused to finance it. Nor could Hutchins find foundation money for it in 1926 or 1927.

The honors program, however, was initiated in the fall of 1926. Seminars were offered, with research opportunities in areas of faculty interest, such as procedure and evidence. The faculty voted to include capable second-year students in the program.[29] With class size limited to one hundred by the end of 1926, Hutchins had two modest victories as a result of his campaign. These accomplishments were not inconsequential for someone who had been teaching for less than two years among a group of faculty members known as "very individualistic, idiosyncratic" characters who clung tenaciously to their intellectual independence.[30]

The law faculty saw in Hutchins a young man with innovative ideas, tremendous energy, and high intelligence. Because his interest and proposals in legal education and scholarship derived from his close work with Clark, the faculty perceived them as partners. Hutchins was also friends with the president of the university and, as secretary, knew many of the members of the Corporation. Despite his youth and inexperience, he was in a fortuitous position as the Law School faced major decisions in 1927.

When Dean Thomas W. Swan was appointed to the United States Court of Appeals for the Second Circuit in December of 1926, Angell refused to allow him to continue as nominal dean until a successor could be found. After a month of deliberation, the faculty decided that Hutchins ought to act as dean until the search committee could find a permanent successor. They chose him for reasons that were intrinsically rooted in the conditions of the Law School at that point.

In his favor, Hutchins had the confidence of the members of the faculty. Swan was doubtful that any of the older members would inspire the unanimity that Hutchins did.[31] Corbin nominated Hutchins, the faculty voted, and the Corporation approved.[32] He took the position in mid-February. With typical self-effacement, Hutchins informed his brother Bill that "this is no particular compliment to me. It is merely that they dislike everybody else more than they do me."[33] There was some truth in this assessment, but the faculty's agreement made him a viable candidate for the permanent position.

Hutchins launched right in to the major and minor duties of directing the Yale Law School. The first meeting over which he presided was a flurry of activity.[34] Throughout March and April he led discussions about possible appointments, candidates for dean, curriculum revisions, and budget allocations.

Some outsiders were skeptical of Hutchins' leadership abilities. John H. Wigmore, dean of Northwestern University's law school and a foremost scholar of evidence, informed Angell that Hutchins' evidence and psychology work indicated that he was an extreme behaviorist whose "jaunty and witty but irresponsible dismissal of the recorded experiences of judges and lawyers" of the last two or three hundred years seemed "to indicate an unscientific and unsafe attitude towards the law." He was afraid Hutchins would give "a false impression" of the university to the outside world, "create unrest among his colleagues," and "unsettle the minds of the young men" who were his students.[35]

Hutchins fueled the indignation of outsiders when he, Clark, and other academic lawyers supported Felix Frankfurter's campaign to have the Sacco-Vanzetti case reviewed by the state of Massachusetts. Their actions called into question the whole of the Boston-Harvard elite including judges, lawyers, and such notables as President Lawrence A. Lowell of Harvard. Reformers concerned with the social context of the law, Frankfurter and his colleagues protested the procedural abnormalities of the case and the obvious prejudice of the judge against ethnic immigrant minorities.[36]

Hutchins and Clark spoke at public meetings and distributed petitions to demand a stay of execution and a retrial. Hutchins was particularly critical of the court's willingness to allow questions that emphasized "in a picturesque and telling manner the political views of a defendant" (known to be sympathetic to anarchist causes) being tried for a crime unrelated to those views. By allowing "cross-examination to an unconventional past," the court had abridged the defendants' civil rights and abused justice.[37]

Theirs was a conservative position; its appeal to uphold the legal principles protecting civil liberties and individual rights was an argument to preserve the structure of the law. In the context of the case, however, it was seen as radical, particularly with widespread opinion supporting the values of American nativism in the period after the first world war.[38] William H. Taft, an alumnus of Yale and a Supreme Court justice, suggested that Angell "restrain Hutchins" in the interest of the Law School, which was too "far removed from the situation" to justify the involvement of its dean in the affair.[39] Charles Stetson, another wealthy alumnus, saw the Sacco-Vanzetti protest as a "Socialistic campaign" with its source in "the prevailing distemper in Harvard."[40] He, too, was afraid Hutchins' and Clark's activities would ruin Yale's reputation. Angell had "no comment to make one way or other."[41]

As the faculty pondered candidates for permanent dean in 1927, Hutchins conducted his work on two fronts. He continued to look for financial support for the Institute of Procedure, and he pursued his research project in psychology and the law of evidence. Angell, whose contacts with the foundation world were extensive, helped him seek funds for the institute. Quite possibly, he also helped Hutchins by directing him to the relevant literature in psychology for his evidence work. Fortuitously, the search for foundation money also netted Hutchins a research partner who was a psychologist.

As early as July 1926 and again in November of that year, Angell had sent letters to Wickliffe Rose, president of the General Education Board, informing him of the institute idea. To put the proposal in the best light,

Angell described the recent bequest from John W. Sterling that would allow the Law School to build new buildings for classrooms and dormitories and to develop a law library.[42] He heard nothing from Rose, so he sent a copy of the proposal to his former University of Chicago graduate student and assistant at the Carnegie Corporation, Beardsley Ruml.[43]

Ruml was the director of the Laura Spelman Rockefeller Memorial (LSRM), established by the Rockefeller boards in 1918. Beginning in 1922, he redirected the spending of its $74 million fund from practically oriented social welfare projects to basic research in the social sciences that might eventually contribute to social welfare. Ruml focused the LSRM's grant giving on universities where scholars were conducting investigations of social phenomena through firsthand observation, the collection of data, and experimentation.

Like Angell, Ruml believed that there was a fundamental unity to social science knowledge disciplines and that interdisciplinary research was the best way to gain a comprehensive understanding of social problems. Much of the LSRM's funding went to the School of Social Service Administration at the University of Chicago, the Social Science Research Council, the University of North Carolina, the National Bureau of Economic Research, and the London School of Economics and Political Science. The remaining money was transferred in 1928–29 to the Rockefeller Foundation, and the work of the LSRM was absorbed into its social science division.[44] To Hutchins in 1926 the LSRM seemed the most appropriate place to seek funds for the Law School's research.

The LSRM staff was hesitant to finance research that might be too "legalistic" or duplicated elsewhere. The Rockefeller-financed General Education Board had recently given Harvard Law School a grant to pursue research in law. However, Ruml's assistant, Lawrence K. Frank, was intrigued by Hutchins and his proposal. Frank thought that Hutchins' work in psychology and evidence might allow the LSRM "to try out the general plan" the Law School had "in mind to see how fruitful it would be."[45]

He directed Hutchins to Donald Slesinger, a psychologist working with the Judge Baker Foundation and the National Commission on Mental Hygiene.[46] Slesinger was interested in the relationship between psychology and criminal law and procedure. After Hutchins found Slesinger, he asked Frank for $3,000 to pay his salary.[47] Due to "matters of policy and precedent," Frank refused LSRM funds at that time. Hutchins managed a Sterling fellowship and a Law School appropriation to cover Slesinger's salary for the 1927–28 school year.[48] Slesinger worked with Leon Tulin for a time on courses in criminal law and with Hutchins in psychology and evidence, eventually collaborating with him on a series of articles.

While the search for funds continued, the Law School faculty came to a decision on a permanent dean. According to William R. Vance, a majority of the faculty had assumed a group self-definition precluding "mid-Victorian theories as to the science of the law and legal education."[49] Rather, they sought a candidate who would pursue a progressive agenda. Oliphant, Clark, Cook, and Hutchins were the choices they considered.

Hutchins had done a commendable job as acting dean. Vance was of the opinion that "the only self respecting [sic] course" for the search committee was to hold off any commitments to others "until it appears more fully whether Mr. Hutchins will grow up to the job."[50] In May the committee recommended Hutchins as permanent dean. He had exhibited the administrative skill, tact, public relations acumen (despite the Wigmore, Taft, and Stetson criticisms), and teaching expertise the committee was seeking. The committee was confident that Hutchins would continue in the new directions the Law School had begun to follow. "His mental powers and personality" were "so unusual," the faculty thought that he would become a foremost legal scholar and educator, capable of attaining great stature in public affairs.[51] Angell was not fully convinced that Hutchins was ready for the job. He delayed confirming the appointment until December of 1927, when the Corporation voted to install Hutchins as permanent dean beginning in February of 1928.[52]

Hutchins continued to work with Slesinger on the psychology and evidence studies, which represent the extent of his scholarly engagement with legal realist thought. Compared to such colleagues as Clark, Llewellyn, Douglas, Oliphant, Jerome Frank, or Thurman Arnold, Hutchins' engagement was neither deep nor extensive. He and Slesinger produced a series of law journal articles on the topic. They explored such issues of evidence as spontaneous exclamations, memory, competence of witnesses, consciousness of guilt, family relations, state of mind to prove an act, and state of mind in issue. Hutchins examined admissible evidence in a variety of cases. Slesinger searched the literature of psychology for conclusions based on experiment and observation that might question the criteria used to judge reliability of testimony.

They argued, for example that the work of Jung, Yerkes, and Münsterberg illustrated numerous possible reasons for spontaneous utterings that were not necessarily indicative of truth or falsity, guilt or innocence. Because there was no definitive way to examine the utterings for veracity (given the contemporary state of psychology research), all of them ought to be admissible in court.[53] Using the experimental studies of noted psychologists including Gates, Titchener, Thorndike, and Ebbinghaus, they probed cases showing experimental findings that refuted commonsense notions about the functioning of memory over time in determining the use of memory as evidence in testimony.[54]

Rather than rely on judges' pre-formed opinions and assumptions about apparent belief in God or the ability to differentiate between truth and falsity, intelligence tests might allow for greater objectivity and accuracy in determining witnesses' competence.[55] To examine such evidentiary problems as consciousness of guilt, state of mind, and family relations, Hutchins and Slesinger used psychoanalytic theory, including the work of Freud, Reich, and Healy, because it explored consciousness rather than behavior. They suggested the variety of possible explanations for the relationships between behavior and consciousness, verbal symbols and state of mind, and loyalty of family members and reliability of witnesses.[56]

Their research was limited to library work. The articles were of fairly high quality, as Schlegel notes, and raised important questions about existing rules of evidence.[57] Yet they did not exhibit the kind of empirical or experimental work Hutchins maintained the Yale Law School ought to be pursuing. As in all of his projects, Hutchins gave the evidence and psychology studies only limited attention before he took up new interests.

However brilliant his colleagues thought him, he was not, by any twentieth-century definition, a scholar. Hutchins' attenuated commitment to legal realist research provides some insight into his understanding of social science scholarship. He did not engage in the experimental work or systematic observation that characterized social science research in 1927. His evidence studies raised important questions but did not generate theory for scholars of the law of evidence. Rather, he pursued legal realist ideas for their potential to reform legal education. He was an administrator rather than a scholar and was "available" to new ideas that could focus his reforms.[58]

The evidence studies were significant for him in other ways. While canvassing the work being done in psychology and evidence, he found a young man who was to have a seminal influence on his thinking as an educational administrator. Mortimer Jerome Adler was a psychology doctoral student at Columbia working with Jerome Michael at Columbia Law School on problems of logic and evidence. Hutchins convinced the Commonwealth Fund to finance both evidence projects as a collaborative study.

There was not much collaboration on the actual studies. Adler and Michael published their work as *Crime, Law, and Social Science* (1933), and Hutchins and Slesinger published their law journal articles. But the grant served other purposes. It enhanced the respectability of Hutchins' scholarly work and suggested his ability to acquire research funds.

However tenuous Hutchins' personal commitment to collaborative research between social scientists and legal scholars, his administrative work in the Law School gave evidence of his professional commitment to such cooperation. Slesinger's fellowship was an official gesture to link psychology and law at Yale. In 1927 he brought in William F. Dodd, political scientist, to teach constitutional law, municipal corporations, and public service law. In 1928 he recruited Walton H. Hamilton, an economist from the Brookings Institution, to teach constitutional law, public utilities, and trade regulations. He also appointed Frederick C. Hicks from Columbia as Yale's first full-time law librarian.

When members of Columbia's law faculty resigned in protest against Butler's appointment of Smith in 1928, Hutchins offered most of them positions at Yale. As Kalman notes, with the Sterling bequest and a boom economy, Hutchins had Angell's backing and near certain approval from the Corporation to recruit realists Oliphant, Yntema, Douglas, Underhill Moore, and Roswell P. Magill.[59] Unfortunately, his grand plan to establish a community of realist scholars at Yale collapsed.

Walter Wheeler Cook had been a visiting professor at Johns Hopkins since 1926 and received funds from that university to create a center of realist research. Before Hutchins could get Corporation approval to hire all of them, Cook recruited Oliphant, Yntema, and Magill to Johns Hopkins' new Institute for Legal Research.[60] Hutchins did bring William O. Douglas to Yale in 1928 and Underhill Moore in 1929. A further instance of Hutchins' interdisciplinary efforts was his recruitment of visiting professors Harold Laski of the University of London to teach political and legal theory, and Morris R. Cohen, the philosopher from City College in New York, to teach an honors course in jurisprudence.

In addition to his Commonwealth Fund grant for the psychology and evidence research, he and Angell acquired another, from the LSRM. In early 1928 Ruml and his staff agreed to support Charles E. Clark's work examining the effectiveness of procedural devices in Connecticut courts. The five-year grant allowed Clark to begin some of the statistical collection mentioned in the Institute of Procedure proposal.[61] Despite Cook's coup, Hutchins had confidence in his own ability to turn the Law School into a major research center with foundation money for law and social science work.

He found a partner in the dean of the Medical School at Yale, Milton C. Winternitz. Winternitz, like Hutchins, was looking for money in 1926–28 to support an institute. His Institute of Human Behavior was to house collaborative research in biological sciences and experimental psychology.[62] He also wanted to develop psychiatry as a discipline in the Medical School. During his deanship, Winternitz had rescued the Medical School from near ruin by raising admissions standards, reducing enrollment, recruiting new faculty, and promoting research, incorporating many of the recommendations Abraham Flexner had suggested in his 1910 report on medical education for the Carnegie Foundation.[63] Hutchins was impressed with the gains Winternitz had made, and, at Angell's suggestion, the two men combined their institute proposals for the Rockefeller Foundation and the LSRM.

Beardsley Ruml was quite enthusiastic about this proposal to establish the Institute of Human Relations.[64] The institute was to be located adjacent to the Medical School and the proposed Law School building. Psychology, psychiatry, and social science researchers were to work in the "graduate, professional, and research center."[65] Scholars associated with the institute would carry on the study of individual behavior, psychobiologically examined, and social behavior, through the problems of family law, criminology, business and finance, labor, and government.

The proposal's success depended on two contingencies. One was the approval of the Sterling trustees for the relocation of the Law School a few blocks from the main campus of the university. The other was financing from the LSRM, in its usual block grant style, to allow for maximum flexibility within the institution and for capitalization of the venture. The Rockefeller Foundation was another source of funds for the specifically medical aspects of the institute's research.

Try as they might, Hutchins and Angell could not meet the first contingency. The Sterling trustees and the building committee of the Law School alumni group wanted the new law building in the middle of the Yale University campus near the proposed Sterling Library. Together the new buildings would match in style and form a quadrangle. Hutchins developed a complicated rationale for changing the plan involving the need to separate the Law School from undergraduate life to guarantee the seriousness and maturity of law work. He argued that the educational benefits to be attained by deliberately bringing law, medical, and social science faculty members and students into physical proximity far outweighed the five-block walk law students would have to make to the main library. Better use of the Sterling money would be secured by spending less on a magnificent building and more on an endowment fund for the Law School.[66] The law faculty supported the plan, and the Corporation approved, depending on the Sterling trustees' response to the idea.[67]

Hutchins campaigned long and hard among the alumni but to no avail.[68] The law faculty, at the time of the bequest, before there was an institute proposal, had chosen the site the trustees favored. This earlier decision weakened Hutchins' case. The trustees' counsel, the three trustees, and members of the alumni building committee clearly expressed their desire for the Law School to be located in a permanent edifice, centered on the main campus.[69] Hutchins had grossly underestimated the psychological reasoning behind such building bequests: a desire for continuity and prominence.

The decision was a stunning blow to Hutchins. He thought the location was crucial to financing and facilitating the institute's and Law School's research. He sent Angell a petulant letter, suggesting that he should put pressure on the Corporation to make a firm statement to the trustees to convince them of the "serious" consequences of their refusal, including possibly losing the institute altogether.[70] Angell was wiser to the ways of alumni and trustees. Arrogance was not the approach to take, especially with one alumnus threatening to transfer his gift to another area of the university. He suggested to Hutchins that his depiction of the consequences of the decision was open to debate. The threat that the institute project could collapse if the Law School site was not moved might best be kept from the Corporation.[71]

During this same period, Hutchins, Angell, and Winternitz met with officials of the LSRM to present a revised proposal for the institute. At that time, the LSRM's future was in question. The Rockefeller boards, in their efforts to consolidate foundation activities, were considering absorbing the LSRM into the foundation and financing social science research separately. For reasons not clear in the correspondence, some officials at the foundation were hesitant, in any case, to finance the social science–law work of the institute proposal. Angell adjusted the request to an annual subsidy rather than a capitalization of the project.[72] When it appeared the LSRM might not consider the social science work of the institute proposal at its November meeting, Hutchins gamely promoted William O. Douglas' project on credit risks and business failures.[73] E. E. Day, later director of social sciences at the foundation, then advised Hutchins to drop any requests for social science research funds from the LSRM.[74]

Whether the foundation was disturbed by the building site controversy or the quality of the projected social science research, or was simply waiting for completion of its reorganization, is a mystery. In mid-November, Hutchins decided to "reopen the matter and to make the proposal one which [would] command the support of the Memorial or the Foundation."[75] In late November, the LSRM trustees decided to appropriate $2 million to finance related research work at Yale in psychology, anthropology, child development, and the social sciences. But they delayed action until the consolidation, thereby transferring authority to the new foundation.[76]

Hutchins then submitted a revised proposal. It described a more detailed project combining psychology, psychiatry, law research, and sociology to examine delinquency and crime in the context of divorce proceedings and family relations. Suggestions Frank had made to strengthen the research design, including control groups, were incorporated in the new proposal. In addition, by using a variety of academic disciplines to examine the problem of delinquency, Hutchins took Ruml's interdisciplinary approach to social science research.[77]

The delinquency project was to be directed by psychiatrist William D. Healy and his colleague Augusta F. Bronner. On the basis of Healy's past psychiatric work with individual delinquents, they planned to use psychiatric clinical casework and family counseling to analyze family relations that might contribute to, or prevent, juvenile delinquency. The law research would investigate court and school records, social service agency files, and divorce cases in court proceedings. The sociology research would articulate the problems of "negro family life," for example, in the New Haven community, as well as "the effects on family life of the impact of two cultures."[78]

Hutchins thought the project would lead to the study of the cultural conflicts immigrant families experienced in New Haven. He argued that the William F. Ogburn notion of "cultural lag" held implications for the "discrepancies between the law and the fact" and might show which "statutes and decisions" had an unintended, or no, effect on behavior within communities.[79] For example, the actual reasons for divorce and the reasons courts cited often differed. Explicating the difference would suggest legal reforms appropriate to cultural change occurring in communities.

The proposal appealed not only to the LSRM but also to the Rockefeller boards. The LSRM was officially absorbed into the newly constituted Rockefeller Foundation on January 3, 1929, and the recommendation on the proposal for the institute was presented then. An additional grant was made at the January 22 meeting of the foundation trustees. Yale was to receive the $2.5 million over a period of ten years. The November grant was to cover building and equipment, an anthropoid breeding station, and the development and operating expenses of research facilities in psychology and psychiatry. The other $2 million was for an annual subsidy, $65,000 for social science and law research, with the remainder allocated to research in psychology and child study.[80]

The establishment and financing of the institute was a major accomplishment for Hutchins, Angell, and Winternitz. Hutchins' subsequent administrative contributions to the institute were less successful. He served on the executive committee with Angell, Winternitz, and others but never managed to establish clear structural or functional relations between the institute and the Law School. William O. Douglas, Charles E. Clark, and Underhill Moore conducted legal research in the early 1930s, financed in part by institute money. Healy and Bronner completed their project in juvenile delinquency with the institute.[81] But the fertile cross-discipinary studies with psychologists, legal scholars, and social scientists yielding comprehensive, interdisciplinary understanding of major social and legal problems never materialized the way Hutchins had predicted they would in his proposals and reports.[82]

He thought, for example, that the law faculty and social scientists would carry out extensive studies of family relations. Beyond Healy's and Bronner's work, this did not happen. He projected the study of the development of small corporations, judicial organizations, and recent trends in corporate development.[83] None of these studies was clearly described. Nor were faculty members inspired to undertake them without Hutchins' persistent encouragement. When he left for the University of Chicago presidency in June of 1929, Clark, appointed his successor, attempted to build on the ethereal foundations Hutchins had laid during his brief tenure.

The law faculty did not make extensive use of the opportunities for cross-disciplinary research, for which Hutchins is not entirely to blame. As Schlegel and Kalman argue, the arrangements for financing projects were weighted toward psycho-biological research. In addition, Clark did not have friendly relations with Winternitz and Angell; he had no power over institute policy decisions.[84] After the stock market crashed in October of 1929, there was little money for research.

Yet some responsibility belongs with Hutchins. He did not give the Law School's research program the sustained attention it needed in those first few months of the institute's organization. In effect, according to Clark, Hutchins left him "in an impossible situation, due to the fact that he had not thought through nor clearly established the relationship of the Law School to the rest of the Institute." Clark was left to try to break through the "vested interests" that controlled institute policy and planning.[85]

Hutchins' deanship of the Yale Law School was a mixed success. On one hand, he used his position to make things happen. His colleagues thought his leadership "clear-sighted, bold and consistent." The establishment of honors work, the incorporation of nonlegal faculty and nonlegal materials in coursework, and his own scholarship represented a strong effort "to give body and form to what was nebulous in the new movement" among academic lawyers to reform education in the law.[86] The faculty unanimously nominated Clark, Hutchins' mentor and close colleague, as his successor to carry forward their reforms. William O. Douglas remembered that, under Hutchins' leadership, "the Yale Law campus was filled with a fervor that no other law faculty experienced."[87]

On the other hand, the curriculum reforms were not securely institutionalized. His promotion of faculty research projects were peripatetic. Schlegel had noted that Hutchins started, but did not complete, many of the curricular and research projects. He could inspire, but seemed unable to sustain, faculty efforts to reform Yale's program. He created opportunities but did not know how to do, or lost interest in doing, what was necessary to support them on a continuous basis.[88]

No doubt his youth and inexperience were partly responsible for his failure to follow through on projects. The brevity of his deanship argues against drawing conclusions about his ability to commit to and engage fully in intellectual projects and institutional arrangements for them. However, many of his later efforts would follow this pattern, marked by a lack of interest in small details, by loosely formulated organizational and administrative arrangements, and by an inability to deal with ongoing personal conflicts among colleagues.

In the case of the institute, Hutchins lacked the commitment to and understanding of social science research required to develop cooperative projects in the Law School and the institute and to command the support of the scientists and social scientists working there. His understanding of social science research was an amalgam of the social science progressivism of Oberlin and the intellectual interests he had acquired from Clark, Angell, and Ruml. In none of his proposals for the institute did he exhibit awareness of the problems of method or the need for developing theory. What they consistently do show is Hutchins' faith that social science research would lead to reform of legal education, legal practice, legal administration, and ultimately the law itself.

In every proposal he wrote for socio-legal research and in every description he presented of the educational program at Yale's Law School was the assumption that tangible, if not immediate, reform of the legal system and the behavior of lawyers would result from careful research and serious study of social factors shaping human behavior. From bringing justice to the poor by better understanding social and economic conditions to instilling ethical values in law students through a better understanding of social life, reform was intrinsic to Hutchins' conception of social science research.[89] He could make a sweeping claim that the institute would make law a branch of the social sciences but apparently had no clue as to how that was to occur.[90] And he went so far as to argue that study of the social sciences was central for undergraduates planning a career in law.[91]

Hutchins' adoption of Angell's and Ruml's arguments for interdisciplinary research indicates a desire not only to understand law more fully but also to set normative standards for the profession. With increasingly complex and specialized academic knowledge domains within universities, the kinds of common values and ethical expectations he had known at Oberlin and that seemed intrinsically democratic and American were threatened. A fundamental belief in Christian morality guiding the laws and customs of the community had bound together the people who lived there. In the increasingly urban, ethnically diverse United States of the 1920s, what could hold communities together and to certain norms of behavior was no longer certain.

As long as cross-disciplinary research held the promise of common intellectual ground and ultimate moral guides to social reform, Hutchins adopted legal realist ideas. When the Depression deepened in the 1930s, social scientists' concerns with methodological rigor, internal coherence of theories, and nonnormative, objective assessment of data seemed meaningless to Hutchins. After Hutchins became president of the University of Chicago, he searched for a more stable tradition to guide his educational reforms.

Interestingly, Hutchins had rejected an offer in 1927 by Abraham Flexner of the General Education Board (GEB) to become the first participant in an experimental program the GEB was contemplating to prepare future university presidents. Flexner offered to support him and his family for three to five years' study of European universities and their problems and then for further study of universities in the United States. Hutchins found the plan intriguing but decided to stay at Yale to pursue his work in the Law School.[92] Flexner undertook the study himself and published *Universities: English, German, American* (1930) based on his observations.

Hutchins had no way of knowing in 1927 that he would become a university president and spend twenty-two years in that position. He might have done well to have taken Flexner's offer, given the subsequent problems he had at Chicago. His deceptive successes with the Yale law faculty did not prepare him for the independent, autonomous research culture of the University of Chicago.

PART TWO *Vocation, 1929–51*

Hutchins was chosen for the presidency of the University of Chicago during the late 1920s boom; the trustees were taking a chance on his youth and inexperience. They fervently hoped that he would grow quickly into his new vocation. But they did not anticipate that he would attempt not only to redefine the role of president but also to reshape the mission of the university. In his encounters with Mortimer Adler and his plunge into the great books reading program Adler had designed from his undergraduate experience at Columbia University, Hutchins found the model of the intellectual community he wanted to create at the University of Chicago. The fact that this model was drastically at odds with the modern university, of which Chicago was exemplary, did not deter him. To him, it was an issue of moral conviction.

The stock market crashed just before he was inaugurated. The Depression persisted through the first decade of his presidency and was followed closely by World War II. Throughout that period, Hutchins managed an institution struggling to maintain its faculty and programs. He reorganized the administration, pushed for a new undergraduate program, supported major changes in the professional schools, and constantly pursued money to keep the institution afloat. He also spoke publicly about educational problems, politics, freedom, and democracy, delivering nearly eight hundred public addresses in the 1930s and 1940s.[1] *His dynamism and oratory shaped the public image of the university as much as did his attempts to change its fundamental mission. Hutchins' charisma and energetic commitment to principled leadership combined with the strong, independent faculty of the university to create a vibrant, ongoing discussion about the purposes of education at the University of Chicago during the 1930s and 1940s.*

This discussion actually had begun before Hutchins' arrival. Undergraduate education had been a concern for a number of years, inspiring experimentation with interdisciplinary courses and, in 1928, a report by Dean Chauncey S. Boucher on the college program. Rather than four different undergraduate programs, Boucher suggested that the university should provide required general introductory courses for the first two undergraduate years and then allow for electives.

Hutchins began his crusade with this report but in an atmosphere not strongly supportive of undergraduate instruction. The faculty body, numbering nearly eight hundred, was largely devoted to research. The student body of fourteen thousand was divided as follows: eight thousand were in graduate and professional schools, two thousand were in the colleges, and the remaining four thousand were in the extension division. This bias toward research, obvious in the numbers and in the departmental framework, was firmly entrenched in the university. Nevertheless, the new plan, based on the Boucher report, was introduced in 1931.

In 1932 Hutchins convinced the faculty and trustees to allow faculty appointments to the college without concurrent appointments to departments. In 1937 he persuaded them to admit high school juniors and shift the age range from eighteen to twenty-two years to sixteen to twenty-two years (including those who entered after finishing high school) and to establish an experimental four-year college, with a four-year general education curriculum, alongside the two-year college. In

1942 he gained agreement for offering the bachelor's degree to signify the completion of a general education (whatever the age of the student), and in 1946 for a fully prescribed, single-degree (bachelor of arts) program in the college.

In those seventeen years of his leadership, the undergraduate program moved from the fringes of the university to center stage, from a largely elective program offering three bachelor's degrees to a fully prescribed program offering one degree, and from ten-week discrete courses to yearlong interdisciplinary courses coordinated across the curriculum. It was an astounding accomplishment, but it cost Hutchins dearly in his relations with the faculty. In combination with his efforts to impose his own plans on the philosophy department in 1930, it created a climate of contention that only rarely abated. He offered to resign once as a result, in the middle 1940s. In 1945 he requested the board to create a chancellorship, and appoint him to it, to allow himself more time to pursue educational policy as opposed to administrative tasks. He took a year's leave of absence in 1946–47 to try to repair his failing marriage and to relieve himself of some of the pressure from the conflicts on campus. But the clashes had been generated in large measure by his own hand.

Hutchins' notorious obduracy, once he made a decision, and the conditions over which he had no control—the Depression and the war—shaped his ability to act and burdened the institution as a whole. Departments lost important faculty members. Enrollments declined in the early 1930s and late 1940s. The neighborhood around the university, in which the institution was a major landlord, became a slum. These problems occurred partly because of the Depression, losses in the market that taxed the university's endowment, and the decline in scholarship funds for undergraduates. But they also occurred because of the tensions Hutchins' administrative policies created and because of the choices he made as leader of the institution.

He chose to focus narrowly on the intellectual life of the university in hopes that such an emphasis would create the kind of questioning, critical community he had left in Oberlin. But the scholastic caste of his definition of what constituted a legitimate intellectual life differed so much from the progressive, empirically oriented tradition of the university and many of its faculty members that his efforts aroused extensive faculty opposition. And he found himself continually compromising in ways that did not satisfy his Oberlin conscience or fulfill his mission.

CHAPTER 4 *An Auspicious Beginning*

ROBERT AND MAUDE HUTCHINS were a young and glamourous addition to the University and the city of Chicago. Men and women alike found Robert's good looks and sharp wit irresistible. Maude's artistic talent and quick tongue soon became legend in the community. They were courted by the socially prominent younger generation on the city's North Side. And members of the board of trustees and friends of the university in the elegant Hyde Park neighborhood on the city's South Side warmly welcomed the Hutchinses when they arrived in the fall of 1929.

The grueling, yearlong search for a new president had been the third for the University of Chicago in less than six years. It was fraught with implications for the university's future. Members of the board of trustees perceived Hutchins' appointment as the beginning of a new era. Faculty members saw a promising young advocate of the research culture they had worked so hard to build, though some of their older colleagues were skeptical because of Hutchins' inexperience and youth. And the city no doubt saw the embodiment of its motto "I will" in the confident and energetic young Hutchins.

Chicago was a city unlike either the close evangelical community of Oberlin or the elite, socially established town of New Haven. Hot in summer and bitterly cold and windy in winter, the city that perched on the southern shore of Lake Michigan was a sprawling, raw, industrial and merchant crossroads constantly redefined by its shifting population. Known for its poets and journalists, it also was a working-class city, populated by diverse groups of European immigrants and a growing migration of African-Americans looking for better economic opportunities. Political and economic power was divided unevenly between a corrupt Democratic machine, run by Big Bill Thompson with a wide base of support in the immigrant neighborhoods, bootlegging gangsters whose most notable representative was Al Capone, and a cohort of wealthy industrialists and philanthropists including the Fields, McCormicks, Hutchinsons, Ryersons, Swifts, Rosenwalds, and Insulls.

This third group had been responsible in the 1880s and 1890s for establishing Chicago's cultural institutions: the Art Institute in 1879, the Chicago Symphony Orchestra in 1891, the Field Museum in 1893, and the University of Chicago in 1982.[1] The source of the university's trustees and some of its students, the group's most socially concerned allied with faculty members to institute better city government and legislation to improve housing, labor conditions, and social welfare for Chicago's less fortunate citizens.[2] Ties between the city's wealthy and the university were firmly in place when the Hutchinses arrived in 1929.

Exemplary of these ties, scion of the meat-packing family and president of the university's board of trustees Harold H. Swift played a significant role in bringing the Hutchinses to Chicago. He provided for many of their immediate needs and, with his friends and associates among Chicago's elite families, introduced Robert and Maude Hutchins to the university and the city.[3]

Finding someone acceptable to both the faculty and trustees and willing to take the University of Chicago presidency was not an easy task for the search committee. The internal politics of the university prolonged the search. A tug-of-war between a trustee-administration coalition that wanted to strengthen undergraduate education and a tenaciously autonomous faculty fully vested in the graduate research culture forced repeated reconsideration of the growing list of candidates. If the trustees had foreseen that these conflicts would be played out continually over the next twenty-two years, and that they would be overshadowed and shaped by a devastating Depression and a demanding war, they might have held out for an older and wiser man.

Most of the candidates they considered from May of 1928 until April of 1929 were closer to Hutchins' father's age than to his and had a wealth of administrative academic experience. Why, then, did the committee choose Hutchins? The answer lies in the connections between the particular qualities the committee desired in a president, the tension on the committee itself over the future direction of the university, the history of the university and its mission, and how that mission had been interpreted by past presidents.

The committee met throughout 1928 and early 1929. Dozens of names were solicited from major philanthropic foundation executives, university administrators, and other friends of the university. Each candidate's ability to spark interest in committee members was a central issue. Hutchins' name appeared on the list in June of 1928 but was taken off. Others were interviewed, but in the end Edmund E. Day, of the Rockefeller Foundation, H. G. Moulton, of the Brookings Institution, and Hutchins were the outside candidates and Frederic C. Woodward, acting president of the university and dean of the faculties, was the inside candidate. Interestingly, Hutchins was reconsidered only after an interview in late December of 1928 when he attended an Association of American Law Schools meeting in Chicago. He made a favorable impression on a number of board members, including Swift, but was dropped again because of his age and inexperience.[4]

In March, Harold Swift received a letter from Edwin R. Embree, president of the Julius Rosenwald Fund. Embree laid out the criteria he thought the committee ought to be considering. Among the important assets any prospective president should bring, he thought, were brilliance and distinction, not simply respectability but the "yeast and ferment" of the Harper years.[5]

William Rainey Harper had been instrumental in the founding of the university. He was a well-known Baptist educator, professor of Semitic languages at Yale's divinity school, and active Chautauqua organizer and teacher. Harper was an avid student of the recent developments in graduate education and research in American universities and an advocate of adult education, through lecture circuits, reading circles, and summer camp meetings, in the Chautauqua organization. He convinced John D. Rockefeller to expand his original donation from $600,000 for the new university to $2 million to support both undergraduate and graduate education and research. He also drew support and money and land for the ostensibly Baptist institution from wealthy non-Baptist Christian and Jewish Chicago citizens.[6] Though the provision for a board of trustees that was three-fifths Baptist was still in effect in 1929, the university primarily was concerned with secular scholarship and education.

The University of Chicago opened in 1892 with an academy, a college, two graduate schools, and a divinity school. It expanded under Harper over the next fourteen years to include numerous affiliations with high schools, an extension program, an affiliate medical school, a law school, and a school of education. Harper recruited aggressively among other universities and colleges, securing for the faculty former presidents, eminent scientists, and heads of departments. Nine women faculty members were brought to the new coeducational university in the 1890s. Under Harper, the faculty and administration established close ties with developing cultural institutions in the city such as the Field Museum, Jane Addams' Hull House, and the Chicago public schools. Reflecting Laurence R. Veysey's model of the modern university, the University of Chicago exhibited liberal culture in undergraduate work, utility in relations with the city of Chicago, and research in the work of the faculty.[7]

Harper's vigorous and enterprising extension, affiliation, and expansion led some skeptics to call his vision of the modern university "Harper's Bazaar." Despite the debt his administration had incurred by the time he died in 1906, there was no doubt that Harper had created a thriving institution. This vitality was what Embree suggested the trustees try to match in their search for a new president in 1929. Harper's successors, all competent men, had continued the university's respectability, but none had brought it to its earlier "pre-eminence."[8]

Harry Pratt Judson (1906–23), for example, had been dean of the junior and senior colleges during Harper's presidency. He stabilized finances during his tenure, increased gifts to the university—by 1910 Rockefeller alone had contributed an unprecedented $35 million—and expanded graduate programs. Ernest DeWitt Burton (1923–25) had been a faculty member since 1892. He taught New Testament and early Christian literature, and directed the libraries. His presidency was eagerly anticipated by a faculty hoping for reinvigoration of the university after Judson's long, and in the end, flagging tenure. Burton encouraged student organizations and publications to enrich college life, which had not been a concern of his predecessors. He brought the Rush Medical College into the university from its prior status as an affiliate and continued some of Harper's affiliations. He also channeled funds into laboratories for the sciences.

After Burton's sudden death, Max Mason (1925–27), a distinguished mathematician and physicist from the University of Wisconsin, took the presidency. He emphasized research in the sciences to build on an already outstanding faculty. Despite the brevity and difficulties of his tenure, including marital problems, conflicts with the faculty, and clashes with wealthy Chicago families, Mason did have an impact. Before his resignation, he established a committee headed by Dean Chauncey S. Boucher to examine undergraduate education at the university.[9]

This last project the trustees thought so critical that they delayed announcement of his resignation for four months to allow the committee to report its findings and recommendations. The desire to reorganize the first two college years was supported by trustees, administrators, and some faculty members. This group believed undergraduate education could promote alumni loyalty and bring in necessary tuition. The plan was both enhanced and complicated by Julius Rosenwald's offer of $2 million for a collection of dormitories across the Midway from the main campus. Reorganization was opposed by faculty members who did not want money diverted from the support of research and graduate study to the development of new curricular programs, personnel, or buildings for the college. The issue had been the source of controversy at the university for most of the 1920s, though its roots lay in the Harper years.[10]

Concern for the status of the colleges shaped the search for the new president because Frederic C. Woodward, the candidate championed by the trustees on the search committee, supported the undergraduate reorganization. To avoid an unpleasant battle, the committee, faculty and trustees alike, turned to outside candidates, most of whom were uninspiring. Swift did not find Edmund E. Day "at all thrilling."[11] As Embree so tellingly noted, qualities that attracted philanthropic foundation money to universities included creative ideas, strong leadership, and an unconventional brilliance, all of which he thought Hutchins had exhibited in his brief, but notable, career.[12] Embree was so taken with Hutchins and so fearful that the university would "settle down to mediocrity" with "some acceptable and innocuous individual" that he requested George E. Vincent, president of the Rockefeller Foundation and former member of the university's sociology faculty, to recommend Hutchins to Swift.[13] Vincent did so, urging Swift to investigate him.[14]

Embree's recommendation seemed worth consideration in light of the difficulties over the colleges and Woodward's candidacy and the strength of the pro-research faculty on the committee. Charles E. Merriam in political science, William E. Dodd in history, Gordon J. Laing, dean of the Graduate School of Arts, and Henry G. Gale, dean of the Graduate School of Sciences, opposed the college plan; Woodward was the only faculty committee member who supported it.

Members of the committee met with Hutchins in early April. They found appealing his competence in discussing administrative matters and his apparent ability to encourage cooperative relationships among faculty members at Yale's law school. His vibrant personality and wry humor and his abundance of ideas charmed his interviewers. Moreover, the trustees perceived Hutchins' great potential for attracting favorable publicity to the university.[15] Swift made further inquiries among administrators at the

Rockefeller Foundation. He received positive assessments of Hutchins' "aggressiveness and willingness to try new things," just the characteristics Embree had touted in his recommendation.[16]

When Swift approached Hutchins' colleagues at Yale, the response was more cautious. Both James Rowland Angell and William R. Vance thought Hutchins brilliant, but "ruthless" and "impatient" with those who disagreed with him or did not think as quickly as he did. Angell pointed out Hutchins' ignorance of and inexperience with general educational problems, despite his "ingenuity in meeting and solving practical problems." Angell deeply admired Hutchins, but thought he needed "five or ten years" to season the talents he exhibited and to temper his impatience and intolerance in his dealings with some colleagues at Yale.[17] Of course, Angell was loath to lose Hutchins' contributions to the Institute of Human Relations and the Law School. Nevertheless, his was a shrewd assessment, in light of later events.

Committee members took Angell's appraisal into consideration but were not swayed in their final decision about Hutchins. That this was the case is a reflection of the problems plaguing the committee and the university. The search committee had already spent a year looking at candidates. As one board member noted in early April, the committee was "at a point where we must act," though at that time he was not in favor of Hutchins' nomination.[18] Even Merriam was willing to see Woodward in the position by April of 1929, though the major holdout by the time the Embree letter arrived was William E. Dodd, who found in Hutchins the perfect compromise.[19] Hutchins' contacts with the Rockefeller Foundation, his ongoing friendship with Beardsley Ruml, a Chicago alumnus, and his work under Angell, another Chicago luminary, all represented continuity for the university and probably helped mitigate trustee and faculty fears about his youth.

His predecessor, Harper, at the age of thirty-four had come to Chicago from Yale. Hutchins' appointment thus represented a historical as well as collegial continuity for the university. What most likely appealed to Dodd and Merriam was Hutchins' apparent interest in social science research. The university's research culture originated with Harper's aggressive recruitment of young faculty in the 1890s. An administrative autocrat, Harper nevertheless allowed faculty members who could raise money for their projects to pursue the pioneering work that built the university's departments and that gradually increased the number of courses offered to all students in the university.[20] He also encouraged departments to develop journals to publish faculty work.

Philosophy and social science scholars explored problems that used the city of Chicago as a laboratory, and they worked alongside such agencies of social reform as Hull House. Rockefeller money and Rosenwald funds for salaries, buildings, and equipment until 1920, and grants Beardsley Ruml allocated from the Laura Spelman Rockefeller Memorial (LSRM), furthered research. Having dealt with Ruml and Angell at Yale, Hutchins was aware of the university's research tradition. Some of the country's most notable scientists and scholars in the social sciences had done their work at the University of Chicago from the 1890s to the 1920s.

Hutchins made clear to a number of faculty members in the months before he assumed the presidency that "the extraordinarily fine social sciences group" at the university was a significant factor in his decision to accept the position.[21] In light of the intellectual and institutional development of the social sciences at the University of Chicago from 1892 to the 1920s, Hutchins' reference to the "social sciences group" was apt. A brief review of the history of this group is essential for understanding Hutchins' appointment and tenure as president.

From the early years, departments had been structurally joined, as in the case of anthropology and sociology until 1929, or intellectually and administratively linked across disciplines and generations, as in the case of pedagogy, philosophy, and psychology under John Dewey from 1894 to 1904.[22] The intellectual connections between scholars at Chicago manifested themselves in a variety of ways. Harper made all the initial appointments in the social sciences department. The department head, sociologist Albion Small, provided the institutional arrangements that allowed a diverse group of scholars to develop their studies of society.

Small recruits George E. Vincent (later president of the Rockefeller Foundation), and particularly, W. I. Thomas pursued some of the most sophisticated empirical work of their time in sociology after they received their Ph.D.'s in 1896 under Small. Charles Henderson was university chaplain, social reformer, and social researcher in the city of Chicago. He encouraged Thomas and Ernest Burgess (Ph.D., 1913) to use the city as a context for social research. Both Thomas and Burgess joined the faculty after receiving their degrees, thus carrying the tradition forward from Small and Henderson. William F. Ogburn, appointed in 1926, extended the department's work to new heights of quantitative research.

Shailer Mathews, still in the Divinity School early in Hutchins' presidency, incorporated a sociological interpretation of the Bible in his scholarly work.[23]

In another vein, John Dewey attracted psychologist James R. Angell to Chicago in the late 1890s. Angell in turn trained John B. Watson, L. L. Thurstone, Walter V. Bingham, and Beardsley Ruml. Thurstone was still on the faculty in 1929 when Hutchins arrived. Ruml was recruited by Hutchins to serve as dean of the social sciences from 1931 to 1934. Dewey's work also influenced the development of sociology and anthropology. Robert E. Park was recruited into sociology in 1913. His social process theory, incorporating some of Dewey's thinking, inspired anthropologist Robert Redfield, who remained on the faculty throughout Hutchins' presidency. With Edward Sapir and Fay-Cooper Cole, Redfield strengthened the department of anthropology in the 1920s.

Dewey recruited George Herbert Mead, a philosopher who later was most recognized for the relevance of his philosophical theories to social psychology. James H. Tufts and Mead were still in the philosophy department in 1929. By the time Hutchins arrived at the university, the philosophy department had long been known for the cooperative work of its faculty. With their students Edward Scribner Ames and Addison Webster Moore, Tufts and Mead (with Dewey as the intellectual leader) had created what William James called in 1903 "the Chicago school" of philosophy and social theory.[24] This Chicago school continued its work until it dissolved in the second year of Hutchins' presidency.

The early political economy department under J. Laurence Laughlin had sponsored Thorsten Veblen and Wesley Mitchell. In the late 1920s, economists Jacob Viner, Frank H. Knight, and Henry Simons began the rebuilding of the department that later led to the Chicago school of economic theory. Political science under chairman Harry Pratt Judson had not advanced until Charles Merriam became chair in 1923. Merriam was able to acquire outside funding for his studies of political behavior and had begun in earnest to strengthen the department's empirical research through faculty appointments, including Harold Lasswell and Harold Gosnell, when Hutchins arrived in 1929.

History, too, had developed a character of its own. Beginning with Harper's appointment of Hermann von Holst in 1892, the department had grown considerably by the 1920s. Such scholars as J. Franklin Jameson, Andrew C. McLaughlin, William E. Dodd, James Westphall Thompson, Samuel Harper, and William T. Hutchinson graced the department's offices and classrooms from the 1890s to the 1920s. Unlike many departments in the university, history always had at least one woman faculty member from 1895 to the 1950s. The department was at its peak in the 1920s, according to Hutchinson, the department's unofficial historian.[25] By the middle 1920s it was clear that philanthropic foundation support was going to projects in the social sciences, inspiring many historians and their students in the department to explore history as a social science, rather than a humanities, discipline.

The connections faculty members saw in their respective researches did little to dispel fears of an increasing fragmentation of academic disciplines, particularly as each field developed distinct methods of research. At the University of Chicago, newer faculty members hired in the social sciences were focusing less on the reform goals of their mentors and more on the kinds of techniques for collecting and analyzing data that fitted their specialized studies.

Beardsley Ruml began to invest LSRM funds in empirical social science research in the 1920s. He favored cross-disciplinary and cooperative research. The university's exploration of the community as laboratory seemed particularly appropriate. It was not surprising that he found the work of Robert Park, Ernest Burgess, Charles Merriam, and Harold Gosnell ideal for the LSRM's purposes. Beginning in 1923, LSRM money was administered through the university's newly created Local Community Research Committee.[26] The School of Social Service Administration received large sums of money. The Social Sciences Research Building, dedicated just after Hutchins took office in 1929, was the culmination of the LSRM's sponsorship of cooperative research at the university.

The significance of the intellectual and structural relationships that had developed at the university from 1892 to 1929 for understanding Hutchins' presidency cannot be ignored. The faculty had known by experience and by legend of Harper's autocratic leadership. Judson's retention of the chairmanship of the political science department during his presidency and his refusal to add anyone to the department in the late 1910s (beyond himself, Ernst Freund, and Merriam) were well known. The faculty's increasing control of departments and policy in the 1920s, spurred by the lack of continuous leadership in the president's office, helped to create an autonomous and powerful body of scholars.[27]

Despite Hutchins' known sympathy for empirical social science research when he came to the presidency, his every move was carefully observed. Every faculty appointment he suggested, made, or blocked was scrutinized by a faculty body known, since Angell's time, for participation in policymaking and recruitment. Not willing to relinquish any hard-won autonomy, the faculty represented an intellectual tradition and political strength with which Hutchins often found himself at odds over the succeeding twenty-two years.

One of the factors that would alternately enhance and exacerbate Hutchins' leadership was the network of personal connections at the university. These connections extended from the University of Chicago to Yale, for example. President and Mrs. Angell had longstanding friendships with many University of Chicago families from their time at the university. Barry Karl notes in his study of Merriam that Mrs. Angell sent Mrs. George Herbert Mead a critical appraisal of Robert and Maude Hutchins, which Mead in turn circulated on campus before the Hutchinses arrived.[28]

Marriages created extensive networks. John U. Nef, an economic historian, was preceded on the faculty by his father. While still a child, his parents were killed in an accident and he spent the remainder of his childhood with the Meads. His first wife, Elinor Castle, was a member of a wealthy Chicago family whose money financed a number of projects at the university, most notably the Committee on Social Thought in the 1940s. Elizabeth Nitze's father, William A. Nitze, was the chair of the romance languages department well into the 1930s. She married Walter Paepcke, president of the Container Corporation of America who later joined the board of trustees of the university. Robert Redfield married Robert Park's daughter Greta, and their son, James, pursued his academic career at the university. Edward H. Levi, whose father was a scholar of Hebrew appointed by Harper, attended university schools, the college, and Law School and married the sister of a member of the Law School faculty. He joined the faculty in 1936, became dean of the Law School in 1950 and president of the university in 1968.

These networks functioned as social and professional grapevines within the university community and as channels of influence for, as well as resistance to, administrative authority. The university was the home of Chicago's "intellectual aristocracy."[29] University-family connections as uniquely characterized the University of Chicago as did the "currents" that flowed back and forth between the university and the "rest of the community."[30] The Hyde Park neighborhood was like a small town—the Hutchinses' activities could not escape scrutiny. This was one of the reasons the trustees were pleased to be assured of Robert's character and Maude's charm and capabilities.[31] Of course, they could not know then that Maude Hutchins' behavior would become a source of embarrassment to the university and to Hutchins over the next two decades.

The trustees offered Hutchins the presidency on April 22, 1929, setting the university on a course as stimulating as its earliest years under Harper. They satisfied the requirements of both the trustees and the faculty members of the committee. Their decision also met the approval of Woodward, who would continue as vice-president and dean of the faculties.[32] His approval was essential. He was to introduce Hutchins to his new position and act as his liaison with the faculty. The majority of university faculty, particularly the younger members, applauded the choice because they saw in Hutchins a champion of research. Members of the higher education community and officials of philanthropic foundations were intrigued with Hutchins' youth and impressed with his accomplishments at Yale.

Hutchins was exhilarated and probably somewhat unnerved by the appointment. The prestige of his new position immediately thrust him into the public eye. He became a national figure. He received letters of congratulations from hundreds of people: old family acquaintances and friends, Army buddies, Yale classmates, and numerous luminaries in the world of scholarship on and off the campus of the University of Chicago.[33] His social position rose immediately along with his standard of living. With a large house on campus, a multitude of babysitters and servants, and her husband's wholehearted support, Maude was free to pursue sculpture and eventually painting and writing.[34]

In the months before Robert Hutchins' inauguration, Maude Hutchins' unwillingness to assume expected social obligations and her self-important demeanor were only intimated. Shortly after the Hutchinses arrived, a leading hostess in the community, Anina (Mrs. William A.) Nitze, invited Maude to a welcoming tea a few weeks hence. Well aware of her own social caché, Maude cavalierly responded that she could not possibly commit herself so far in advance of any social event. Such behavior would become more frequent during Hutchins' tenure, but in the beginning Maude's rudeness was overshadowed by her intelligence, style (she only wore black and white), and supreme self-assurance.[35] And the invitations from Chicago's leading lights continued.

The trustees decided to hold a formal inauguration, the first for the university, to capitalize on the publicity and to introduce the new president and his striking wife to the alumni and citizens of Chicago. The inauguration was held four and a half months after Hutchins took office, with ceremonies stretching over two days beginning on November 19, only weeks after the stock market crash. Twenty-three thousand guests were invited, including nearly fifteen thousand students, over a hundred presidents of universities and colleges, other delegates from educational institutions, Chicago's prominent citizens, alumni of the university, and notables from the foundation world and learned societies.

On that cold and cloudy morning at eleven o'clock, the long procession of faculty and trustees marched from Ida Noyes Hall along the Midway Plaisance to the University Chapel. The audience and participants nearly filled the two-thousand-seat chapel. James Rowland Angell opened the investiture, commending Hutchins for his energy and brilliance and for his gracious and charming wife. When Hutchins took the pulpit, there was no clumsiness or searching for words. His "dry, clear monotone" was the "perfect vehicle for his lucid" thoughts.[36] His audience was captivated by his humor, his radiant smile, and his verbal acuity. Hutchins remarked on the university's historic connection to the city of Chicago, primarily through cooperative faculty research into city problems, an arrangement he wanted to see continued because it brought together interdisciplinary scholarship and "life as it is being lived today."[37]

Hutchins had the task of bestowing honorary degrees on two dignitaries at the inauguration. Martin Ryerson was one. He had been a cofounder and original trustee of the university, and he had served as director of the Art Institute and on the boards of the Chicago Symphony Orchestra and the Field Museum, as well as the Rockefeller Foundation. The choice of trustee Ryerson fittingly brought the university's past together with its present and future. The other recipient was William James Hutchins. In a touching moment Robert honored his father for his service as a minister and educator.

The activities continued throughout the day, taking full advantage of the opportunity to display the Hutchinses and the university. A luncheon at Ida Noyes Hall included speeches by Gordon J. Laing and Harry Woodburn Chase, president of the University of North Carolina, and a brief comment by Hutchins. Dinner at Chicago's elegant Palmer House followed. All the speakers, including George E. Vincent, president of the Rockefeller Foundation, had received at least one degree from Yale. Vincent noted the growth of the University of Chicago since John D. Rockefeller's original bequests. He pointed to the increasing proportion of gifts from the people of the city of Chicago ($16 million) and from the various Rockefeller boards ($10.5 million, mostly for graduate training and faculty research) from 1924 to 1929. Vincent also remarked on the university's vitality as of 1929: an annual budget of $7.4 million; an income-producing endowment of $51 million; a staff of 789; a student body of 14,000, including 8,000 graduate and professional students, around 2,000 in the college, and the rest in extension classes; and a physical plant consisting of fifty-six buildings on eighty-one acres on the city's South Side.[38] Most of these assets would decrease alarmingly in the succeeding ten years as the Depression eroded endowment, staff, and student enrollment.

Referring to all his recent speechmaking, Hutchins introduced himself at the dinner as "the lineal descendant of John Bunyan's notorious character, Mr. Talkative, the son of one Saywell, who lived in Prating Row," finishing the day the way he began, by making the guests laugh.[39] He addressed in his presentation two interests that would become major themes of his administration over the next twenty-two years. One was his interest in interdisciplinary research. The other was academic freedom.

With hundreds of Chicago businessmen in the audience, he described the object of scholarship as understanding, not immediate reform or predetermined utility. In the studies of businesses in the Chicago area by the School of Commerce and Administration, or of schools by the School of Education, or of social welfare by the School of Social Service Administration, or of regional planning by the Local Community Research Committee, neither the citizens nor the businessmen should determine the problem to be studied. The scholar should choose the problem. Fortunately for the city and the university, Hutchins noted, scholars from a variety of disciplines had chosen problems that also seemed to be the most significant for the welfare of the city. This interdisciplinary interest would be manifest in Hutchins' promotion of the college program, cross-departmental committees, and incorporation of the Medical School in the biological sciences division.

Shielding scholarly work from outside interference was to become one of Hutchins' more important crusades at the university. The protection of academic freedom was a family tradition—his father served on the American Association of University Professors' Academic Freedom Committee in the 1920s. At the university, Hutchins would be dogged in defending professors' rights against outside interference. Alternatively, on various occasions over the next twenty-two years, when faculty members attempted to determine the future of their departments or of educational policy at the university, he would exercise presidential authority to try to reorient the educational and scholarly mission of the university, often contrary to their wishes.

Hutchins' last hortatory obligation during the inaugural celebration was to the students. To the two thousand who came to Rockefeller Chapel to hear him on that Wednesday morning, Hutchins remarked on his great satisfaction and pleasure that he was older than they and would "continue to be."[40] He described his own frustrations as a student with such rules as required attendance, weekly tests, and semester examinations; he preferred self-motivation to external compulsion. He told them that the only criteria for admission to university study ought to be strong interest in further studies and competence to carry out those studies. Scholarships for qualified students ought to be available, he argued. Finally, he suggested a "pass and honors system" for the curriculum, including independent study in the fields of most concern to students.[41] Minimal supervision would enable them to develop initiative and explore their interests, much as Hutchins had in the Law School at Yale. For other studies, students could attend large lecture courses and exercise the option to transfer into honors work.

It was a vague proposal that reflected contemporary discussions of honors programs and Hutchins' own experience more than any thoughtful consideration of how universities worked or the range of learning styles students exhibited. But elements of this plan along with comprehensive subject-matter examinations were two innovations that would shape the future of undergraduate education at Chicago.

Hutchins was never to develop close relations with students at the university—he grew increasingly remote as the years passed, but he kept endearing himself to them. His homiletic talents were most inspirational when he spoke of the materialism of American society, the moral laxity of businessmen and politicians, and the problem of placing means before ends in much of human activity. His identification with youthful idealism kept him in the students' good graces throughout his presidency, no matter what his arguments were with other constituents of the university.

Hutchins began to address the university's immediate needs before he officially took office. A variety of positions required filling in 1929. The search for chairs for the art and economics departments, faculty appointments in chemistry, education and psychiatry, deans for the Library School, the School of Commerce and Administration, and the Law School demanded much of Hutchins' time right after his appointment. It is not clear whether he tried to address Harold Swift's priority of "more women of charm and accomplishment on our faculties," but other efforts paid off handsomely.[42]

His colleagues in law saw his appointment, as he did, as an opportunity to establish "a first class center in legal investigation" at the university.[43] He began by securing faculty member Harry Bigelow as dean, a feat Frederic Woodward had been unable to accomplish.[44] Interestingly, the Law School would develop a unique and innovative interdisciplinary approach to legal education and scholarship and a rigorous program in jurisprudence during the Hutchins years. It was to be an area in the university where Hutchins' influence would endure.

Hutchins discussed with the Rockefeller boards funding possibilities for the study of education. He had in mind his own ideas about training for the Ph.D. and college teaching and wanted to combine these with the needs of the university in his proposals. The School of Education needed a new faculty member. The university needed action on the faculty senate committee's report on undergraduate instruction, which had been completed in 1928 and shelved when Mason resigned.

Hutchins was familiar with the report and knew he had to proceed with it, but he had not thought much about undergraduate education except in light of his own experience, as his speech to the students revealed. His proximity to Rockefeller and Carnegie Foundation officials suggests that he was aware of their concerns about collegiate and graduate education in the 1920s. The vocationalism of undergraduate aims, the preoccupation with extracurricular activities on campuses, and the growing numbers of students entering colleges were all interpreted as symptoms of the decline of quality in higher education. Honors classes were one proffered means of restoring academic excellence in colleges and universities.

Hutchins' first public declaration at the university after his appointment was at the June 11, 1929, convocation. In that speech he echoed Angell's first address to the Yale students in 1921. Elements of Hutchins' past speeches, including his class day oration and his talk to Yale's class of 1896, also were evident. He argued that the purpose of higher education was "to unsettle the minds of young men, to widen their horizons, to inflame their intellects." (No doubt seeing the hundreds of faces of young women in his audience compelled him to amend his definition to include "young people" and "men and women" by the end of his talk.)[45]

The way to accomplish such unsettling teaching was to train better teachers, a task that should be differentiated from the training of scholars, he thought by the end of 1929. In his second convocation address he suggested that future college teachers should focus on the study and investigation of educational problems. They should produce a thesis and give equal weight to supervised clinical training to earn their Ph.D.'s. Those who decided to be scholars should be awarded another degree for their research and study.[46]

George E. Vincent informed him of the Rockefeller Foundation's interest in "genuine experiments" in collegiate education.[47] Accordingly, the General Education Board (GEB), the Rockefeller board that dealt with educational institutions in the United States, had recently made a policy change. Having appropriated large sums for selected colleges and universities, the GEB opted to try to raise standards of scholarship (through, for example, honors courses and research fellowships) in the middle 1920s. Then, in 1928, Trevor Arnett, the president, and members of the board of the GEB, including Angell, Vincent, and Anson Phelps Stokes, decided to shift focus to improving the quality of collegiate education. Dismayed that the great increase in college enrollment (250 percent since 1900) had crowded colleges with students whose motives included social and occupational mobility, the GEB began to finance institutions reorganizing curriculum, teaching, and administration to deal with large numbers of students without sacrificing academic quality.[48]

An enterprising young man, Hutchins went to work to develop a genuine experiment in undergraduate education. His incorporation of honors work in many of his plans, particularly in those early years, spoke the language of foundation officials. Trevor Arnett of the GEB was impressed.

Hutchins' earliest grandiose plans, incorporating all the needs he saw in the department of education and in university undergraduate programs, involved raising millions of dollars from local sources as well as foundations.[49] Such funds never materialized. But the college of the University of Chicago ultimately benefited from a large grant from the GEB to the School of Education in November of 1929. These funds were to develop the school's endowment, buildings, equipment, and maintenance, contingent upon an annual $75,000 increase in the university's budget allocation to the school. The grant was a way for the GEB to invest in both the child study research the school was already conducting and the new undergraduate curriculum that the Boucher committee had recommended in its report. The grant made $1.5 million immediately available to the school.[50]

The School of Education was abolished in 1931 at the request of the faculty, but most of the terms of the grant continued to be met by the department of education.[51] The training of elementary and secondary teachers was administered by a committee on teaching and assumed by the whole university. The department of education conducted graduate research and training. Among its functions were the study and evaluation of the new college plan and the design of innovations that gave the college its unique characteristics, including comprehensive subject-matter examinations.

The reorganization of the university Hutchins and his deans accomplished in 1930–31 also received GEB funds.[52] Unfortunately for Hutchins, his golden touch with foundation officials was to fade in the next few years. The foundation whose benefactor had contributed so significantly to the development of the university undertook a fundamental shift in its policy of giving in 1934. Rather than finance general endowments or budgetary expenses, the Rockefeller Foundation began to limit grants to specific research projects.[53] The onset of the Depression made the university's needs more acute at the same time that the Rockefeller Foundation boards were stubbornly withdrawing support from the general budget. Hutchins' fondest hope, to raise faculty salaries immediately, was dashed when the stock market crashed on October 29, 1929. As the Depression deepened, it became increasingly clear that the university would have to consolidate and retrench, with only limited help from such agencies as the Rockefeller boards. Hutchins' creative efforts to carry out these tasks in the early 1930s gained a great deal of attention from the world of higher education and from the general public.

A pragmatic man, available to ideas that made sense and seemed creative and important to him, he was to use the effects of the Depression to provide a rationale for an administrative restructuring the university. Many of the ideas that would explain that restructuring, especially for the college, developed in his conversations with his friend Mortimer Adler. Adler directed him to literature that shaped his thinking about the function of universities in those crucial early years of his presidency. His and Adler's intellectual partnership was one of grave significance for his presidency, particularly when he brought Adler to the campus of the University of Chicago.

CHAPTER 5 *A Meeting of Minds*

ROBERT HUTCHINS MET MORTIMER ADLER on a warm August morning in 1927. Hutchins had heard about Adler's work from C. K. Ogden, an enterprising British philosopher and editor of the International Library of Philosophy, Psychology, and Scientific Knowledge. Ogden was in process of publishing Adler's *Dialectic* and showed Hutchins some of the work in page proof. Intrigued by a reference Adler had made to legal casuistry, Hutchins wrote to Adler, who was completing a doctorate at Columbia in psychology, suggesting that they might have a mutual interest in the logic of evidence in the law. Adler, not having thought much about evidence, read J. H. Wigmore's treatise on the subject. Characteristically compulsive in his approach to intellectual matters, he probed the two volumes for all the logical inconsistencies he could find.[1]

Assuming the dean was a typical elderly academic administrator, Adler (only in his middle twenties at that time) arrived at Hutchins' office at the Yale Law School dressed somberly in a black suit and hat. He was quite shocked when Hutchins, a man near his own age, greeted him in a white tee shirt, ducks, and tennis shoes with the information that he was, indeed, the dean of the Law School. His friendliness, intelligence, and breezy humor immediately won Adler's affection.

What attracted Hutchins to Adler is less clear, since Hutchins left no account of his impressions. Quite probably, he was taken with Adler's intellectual self-assurance, his quick mind, and his willingness to battle to the end to make a point. Their conversation came easily, stretching through dinner and into the evening. Subsequent communications were on the topic of evidence, mingled with the problems of logic and psychology. A warm friendship grew, evident in their sardonic exchange of gossip about Columbia's and Yale's law schools and in their interest in one another's work.

Hutchins' and Adler's immediate liking for each other is curious in a number of respects. They were a study in contrasts. Hutchins was tall and lithe. Adler was short and rather ungainly. Where Hutchins' upbringing was unquestionably American Protestant, Adler was raised with a sister in an extended German Jewish family in New York City. His father, Ignatz, ran a jewelry business with Adler's uncle. His mother Clarissa had been a schoolteacher after her graduation from Hunter College until she married. The Adler family was comfortable but not wealthy. When Mortimer decided to attend Columbia University, his mother taught immigrants English to help pay his tuition and expenses. By his own account, he was raised to be respectful of his elders and to do well in school. From his earliest years he manifested an imperious compulsion for neatness and order that marked his whole life, significantly shaping his intellectual development and his relationships with others.[2]

Unlike Hutchins', Adler's formal education was not a smooth progression from one level to the next. At the age of fourteen, Adler lost interest in classes at De Witt Clinton High School when he was barred from work on the school newspaper. He had broken a rule and allowed a failing student to continue on the staff. Shortly afterward, he dropped out of school and took a job as copyboy at the *New York Sun.* He tried his hand at writing editorials, leaving his efforts on the editor's desk. At least one of his pieces was actually published.

An autodidact by nature, Adler continued his own program of reading, at the same time seeking more structure for his study by enrolling in Columbia University's extension division. He had discovered John Stuart Mill's autobiography and decided to read the books Mill had read. In this way he encountered the dialogues of Plato for the first time. He completed a year's worth of courses and applied to Columbia College for admission as a fully matriculated undergraduate. Columbia accepted him as a sophomore in 1920 at the age of sixteen.

Like his early disillusionment with high school and subsequent brief career in journalism, Adler's college education followed lines different from Hutchins'. He studied philosophy with John Dewey and F. J. E. Woodbridge, reading Aristotle for the first time in Woodbridge's course. Hutchins remembered little direct exposure to primary material at Oberlin or at Yale, beyond reading a dialogue of Plato, the Bible, Goethe's *Faust,* and Shakespeare.[3] Adler's reading of classic works of Western culture took firm root when he was accepted in a new course offered at Columbia in 1921. In 1918 John Erskine, professor of English, had developed a reading course of great books in an education program for the idle Army recruits who remained in Europe for some months at the war's end. He gained the faculty's approval to offer the course on a limited basis at Columbia during Adler's junior year. Called "general honors," the class was the most significant of all Adler's undergraduate classes. It presaged what would become the abiding theme of his educational ideas and programs for the rest of his life. Through Adler, it shaped Hutchins' definition of formal education.

The class met for sixty two-hour sessions throughout two academic years. Students read one classic of Western thought a week, beginning with Homer, Herodotus, and Thucydides and ending with Darwin, Marx, and Freud. Not only the books but also Erskine's manner of raising questions and stimulating the weekly discussions profoundly shaped Adler's conception of what a college education ought to be. When Robert Hutchins was searching for a programmatic approach to undergraduate education in the months after he became president of the University of Chicago, Adler's account of his general honors class appealed to him. Such a course was a potential weapon against early specialization at the undergraduate level.

Adler finished college without obtaining a degree, having refused to complete the fours years in physical education Columbia required. With sufficient course credit to enter the graduate school but faced with imminent rejection by the philosophy department, he undertook graduate work in psychology. The philosophy department's refusal to admit him to the Ph.D. program came as a blow. It occurred, according to his own account, because of his continual and contentious effort to debunk pragmatism in favor of metaphysics at department gatherings. Philosophy, he thought, ought not be concerned solely with man's relation to man. His arguments ran directly counter to the work of John Dewey and some of his colleagues in the department.

In 1923 Adler began to teach in the psychology department, as was the custom for graduate students. In addition, he was invited to co-lead the general honors seminar. His first partner in this venture was Mark Van Doren. As the course developed over the next few years, Adler gave vent to his penchant for categorizing by helping to reconstruct the lists of books to be used in the course. The staff then voted on them. This pattern of constructing and arguing over lists would manifest itself in all of Adler's subsequent great books ventures.

A number of people Adler met in the 1920s, either in connection with the great books seminar or with the Columbia philosophy (where he continued to take courses) and psychology departments, would remain lifelong colleagues. Many would be included in various great books or interdisciplinary experiments at the University of Chicago with Hutchins, but three in particular had a notable impact on Hutchins' life.

The least influential of the three, Arthur Rubin, was a Ph.D. student in psychology whose idea of argument included a dogged, incessant, often rude interpretation of Socratic questioning. He continually posed philosophically oriented challenges that intrigued Adler, who could be as dogged as Rubin. In the 1930s Rubin would become a temporary faculty member on the Committee on the Liberal Arts at the University of Chicago. He helped to secure funds and participated in the committee's activities. His argumentative style alienated many faculty members. Independently wealthy, he never finished his degree because of family business commitments and so never gained a permanent faculty appointment.

Scott Buchanan had studied under liberal educator Alexander Meiklejohn at Amherst College. He was a Rhodes Scholar and had received a doctorate in philosophy from Harvard. Adler met him when he was an instructor at Columbia. As assistant director at the People's Institute under Everett Dean Martin, Buchanan organized evening lecture and discussion classes for working adults. He drew Adler into the institute by inviting him to deliver a series of lectures in psychology. When Buchanan left for an assistant professorship at the University of Virginia in 1929, Adler took his position as assistant director. Buchanan's playful intellect and gentle, persistent questions aroused Adler's lifelong affection and loyalty. These same qualities endeared Buchanan to Hutchins.

Richard McKeon, a classmate of Rubin, had studied medieval philosophy under Étienne Gilson at the Sorbonne. He returned to Columbia to take an assistant professorship in philosophy. Adler met McKeon while searching for English translations of Aquinas' *Summa Theologica.* McKeon occasionally joined the group, including Rubin, Buchanan, and Adler, that met in one another's apartments for informal discussions of Aquinas and other works. Eventually, they all joined forces with Van Doren, Jacques Barzun, and Clifton Fadiman to hold great books classes at the People's Institute. Their experiences with the adults and the great books convinced them that the books could be a viable tool for education, no matter what the background of the students, if the students themselves were committed to reading and discussion.[4] Hutchins would call upon their liberal arts expertise in the decades to come.

Adler's involvement with the People's Institute was only of superficial interest to Hutchins between 1927 and 1929. Rather, Adler's exploration of what he saw as philosophical and logical issues of evidence, the relationship between British empiricism and English law, for example, and his criticisms of Hutchins' overreliance on behaviorist psychology to explore exceptions to the law of evidence piqued Hutchins' interest.[5] As a practical man, Hutchins was concerned about what might further his own explorations of evidence. Moreover, Adler's ability to move in a variety of realms, including general honors at Columbia College, psychology in the graduate school, and the People's Institute, quite likely attracted Hutchins.

At a deeper and related level, Hutchins was impressed with Adler's familiarity with philosophical works and his prodigious reading in the literature of psychology. Both practically and intellectually, Adler's competence in these different domains appealed to an aspiring interdisciplinarian like Hutchins. As a result, Hutchins offered Adler a Sterling fellowship at the Law School similar to the one Donald Slesinger took in the fall of 1927.[6] Adler turned the fellowship down but used the offer to solicit a position at Columbia Law School.

It is quite probable that the differences in their life and educational experiences underlay Hutchins' initial attraction to Adler. Their personality differences might also have contributed. Hutchins' unfailing courtesy, cool rationality, and elegant bearing were foil to Adler's abrupt manner and his obvious desire to win arguments. Perhaps Hutchins was attracted to Adler's passion. There is no question that they shared a fascination with ideas and that they both perceived themselves as iconoclasts. By the 1930s Adler would become preoccupied with taking ethical and philosophical positions because he believed they were right. In the late 1920s, though, he informed Hutchins that he liked to raise "hell with ideas rather than [be] right about them." He gloried in questioning and challenging "pet prejudices" in people's thinking.[7]

Hutchins always tended to argue with moral, if not intellectual and practical, certainty. But the questioning of prejudices (other than his own) had been one of his legacies from Oberlin. Unsettling the minds of young men was the purpose of education. Clues as to why their friendship developed so quickly and strongly can be found in the highly developed verbal acuity, intellectual precocity, and need to challenge the status quo both men exhibited.

Beyond the attractions that made them friends, one must ask why Hutchins was so available to Adler's ideas about the substance of a college education and about philosophy's central role in university scholarship. To be sure, when Hutchins approached Adler in October of 1929 with the casual question about his own education that led to the story of Erskine's course, Adler had not given much thought to education per se. However, he had given some thought to Hutchins' interests in cross-disciplinary research. Moreover, with Hutchins as president of a major university, Adler began to fantasize the kind of philosophy department he, Buchanan, and McKeon could develop together. Within a month of Hutchins' appointment, he and Adler discussed such a department.

As Adler saw the situation then, the three of them represented interdepartmental competence: McKeon as philosopher and historian, Adler as philosopher in the Law School, psychology department, and possibly physical and social sciences, and Buchanan as philosopher and mathematician. Beyond using philosophy and logic in other disciplines, they might also incorporate in their teaching the honors part of Hutchins' pass and honors idea for the college.[8]

As the plan developed over the first year of Hutchins' presidency, it combined Hutchins' sparse educational ideas and his administrative hopes for distinguishing himself at the university with Adler's grandiose desire to create a community of philosophers. These men would be dedicated to a dialectical examination of contemporary academic knowledge disciplines. At the same time, they would create a new center for philosophy at the university, not unlike the University of Paris in the Middle Ages.

At Columbia Adler was appointed by Dean Smith to observe law classes during the 1929–30 school year. He submitted a critical assessment of Young B. Smith's, Karl N. Llewellyn's, and Richard R. Powell's teaching, and of the case method itself for teaching torts, contracts, and real property, all first-year courses.[9] From that experience in combination with his ongoing conversation with Hutchins, he determined that law students were too narrowly educated. Indeed, all students were too narrowly educated. Moreover, all members of all faculties were too narrowly educated. A good example of the latter assertion was his experience with faculty members at Columbia in the social sciences and in general honors classes.[10]

To counter such limited preparation and develop a unique program, Chicago might recruit some student "misfits" who were "intellectually inclined" but uninterested in typical professional or graduate studies. They could spend three years moving from one school or department to another, acting as critics and acquiring cross-disciplinary exposure to a range of academic fields. Adler suggested an honors reading course to give the group of at-large students a common foundation in their junior and senior years.[11] He compared the idea of such a program to Alexander Meiklejohn's Experimental College. A unique exploration of historic and contemporary ideas with a self-selected body of students, the Experimental College brought the University of Wisconsin recognition for its new approach to undergraduate education.[12] As a self-perpetuating training ground in critical, cross-disciplinary education, Adler's department of philosophical studies similarly might bring educational renown to the University of Chicago.

Hutchins found the idea very appealing. Right after he returned from Europe in the fall of 1929 he pressed the philosophy department to consider Adler's appointment. He also urged the department to compile assessments of McKeon and Buchanan. The department considered all three men's work interesting. However, the members were concerned with maintaining a balance between the department's two emphases: logic and metaphysics, on one hand, and ethics and social and political philosophy, on the other. At that point, the department was weighted toward logic and metaphysics. With the projected retirements of James H. Tufts and George Herbert Mead in the next few years, the balance would be tipped further in the direction of logic and metaphysics, the areas of Adler's and McKeon's work.

There were other concerns. The younger faculty wanted assurance that an older scholar of outstanding ability would be appointed to ensure continuity of the department's reputation when the two most senior members retired. Members of the department also thought its own Ph.D.'s ought to be considered. Only two of eight faculty members at that point had a Chicago doctorate. Chairman Tufts voiced the opinion of the department when he stated that Adler, McKeon, and Buchanan "are men of scholarly promise." However, he noted, the department was not convinced that any of the three would be "the best available for the needs and purposes of the department."[13] Clearly, the department's agenda did not mesh with Hutchins'.

Despite these misgivings, Hutchins was determined that his friend Adler should be in the department of his choice. Because Adler perceived himself a philosopher, Hutchins wanted him in a position to begin building a department of philosophical studies at the University of Chicago. The history and tradition of the philosophy department held no stock with Hutchins in these first few months of attempting to shape the institution. In a spirit of accommodation to the new president, and unaware at that point of Adler's grand plan, the department agreed to take him.

The agreement was conditional. First, the permanence of the appointment was left for later decision by the department. Second, Adler was slated to do only one-third of his teaching in the philosophy department, the balance to be in psychology and law. Adler received his appointment in December of 1929, to begin in September of 1930. Much to the department's dismay, it was announced that Adler's rank would be associate professor and that his salary would be nearly one thousand dollars higher than the salaries of all other full professors in the department, with the exception of Chairman Tufts.[14]

Collegiality among philosophers was not limited by campus boundaries. As in all the academic disciplines, communication between scholars was national, often international, in scope. Adler could not keep his hopes, dreams, or opinions to himself. In the months before he assumed his new position, rumors and gossip about his plans for the department and his less than flattering assessment of his future colleagues reached the University of Chicago. These rumors did not portend a warm welcome for Adler. More to the point, they greatly damaged Hutchins' credibility with the department of philosophy and, eventually, in the whole university.

Adler's opinions of his future colleagues were rooted in his earlier studies in philosophy with Dewey and others at Columbia and had developed during his work with Jerome Michael at Columbia Law School. Adler had decided that philosophy ought to be concerned with metaphysical as well as empirical problems of human existence. He thought pragmatism focused too much on "man-centered' thinking and not enough on "god-centered" thinking.[15]

If he had restricted his comments to scholarly criticism within the accepted forums, Adler's contributions to philosophy and the logic of social science theory might have been welcome. Instead, his social and intellectual exchanges with his fellows were marked by an obsessive, arrogant conviction of the righteousness of his opinions. He disregarded Hutchins' request to restrict himself "to naive inquiry and intelligent humility" in discussions with and about colleagues, and, indeed, he may have been constitutionally incapable of doing so.[16] He wrote to Hutchins in late 1929, for example, complaining about a departmental course in reflective thinking Tufts had asked him to teach. He described it as "goddam Deweyized bunk."[17]

Adler's perceptions of pragmatism were shaped by his opinion of the social sciences, an opinion that had a profound effect on Hutchins' thinking about university scholarship. In the process of investigating truth claims while studying social science research of criminal behavior, Adler had concluded that the social sciences lacked methods of research and analyses of data sufficiently rigorous to support claims to truth.[18] Because social scientists had little or no training in the precise thinking and expression required by logic, mathematics, and physics, their work was a "mess."[19] His criticism was two-pronged. He thought the social sciences were not scientific enough. Sociologists' work, he informed Hutchins, for the most part should "be classified as literature" rather than science.[20] Because social scientific studies lacked clearly testable hypotheses, precise research methods, and meticulous conclusions, their claims to authority were no greater than much that passed as observation and description.

Compounding the problem, the social sciences had displaced philosophy as a legitimate mode of inquiry. Philosophy, particularly as conducted by Plato, Aristotle, and Aquinas, presented rigorous analysis of important questions and treated issues of greater import than the social sciences did. The subject matter of philosophers' studies was being, or existence. Adler thought this was of far greater intellectual consequence than studies of man's sociopolitical relation to man.[21] Such an argument for intellectual significance appealed to Hutchins.

The method of philosophy, which Adler obscurely perceived in 1930 to be dialectical examination of the academic disciplines to discover their logical inconsistencies and, presumably, faulty claims to truth, was as legitimate and important a pursuit of truth within the university as any mode of scientific inquiry. Philosophy, to Adler, was rational science as opposed to empirical science. While empirical research could lead to "knowledge of matters of fact," metaphysical research could lead to "knowledge of the relation of ideas" and, by exploring "the ultimate nature of the universe, reality or being," to wisdom.[22]

Adler articulated a role for the University of Chicago in the restoration of philosophy (or metaphysics) as the preeminent science in the work of the university with his scheme for a department of philosophical studies. Not just students would engage in interdisciplinary work. Professors "'dialectizing' the various subject-matters" would "do for the science and culture of the twentieth century what Thomas did for . . . the thirteenth in the Summa Theologica."[23] The final product might be "a Summa Dialectica" that would promote the creation of "philosopher-kings."[24]

Hutchins was drawn to the idea of shaping a distinctive and significant role for the University of Chicago under his presidency. Rather than promoting research of facts, the domain of the social sciences, he thought Chicago could begin the study of intellectually essential questions like those of existence and the purpose of human existence. He thought that under his leadership, with Adler in the philosophy department, there was "going to be no university in the world like Chicago."[25] For these reasons he was willing to brave the philosophy department's displeasure.

Adler's colleagues at Columbia were aware of his attitude toward their work. His future colleagues at Chicago heard about his opinions because he openly volunteered them at a party in New York in the spring of 1930.[26] If he was as unrestrained in public as he was in his correspondence, it is no wonder the Chicago philosophy department did not welcome him. He informed Hutchins, for example, that Arthur Murphy was a "dud" and that the work of Tufts, Mead, Edwin A. Burtt, and T. V. Smith was "slop and bilge."[27] Though Smith and Burtt were not pragmatists of the Tufts and Mead school, Adler lumped them all together. In his opinion, their work had "corrupted" the first-rate work of such social scientists at Chicago as Harold Lasswell in political science and Edward Sapir in anthropology.[28]

As much as his opinions were the fodder for cross-country academic gossip, so were his hopes for the philosophy department's future. His rumored plans for intellectual reorientation and new personnel alienated the members of the department. Tufts and Mead had devoted their lives to building the philosophy department. As a departmental faculty, they, with Smith and Burtt in the 1920s, had gained increasing autonomy in determining the department's emphases and in maintaining its links with social science departments and the Divinity School (through Edward Scribner Ames).[29] The suggestion of replacing what was left of the Chicago school of philosophy with an Adlerian brand of metaphysics and logic might have been laughable as the grandiose plan of a self-inflated upstart. Unfortunately, Adler was a close friend of the new president of the university, and the president's behavior had begun to reflect Adler's influence.

Hutchins had denied Tufts' request to raise all salaries in the philosophy department commensurate with Adler's. When the members of the department heard about Adler's plan "to effect a radical change in its make-up," they grew increasingly suspicious of Hutchins' motives. Sensing that Hutchins lacked confidence in him, Tufts resigned as chair. Mead succeeded him with Hutchins' reassurances that the department could determine its own future. Still, Hutchins would make no guarantees about new appointments to the faculty in accordance with departmental plans.[30]

In the summer of 1930, rumors reached the department indicating that Scott Buchanan fully expected to come to Chicago. In the fall, shortly after Adler's arrival, Hutchins informed the department that he would not act on appointments because of the financial uncertainty created by the Depression. Shortly afterward, he requested that the department accept Buchanan, not necessarily permanently, so that he could do work in mathematics and biology, as well as philosophy. He claimed that the money for Buchanan's salary was to come from an outside source.[31]

It is no wonder that the department was suspicious. The whole time Hutchins had been reassuring the department faculty members that they would determine their own future, he and Adler had been trying to figure out how to bring Buchanan and McKeon into the department.[32] By 1931 philosophy faculty members felt they had been had by the president of the university. Hutchins continued to resist requests to consider their preferred candidates in 1930 and early 1931.[33]

Hutchins' intimation in late 1930 that he was unsure of his commitment to the department based on its "present membership" deepened their suspicion, despite his protests that he had no desire to control the department. It is a measure of the department faculty's willingness to come to some agreement with the president that they consented reluctantly to an outside review of their work and of the work of potential appointments. Hutchins sent letters to some of their suggested reviewers and to an equal number of his own choice, hoping, no doubt, to find support for the appointment of Buchanan and McKeon from outside the university. The result of this "humiliating" procedure was national exposure of Hutchins' first major blunder in his dealings with the faculty.[34]

James Rowland Angell's warning to the trustees about Hutchins' immaturity, impatience, and ruthlessness must have haunted Harold Swift that spring. Hutchins' virtual lack of understanding of, and indifference to, the traditions and culture of the university as embodied in the philosophy department destroyed his hopes that a forum for Adler's philosophical work could be created at the university. Moreover, his credibility with a faculty constitutionally watchful of administrative coercion was badly damaged. By nationally soliciting the opinions of philosophers about their colleagues, who had trained a sizable group of well-respected academic philosophers and who had a longstanding reputation in American philosophy, Hutchins found not his judgment but the department's judgment confirmed.

His actions put on the alert anyone who might have considered appointment to the department at the University of Chicago. McKeon, for example, asked Hutchins to withdraw his name from the list.[35] But the most problematic result was the breach between the president and his faculty that would never be completely healed. Anyone who might have plans for their department or whose judgment of scholarly competence differed from the president's was forewarned of potential obstacles in the new administration.

With the intervention of Dean Laing of the humanities division and other respected faculty and administrators, the conflict was diffused. Hutchins was compelled to apologize to the philosophers and to move Adler to the Law School in order to appease the faculty. Because he continued to refuse to act on their suggested appointments, including Charles Morris, or to accept their assessment of junior faculty, Mead, Burtt, Murphy, and Hall resigned. They felt they had fundamental differences with Hutchins in the evaluation of scholarly competence in philosophy. They also thought the damage to the department's standing in the academic world was irreparable in the near future.[36] Edward Scribner Ames agreed to take the chairmanship. T. V. Smith, who preferred "Chicago troubled to many another place quiet," agreed to help restore the department.[37] Mead died shortly after he left Chicago for Columbia University. The others went to positions elsewhere. And Hutchins had to appoint Charles Morris after all.

Hutchins persisted in opposing the philosophy faculty for a number of complicated, but related, reasons. He found Adler's ideas exciting. Adler incorporated Hutchins' desire for cross-disciplinary exploration in his plans. He used Hutchins' nebulous ideas about academic quality. Moreover, his appeal to Hutchins' rebellious nature was probably irresistible. The discovery of someone who could translate his amorphous hopes into a methodical program, and the desire for a sympathetic ally within the institution, outweighed the discomfort of what might only have turned out to be a momentary protest of a single group of faculty. In addition, Hutchins had great faith in the power of his own persuasive reasoning. When he thought he was right, he became fully committed to a cause. It was difficult to convince him otherwise without also suggesting that his integrity or his judgment might be in question.

He likely was acting on a negative lesson he had learned from Angell's presidency at Yale. Rather than cautiously gathering support over time before instituting policy as Angell had, Hutchins moved quickly and impetuously. He later admitted he firmly believed that any change he wanted to effect would have to be in the early years of his tenure; otherwise the forces of institutional inertia would outweigh his powers of persuasion.[38] What appeared to Angell's observers as tolerance might well have appeared to Hutchins as indecision.

To lead a community with strength, one took unpopular positions and stood by them. More than on Angell, Hutchins may have based his behavior on the example of Henry Churchill King, a moral and intellectual power in the Oberlin community, who, like Angell, had also contended with faculty opposition. Whatever the factors influencing his behavior, Hutchins' attitude toward the philosophy faculty revealed a developing pattern of treating faculty members as employees subject to his managerial policy decisions.[39]

Hutchins' invitation to another close friend to join the faculty in 1930 offers some interesting comparisons. Thornton Wilder also received his appointment to the English department by presidential fiat, but as a visiting professor. Wilder's tenure was quite different from Adler's. He had no Ph.D., but he did receive the Pulitzer Prize in literature in 1928 for *The Bridge of San Luis Rey.* Though initially members of the department resented his presence, he eventually was fully accepted. Personable, eminently tolerant, and gracious, he was well liked. He fit into Chicago's North Side upper-crust cultural and social circles as well as the university's South Side student groups. He refrained from speaking for Hutchins at the university or from becoming involved in any faculty-president battles. Never an explicit ambassador for Hutchins in the community in the way Adler was, he nevertheless remained one of Hutchins' closest lifelong friends.

Hutchins' position, by virtue of his power of appointment and duty to attend to the whole of the university, separated him from the community of scholars he was responsible for sustaining. His aristocratic elegance further distanced him from the hoi polloi of the university community as did Maude Hutchins' refusal to entertain on a frequent basis. Annual New Year's teas and springtime recitals in his home did little to close the personal distance he created between himself and others.

A sophisticated showman, he skillfully used his homiletic talents to engage, provoke, and exhort the university community from his presidential platform. At the same time, in his face-to-face contacts with members of the community, he employed his wit and dry humor to measure others and then to maintain or to close the distance, depending on how they placed in his estimation. He was "a most sweetly reasonable man,"[40] engaging, even kindly, with those who stimulated him or appealed to his sensibilities. Alternatively, he was cool, distant, and unmoving with those who did not.

Hutchins' friendship and collaboration with Adler, a man who in his youth lacked the conversational grace and unfailing courtesy that was bred in Hutchins, increased the perception that Hutchins could never be a full member of the tightly bound community. Those who were able to break through his reserve or persist despite the off-putting rejoinders in his conversational repertoire were rewarded with Hutchins' tenacious loyalty and prodigious ability to bring together resources to initiate their projects. Those who were unable or unwilling to break through his reserve or respond to his wit either confronted the president rarely or minded their own business. Otherwise, they would have been continually frustrated in their efforts to shape educational policy at Chicago.

One source of frustration was Hutchins' proposal early in his presidency to distinguish the undergraduate program at the University of Chicago in certain ways. He was intrigued with Adler's casual description of the Erskine general honors seminar at Columbia College. Conscious of gaps in his own education, particularly in comparison with Adler's, he decided he ought to begin reading some of the books in that seminar. He was aware that the additional pressures of his new position would leave little time for such reading unless it was structured into his schedule as a formal commitment. For that reason, he asked Adler if he would be willing to coteach with him a seminar for freshmen in the college using those books. Adler agreed. According to his account, the news that the president planned to hold an honors seminar for freshmen created quite a stir on campus.[41]

Since Hutchins had not yet read any of the books, the two men worked with Adler's materials from the Columbia course, including book lists and analyses of staff discussions to plan their seminar. Adler warned Hutchins of the problems such a seminar could raise within the university. He had found at Columbia, for example, that staffing was difficult and expensive, with two instructors for every ten or fifteen students. Some faculty members resented the seminar. "Departmentally-minded individuals" and scholars thought it pretentious. Yet, Adler argued, it provided an antidote to poor texts and a counter to "specialism." In addition, general honors constituted "the backbone of a liberal education" and created "an intellectual community within a college."[42]

Undeterred, Hutchins began his reading in the summer of 1930 to prepare for teaching in the fall.[43] Adler began the fall term by interviewing the eighty freshman applicants whose school records met his standards. He chose twenty who appeared capable of doing the work. The class met once a week for a two-hour discussion of the book of the week. Normal semester course credit and examinations were suspended, as the course lasted over two school years. The class met in a special room around a long oval table.

Students also used the room as a reading room. At the end of each year, students submitted to oral examinations by such invited outsiders as Scott Buchanan and Richard McKeon. These examinations were open to university faculty observers and stirred up "considerable interest, argument, and discussion."[44]

The honors class drew attention to the university. Classes often were open to visitors who wanted to observe the discussions. After the initial two-year experiment, part of the first group petitioned to extend the class over two more years to reread the books. Their request was granted because Hutchins and Adler convinced Dean Chauncey Boucher that a second reading could only enhance the students' college education. Eventually, Hutchins and Adler extended the class down to the University High School, up to the Law School and departments in the divisions of the humanities and social sciences, and out to the extension division of the university.

Over time, a core group of faculty and staff participated as teachers in the classes. Discussion groups formed in the Chicago area. In the early to middle 1940s, the great books movement (as it came to be called) was promoted by Adler and financed by the university's recently acquired *Encyclopaedia Britannica* (EB) company. The movement spread throughout the Midwest and to the East and West coasts. Groups gathered in private homes, churches, and public libraries to read and discuss the books. John Erskine participated in the 1940s as an editorial adviser to the EB's publication of a set of the books entitled *Great Books of the Western World* (1952).

At issue here is not the growth and spread of the great books, possibly a fascinating study in itself. Rather, the issue is what attracted Hutchins to the reading and discussion of the books and what compelled him to advocate such a program as the curriculum of the college at the University of Chicago. A man who in the late 1920s had touted study and research in the social sciences as the primary means of understanding human activity was trying, by the early 1930s, to convince the college curriculum committee to adopt the great books as the basis of the curriculum. A number of factors figured in Hutchins' attraction to the books as an educational program.

Teaching with the books was an intellectual and pedagogical challenge for Hutchins and Adler. One observer noted that in the early years their manner in the class was extremely didactic; had she been a student, she would have found it humiliating.[45] More often, Hutchins' style offered a balance to Adler's. Adler slapped the table and badgered students. He pushed students to see the "errors" in the books and contradictions between different authors' claims to truth.[46] Just any response by students did not suffice. One had to take a position in light of the reading and present a logical argument for it that could withstand the assault of his aggressive questioning.

By contrast, Hutchins was remote but kind with the students. When they experienced difficulty with their interpretations, he tried to help them clarify their responses. At the same time he, too, pushed them to grapple more fully with the issues the books raised, usually with humorous and sometimes acerbic bantering. He and Adler often performed for the students, demonstrating the art of argument. But the predominant pedagogical method was discussion of the meanings of words and ideas, using cultural associations, students' personal experiences, and questions.[47]

As Hutchins read and discussed the books with Adler and the class, he found them to be a potent educational tool. They demanded rigorous intellectual engagement. They explored the most fundamental of spiritual, social, and political problems. The logic of their ethical and moral arguments seemed to transcend the contexts in which they were written. And they represented a cohesion and seriousness that Hutchins had found lacking in his own college education at Yale, where the emphasis was on elective courses, clubs, football, and social accomplishment.

What else, beyond his direct intellectual experience with the books, allowed Adler's iconoclastic ideas to play such a definitive role in Hutchins' thinking about education and scholarship in the early years of his presidency at the University of Chicago? His childhood in the evangelical Protestant culture of his father and Oberlin suggests a powerful source for his attraction to Adler's ideas. In light of this early training, the practical problems he faced in the 1930s demanded a fundamental reconsideration of his role as an educational leader.

As already noted, an examination of the Hutchins family and Oberlin community suggests the powerful influence these two contexts had in the formation of Hutchins' character and predilections. The principles of conduct he had learned to respect were firmly rooted in the Protestant evangelical tradition. The virtues of "courage, temperance, liberality, honor, justice, wisdom, reason, and understanding" were virtues he had found in the living example of his father.[48] They were virtues held in high esteem in the Oberlin College community. And they were virtues much discussed in the literature that most moved him: Plato's dialogues, Aristotle's *Ethics* and *Politics,* Aquinas' treatises, and John Stuart Mill's work.[49]

By teaching with the great books, Hutchins envisioned a secular educational program that embodied discussion of these virtues. The principles of conduct and the discussions about them were explicitly stated, not left to haphazard deduction based on individual experience in a specialized elective curriculum. At the same time, the program did not rely on religious authority in the way the teachings of Will Hutchins and Oberlin had. Rather, the discussion could be rooted in the intellectual authority of the Western cultural tradition. The idea of this kind of liberal education in the great books resonated with Hutchins' own moral education but was more suited to the secular modern university he led.

In addition to the education Hutchins had received from his family and Oberlin, his experience reflected models of the purpose of higher educational institutions and the role of educational leader. Oberlin's most important task was the education of each new generation of students, who would, in turn, serve communities and the larger society with the knowledge and habits thus acquired. The social, moral, and intellectual aspects of that education were virtually the same. In effect, when Hutchins argued for a liberal education in the college in the 1930s, he was arguing for a secular mission for the University of Chicago. It was a contemporary translation of Oberlin's nineteenth-century religious mission, embodying Hutchins' desire for unity, coherence, and a framework of principles to guide the institution.

For models of educational leadership Hutchins had his father and Henry Churchill King, both paragons of virtue. They articulated beliefs and ideals for their institutions, whether or not the community agreed with their ideas. Of course, both men had been trained for the ministry, and their leadership reflected the expectation that they would provide spiritual, as well as intellectual, guidance in educational policy.

Robert Hutchins never understood why the faculty at the University of Chicago might consider him arrogant and authoritarian when he tried to overrule the proposals of the philosophy department in 1930 and 1931, or when he continued to advocate great books for the college despite the faculty's refusal to follow his program, or when he made recommendations for university educational policy that bypassed the faculty. His duty was to lead the faculty and define the mission of the university.[50] The great books and philosophical reasoning offered a means and an end, rooted in Western culture, that was both distinctive in the 1930s and sensible to Hutchins. His belief in the power of rational thought and discussion became a theme of all his educational proposals. As a primary route to knowledge, this belief reflected an older, theological approach to intellectual work. In this vein, Hutchins perceived the social, political, and economic problems of the Depression to be, at root, moral problems.

When Hutchins arrived at the University of Chicago in 1929, the country was still riding on the stock market boom. In the next four years, the same four years of his growing friendship with Adler, his reading and teaching of the great books, and his early efforts to shape the college, the country experienced the worst depression in its history. Hutchins served in a variety of public and quasi-public capacities that gave him direct contact with the effects of the Depression and a platform on which to argue about public policies. As chairman of an advisory council of the National Reemployment Service, he mediated labor controversies in 1933 and learned of the effects of unemployment in the Chicago area. He also worked with Chicago's joint emergency relief fund, an organization of businessmen. He found that private charity would "not meet this situation" and argued for increased public funding for Chicago's hungry families.[51]

Hutchins served on the Rockefeller-financed Commission of Inquiry into National Policy in International Economic Relations. The commission, after months of hearings, suggested future economic policy for the United States, which President Hoover chose to ignore.[52] Finally, he watched aghast as the politically corrupt Chicago school board reduced funds to elementary and high schools, firing teachers and cutting their salaries, and closed one of the city's junior colleges, but refused to negotiate over janitorial positions and salaries.[53] He argued locally and nationally for federal support for public education, more equitable distribution of funds to schools, and a cabinet-level post for education.[54]

Hutchins' 1932 speech to the Young Democratic Club in Chicago just before the national convention further outlined responsibilities for political leaders. With pungent wording and passionate rhetoric, the speech presented a moral and political condemnation of the Republican party's performance throughout the 1920s and early 1930s. More than that, it embodied a clear set of principles framing the Democratic party's commitment "to advance the happiness and well-being of the community" with a focus "on the needs of the majority of the community rather than on those of the powerful few."[55] The speech reflected Hutchins' perception of himself as a moral critic in a deeply troubled social order.

The Depression itself, as well as the refusal of public officials to conduct public policy in a principled way, appeared to Hutchins a clear example of the need for a more authoritative basis for making public decisions. Economics, sociology, and political science had neither predicted nor prevented the Depression. Nor had they presented clear means and ends, or practical guides, for deciding what to do about it. For defining the university's role in relation to these policy problems, philosophy was the key. In the realm of moral and ethical education, philosophy promised far more than the social sciences could deliver. Description of the facts or the conditions of existence was not adequate to provide a rational foundation in ethics and politics or to investigate the ends of the behavior, rules, and social arrangements the social sciences described.

In addition to the subjects of its investigations, the methods of philosophy promoted the development of such skills as logic, rhetoric, and grammar. These skills could enable scholars to choose and engage in systematic exploration of important questions, inform the work of social scientists, and provide a common language with which scholars could communicate, no matter what their particular academic discipline. "Masses of social, political, economic, and psychological data" provided information but did not explain how to use it.[56] To bring order to the "chaos of the modern world" required not the teaching of facts but rational inquiry and discussion.[57]

Quite possibly, too, the rise of fascism in Europe in the 1930s further suggested the need to introduce students to an authoritative tradition whose lessons might help to counteract authoritarianism.[58] By exposing students to the great books, Hutchins hoped to accomplish this goal. Reading works exploring ethics, philosophy, and political theory, reaching back to the earliest recorded discussions of democracy and self-determination, would enable students to develop and articulate their own positions. They would be prepared to resist pressure to conform to dominant (or totalitarian) political creeds and movements. Development of the "intellectual virtues" was a means to cultivate "correctness in thinking," leading to "intelligent action."[59] The twofold exigencies of worldwide depression and political fascism may well have shown Hutchins that old truths held new meaning for students of the liberal arts through the great books. Hutchins' desire to use a conservative conception of culture to counter cultural deterioration was not an isolated phenomenon in the 1930s.[60]

Within the university, the effects of the Depression and the need to address the undergraduate problem that he had inherited from Max Mason might well have made Hutchins receptive to the great books as a distinctive educational program. The university lost more than one-third of its endowment income between 1930 and 1934 as a result of the Depression.[61] Hutchins felt compelled to provide a rationale for the college program. If the rationale were distinctive and gave promise of dealing with a varied student group, foundation money would become available to facilitate collegiate programs. In the world of higher education, a number of colleges and universities had begun to experiment with and develop justifications for their programs.

Higher educational institutions were increasingly dealing with students from a variety of economic, social, and ethic backgrounds. With the fragmentation of academic disciplines in the years since 1860, courses and departments had formed around scholarly research. Meeting various needs and providing a common intellectual experience were the criteria of the Experimental College at the University of Wisconsin, the Contemporary Civilization course at Columbia University, and the General College at the University of Minnesota, to name a few within universities.[62] None of these programs tried to establish the single required curriculum that Hutchins attempted at the University of Chicago in the 1930s and 1940s. Yet all were a response to what appeared to be a chaotic offering of coursework whose coherence depended on the haphazard ability of the individual student to give it unity and meaning.

Hutchins' advocacy of the great books and his disaffection with the social sciences as the central disciplines of the curriculum make sense, in light of the pressing demands he faced and his own educational and intellectual needs. In Adler, Hutchins had a friend and an intellectual adviser. The demands of the presidency left him with little time for serious study and reflection. Over the years, Adler provided him with suggestions of books to read. He found quotes in texts and listed them for Hutchins to use in his speeches. He suggested speech and essay topics. He edited Hutchins' essays. He was Hutchins' confidant in times of trouble.[63]

Hutchins also advised Adler, provided him with forums for his work, and stood by him with tenacious loyalty, despite all the criticism in the university community. One of Hutchins' major concerns when he was contemplating leaving Chicago in 1938 was that Adler be tenured before he resigned.[64]

Adler helped Hutchins to construct an educational philosophy. Formulating a rational argument for a program was a difficult task for such a young man in such a demanding position. Hutchins had neither the time nor the need to explicate his own rationale for education before he was called to the University of Chicago. Adler was there when he needed him.

C H A P T E R 6

Defining the College: Administration and Curriculum

THE STORY OF THE COLLEGE of the University of Chicago and Robert Hutchins' role in it in the 1930s and 1940s is a complicated one, full of irony and contradiction. Hutchins began in 1929 with three goals. One was to simplify the administrative organization of the university, which had grown increasingly unwieldy since the Harper years. Another goal was to find means to encourage existing and future cross-disciplinary research. The third was to address trustee and alumni demands to improve undergraduate education by raising the quality of the program and increasing enrollments. Hutchins intended to use the Boucher committee plan, developed during Max Mason's presidency, as the basis for curriculum revisions in the freshman and sophomore years. Although these began as practical tasks, they became Hutchins' most challenging crusades as president of the university.

By the middle 1930s Hutchins' goal was to create a viable, intellectually coherent four-year liberal arts college within a university primarily devoted to research and scholarship. Throughout the 1930s and 1940s he battled powerful members of the predominantly graduate faculty to yield some power and control over educational policy to the college. Teaching great books with Adler fostered his belief in a liberal arts undergraduate program. But he was unable to convince the faculty to institute a fully required four-year great books curriculum in the college. It was a failure he never understood.

To the extent that Hutchins encouraged the college faculty to develop a fully required four-year curriculum (though not in the great books), he had made great gains by the time he left the University of Chicago in 1951. To the extent that he inspired and reinforced a commitment to undergraduate education at the University of Chicago, Hutchins' work for the college was a resounding success. But his relentless zeal to institute an ideal, coherent, fully prescribed curriculum meant, in the end, that the college could only survive for the duration of his presidency.

When Hutchins took office in 1929, the administration of Chicago had so expanded that the president was required to oversee seventy-three budget lines. Deans had little control over educational policies and budgets but were responsible for student activities. A separate committee on expenditures composed of the president and other administrative officers made allocations to departments. Thirty-five separate departments offered graduate and undergraduate courses, some at the junior college level (freshman and sophomore) and some at the senior college level (junior and senior). Cross-disciplinary study at the graduate level was carried out informally or on an ad hoc basis. The teaching of undergraduates was not well coordinated between departments. To earn the bachelors' degree, students were required to complete eighteen major courses each in the junior and senior colleges in the programs of their choice.

Hutchins' primary accomplishment during his first year was gaining support for a major reorganization of the university from Gordon J. Laing, dean of the Graduate School of Arts and Literature, Henry G. Gale, dean of the Graduate School of Science, Chauncey S. Boucher, dean of the Colleges of Arts, Literature, and Science, and the board of trustees. The genius of Hutchins' proposal was its efficient encompassing of the administration problem, the interdisciplinary research problem, and the undergraduate problem, each of which concerned one or more of the university's constituencies. The faculty senate (full professors with educational policymaking powers) accepted the plan, and the board approved it in October of 1930.

The plan's structure was simple. The academic departments were organized into four divisions: the humanities, the social sciences, the biological sciences, and the physical sciences. In some cases, a department had members in two divisions. For example, after much debate among the historians, the department decided to divide members between the social sciences and the humanities divisions. Anthropology placed representatives in the biological sciences division as well as the social sciences division.

A fifth division was the college, which was to "do the work of the University in general higher education" in the freshman and sophomore years.[1] Students wishing to continue toward a bachelors' degree were to apply for admission to one of the other four divisions. Each division had a dean. The dean was to be relieved of responsibility for students to focus on the needs of the division, including budget, curriculum, staff, and organization problems. Hutchins consolidated all student activities under a dean of students. The number of offices reporting to the president on budgetary and other matters was reduced from eighty to fourteen. These included the division deans, the University College (extension division) dean, professional school deans, and the heads of the Oriental Institute, the library, and the University of Chicago Press.

In addition to reducing administrative confusion, no doubt the new president's primary worry in that first year of the Depression,[2] the new divisional organization accomplished other ends. First, by grouping departments into divisions, Hutchins encouraged formal arrangements for the cross-disciplinary research that faculty members had conducted in the 1920s. One immediate result was the Committee on International Relations. Other such committees followed in the 1930s and the 1940s: Child Development (later Human Development), Nursing Education, Teaching, Psychiatry and Mental Hygiene, History, and the Committee on Social Thought. This move had long-term consequences for the conduct of scholarship at the university.

Hutchins hoped the interdisciplinary research in the social sciences, financed by the Laura Spelman Rockefeller Memorial, and in the biological sciences and medicine, financed by the Rockefeller Foundation, would continue more consistently and formally under the new organization. His inaugural address had alerted the community to his interest in furthering such work. Beardsley Ruml, also committed to interdisciplinary research in the social sciences, helped Hutchins acquire foundation support in the first two years of his presidency. Hutchins appointed Ruml the first dean of the social sciences division in 1931.[3]

Another result of the reorganization was a redistribution of power over educational policy, budgets, staffing, and curriculum. The committee on expenditures, in existence since 1898, had overseen all spending by departments. By granting deans more budget-making power, Hutchins' plan shifted some of this power from the administration and placed it with those who had direct contact with department chairs and faculty. But greater power for the deans over these decisions meant less power for department chairs.

Why the faculty senate was willing to allow reallocation of control from departments to division is unclear. But Hutchins had a few factors in his favor. One was the support of Gale and Laing. He was able to convince them of the need to have knowledgeable, competent representatives of the faculty arguing for resources for divisions and departments. Beyond that, the logic and efficiency of the plan were persuasive. Quite likely, an additional factor played a role: the condition of the colleges and the ongoing debates at the university over what to do about undergraduate education.

Chauncey S. Boucher's committee developed the college plan between March and May of 1928. It was the result of years of discussion at the university about the fate of the junior and senior colleges and of Boucher's investigation of a variety of curricular experiments in other universities in the 1920s. The University of Chicago was not alone in raising questions about undergraduate education in that period. Expanded enrollments and the growth of a collegiate youth culture moved many institutions to reexamine their programs.[4] Boucher hoped to take advantage of this enrollment growth and develop a general curriculum that would satisfy faculty demands for rigorous standards. The University of Chicago's comprehensive solution to the problem was exceptional because the education of undergraduates since 1892 intentionally had been a secondary function of the institution.

In the Harper years, undergraduates followed one of three programs, each offered by one of the colleges: the College of Arts, the College of Literature and Philosophy (which separated and rejoined in later years), and the College of Science.[5] In 1898 the College of Commerce and Administration was added to the senior college options. The College of Arts offered classic languages to lead to the bachelor of arts (B.A.) degree. The College of Literature and Philosophy offered modern languages, literature, social studies, and philosophy to lead to the bachelor of philosophy (Ph.B.) degree. The College of Commerce and Administration also offered the Ph.B., and the opportunity to study with economists Wesley Mitchell and Thorsten Veblen in its early years. The College of Science offered natural and physical sciences to lead to the bachelor of science (B.S.) degree.

The first two years of undergraduate study were conducted in the junior colleges, each with its own faculty, and administered separately by assistant deans (until the junior colleges joined with the senior colleges in 1920 under one dean). Requirements in each college were based on what students had studied in high school and on what was needed to move from the junior to the senior college level. Three electives were the maximum allowed. Latin was required. The senior college programs, administered by a single dean, were largely elective, with some limitations depending on distribution requirements in departments and the number of departments in which students had studied over the course of each thirty-six weeks (three one-quarter terms).

Between 1905 and 1912, at the request of junior college faculty, the curriculum was revised to allow for more elective choice, to reduce foreign language requirements, to permit further concentration in departments, and to raise standards for graduation. This was a considerable shift in educational policy and reflected the influence of the university model on the colleges.

Between 1912 and 1931, under Judson, Burton, and Mason, minor changes that presaged the Boucher committee's curricular reform proposal were introduced. A division of knowledge component was instituted, requiring students to cover a minimum amount of course work in history, philosophy, the social sciences, modern languages, mathematics, and natural sciences; to exhibit proficiency in written and spoken English; and to display a reading knowledge of French or German—all to provide breadth at the junior college level. Senior college students were expected to take sequential courses in a major and a minor field of study, within either a department or a group of departments, but there was considerable elective latitude in both the major and minor fields.

Structurally, the junior colleges served either as terminal education or as conduits to the senior colleges, which, in turn, offered a final degree (the B.A., the Ph.B., or the B.S.). At the undergraduate level, classes tended to consist of large lectures. Academic advising existed but was not systematic until 1913, when Dean James Rowland Angell instituted an advisory system to help students choose major and minor studies in their last three years and to ensure that they had one adviser from the beginning of their programs to the end.[6]

Like other universities, including Yale during Hutchins' undergraduate years after World War I, the University of Chicago suddenly faced larger enrollments and overcrowded classrooms and dormitories. An orientation week for freshmen was introduced in 1924, a practice never before tried. Some members of the administration and faculty continued to raise questions about how to treat this increasingly heterogeneous group of students, but their concerns were overshadowed by the priorities of the graduate faculty and the undergraduate dean.

Typical of the emphasis on research, the increased tuition income was seen as a boon for graduate research rather than as funds to enhance the colleges. The university senate formally declared in 1924 that the university ought to develop a clear policy limiting the expansion of the colleges and developing the graduate and professional schools.[7] Of course, at that point the faculty senate did not know just how much the university would come to rely on undergraduate tuition income in the 1930s. Dean David Allan Robertson defined the colleges' mission as efficient preparation for occupations, probably reflecting many students' aspirations in the early

1920s. In sum, the policy commitment to undergraduate education was slight even while enrollments grew in the early 1920s.

During Ernest DeWitt Burton's presidency, a constituency of the faculty suggested that a junior college be segregated across the Midway from the rest of the university. With its own faculty, deans, buildings, and budget, it could bring in needed tuition but leave the important work of the university undisturbed. The group advocating such a move included trustees and administrators who perceived this as an opportunity to enhance undergraduate education without the traditional objections from the faculty.

Those favoring the idea had good reasons to strengthen the colleges. The colleges' alumni earned more than the graduate alumni and were in a better position to continue to support the university, a primary concern of trustees and administrators. This line of argument was strengthened by President Burton's successful development campaign in 1924 and 1925. He raised $10 million for buildings and programs, much of it from college alumni. Undergraduate tuition was a continuing source of unrestricted annual income for research, instruction, and other faculty needs. Though unforeseen in 1925, tuition income during the Depression would outpace endowment income, making the college a vital element in the financial survival of the university. Finally, the undergraduates were a source of promising graduate students for faculty in the departments. By 1929 less than 20 percent of the colleges' graduates went on to graduate school; however, that percentage was to grow.

By the middle 1920s, the continuation of undergraduate education was no longer in question, but heated debate over the apportionment of resources and the locus of educational policymaking for the colleges persisted. Dean Ernest Hatch Wilkins (1923–26) gained the support of President Burton and eminent members of the sciences faculty to introduce survey courses into the undergraduate curriculum. The geology department developed an introductory course for any undergraduates and a sequence for those planning to continue in the department; these courses provided the basis for the physical sciences course under the New Plan after 1931. A survey course in the arts and one on man and society were tried but did not survive. Another, entitled "The Nature of the World and of Man," was offered over two quarters in the freshman and sophomore years; it explored physical, chemical, biological, and geological properties of earth and the evolution of plants, animals, and humans. Like Columbia College's Contemporary Civilization course and Dartmouth's Evolution course, it functioned as a general introduction to academic fields of knowledge. Other plans for survey courses came to nought. Deans and department faculty members in the arts and sciences continued to resist any suggestion to provide increased resources to the undergraduate program.

Wilkins' successor, Chauncey S. Boucher, found a supporter of the colleges in the late 1920s in President Max Mason. By then, freshman enrollments had declined slightly, and the impetus to redesign the program to meet undergraduate needs was augmented by the desire to increase enrollments. Mason focused the debate on the kind of undergraduate education the university should offer, appointing a committee under Boucher to recommend reforms. Boucher's committee suggested that comprehensive examinations be substituted for course credits, with admission to the senior college contingent on the passing of five (English composition and literature, a foreign language, natural science and mathematics, social science, and one elective). The bachelor's degree should depend on the passing of an additional three (one in the major field and two in minor fields). Rather than using traditional departmental introductory courses, new sequential, year-long courses should be developed by the faculty. Finally, a special board of examiners should design the examinations. This was the report Hutchins read shortly after his appointment.

In his inaugural address, Hutchins framed the problem as one of defining undergraduate education in an institution where the focus was on research and graduate instruction, but where fewer than 20 percent of those receiving the bachelor's degree pursued further formal study. He suggested that the university ought to welcome the challenge of determining how to treat the first two years of college in relation to high school education, on one hand, and to advanced study, on the other.[8] To this end, he charged Boucher with developing some of the comprehensive examinations and junior college courses along the lines recommended in the report.

To capitalize on the GEB's interest in genuine educational experiments, Hutchins also acquired GEB funds for the department of education to study collegiate education.[9] A number of four-year colleges had initiated such experimental programs. They reflected a progressive interest in integrating studies to prepare students for the complex interrelatedness of modern life and, at the same time, accommodate individual differences.[10] Swarthmore offered honors classes; Stephens College in Missouri coordinated the last two years of high school with the first two years of college; Antioch integrated classwork with practical experience.[11] Other experimental programs were a more direct response to the elective system, which had become standard in higher educational institutions by the twentieth century. Alexander Meiklejohn introduced a required interdisciplinary freshmen course at Amherst as early as 1914. Reed College reorganized the faculty into divisions, designed a mix of requirements and electives for freshmen and sophomores, and instituted a required senior colloquium, a twentieth-century version of the nineteenth-century moral philosophy course.[12]

The innovations at the University of Chicago were inspired by those of the 1920s and occurred in the context of others in the 1930s. Independent study plans where students worked with advisers to construct their course work were incorporated at Stanford. Vassar did the same with tutors. Bard, Sarah Lawrence, and Bennington, in the tradition of progressive reforms, encouraged student initiative and freedom by offering individualized instruction based on student interests and college resources. Black Mountain and Berea joined Antioch with a combination of practical experience and book learning. Bryn Mawr introduced field work for undergraduates in line with faculty research projects. Many institutions offered survey courses. Some, including Reed, Rollins, and Sarah Lawrence, provided seminars for undergraduates.[13]

Universities as well as colleges innovated. The University of Chicago, Columbia University, the University of Wisconsin, the University of Minnesota, and other institutions where the priorities of research and graduate instruction competed with undergraduate programs for attention and resources engaged in curricular experiments. They bear mention here as contrasts to the uniqueness of Chicago's program and as examples of less comprehensive, but in some cases longer lasting, innovations. With intellectual as well as institutional goals, these programs were designed to deal with student interests and provide a common educational experience for undergraduates. They also were intended to maintain enrollments in competition with other institutions. One concern was to retain students capable of doing advanced work by offering seminars and more challenging courses while continuing to attract less intellectually driven, but still capable, students. Columbia College's program, particularly, inspired the Boucher plan at Chicago.

In 1917 Columbia College was charged with developing a War Issues course for students in the Student Army Training Corps. Shortly after the course was initiated in 1918, members of the faculty suggested a Peace Issues course to complement or succeed War Issues. In 1919 Columbia's yearlong Contemporary Civilization course first was required for freshmen. Its success in providing undergraduates a common intellectual experience and a modicum of general education led to a second yearlong sequence, added in 1929. The great books course of Adler's undergraduate experience developed into Columbia's Humanities course by 1937.[14] They are among the experiments of the period that have survived.

Boucher examined Columbia's program in 1928 while writing the report on the colleges. At Hutchins' request in 1929, Adler sent him samples of psychologist Ben Wood's Pennsylvania tests for the Boucher committee to use to prepare the comprehensive examinations. He also outlined for Hutchins Columbia's scheme of distributing requirements and electives.[15] It was an appropriate model because Columbia maintained selective admissions and managed to attract 60 to 70 percent of the undergraduates into graduate and professional programs. Both of these were goals of the University of Chicago.[16]

The University of Wisconsin tried another kind of program under philosophy professor Alexander Meiklejohn. Beginning in 1927 the Experimental College accepted a self-selected group of young men to work with professors in tutorial and discussion settings. They studied Athens during the time of Pericles and Plato in their freshman year and the contemporary United States in their sophomore year. They focused on the philosophical and political problems of citizenship, community membership, and governance during both eras. In an intensive mixture of real life and study, the dormitory and professors' offices were in the same building. The intellectual and social activities of the college provided the coherent education Meiklejohn sought. But a decline in enrollments and hostility from other college students and professors who resented differential treatment of the experimental group, as well as adverse public opinion about radical students and socialist professors, contributed to the university's decision to close the college in 1932.[17] If the Experimental College's decline in enrollments and hostile response within the university held any portents for the college of the University of Chicago, Hutchins ignored them.

Other state universities explored special programs for undergraduates in the 1930s. Two of them informed, and were informed by, Chicago's program. The University of Virginia conducted a study of the feasibility of an honors course for undergraduates. Scott Buchanan, whom Hutchins had tried to bring into the philosophy department, and his fellow Rhodes scholar Stringfellow Barr drafted a report on the study in 1935. They suggested instituting a new college within the old one, devoting the first two years to a liberal arts education in the great books and the last two years to tutorials in specialized study. Their plan died with the president who sponsored it at the university, but Barr and Buchanan joined Hutchins and Adler a year later on the Committee on the Liberal Arts at the University of Chicago to study the problem anew. The following year, they established the fully required great books curriculum at St. John's College in Annapolis.[18]

The University of Minnesota under Lotus Delta Coffman created a different kind of experiment. Its varied student body and its commitment to admit any accredited high school graduate from the state generated three kinds of undergraduate education. Coffman's primary goal was to keep students with a wide range of abilities and interests enrolled in the institution. The traditional offering of electives and majors through the departments and schools of the university addressed typical students' expectations. The College of Science, Literature, and Arts was an honors plan begun in 1932. It allowed selected students intensive advisement and enrollment in classes all over the university. The third, the General College, was a two-year general education program for any student who could not gain admission to the traditional program.

The General College provided orientation and academic and vocational guidance. Courses were designed to serve the needs of a general population. Health problems, for example, were addressed through a comprehensive human biology course. Citizenship issues were studied in a course called Public Opinion. Contemporary society was the topic of a course that explored the Background of the Modern World. Pedagogical tools such as film, radio, record players, lectures, discussions, and student experiences were the media of instruction.

Enrollment grew throughout the 1930s and 1940s, but problems plagued the program. Fewer than one in five completed the two-year course in the 1930s, and clear status distinctions between each of the student groups belied the democratic promise of the undergraduate program. Nevertheless, the General College was a unique experiment that gave many Minnesota citizens access to college. Moreover, it prepared a large and loyal citizen-alumni constituency ready to defend the university when budgets were threatened.[19]

Hutchins' desire to develop a single program for all students differentiated the Chicago plan from Minnesota's. But the plan shared a similar goal with others: to provide undergraduates with a coherent general education within an institution primarily dedicated to research and specialized instruction. The conditions that spurred these efforts included an increasingly heterogeneous student body, mostly from the middle class, with social and occupational aspirations that exceeded their parents' attainments. Although many of these new students were absorbed by junior colleges, normal schools, and other teachers' colleges, a significant proportion applied to public and private four-year programs like Chicago's. In short, this was the pool from which the University of Chicago drew its applicants. And the university's administrators were hoping to attract the capable midwestern students who otherwise would choose to attend the elite eastern institutions.

According to historian Colin Burke, one in five Americans of college age was enrolled in college-level educational institutions in the 1920s. Moreover, by 1927–28, Illinois, the state from which the University of Chicago drew the majority of its undergraduates, exhibited the highest college enrollment percentages of any state.[20] This increasing social heterogeneity, and the fear that colleges might lower standards to accommodate the expanding collegiate population, concerned the philanthropic foundations financing the experiments, including the Carnegie Foundation for the Advancement of Teaching, the Carnegie Corporation, the GEB, the Rockefeller Foundation, and the Mellon Foundation.

When the reorganization plan was accepted at the University of Chicago in 1930, Hutchins applied for and received $96,700 from the GEB to cover initial curriculum reorganization expenses. An additional $275,000 was awarded to assist with instruction and administration costs over the first five years of the new plan. The Carnegie Corporation provided the college $75,000, also over five years.[21] The GEB had already invested in a massive survey of the university's financial organization, begun in 1924 and completed in 1932.[22] The new plan took advantage of the information provided by the survey, the climate of collegiate experimentation in the 1920s and 1930s, and the increasing commitment of the program's most powerful spokesperson, Robert Hutchins.

Shortly after the reorganization was accepted in 1930, Boucher chaired a curriculum committee composed of representatives from each of the four divisions. In January of 1931 he appointed Mortimer Adler to the committee at Hutchins' request. Adler's primary contribution was to submit and argue for four lists of books corresponding to the divisional academic fields. Most of the books were written before the twentieth century, and excluded much of the work by University of Chicago faculty in the sciences, humanities, and social sciences. With Hutchins' backing,

Adler urged the committee to consider basing the four introductory general courses on syllabi containing the great books.[23] The social sciences course, for example, might cover Homer to Keynes, physical sciences Euclid and Nichomachus to Whitehead and Scott Buchanan, humanities Hesiod to Thomas Mann, biological sciences Plato and Ovid to Rabelais and modern histories of science.[24]

The curriculum committee was neither impressed with nor swayed by the book lists. Its recommendation to the college faculty, members of departments and divisions who taught courses in the freshman and sophomore years, laid out requirements for the associate of arts degree and the first two years of undergraduate work. The college faculty and the university senate approved the curricular plan. Five required comprehensive examinations, one each in the divisional fields and one in English composition, were to test basic factual information and introductory level understanding of theory and methods. Two elective examinations, based on yearlong or sequential courses offered in departments, were also required to indicate completion of junior college work. The divisional introductory courses were intended to provide breadth of exposure to subject matter, and the electives were to allow deeper pursuit of interests. As in the original Boucher plan, students wishing to continue after the sophomore year entered a division.[25]

Instituted with the 1931 entering class, the new plan received wide press coverage, in part because Hutchins was newsworthy.[26] Beyond that, the new plan manifested characteristics that many colleges were seeking to incorporate in the 1930s: attention to individual needs, egalitarian treatment, and a common curriculum.[27] Few attained them in the time Chicago did. Comprehensive examinations were one of the most innovative aspects of the program. These examinations, rather than course credits or attendance, were used to certify educational accomplishment. Hutchins made much of the fact that students could study the material on the syllabus, take a comprehensive examination, and pass without having to attend class, if they wished. They could take the tests when they chose and retake them if they failed or wished a higher score. The two elective sequences allowed individuals to pursue their interests. If a student satisfied the examination requirements and wished to do so, he or she could pursue specialized study in one of the divisions before entering the junior year.

Once a student was admitted to the college, an inherent egalitarianism pervaded the program. No longer could grades be based solely on a professor's response to a student or a student's work. Ongoing faculty and adviser assessment was incorporated in judging student progress to catch academic problems and intercede when necessary. Lectures and discussions constituted in-class work, but student initiative, academic competence, and self-motivation determined speed and success in completing requirements.

The introductory courses exposed students to cultural knowledge through a common curriculum in the first two undergraduate years. The syllabi for the courses were approved only after numerous reviews by divisional faculty and revisions by the curriculum committee. They were published and sold in the bookstore. Respected faculty members delivered introductory course lectures and supervised instructors with the discussion groups. Students were inspired by particular lecture and discussion topics to form extracurricular study groups and to invite eminent faculty members to speak at their evening meetings.[28] In short, the opportunity to belong to an intellectual community was no longer restricted to departmental graduate work at the university but also was available in the first two years of the college.

During Hutchins' presidency, the college engaged in a series of administrative and curricular reforms that increased its autonomy and distinction within the university. This transformation was nothing short of astounding, and it occurred because Hutchins determined that it should.

Hutchins first addressed the power of the dean. In 1929 Chauncey Boucher complained to Frederic Woodward that he had had no official power as dean of the colleges. He had no voice in the appointment of faculty members to departments, even those teaching courses in the colleges. He therefore had little authority to strengthen weak courses or influence departmental collegiate activities when department heads were making plans that affected undergraduate courses. He had no means of assuring gifted young teachers continued positions at the university. He had no access to budgetary decisions—they were made on the basis of departmental faculty time spent teaching freshman and sophomore courses. In short, he had little to say about educational and administrative policies affecting the colleges.[29]

By establishing the college as one of the five divisions in the university and providing the dean the same access to the president as all other deans (weekly meetings and regular consultations on policy), Hutchins changed the situation. He refrained from direct interference in curriculum policy, except to suggest repeatedly that the great books be on the syllabi.[30] Rather, he employed or encouraged administrative actions to protect the work of the college in general education from encroachment from the rest of the university. These ongoing reforms met with mixed reactions in the departments and divisions that were a complex combination of responses to Hutchins' administrative and curricular goals. They reflected faculty members' perceptions of Hutchins' attempts to redefine the college's relationship to the rest of the university.

Instead of departments, each divisional introductory general course had a staff headed by a director interested in the college. The divisional reactions to the administrative and curricular changes differed according to the deans' and faculty members' relationships with Hutchins. The biological sciences division welcomed the reorganization because it provided an opportunity to bring clinical and biological sciences into one unit. Incorporating the Medical School into the division was perceived as a "new and daring" experiment.[31] Yet the division exhibited little commitment to general education in the college. Under deans Scammon (1931) and Lillie (1931–35), the division developed "unsatisfactory" general examinations but abolished even those in the preclinical subjects in 1935.[32]

Anton J. Carlson, professor of physiology in the division, was on the college curriculum committee, the divisional curriculum committee, and the divisional committee on educational policy. His influence on the division's development of general courses was crucial. He not only disagreed with Hutchins' ideas about general education and the great books but also debated the president's ideas about education with Mortimer Adler at a well-advertised campus gathering in Mandel Hall in 1934.[33] Carlson was first a scientist, and any effort to deemphasize experimental research in favor of reading original sources in the sciences had to pass his scrutiny and was unlikely to receive his support.

Hutchins received more cooperation from Lillie's successor, William H. Taliaferro (1935–44). Taliaferro agreed with the principles of the college plan, including the general courses and the provisions for student initiative. As he noted to Hutchins, however, in any totally prescriptive program the division faced the problem of meeting professional and state requirements for students to qualify for admission to medical school. Because of the tenacity of the older faculty's commitment to the existing program, Taliaferro encouraged younger faculty members to reform the curriculum.[34] Despite Taliaferro's cooperation with Hutchins, in 1938 the biological sciences faculty decided to deviate from the college plan and allow students to receive the B.S. degree with a C average in the divisional courses and without taking the comprehensive examination.[35] But a number of younger faculty members participated enthusiastically in designing new courses. One, Joseph Schwab, joined the core of college faculty who created a fully prescribed four-year curriculum in the 1940s.

The division of physical sciences cooperated in the college program to the extent of offering an introductory course, developing films to accompany it, and designing departmental sequences for the bachelor's program.[36]

The social sciences division moved quickly to institute Social Sciences I and then Social Sciences II. Beardsley Ruml appointed the course staff members and left them to design the course and the examinations. Harry D. Gideonse, associate professor of economics who chaired the committee, not only agreed in principle with the purposes of general education but also wished to preserve the social sciences courses from incursion by Hutchins or Adler. Louis Wirth, sociologist, and Jerome Kerwin, political scientist, worked with Gideonse. They cooperated because they were wary of administrative pressure from Hutchins to include mostly great books in the syllabi.[37]

Gideonse was pleased with the first course syllabus, the field study component of the course, the examinations, and the resulting common intellectual experience of freshmen.[38] But according to Ruml's successor, Robert Redfield (1934–46), divisional faculty wished to have the course more integrated with divisional studies so that students entering the division after the sophomore year would be better prepared.[39]

These problems diminished in the late 1930s after Edward Shils, a doctoral student in sociology who later joined the Committee on Social Thought, reorganized the Social Sciences II course with more great books on the syllabus (though not necessarily the books Hutchins would have selected). He was able to generate college faculty members' enthusiasm for designing the third-year course in the 1940s.[40] By then, the college had a strong, loyal young faculty and the courses were sufficiently integrated to please Hutchins. Although the departments in the division offered a lecture series entitled "The Nature of the Social Sciences" in the 1930s, the departmental faculty had responded slowly to his urging to redesign the sequential courses so that the college-to-department transition could occur smoothly for students.[41]

The humanities division faculty under Dean Laing (1930–35) initially was split over the college plan. The difficulty of constructing adequate examinations was one point of contention while the possibility for interdisciplinary cooperation was an attractive feature of the plan. The division contributed to the formulation of the humanities introductory course despite this split and despite residual hostility from the Adler–philosophy department fiasco. One reason some members of the division participated was the support and encouragement given the new plan and Hutchins by Ronald S. Crane, a widely respected professor of English. Crane went so far as to assist Adler in constructing the great books lists for the curriculum committee.[42] He also initiated regular meetings in his home with young humanities instructors to discuss texts and humanities-related issues. Adler has recalled that this group later instituted Clarence Faust's curricular innovations in the college.[43]

Crane's endorsement was crucial when Laing resigned the deanship and Hutchins wished to appoint Richard P. McKeon to succeed him. Three years after the Adler–philosophy department conflict, McKeon was invited to the university as a visiting professor of Greek, due largely to Crane's efforts. Upon Laing's resignation, Hutchins met with department chairs in the division and with other faculty members.[44] He found enough support to appoint McKeon without fear of backlash from divisional faculty. Hutchins thought McKeon's deanship (1935–47) would encourage the division to make greater contributions to the college program by developing courses under three disciplinary areas: philosophy and science, history, and the fine arts.[45]

Hutchins attempted to address the problems he encountered in the divisions through administrative measures. To promote integrating and coordinating courses, he proposed moving the University High School from the education department to the college and linking the two units in a four-year program of general education. Faculty members teaching in the college felt they already were invested in the curriculum and feared they would be relegated to high school teaching by this proposal.[46] Because of this response, Boucher moved slowly. He was hesitant to assume responsibility for admissions procedures, curriculum development, and staffing until a committee had time to study the problem. In 1932 the board of trustees approved the venture in principle but delayed action on the plan. Hutchins grew increasingly impatient.

He gained senate approval in 1932 for the college dean to appoint faculty members to the college without requiring that they also be appointed by departments. The dean only exercised the option once before he retired in 1935.[47] With these two actions, combining the high school and college and allowing the dean greater powers of appointment, Hutchins clearly was pushing the university to grant more responsibility and autonomy to the college and more extensive general education than the freshman and sophomore years alone could provide.

To apply more pressure, Hutchins prodded the faculty to think differently about undergraduate education. The college years, he thought, ought to be spent in serious study and discussion of important ideas, "training the mind." These years were crucial in the preparation of "intelligent" citizens, people who had "learned how to think" in order to solve their own problems and "to share in the solution of those of [their] generation."[48]

Whether students planned to terminate their education with the bachelor's degree or go on to further education to prepare to become their generation's experts and leaders, an essential aspect of the university's public service role was this rigorous training of the intellect through common exposure to the greatest works of Western thought. The university had a unique contribution to make in educating future leaders and citizens. Its experiments in general education and in clarifying the relationship between, and special functions of, each level of education asserted "the leadership of the University in a confused and critical area of education" in the United States.[49]

In *The Higher Learning in America* (1936), Hutchins argued for a four-year liberal arts curriculum at the college level to counteract over-specialization, crass vocationalism, academic disciplinary isolation (and self-interest), and anti-intellectual tendencies of universities. A program of "permanent studies" based on "our intellectual inheritance" (the "greatest books of the western world" presenting "a common stock of ideas") would cultivate the "intellectual virtues" useful "for a life of contemplation or a life of action."[50] A fully required liberal arts curriculum would re-create an intellectual community where learning was justified as an inherent good.

The Higher Learning elaborated arguments he had begun to develop in 1931 on the basis of his general honors experience, discussions with Adler, the need for a distinctive rationale for the college, and fears about the state of public affairs during the Depression. The book reflected a concern similar to that of the Yale Report of 1828, which argued for a classical curriculum in the face of increasing higher educational options offered by the antebellum colleges in the United States. There were similarities, too, to John Henry Newman's *Idea of a University* (1852), which proffered theology as a means to unify the curriculum at a time when Great Britain's secondary and postsecondary institutions were expanding their offerings to include technical and modern science subjects. An echo of Thorsten Veblen's suggestion in his book under the same title, *The Higher Learning in America* (1918), that business values should not dictate educational or administrative policy in universities, was also present in Hutchins' argument.[51]

Much as the others had done, Hutchins' book raised a considerable uproar in the world of higher education. John Dewey, for example, questioned whether a program of "permanent studies" embodying "*the* truth" was either appropriate or desirable in the twentieth century. He suggested that the assumption that "truth only needs to be taught and learned," implicit in Hutchins' recommendations, suffered from a faulty understanding of the role of experimental science and empirical research in generating new knowledge and in "the constitution of authentic knowledge."[52]

Hutchins' arguments in *The Higher Learning* forced the University of Chicago community to deal with a strong president firmly committed to an autonomous college providing a common, general education for future citizens and leaders. Discouraged with Boucher's slowness to convert the college into a four-year institution, Hutchins wanted to replace him, when he left for the chancellorship of the University of West Virginia, with someone more sympathetic to the idea. Already wary of Hutchins' efforts to institute his great books program, a few hostile faculty members suggested Harry D. Gideonse, whose experience with the Social Sciences I and II course committee made him a suitable candidate. They thought Gideonse, who was nearly as striking as Hutchins in appearance and as unafraid to express his intellectual convictions, might effectively interpret the president's ideas to the faculty and, more important, the faculty's to the president.[53]

Hutchins thought Gideonse's Social Sciences II syllabus was insufficiently general. Though it broke through departmental divisions, it reflected too much contemporary research and too little exploration of the theoretical problems underlying the research.[54] Classic works in political economy, social theory, and political philosophy written before the twentieth century would have been more to Hutchins' liking. Another factor against Gideonse was his philosophical opposition to Hutchins' ideas. Beginning in 1933 in response to the editorials of John Barden, a student from the general honors class and an advocate of Hutchins' beliefs about the aims and methods of liberal education, Gideonse's criticisms were posted on the bulletin board outside his office. Some of them were published with Barden's editorials in the university's student newspaper the *Daily Maroon*.

Their disagreement was public in the two years before the deanship was vacant, but it culminated just as the appointment was made in 1937 when Gideonse published his response to Hutchins' *Higher Learning* position as *The Higher Learning in a Democracy.* His arguments carefully distinguished the actual college program from Hutchins' great books ideal. He indicated that faculty members were searching for a balance between enduring ideas and contemporary research in a curriculum they hoped would be attentive to the "significance and relevance" of scholarly research and theory for students facing twentieth-century American society.[55] Clearly the recommendation to appoint Gideonse represented a struggle for control of the content of the college program. Under the circumstances, with Hutchins' tenacious adherence to an idea once he professed it, it was virtually impossible for Gideonse to be appointed dean of the college.

Hutchins' first choice for dean was historian Stringfellow Barr, Scott Buchanan's colleague at the University of Virginia. Hutchins and Barr were in fundamental agreement about the structure and content of undergraduate education. In 1935 Hutchins had tried unsuccessfully to have Barr appointed to a history position in the college, bypassing the department.[56] After this plan failed, he asked Barr and Buchanan to spend the 1936–37 academic year as visiting professors with the Committee on the Liberal Arts. Arthur Rubin and a small group of graduate students also joined that committee.

Adler had suggested the previous year that Hutchins bring together "a gang of men" with "the intellectual competence and the proper passions" to develop a liberal arts program for the college and that he publish a "manifesto" on educational reform.[57] The Committee on the Liberal Arts and *The Higher Learning in America* were the results. The committee was created by Hutchins and financed by private donors to stimulate "the study of the curriculum in the College and in the Humanities Division" and to "consider the place of the seven liberal arts in modern education."[58] McKeon sponsored the committee in the division of the humanities.

The committee was perceived by many faculty members as Hutchins' attempt to bring Buchanan and Barr to the campus through a back door rather than through the normal departmental channels. There is some evidence in the Hutchins-Adler correspondence to support this supposition.[59] Moreover, the committee appeared to represent presidential pressure to institute a liberal arts program at the university without explicit faculty senate approval. The timing of the venture, concurrent with the publication of *The Higher Learning,* made it appear to be another effort of the president to foist his own men and ideas on the division, which, of course, it was.

Within the first few months, despite Adler's high hopes for bringing his friends together again, the committee began to disintegrate over disagreements about which books were the most appropriate to read, how they ought to be interpreted, and how to teach philosophy.[60] These internal problems, coupled with hostility from the divisional faculty, who perceived the committee as an affront to their contributions to the college program, led to the committee's demise.

The senate committee on university policy and the division of the humanities committee on policy termed the establishment of the Committee on the Liberal Arts an educational policy problem. The members recommended that any future Hutchins appointments require the approval of the appropriate faculty, either in the division or in the senate. To protect his credibility with the division and his work on curricular reform of the undergraduate program, McKeon resigned from the committee. He asked Hutchins to remove the committee from the division and make it a presidential committee.[61]

Foiled in his attempt to institute the liberal arts through the great books in the humanities contribution to the college program, Hutchins worked with Buchanan and Barr when they left the university in 1937 to reorganize St. John's College, instituting a fully prescribed great books–based liberal arts program. He served on the board of St. John's, advised Barr, who was president, about administration and fund raising, and contributed one hundred dollars a month to the college in the early years.[62] As a result of the faculty's reaction to the Committee on the Liberal Arts and Barr's subsequent departure for St. John's, Hutchins did not have a hope of making him dean.

Instead, he finally appointed Aaron J. Brumbaugh, formerly assistant dean to Boucher and then acting dean in 1935 and 1936. Brumbaugh had steered the committee, which included Gideonse, Charles Morris of the philosophy department, and H. K. Loomis of the high school, on the ideal program. Because the program provided for a four-year curriculum in general education, Hutchins was satisfied, but he would have preferred faster action by the committee and the inclusion of more great books in the course syllabi.[63]

In 1937 the college faculty adopted the four-year course of study to operate alongside the two-year college. To complete the program, students were required to pass fifteen comprehensive examinations. The tests were based on a three-year humanities course, a three-year natural sciences course, with the option to spend more time in either biological or physical sciences, a three-year social sciences course, a three-year reading, writing, and criticism course, a one-year philosophy course, and two elective sequences from departments.[64]

Initially, most of the students who entered the college at the end of the sophomore year in high school were from the University High School and other local schools. Classes were held in a building separate from the two-year college, and no degree was awarded. Because total enrollments were low, classes were small, allowing a high level of contact between students and instructors and a variety of pedagogical approaches, including discussions and laboratory work in the sciences.[65]

The program was never free from faculty criticism. For example, divisional examinations, faculty members argued, provided a limited basis for grading students and required a great deal of faculty time to design. In addition, administering them reduced the number of class meetings in the spring.[66] Despite the criticism, there was enough support for the examinations to keep and improve them. Hutchins recruited Ralph Tyler to head the department of education in 1938 and to act as university examiner. Tyler worked with the divisional faculty to redesign examinations that tested the objectives of their courses.[67] Such ongoing reform and improvement had become a hallmark of the college program by the late 1930s.

In keeping with Hutchins' original charge to view the college as an experiment in general education, the faculty continued to refine courses and explore administrative policies to enhance their initiatives. Because faculty members were organized according to course staffs rather than departments, cross-disciplinary approaches to the curriculum were officially sanctioned. Few opportunities for departmental rivalry existed by the late 1930s. Teaching was treated as a primary activity in the college. In 1932 awards for excellence in college teaching were instituted; in 1937 an anonymous donor expanded the awards; and in 1943 an alumnus donated $100,000 to be used for the continuing development of the teaching staff of the college.[68]

By 1941 Brumbaugh had designed a regimen, including clarification of the purposes and philosophy of the college program, for training new faculty to teach the general courses and the English course. Faculty members were to participate in an ongoing critical assessment of the curriculum, facilitated by weekly staff meetings and occasional all-college faculty meetings. Most new staff members were expected to attend the lectures and sit in on some of the discussion groups led by senior faculty members. They were obligated to participate in revising syllabi, preparing examinations, and assisting students with special academic needs.[69] With such intensive involvement, faculty members were largely responsible for creating the intellectual community that existed in the college.

Faculty criticism continued to be aired as faculty allegiance to the college came to full flower in the 1940s under Dean Clarence H. Faust, whom Hutchins appointed to succeed Brumbaugh in 1941 when Brumbaugh became dean of students. Faust had taught in the college and in the English department for eleven years. He was as committed as Hutchins was to a general, nonvocational curriculum in the college. One of his major goals was to elicit from the faculty a more thoughtfully integrated, fully required curriculum for the four-year college. Another was to make the college and its faculty as autonomous as the other divisions. Hutchins not only supported these goals but also was instrumental in accomplishing them.

In early 1942 Hutchins proposed that the B.A. be awarded by the college faculty, rather than the divisional faculty, at the end of the general education program and that the Ph.B and B.S. be abolished. Instead of operating two undergraduate programs, the university ought to combine the two-year and the four-year colleges, he thought. The timing of his suggestion, a month after Pearl Harbor was bombed, was deliberate. Colleges and universities were preparing for student military training programs. Granting the B.A. after taking the required comprehensive examinations would allow students planning to enter the military to finish as quickly as they chose before enlisting.

The university senate debated for two weeks, finally agreeing that the power to award the B.A. and the Ph.B. be transferred from the divisions of the humanities and the social sciences to the combined four-year college. The definition of general education in the university was left to the college faculty. B.S. degrees, however, were still the responsibility of the divisions of the biological and physical sciences for the duration of the war. The science faculty members had opposed the president's suggestion, in part because the general education program did not provide science students with the necessary exposure to chemistry and mathematics they needed for a B.S.

During six weeks of debate by the college faculty, the policy committee devised a four-year program. It represented a compromise between Dean Faust, who desired a fully prescribed curriculum, and others, who advocated earlier opportunities for specialization. Two degree options were established, the fully prescribed option for the B.A. and provisions for two electives for the Ph.B. The committee also outlined requirements for those entering from the sophomore year in high school and those entering after completing high school, thirteen and eight comprehensive examinations, respectively. The examinations, as in the past, covered material in the divisional and English courses. A committee chaired by Richard McKeon designed a new one-year course called "Observation, Interpretation, and Integration" (O.I.I.), which replaced the philosophy course as the culmination of the general program.

Ph.B. students were permitted to substitute two elective examinations, based on yearlong departmental sequences, for a humanities or social sciences or O.I.I. examination. This substitution was allowed because a significant fraction of the committee and the college faculty believed that students ought to be able to pursue special interests before receiving the B.A.

By its inaction on the committee's curriculum proposal, the senate allowed it to become legislation. Conflict between college and divisional faculty members in the senate focused on whether the two degrees should be called "bachelor's" degrees. Divisional faculty opposition to granting the B.A. for completion of a fully prescribed general education program was so intense that the senate twice sent the program back to the college for reconsideration. The second time, a final motion to rescind the senate's approval of the college program failed by a tie vote. The president of the university, by creating the tie, cast the deciding vote and enabled the college faculty to institute the program and assume responsibility for granting the terminal degree.[70]

The decision to delay abolishing the Ph.B. until after the war allowed a core of college faculty to build. Because Dean Faust had both the power and the mandate to search for new faculty, many of the young instructors he hired to teach in the college believed in a general, liberal education. Moreover, Hutchins consulted with key faculty members who supported his and Faust's program before making appointments to the college.[71] By 1944, of the 131 college faculty members, 29 were not also members of departments, a significant increase in the nine years since Boucher had left the university.

The faculty initiated a number of adjustments in the program in the early 1940s. Placement examinations enabled staff to determine where best to situate students in the program, especially important with the age range, the students' differing educational levels, and some students' plans to enlist in the military. Between 1943 and 1950 the program expanded considerably. Three-year courses in the humanities, social sciences, and sciences and one-year courses in mathematics (with an optional additional year), reading and writing, foreign languages (elective), history, and O.I.I. made up the prescribed curriculum.

The humanities courses focused on exposing students to great works in the arts, literature, and music; to analysis of works with methods appropriate to the humanities; and to tools for criticizing the values and interpretations present in humanities productions. The social science courses avoided a survey orientation by centering on American political institutions, on personality and culture (or human nature and society), and on problems of policy in relation to concepts of freedom, democracy, order, and equality. The science courses encompassed physical and biological sciences and were coordinated with the humanities and social sciences. Students critically read and discussed original research papers, using textbooks to bridge gaps in knowledge and context, and conducted laboratory experiments. Studies were organized around the understanding of processes, explorations of inquiries and problems, and experiment and observation.[72]

The History of Western Civilizations course was placed at the end of the curriculum to relate students' prior course work to it and to coordinate it with O.I.I., which drew connections between prior course work and philosophy. The history course began with the Greeks and ended with the Russian Revolution. It tried to balance a particularized approach, focusing on special topics in historical periods deemed appropriate for exploring each topic, with a more comprehensive understanding of context, events, people, and ideas, by using general and specific texts and exploring themes (conceptions of time and space, for example). O.I.I. used philosophical texts to examine and discuss organization, methods, and principles in fields of knowledge.

After the war, Faust pursued his plan to institute a fully prescribed curriculum offering a single degree. He again proposed to the college policy committee members that they award only the B.A. Because the action affected the divisions, the discussion was also carried on in senate council committee meetings in January of 1946 and in divisional meetings. When senate council committee members objected to the lack of options for predivisional specialization, Hutchins, who was at the meeting, argued that it was not the divisions' but the college faculty's obligation to define general education. Faced with growing opposition from three of the four divisions, the college faculty quickly abolished the Ph.B. in early February by a vote of sixty-five to forty-three.

To defend the college faculty's decision and to counter objections to it, Faust and Hutchins attended subsequent meetings of the senate council committee. They asserted the college's autonomy from the divisions. Hutchins suggested that the council had no confidence in the college faculty's ability to make policy. Faust argued that the college was not responsible for offering specialized courses or electives. In the meantime, the humanities division met and urged the senate council to withhold approval of the college's action. At the end of February, the council recommended that the college reconsider. In early March the council voted (thirty to ten) to establish a joint committee of the college and council to study the issue. This vote was a response to protests by the physical and biological sciences divisions and the negative vote of more than a third of the college faculty on the early February decision.[73] Faust objected to the delay.

Hutchins vetoed the council action, arguing that such a committee would slow the college's progress and discourage the college faculty's curriculum and policymaking initiatives. He suggested that the council should first support the decision and then appoint a joint committee, with college faculty members advising in the process. Council members objected to the veto and reaffirmed their action. In a statement to the board of trustees, to whom the faculty always turned when they could not move Hutchins, the council described the controversy and requested support for further discussion between the council of the senate and the college within a committee appointed for that purpose.[74]

The result of all this was a compromise. Hutchins withdrew his veto. The senate council withdrew its two actions, stayed the college vote, and formed a joint committee with the college to discuss the meaning of one degree in relation to divisional programs. The Ph.B. was slated to be abolished in 1947. A new general physics course was an option for the examination in the physical sciences and for students planning to study medicine. A foreign language component was included in the humanities third-year course for those desiring such an alternative. And students were allowed to register in both the college and an upper division while completing college requirements, but could not pursue graduate work until receiving the B.A.

Faust left the college to become dean of the Graduate Library School once his task of securing a fully prescribed program and a single degree, symbolizing college faculty autonomy from the divisions, had been accomplished. Frederick Champion Ward, a graduate of Oberlin and Yale and an assistant professor of philosophy since 1945, became dean of the college in 1947. Ward focused on the curriculum of the college. He oversaw the development of the history course, the English course, and the third-year natural sciences course. In addition, he encouraged the faculty to raise questions about the courses and to experiment with them.

By 1950 the expanded four-year curriculum was in place. Taking four required courses per year allowed a student two elective courses in the fourth year of the four-year course. Considering the fact that before 1931, college courses were offered on a quarterly calendar and each quarter's offering tended to be a discrete unit (unless it had or was a prerequisite for another course), the institution of yearlong courses that integrated divisional subject areas in a full undergraduate curriculum was an extraordinary accomplishment. But this administrative and curricular autonomy did not last long past Hutchins' departure from Chicago in 1951.

Two major changes were made in the 1950s by Hutchins' successor, Lawrence Kimpton, that thoroughly undid Hutchins' and the college deans' work. The first, to admit only high school graduates beginning in 1953, occurred despite Ward's protests. When Ward left the university for the Ford Foundation, the university reorganized the college into a lower division with two years of required core courses, some of which students could forgo, and an upper division, with a year of specialization and a year of electives contributing to a departmental major. This decision in 1957 began the dismantling of the carefully constructed, interrelated general courses and O.I.I. Though some of the remaining courses provided a common intellectual experience for students, the exceptions that students were allowed removed the guarantee that all would share in a common curriculum.[75] But a tradition of commitment to undergraduate education had been established at the university. The quality of this commitment simply had not been there before 1931. And reforms propelled by concerns about the coherence of the undergraduate program continued long after Hutchins left.

For more than twenty years, most under Hutchins' presidency, the University of Chicago maintained a genuine experiment in undergraduate education. Hutchins attempted to ensure the creation and survival of the college by encouraging an enterprise that clearly was at odds with prevailing and entrenched conceptions about the twentieth-century university.

The fact that Hutchins never achieved his great books program as the required curriculum at Chicago is as important here as what he did accomplish. The college of the 1930s and 1940s was a significant alternative to the university model of education. It was established at the University of Chicago because Hutchins was determined to do everything in his power to provide and maintain the autonomy of the college faculty. That it did not survive his tenure is a testament to Hutchins' stubborn idealism, his failure to understand the university model, and, finally, his ignorance of the needs and desires of the students who were enrolling in higher educational institutions in the 1930s and 1940s. In combination, these factors proved fatal to the college program when it lost Hutchins' stout protection.

CHAPTER 7 *Defining the College: Students*

THE GENIUS OF THE UNIVERSITY OF CHICAGO COLLEGE and the commitments that enabled its birth and development as an intellectual community are also the keys to its demise. An exploration of the faculty and the undergraduates at the university shows this to be the case. The establishment of a viable, coherent undergraduate program at the University of Chicago was a major success for Hutchins. Yet, if one judges his accomplishment by enrollment or retention rates, or by the longevity of the prescribed curriculum of the college, his effort was less successful. Despite the college faculty's full commitment to the program into the 1950s and despite the national reputation for academic rigor the college had acquired, the administrations subsequent to Hutchins' dismantled the college program.

Why did the Hutchins college fail to survive the 1950s? The primary reason was the difficulty in attracting and keeping enough students to justify the college program at the university. Like Chicago, many higher educational institutions suffered some decline in enrollments during the Depression years. Many experienced some increases in enrollment during World War II, as did Chicago. Where Chicago differed was in postwar enrollments. Most institutions experienced marked increases in the late 1940s, including G.I. Bill enrollments and the children of the expanding college-going population of the 1920s. Yet Chicago's undergraduate enrollment continued to decline into the early 1950s. Divisional faculty complaints about the program, which Hutchins discounted to preserve the college's autonomy, indicate that the faculty had a far more realistic grasp than Hutchins of who was attending the college and why. The tremendous loyalty of the college faculty to the program, in contrast to the divisional faculty in the 1940s, is one irony in the college's story.

The reasons for this enrollment decline are numerous and complicated, but the key to explaining it is the students. In order to understand the demise of the Hutchins college, it is important to understand who went to college in the 1930s and 1940s and, more particularly, who went to the college of the University of Chicago and why. It is equally important to understand Hutchins' contribution to change in the college to explain why fewer and fewer students chose to enroll. Precisely the changes Hutchins made to ensure the college's autonomy from the divisions contributed to its demise.

Its curricular and administrative independence, and singular program, made it difficult for students to move from the college to graduate and professional programs at other institutions. Moreover, because of its academic rigor and uniqueness, students tended to self-select in the admissions process. In an institution already suffering chronic enrollment problems, Hutchins' reforms reduced the college's ability to compete locally and nationally with other higher educational institutions.

Throughout his presidency, Hutchins faced a powerful core of faculty resistance to his ideas and policy recommendations. Some of that opposition was rooted in the Adler–philosophy department controversy and was manifest as suspicion of Hutchins' motives. But the faculty resistance to Hutchins' vision for the college of the University of Chicago also illustrates the faculty's awareness of, and Hutchins' refusal to see, the role of undergraduate education in a modern American university. A fundamental difference in conception of this function was evident at every turn in Hutchins' ongoing struggle to institute college policies. The departmental faculty in the early 1930s viewed the college primarily as preparation for the graduate school. Hayward Keniston, professor of romance languages, for example, resigned from the curriculum committee because he held this view.[1]

By contrast, Hutchins in the beginning was faced with the hard fact that fewer than 20 percent of the colleges' graduates went on to graduate or professional school. From a practical perspective, to perpetuate a program that ignored this fact would not be an efficient or wise use of university resources. Moreover, it was a program that lost one-quarter to one-third of every freshman class to academic failure and from which fewer than one-half of the original members of each freshman class eventually graduated.[2] As endowment income decreased by one-third in the first four years of the Depression, the university relied increasingly on tuition income.[3] In conjunction with these practical concerns, Hutchins became a missionary for the cause of general education in the great books. By the middle 1930s his prudence was overtaken by his crusade to create a model of general education suitable for any future plans graduates might have.

The faculty did not object to the university's assuming a leadership role in general education. Nor did most faculty members object to offering a general education in the college. Some resented having to spend extra time on divisional courses and examinations in addition to their ongoing departmental duties.[4] Some were most concerned with preserving the courses they already offered, yet welcomed the opportunity to develop a cross-disciplinary course.[5]

In 1939 divisional faculty members were asked to evaluate the performance of college students after they entered the divisions from the general program. On the whole, they found the students at least as well prepared for divisional work as transfer students from other universities and colleges.[6] Two years of general education was fine, most thought. Rather, the faculty objected to four full years of a fully prescribed general education. The science faculty's campaign against the single degree in 1942 illustrates this disagreement with Hutchins about the function of a college education within a university.

Physicist H. I. Schlesinger, for example, thought the comprehensive examinations and the general courses led to a "deterioration" in students' ability to master a topic thoroughly and to focus on specific rather than proximate knowledge.[7] The science faculty had to compensate for the preprofessional training the divisional students lacked. Physiologist R. W. Gerard agreed with the basic purposes of the college program, developing a critical perspective, standards of judgment, and problem-solving skills, but did not understand why specialized study could not proceed concurrently with general education.[8] Zoologist Carl R. Moore, on behalf of his department, agreed with the need for broad training in the college. He suggested the real issue for the college was to define the relationship of science to general education and specialized training rather than to discount the kind of focused work science students needed. Two years of general education were adequate, he thought.[9]

The 1946 debate about awarding only the B.A. upon graduation from the college was not over whether the College ought to offer only one degree. Nor were the differences solely attributable to divisional versus college faculty interests, for, despite Faust's and Hutchins' appointment policies, a large minority of the college faculty voted against the proposal. Rather, the dispute was about the program leading to the degree: a single, fully prescribed general curriculum.

Political scientist Leonard White, representing the senate committee on policy, spoke for many faculty members when he said he was "not persuaded that any single curriculum is the necessary and only road to a general education." Ronald S. Crane, who had been such "a sympathetic friend of general education" in the 1930s, did not favor a "highly rigid and inflexible" program that would interfere with the "selection and early training of bright young students who wish to become scholars."[10] Others believed that a single program handicapped science and humanities students, who would have to study an additional two academic quarters after the B.A. before admission to divisional study.[11] Their objections implied that the policy would create such distinction for the college program that it no longer would function as an integral part of the university.

H. I. Schlesinger may well have spoken for the majority of students in the college when he noted that 80 percent of the students entering the college opted for the Ph.B. program. Because it allowed for electives, this choice was an indication of their wish to pursue their own interests apart from the single curriculum of the B.A. program. Furthermore, the proportion of the college's graduates going on for further study in the divisions of the university had increased to 50 percent since the 1930s. He thought a single program threatened to be dogmatic, and it would most likely lead to a gradual elimination of high school graduates from the college.[12] With fewer options, he suggested, high school graduates would reject the university's undergraduate program in favor of other institutions and the graduate programs would lose a major source of students.

The acknowledgment of the role of individual interest in learning processes had been the hallmark of the progressive movement in education.[13] The faculty clearly recognized the importance of providing for individual intellectual development by maintaining some choice in the curriculum. They also realized that the growth of occupations and professions in modern society necessitated more varied college-level preparation if the university was to continue to maintain a functional relationship with society. Furthermore, the continual growth of new knowledge made the question "What knowledge is of most worth?" subject to ongoing discussion. It is surprising how diligently Hutchins chose to ignore educational research and social change in the interest of continuing to try to develop an ideal curriculum that would serve "at any time, in any place, under any political, social, or economic conditions."[14]

He was unable to establish his fully prescribed great books program at the university, but he did inspire college faculty members to believe in the viability and desirability of a single program. And these members of the university community were able to develop the program under Hutchins' protection. One, Ralph Tyler, was chairman of the education department and acting dean (and later dean) of the division of the social sciences (1946–53).

Tyler was well versed in the progressive education movement and in the ideas of John Dewey. But where Dewey was critical of Hutchins' narrow ideas about the intellectual role of undergraduate education, particularly the focus on a canon of great books, Tyler found the program less one-dimensional than it appeared.[15] On the basis of his experience with the college faculty he believed that most of the senate council members' fears were unfounded. Research on the performance of college graduates in the divisions had indicated that they were better prepared than transfer students for graduate work. He thought rigidity in the curriculum would be prevented because college faculty members were engaged in continual critical assessment and revision of the course content. Furthermore, greater attention was given to college courses than to most courses in the division. Finally, flexibility and regard for student interest were inherent aspects of the program. College faculty members developed a variety of teaching methods and explored ways to link different methods with specific content.[16]

This vitality in the college program and the challenge of creating a truly coherent, integrated curriculum inspired great commitment and loyalty from college faculty members, particularly those whose primary duties were in the college. By the late 1940s the predominant method of instruction was discussion rather than lecture.[17] Some problems persisted: inadequate facilities for staff and students (offices, lecture rooms, and laboratory space) and the difficulty of training a large number of recent appointees. Yet faculty and students had experienced strong intellectual excitement, fed by the demands of a rigorous curriculum and faculty members' efforts to inspire students to grapple with the content. The opportunity to participate in the program was a unique experience for students and for faculty members within a major university.[18]

By gaining autonomy for the college, Hutchins and the deans consolidated the college's position and created an intellectual community in the university. The dean's office had the personnel necessary to administer the college. Better facilities had been provided, and more laboratory space was planned. The curriculum was established and undergoing minor revision. One thousand copies of the college staff's publication "Teaching by Discussion in the College Class" had been sent to soliciting institutions. Syllabi were distributed by request outside the university or sold in the bookstore as quickly as they were published.

Some course staff members were holding regular seminars to explore further the intellectual content of their subject areas. The college attracted increasingly competent new faculty, retained some senior faculty members whose major interests were teaching and curriculum development, and acquired the *Journal of General Education* to publish college faculty work.[19] The faculty was a recognized, autonomous body in the university. Hutchins and his deans had accomplished a feat that had looked impossible twenty years earlier. They had created a college offering a fully prescribed general education within a modern American university.

It is impossible to know how long the college program might have survived had Hutchins stayed at the university beyond 1951. By the late 1940s the university was suffering an overall decline in enrollment, salary adjustments for faculty members, and budget cuts.[20] Tuition from the college became a significant proportion of the university budget in the 1930s. When enrollment in the college alone declined by 18 percent between 1940 and 1951, the administration under Lawrence Kimpton began to dismantle the college program.[21]

Changing student demographics was a key factor in the decline in college enrollment. An exploration of who the students were and why they chose the college helps to explain why enrollment declined so drastically at a time when other colleges and universities were experiencing enrollment growth. While there are various worthy considerations, such as the condition of the university neighborhood, that undoubtedly played a part in students' (and their parents') choices, the pattern of the decline suggests that two other elements played a larger role: the institution of the fully prescribed curriculum and the autonomy of the college in relation to the divisions. In the end, it was the students who rejected the Hutchins college, in much the way many of the divisional faculty members had feared they would.

Hutchins noted in his 1939 President's Report that the university "is predominantly a middle western, an Illinois, and a Chicago institution."[22] The college was especially so. According to the *University of Chicago Survey,* nearly 90 percent of the alumni of the university came from the Midwest and over 50 percent came from the state of Illinois alone.[23] By 1937 two-thirds of all living alumni of the university were living in the Midwest, and one-half of the total in the Chicago area.[24] Though there were slight fluctuations in the exact percentages throughout the 1930s, the Midwest—Chicago particularly—supplied the majority of the undergraduates of the university, possibly because the economic uncertainty during the Depression led many families to choose a college close to home (see appendix table 1).[25] The university continued to draw predominantly on local students into the 1940s.[26] This dependence had numerous implications for the college. Two of the most significant were local perceptions of students' social backgrounds and local understanding of the college's aims.

The college relied on Chicago area high school officials to direct applicants to the university. The reputation of its program, the quality of its social life, and the condition of its neighborhood were crucial factors in recruiting students. The admissions office recognized this problem by, for example, reducing admission of Jews and possibly of African-Americans during the 1930s when complaints about the number of Jews, African-Americans, Catholics, and Communists on campus reached the office.[27]

There is no evidence that discriminatory admission policies existed against Catholics, because Catholics were not noted separately from others in the "Gentile" category of enrollment figures after 1930. The proportion of Catholics seems to have risen through the 1920s. Conversely, though statistics were not kept for blacks before 1930, there is no doubt that the number of black undergraduates was extremely small throughout the 1930s. Alternatively, the proportion of Jews increased steadily to approximately 26 percent of the undergraduate student body by 1930, held steady until the middle 1930s, then declined to 18 percent in 1939 and rose slightly to almost 21 percent in 1940 (see appendix table 2).[28]

These statistics indicate that there was some heterogeneity by race and ethnicity among students in the college, but, particularly in the case of African-Americans, it may have been sacrificed to enhance the university's image locally in order to increase enrollment. The question of admitting black students was exacerbated by the university's dealings with the neighborhood around Hyde Park.

To protect the university from the growing slums on the South Side, populated largely by African-Americans who had migrated from the South looking for work, the university honored restrictive covenants, which were legal in the state of Illinois. Called upon to account for the university's participation in discriminatory activities on the South Side, Hutchins (who did not hesitate to defend the university's scholarship and teaching from intrusion) made an eloquent statement in the *Chicago Defender* against racism as contrary to "the light of reason." He enumerated the ways the university had studied the economic and social problems African-Americans faced on the South Side. And he insisted that the university did not discriminate by race. Yet he defended the university's actions to assist local housing organizations to improve the neighborhood surrounding the university.[29]

The fact was that the university did discriminate through the restrictive covenants and through treatment of some of its own buildings that housed African-American families.[30] Hutchins personally found such activities morally offensive enough to write his father for counsel on the matter, but he did not fight the board of trustees on the issue.[31] Instead, he acted in other ways. For example, when Allison Davis, assistant professor of education, was denied membership in the faculty and administration's Quadrangle Club because of his race, Hutchins threatened to resign unless Davis was admitted.[32]

Of course, the small number of African-American students enrolled in the college may not have been due to deliberate discrimination by the admissions office, and there is only circumstantial evidence to suggest that was the case. The application form requested a statement of race, and the reduction in the already small number of black students occurred in the same period the university was being criticized. But other considerations may have contributed to the low enrollment of African-American students. The Depression forced many potential black and white college students to sacrifice their plans in the early 1930s. The university offered scholarships, but the amounts were reduced as the endowment shrank and were most often in the form of tuition remission, the average grant being $147, or half the tuition cost. Other institutions in the Chicago area had lower tuition, including Northwestern and the University of Illinois.[33] Beyond these practical reasons, African-American students going to the University of Chicago had to be prepared to live in a racist environment.

Racial discrimination was widespread on campus in the 1930s. African-American students were denied haircuts in a barbershop in Reynolds Hall until Hutchins threatened to close the barbershop. African-American students could not rent apartments in university-owned buildings near campus because of the restrictive covenants. Black fraternities disbanded because they could not rent houses in the neighborhood. African-American students were denied equal access to treatment in university hospitals. No African-American children were admitted to the nursery school until the 1940s, or to the upper grades of the Laboratory School until 1944.[34]

There were few black professors as role models for students in the university; their presence depended on the racial tolerance of department heads and division deans.[35] Racism was present in the administration as well. Emery T. Filbey suggested to Wilbur Munnecke (both were vice-presidents) that, when black students brought their families to receptions at the university, their presence was "very conspicuous." Such "over-representation" could have "a tendency to kill off" other students' "enthusiasm," stretching the limits of social tolerance, particularly given the university's "proximity to the Black Belt" on the South Side. He also mentioned the "vigilance" administrators ought to exercise over those faculty members who discriminated "in favor of negroes and Jews."[36]

The university did little to deal with the deteriorating neighborhoods on the South Side, despite suggestions that it do so from faculty members Louis Wirth and Ernest Burgess.[37] Hutchins was "perplexed" by the situation and, as he noted later, preferred to focus on the educational program rather than spend most of his time solving the problems of the neighborhood.[38] However, when Munnecke suggested that "there unquestionably is a percentage of Negro [and Jewish] students that we cannot go beyond at this time," Hutchins finally made a definitive statement of policy.[39]

"A university," he stated, "cannot talk about the limitations of social tolerance. A university is supposed to lead, not to follow." Rather than allow economic security to dictate its moral policies, "a university is supposed to do what is right, and damn the consequences." Some in the university had tried to justify a varied policy with respect to its hospitals, its property usage, and its student admissions, which he did not understand. "As long as we are a university, and not a club, we cannot invoke racial distinctions as a basis for the selection of our students," he informed Munnecke in 1944.[40] How such a statement if made earlier might have affected the heterogeneity of the student body or the racial climate on the campus is impossible to know.

Other data on the students suggest that they were highly motivated and academically well prepared when they participated in the college program in the 1930s and 1940s. Judging by their fathers' occupations, by their parents' education level, and by how many expected to work while in college, they appear to have come from the growing middle class, with high occupational and social aspirations. This pattern was carried forward from the 1920s, when over 70 percent of students' fathers were in professional, commercial, and managerial positions and nearly 30 percent in manual occupations. The colleges had prepared an overwhelming proportion of graduates for professions, though only one-quarter of their fathers were in professional occupations.[41]

Between 60 and 70 percent of the 1932 entering class had fathers in middle-class occupations, indicating some broadening of access to lower-middle-class students. Only 20 percent of the fathers were in professions, and all of 36 percent were in business and trade. Most students, though, had occupational aspirations different from their fathers'. Over 64 percent planned to enter professional service, and only 8 percent planned to enter business.[42]

During the 1930s the educational level of the parents of entering freshmen rose. The percentage of non–high school graduates among parents decreased, and the percentage of those who had graduated from college increased (see appendix table 3).[43] These changes indicate that the parents' educational level was high in comparison to the national average.[44] They also show that a significant proportion of University of Chicago college students were pursuing an educational level beyond the schooling their parents had received. And they raise questions about the soundness of Hutchins' ongoing attempts to establish a single prescribed curriculum for a cohort planning to pursue a variety of professional occupations.

Further signs of an increasingly middle-class student body are found in the proportion of students who planned to work while in school. In the 1920s, for example, close to 25 percent of the students were fully self-supporting, over 40 percent worked part-time, and close to 29 percent were fully supported by their families or other private sources while in school.[45] By contrast, in the 1932 freshman class just under 3 percent expected to be fully self-supporting, 32 percent planned to work part-time, and 65 percent planned on total private support while in school.[46]

Not surprisingly, the Depression affected the work plans of students. In 1937, the same year the administration expressed great concern about the continued decline in enrollment, approximately 3 percent of the freshman class expected to be fully self-supporting. Over 38 percent expected to work part-time, and just over 57 percent planned on full private support (see appendix table 4).[47]

The increase in the percentage of students who received full private support from the 1920s to the 1930s is significant. Though it dropped during the 1930s, it was still twice as high as the 1920s. Examined in conjunction with the university's concern about the decrease in enrollment in the 1930s and increasing dependence on tuition fees, this rise in middle-class students suggests that the university focused on enrolling students who could pay their own way.[48] As the educational attainment of families increased, the degree of self-support seemed to decline among college students at the university from the 1920s through the 1930s, indicating a solidly middle-class caste to the students who chose the college at the University of Chicago. Yet these students were not wealthy. They expected to support themselves after they finished formal schooling, and it is highly unlikely that they perceived their higher education in isolation from these future plans.

Beginning with the new plan and continuing throughout the 1930s, the academic preparation of entering freshmen was consistently high, despite the relaxing of admissions standards and the low rejection rate of applicants.[49] In the 1932 entering class, for example, over 40 percent came from the upper one-tenth of their high school class and over 70 percent from the upper third. In 1937 nearly 46 percent came from the upper one-tenth of their high school class and over 77 percent from the upper third (see appendix table 5).[50]

These figures suggest a high degree of self-selection by students who also manifested strong academic motivation and commitment to professional preparation before they came to the university. Considering the uniqueness of the Chicago program for undergraduates in comparison to other institutions, it is quite likely that applicants chose very carefully when they chose the University of Chicago. Indeed, when questioned about what brought them there, nearly half of the freshmen entering in 1936, for example, claimed that it was the university's reputation and faculty and nearly another quarter named the college program.[51]

The data on gender are less suggestive of motivations and plans. Between 1893 and 1930, out of a net total of 27,407 alumni receiving degrees from the university, 12,292 were women.[52] In the first decade, women attended the university on an equal footing with men; they enrolled in the same classes and many of the same academic programs. Moreover, the University of Chicago appointed more women faculty members than any other coeducational university in that period. However, in 1902 women outnumbered men at the junior college level. The administration, worried that women's high academic performance in combination with their wide social influence would effeminize the university, set off a national controversy by instituting sex-segregated classes, despite protests from a significant body of faculty members, alumnae, and various women's organizations. This practice did not affect all, or even a majority, of the undergraduate classes, and eventually it fell into disuse.[53]

The proportion of women to men admitted decreased after 1902, and this trend continued throughout the 1930s, from four men to three women admitted in 1932 to less than one and a half men to one woman in 1940. The ratio of male to female undergraduates overall was about eighteen to ten in 1940.[54] Slightly more women than men were from the central states among alumni while a significantly lower proportion of women came from outside Illinois to join the freshman classes throughout the 1930s. Women students tended to be more local in origin than men students in the 1930s. They also enjoyed greater family financial assistance and were more academically competent as a group than men entering the freshman classes (see appendix tables 1, 2, 4 and 5). Moreover, there is some evidence to suggest that they participated extensively in the political, social, and intellectual debates on campus in the 1930s.[55]

It is reasonable to conclude that the women who enrolled in the college in the 1930s, like the men, came predominantly from middle-class families, enjoyed significant private support for their education, and reflected the ethno-religious and racial heterogeneity of the student body. They not only were academically talented but also were seeking the academic rigor of the college program. They selected the college for its location, uniqueness, and, possibly, its coeducational character.

Clearly, the university relied increasingly upon local, middle-class, highly academically motivated students to increase enrollments when endowment declined and tuition income became essential to the budget. Enrollment and retention were not new problems for the college in the 1930s. Before 1931 enrollment in the junior colleges grew slowly and peaked in the 1931–32 academic year. As in many institutions, enrollment declined in the early years of the Depression and then began to grow in the latter half of the 1930s.[56] Admissions policies were liberal, as the university relied upon rural and urban midwestern high schools with diverse curricular programs. When selective admissions policies were instituted in the 1920s, they were geared toward academic, rather than social, selectivity. The faculty hoped to bring the percentage of students electing to continue in the graduate schools closer to Columbia University's unusually high 60 to 70 percent from its own meager 15 percent.[57]

When enrollment declined by nearly one-sixth of the student body in 1932 and then fluctuated throughout the 1930s, the college's admissions requirements eased. The admissions office began an aggressive recruitment program in the Midwest, comparing enrollments with the state universities as well as with Northwestern and Washington University, the major secular private universities.[58] The financial strain on families during the Depression was a constant, but unpredictable, variable the university faced. When 47 percent of the students admitted to the freshman class of 1939 did not enter, the admissions office surmised that other institutions offered them better scholarships.[59]

As noted previously, students selected the university for its academic program and reputation. Their academic qualifications were high, even with relaxed admissions requirements. Yet the attrition rate also remained high. In the late 1920s the problem of student failure persisted, despite selective admissions policies. A segment of the faculty continued to grade on the same curve, regardless of the increasing academic qualifications of students. As Reeves notes in the *University of Chicago Survey,* between one-quarter and one-third of the students admitted failed in the 1920s.[60]

The reasons for such attrition were not only academic. In 1931, a Depression year, 60 percent of the freshman class left the university. In 1932 53 percent left. The proportion of bachelor's degrees offered by the university to transfer students (between 58 and 63 percent), as opposed to those who had attended the college for four years, suggests a continuing high attrition rate throughout the 1930s.[61] Attrition and enrollment problems appear to have been closely related.

According to Dean Brumbaugh, the attrition rate contributed to the perception by local school officials that the program was very difficult, suited solely for the most academically able students. High school officials, he thought, recommended the college only to "superior" students, for a number of reasons.[62] They did not want to endanger the reputations of their institutions by sending potential failures to the University of Chicago. They sincerely believed that students of average ability could not succeed there. And they themselves may have experienced great difficulty finishing at the university.

He also suggested that students' fears about their performance on the comprehensive examinations may well have affected their own enthusiasm about the college in discussions with their peers in the weeks before they received their examination results. Brumbaugh's reasoning was speculative, but Dean Huth of Chicago's University College had found similar reasons for declining enrollments in the extension division of the university in his survey of students, parents, and other members of the public.[63] Such local perceptions were a crucial factor in the university's ability to continue to draw students from the local area.

Students who had studied under the new plan between 1931 and 1935 were surveyed by the university in 1938.[64] Of the 1,065 questioned, over 88 percent thought every student ought to be required to take the general introductory courses. Over 70 percent thought that instruction was well organized, the comprehensive examinations were fair, and their studies were fulfilling. In addition, they appreciated the freedom of the plan.

The survey results suggested that the problems with the college were more practical than academic. Only 13 percent of those surveyed thought the college had helped them choose a vocation, though over 40 percent claimed it had helped them articulate other goals. Nearly 47 percent thought there was too little "college spirit" while another 47 percent thought there was enough. Almost 60 percent thought the college plan was a good means of education for many; but fewer than 29 percent had recommended the college to all of their friends while 64 percent had to some of their friends. Over 28 percent found the social life at the university unsatisfactory while slightly more than 47 percent found it satisfactory.

The 179 students questioned who had transferred to other colleges and universities were asked to compare the University of Chicago to these institutions. Over 90 percent of this group thought the college provided better breadth of training, and over 78 percent agreed the college provided better instruction and better preparation for graduate work. By contrast, 50 percent thought the college provided fewer opportunities for social contact, and 26 percent thought opportunities were the same.

This last criticism reflected a widely held belief both on the campus and off that the college was a place for grinds, that the administration was interested only in the intellectual development of students. Hutchins' speeches and publications contributed to that perception. Those not familiar with the college program assumed that it was based on Hutchins' arguments about providing a liberal arts education in the great books. This misconception, university officials thought, also drove some applicants away from the program.[65] David Riesman, a member of the faculty in the 1940s, has suggested that the college's program appeared monolithically academic to prospective students. With only one criterion of success and one means of relating to the community, students chose other institutions, like Harvard, because they offered more varied opportunities for growth and accomplishment.[66]

By the end of the 1930s, only 40 percent of the freshman entrants were finishing their bachelor's degrees at the university. The college continued to depend on the local area for students. Hutchins persisted in challenging the college faculty to design, and the university to accept, a unique, fully prescribed program. Judging by his determination and tenacity, the hope of developing an ideal college program within a research university far outweighed the practical necessity of attracting and keeping undergraduate students. In 1937, referring to Hutchins' ideas about collegiate education and the discussion they aroused, one dean queried: "Are we in a position to wait for their acceptance?"[67]

The enrollment problems and high attrition rates were more extreme in the four-year program from 1937 to 1942. These problems continued to escalate throughout the 1940s as the prescribed college program absorbed all the undergraduate options in the university. A brief surge in undergraduate enrollments in 1942–44 convinced Dean Faust of the soundness of the decision to combine the two- and four-year programs.[68] Yet, as postwar enrollment again declined, few administrators questioned the program itself and its relation to other higher educational institutions, despite the warnings by the graduate faculty members. Rather, they were persuaded by Hutchins and the deans and faculty members he had appointed to the college that adequate recruitment efforts would find the particular students who were suited to the college program.

Most of the first-year students who entered the four-year college program between 1937 and 1941 were from the University High School and local public high schools. When the size of the University High School tenth grade classes declined from 1939–40 to 1941–42, the number of first-year students in the college declined (from 106 to 80). Approximately half of them left by their fourth year in the college, and less than a quarter of the entering class of 1940–41 remained four years later.[69]

When first-year enrollment increased in 1942–43 (to 122), Dean Faust attributed it to parental desire to keep children close to home rather than send them to eastern preparatory schools during the war. He also thought parents were "eager to have their sons complete a college education before being called to military service." This motivation made the college's recruitment program less one of "public enlightenment" as to the benefits of the curriculum than one of illustrating the wartime advantages of the program.[70]

A high of nearly three hundred students enrolled in the first two years of the college during the 1943–44 school year. An increasing percentage of them were not from University High School, and most of them entered in the second year. This wartime response bolstered the administration's hopes for the four-year program. Yet the majority of undergraduates at the university were not enrolled in the prescribed four-year program at that time. More than a thousand students enrolled in the third and fourth years, a reflection of their preference for finishing high school before entering college.[71] In 1944 this enrollment represented almost 65 percent of the students, and in 1945 it represented almost 70 percent.[72]

As H. I. Schlesinger argued, the majority of undergraduates opted for programs that allowed some choice. The number of bachelor's degrees declined rapidly for those entering freshman classes of the late 1940s after the college's single program became the primary vehicle for undergraduate education and G.I. Bill students finished their undergraduate work. In 1929–30 930 bachelor's degrees were awarded by the university. In 1951–52, a year after Hutchins left and four years after the Ph.B. was abolished, 490 were awarded. In the following four years, reflecting the drastic drop in enrollment in the college, the number of bachelor's degrees stayed in the three hundreds.[73]

The staff of the college attributed this decline in the late 1940s to a variety of factors, all the while confident that enrollment could be expanded with aggressive enough recruitment procedures and attention to such factors as the university was capable of addressing, including better housing and supervision.

Examining other Chicago institutions to discern where college students enrolled, the staff found that roughly 50 percent enrolled at local junior colleges and slightly more than 37 percent enrolled at public four-year institutions. Almost 9.5 percent enrolled at the area's other private university, Northwestern, and slightly over 3 percent enrolled at the University of Chicago. "Low cost and relative convenience" were the reasons given for choosing from among the college's competition.[74] This manifestation of student choice was a clear indicator that the college could no longer depend upon local students to fill its classes. At that point, the condition of the neighborhood and the structure and content of the program became crucial factors in enrollment.

The neighborhood was cited for two primary reasons. First, the high schools that had supplied commuting students were in neighborhoods in economic decline on the South Side. Fewer students continued on to college from these schools than had in the past, and those who did tended to choose junior colleges and public institutions. Moreover, the principals in these high schools discouraged students from applying to the university, staff members thought.[75]

Second, the condition of the neighborhood deterred applicants. The growing slum on the South Side not only was unattractive when compared to many other campus locations but also quite probably frightened away prospective students and their parents, who associated slums with crime.[76] It is unfortunate that the university did so little to address the problems in its neighborhood in the 1930s when faculty members and neighborhood organizations from the black and white communities were willing to work on them. Hutchins' avoidance of the issue may well have contributed to the enrollment decline in the college in the late 1940s.

Other factors played a role in declining student applications, according to college records. Rumors of a lack of social life, while unfounded, persisted. Particularly as the student body decreased, student activities seemed to be dominated by a small group of the same students, most of them from the University High School. Parents were worried about adequate supervision of their teenaged children. The university allowed third- and fourth-year students, many between eighteen and twenty years of age, to live in rooming houses off campus because of a lack of dormitory space. "Lurid tales" followed students home, and parents worried about the mixing of supervised and unsupervised students. They perceived "indifference" on the part of the college administration.[77] Clearly, the perception was that the university cared almost exclusively about the intellects of the students and ignored other aspects of their development.

Few complaints came from outside the university about the curriculum. Most local principals and guidance counselors had "a high regard" for the program, including those who held a low opinion of the social life of the college.[78] Dean Ward was confident about the soundness of the curriculum. He suggested the purpose of the college enrollment service, established in 1948 to increase enrollment, was "to discover whether a very good college can also be a very large college."[79] Educators at other universities thought that the curriculum was worthy of emulation. According to Faust, Northwestern claimed to offer a similar general education. A faculty committee at Stanford recommended a plan similar to Chicago's in general education, and the faculty at the Berkeley campus of the University of California expressed considerable interest in Chicago's general courses.[80]

Indeed, former students of the college in the 1930s and 1940s remember the intellectual challenges of the program. They were required for the first time in their formal schooling not to memorize facts but to analyze ideas in books they read and to develop and express thoughtful reactions to the curricular material. They recall being able to talk to classmates "about the professors and the lectures and the readings" because they all took the same classes. They remember being part of an important experiment, an undergraduate college with a faculty devoted to teaching, in the midst of "that great research-oriented center of graduate studies in physics, medicine," and other fields.[81] Clearly, they were students looking for exceptional intellectual challenges.

Among those who criticized the college were students of the late 1940s who appreciated these challenges. Their criticisms articulate some intrinsic characteristics of the program that suggest why others may have chosen not to enroll in the college in the late 1940s or, if they enrolled, chose not to stay.[82] They thought the college emphasized intellectual development to the detriment of social and emotional growth, resulting in psychological problems particularly in the younger (fifteen- to eighteen-year-old) students. Students constantly felt the burden of keeping up with their work and facing impending comprehensive examinations.[83]

The forms of intellectual engagement the college program fostered, intense analysis and criticism of ideas and course literature, made it harder to find one's own voice and define one's own values, these students thought. The transition from the rarefied atmosphere of college classes to normal social situations was fraught with feelings of uncertainty. In addition, the structure and nature of the program, a single prescribed curriculum with broad exposure to academic disciplines, increased the difficulty of making vocational choices. Despite the efforts of the vocational guidance staff of the college, students who had no special interests had trouble finding them and students who had special interests experienced difficulty pursuing them.

Finally, these students thought the curriculum was not ideal. The college purportedly was searching for an ideal curriculum for all students; but, the students claimed, the program as it stood was elitist and overly narrow, a problem exacerbated by the administration's laissez-faire attitude toward the social and emotional experiences of students. They suggested bringing a team of psychologists in to study the college situation. Creating cooperative work experiences to keep students in touch with "reality" and to enhance their intellectual development with exposure to concrete training situations would address many of the problems they perceived in the program.[84] These perceptions were echoed in David Riesman's description of the "hegemony academic matters held" in the "enclave of the University of Chicago."[85]

There were other, related problems that affected more than a few students. By the late 1940s the percentage of students who chose to pursue graduate or professional study after receiving the B.A. rose. According to one estimate, almost 89 percent of the college graduates from June of 1945 to September of 1948 whose records could be found went on for further study. Over 66 percent of these did graduate work at the University of Chicago.[86]

Yet many institutions, particularly after 1947, would not accept the Chicago B.A. on its own merits. Students found they had to complete from two quarters to two years of additional undergraduate work, depending on whether they had taken divisional courses in their senior year or had spent only two years in the college. Comprehensive examinations were not accepted as the equivalent of disciplinary study. Direct admission of students with the Chicago B.A. into graduate schools was rare.[87] As the faculty had warned in 1946, even within the university in the graduate divisions and the professional schools, graduates of the college were required to complete extra work before admission.

To establish an ideal, coherent, fully prescribed, wholly common curricular program in the college, Hutchins, the deans, and members of the faculty (many of whom were his appointees) made some sacrifices. In that era of expanded enrollments and access, particularly for young people from the growing middle class, the first and most obvious sacrifice was the loss of prospective college students who desired curricular choice in their quest for a future vocation. When faculty members voted to award a single degree to certify completion of a single kind of program, they effectively narrowed the applicant pool.

As historians of higher education have argued, more young people went to college in the 1920s and they went for a variety of reasons.[88] Despite some reduction in enrollments in the 1930s, the trend of expanded enrollments continued in the 1940s. As the need for expertise grew and white collar occupations diversified, a college education became essential for social and occupational mobility. Moreover, a college education was increasingly viewed as a right, particularly after the G.I. Bill was passed in 1944.

When students rejected the college at the University of Chicago in favor of other institutions, in effect they were saying that they wanted greater choice in their educational program.[89] Whether they planned to enter occupations immediately upon receiving the B.A. or to pursue graduate study, the University of Chicago college did not satisfy their diverse needs or desires. Its reputation for excellence and inspired idiosyncrasy notwithstanding, college-bound students were not persuaded of its exceptional benefits in light of their own educational or career plans.

Curiously, the administration and college faculty seemed unaware of the ongoing effect of the various institutional measures enacted to limit the program and guarantee autonomy from the divisions, perhaps because of the enrollment increase just after World War II. Counting summer enrollments, the number enrolled in 1945–46, 1946–47, and 1947–48 exceeded 3,000. Again, however, consistently fewer than one-fifth of those undergraduates enrolled in the first two years of the college. And the total increase as a result of the G.I. Bill did not hold. Enrollment declined overall from 2,570 in 1942–43, the year the two- and four-year programs were joined, to 1,450 in 1952–53, just before the university limited enrollment to high school graduates.[90] Beginning in a more normal (nonwartime) year, 1940, the overall decline amounted to 18 percent by 1951, at a time when other institutions were experiencing steadily increasing enrollments.[91]

Yet the college administration and faculty tinkered with the curriculum, added guidance services, and expanded dormitory space instead of assessing the structural and programmatic assumptions of the Hutchins college. Extensive recruitment efforts in the late 1940s were unsuccessful, another instance of prospective students' rejection of the program. For some time the admissions office had not limited enrollment to the top 20 percent of the high school class but had expanded the definition of eligibility to include "all reasonably competent persons who apply."[92] The fact that fewer chose to apply was another indication that students simply were not interested in Chicago's single, prescribed undergraduate program.

Had the university been able to afford to forgo tuition income from the college, the program might have continued. But a million-dollar annual deficit in the early 1950s forced officials to examine ways to increase revenues. One means was to make the college more like other collegiate institutions to appeal to the expanding cohort of college-bound high school graduates. When the administration proposed changes, Dean Ward tendered his resignation and faculty and students protested. Limiting admission to high school graduates was the compromise.[93]

Loyalty to the college was such that Ward's proposal in 1952 to establish a branch college in Aspen, Colorado, was seriously considered by the board of trustees. Hutchins and Walter Paepcke, a member of the board, had held a festival in Aspen in 1949 to commemorate the bicentennial of Goethe's birth. A celebration of Western culture, the Goethe Festival offered music, discussions of literature and the arts, and great books sessions, along with talks by such notables as Albert Schweitzer, José Ortega y Gasset, and Thornton Wilder. Shortly afterward, Paepcke,

Hutchins, and Mortimer Adler established the Aspen Institute, with a music school and seminars on Western culture held in the summertime.[94]

The proposal to locate a branch college in Aspen promised such advantages as escape from the South Side, a more geographically diverse pool of students for recruitment, and the cultural and recreational advantages of Aspen. Most important, a branch college would allow the experiment to continue away from the pressure of the university's demands.[95] The board apparently was not convinced of the merits of the plan, for a branch college was not established. The single fourteen-course curriculum of the Hutchins college gradually was dismantled beginning in 1957 when students were allowed to choose some of their courses. Departments began offering their own degree programs for students who had completed a portion of the college program, and faculty members were appointed jointly to the college and the graduate divisions.

First-year enrollment after 1953 gradually increased, as did the overall enrollment in the college, reaching into the four and five hundreds for the remainder of the decade. These enrollment figures exceeded the total enrollment of the first two undergraduate years in the 1940s. Attrition, however, remained high, as it had throughout the history of the university.[96]

When Hutchins, the deans, and the faculty members he appointed secured the administrative autonomy they had sought for the college, they virtually guaranteed its demise. At the same time, their good intentions—to present coherently the knowledge they deemed necessary for educated citizens in the twentieth century and to provide students with an intellectual community sharing a common adventure in learning—furnished University of Chicago undergraduate students with an intense, rigorous, and exciting educational experience in the 1930s and 1940s.

It was an experience that grew into a tradition at the university. Notwithstanding the earlier curricular innovations of the 1920s, those of the 1930s and 1940s established precedents that continue to shape undergraduate instruction at the University of Chicago. Yearlong courses continued, as did the syllabi published in booklets that could be purchased in the bookstore. The Social Sciences II course is no longer required, but core courses that resemble it are still taken by hundreds of students each year. Core courses linking biology and physics are reminiscent of the Natural Sciences I and II courses. And a program called "Fundamentals" bears some resemblance to the Humanities I and II courses.[97] The difference, of course, is that none of these is required of all students wishing a B.A. from the university.

Among the many innovations introduced in colleges and universities from the 1920s through the 1940s, with the similar purpose of countering the negative effects of trivial courses and elective curricula constructed without thought to their integrity, that at the University of Chicago was unique. The college's program was fully prescribed, designed by a faculty whose primary responsibility was to teach, and consciously integrated across academic disciplines. Against great odds, it was instituted in the midst of a modern university with a wide range of disciplinary and professional study, a faculty whose primary responsibility was to do research, and an organization designed to promote discrete specialized studies.

This disjuncture between the college and its goals and the university and its goals, and the administrative structures established to ensure the college's self-determination, may have been based on sound educational objectives. However, as a policy initiative at the University of Chicago it ultimately failed because it did not take into account the whole institution's needs. Nor did the program take account of who the students were and what they wanted from higher education in those years. Without enough students to maintain the program and contribute to the whole institution, it could not survive.

For Hutchins, these practical concerns were not at issue. Of importance was the establishment of an ideal program. If it was good enough, if faculty and staff members were persuasive enough, and if the administration was supportive enough, the students would come. When they did not, he suggested that President Kimpton's reorganization of the college in 1953 was a failure of will and of commitment "to do what ought to be done in education without regard to what other people are doing or what the public thinks."[98]

Ironically, the college that resulted from Hutchins' support and fierce protection was not even the program he wanted. There were some common characteristics: an integrated, thoughtfully planned set of courses that cut across academic disciplines, the inclusion of some original sources in the syllabi, the liberal use of discussion groups for all students, not only honors students, and the prescribed, common curriculum. There also were differences. And from the late 1930s to the early 1950s, he continued to entertain the possibility of establishing the college he really wanted.

In the summer of 1936, when the faculty protested the establishment of the Committee on the Liberal Arts, Hutchins and Adler discussed establishing "Cornwall College" as their ideal undergraduate institution, and considered the potential of the chancellorship of the City College of New York for creating an institution for the study of the seven liberal arts.[99] In 1937 Adler suggested that Hutchins would never get the program he wanted at Chicago and should seriously consider taking the presidency of St. John's College. Hutchins responded that the challenge of trying to be a philosopher and an administrator meant that stating "eternal truths" and getting "practical results" were not always congruent endeavors. He thought he "would be using about half [his] cylinders at St. John's" as an administrator, but if foundation money could be found, he would consider resigning for "a chain of St. Johnses."[100]

In 1939 Hutchins discussed with University of Chicago officials establishing a separate college, based on a clear philosophy, with its own board of trustees. This college could undertake an eight-year program beginning in the seventh grade. By using the existing college as a control, his and others' ideas about undergraduate education could truly be tested and refined without the constraints imposed on the college by the graduate faculty.[101] In 1949, Ward was persuaded to consider the branch college idea. Initially, he explored acquiring a campus, like the Frances Shimer College in Lake Forest, Illinois, which eventually adopted the curriculum scheme, but remained independent. Then, in the early 1950s, he explored the Aspen college idea.[102] None of these plans came to fruition.

St. John's College, the institution with a program closest to Hutchins' ideal, survived precisely because it has always drawn on a small group of students seeking that particular type of education. Moreover, St. John's had no competing interests within the same institution that depended upon the attraction of undergraduate students. The idealism guiding the St. John's program was also manifest in Hutchins' plans for the college at the University of Chicago. Though the content of each of the programs was different, the notion that students would engage for four years in a fully prescribed curriculum, setting aside career concerns to acquire an education as an end in itself, underlay both programs and limited the pool of students from which they could draw. In the case of the Hutchins college, too few middle-class students existed who wanted to sacrifice practical concerns for the full four collegiate years.

Yet Hutchins' persistent arguments for his program accomplished two ends. He provided the college faculty and administration with a sense of mission that was empowered by the head of the university. And he succeeded in alienating faculty members who feared his administrative efforts to dictate educational policy. For it was this ongoing battle over the autonomy and mission of the college program that placed Hutchins at odds with the modern university. His recurring disputes with faculty members over educational policy, the merits of appointments, and the aims of the university grew out of those battles over the college and were further manifestations of this adversarial relationship.

The demise of the college represents a reality with which American higher educational institutions have had to contend since the nineteenth century. That reality has been the need to attract and keep students in competition with other higher educational institutions. Hutchins chose to ignore this tension between mission and market when he sought to encourage a singular program that was independent of the graduate and professional schools of the University of Chicago and other universities. But the creation of such a program, within such a context governed by such a tension, was nothing short of remarkable.

CHAPTER 8 *At Odds with the Faculty: Departmental Needs and Goals*

THE CENTRAL, FUNDAMENTAL ACTIVITY of the University of Chicago continued apace in the 1930s and 1940s, despite all the controversy over the administration and curriculum of the college. Research was the primary enterprise occupying faculty members; graduate students outnumbered undergraduates by two to three times in the 1930s and 1940s. The exigencies of the Depression forced some accommodation from scholars, including extra teaching duties and less university money for research. Yet the work continued. Hutchins, for all his attempts to redefine the mission of the university, recognized the importance of this work. He supported and protected scholarship when it was threatened from outside the university. And, characteristically, he tried to shape it from within. He possessed some means to do so. The power of appointment and promotion, the allocation of budgetary resources, and the acquisition of funds from philanthropic foundations were functions under his purview.

Hutchins is as remembered for his tenacious defense of academic freedom as he is for his relentless advocacy of liberal education in the great books. During his presidency, he protected individual faculty members from disgruntled, politically conservative trustees. More significantly, he put himself in the line of fire in 1935 and 1949 to protect all the scholars at the university from state investigating committees. He instructed the trustees on the reasons for protecting scholarly work and rallied them to his cause. For this reason, the faculty held him in high esteem and students held him in awe.

The same moral and ethical conviction that generated such strength of character also fueled his decisions about institutional policy on appointments and promotions. He ignored many departmental requests for appointment and promotion, occasionally offering his own alternative candidates. In some cases, departmental curricular and program needs were subordinated to his rarely explained judgments about scholarly excellence. Throughout his presidency, the university lost promising young scholars, particularly in the social science and humanities departments, with which he had fundamental disagreements over scholarship. He tended not to argue with the physical and biological scientists over these issues. At the same time, he brought stellar scholars to the university when he received persuasive advice from deans and key faculty members.

Many of his disagreements with departments were complicated by his reliance on these key people to the exclusion of departmental faculty. He met regularly with the deans and usually attributed his personnel decisions to agreement with the appropriate dean. In cases when the whole department supported a rejected candidate, the deans were perceived to be the president's men rather than representatives of divisional faculty interests.

Whether or not the deans actually acted more in the interests of the administration than of the faculty is a moot point. The effect of Hutchins' actions on personnel decisions during the Depression was to damage faculty morale and provide the basis for continued faculty resistance to many of his ideas about education and scholarship.

Presidents before Hutchins had been autocratic. Harper never hesitated to exercise his authority over administrative and educational decisions, although he allowed some autonomy to faculty members who raised money for their research. Judson controlled policy and resource allocation with a similar tight rein. But faculty members who had endured the transitions of the 1920s, the decline of Judson's control, Burton's short presidency, and Mason's problems had begun to exercise more power over the decisions that affected their particular departments.

Charles E. Merriam, for example, assumed the chairmanship of the political science department in 1923 upon Judson's resignation. He elicited support from the Laura Spelman Rockefeller Memorial for the Local Community Research Committee in 1924 and began building a "community of researchers."[1] He recruited faculty members who had been public service officers. He brought into the department its most promising graduates to initiate and continue research projects he perceived as significant. Because Merriam was able to raise from outside sources the funds he needed for the department's research, he was successful in shaping a department of national renown largely free of presidential interference until Hutchins began to develop contrary ideas about what constituted legitimate scholarship in political science.

From the announcement of his appointment of Adler to the philosophy department, Hutchins' presidential demeanor cumulatively signaled to the faculty a return to the autocratic presidential control of an earlier era.[2] His participation in the honors class was no cause for alarm until he began to recommend such a program for all undergraduates. His public image as an advocate of a great books curriculum combined with his overt and covert attempts to bring Scott Buchanan and Stringfellow Barr to the campus and his establishment of the Committee on the Liberal Arts increased the faculty's suspicion of his conduct.

Faculty members' perceptions of his power were rooted in their awareness of his charisma as much as in their observations of his conduct within the institution. He attracted attention. The popular press found him fascinating. Many of his speeches were covered in the *New York Times* and his activities were detailed in *Time* magazine. His authority seemed to grow as his national image did, particularly from 1933 to 1939 when he was being courted by Franklin D. Roosevelt for positions in various New Deal agencies.[3] It is within this context that Hutchins' relations with the faculty at the University of Chicago must be viewed.

When the reorganization of 1930–31 was complete, the patterns of conflict and control also were altered. Department chairs no longer had direct access to the president in their budget negotiations. Rather, they worked through the dean of the division in which their department was located. Where the dean stood in relation to the department chair (and particular faculty members) was crucial in the appointment and promotion process and in budget allocations. With Hutchins responsible for appointing deans in consultation with departmental faculty, avenues to policymaking within the university were more concentrated than they had been before the reorganization.

Whenever there was a conflict over the president's conduct of policy, faculty members acted through their governing body, the faculty senate. In 1931 after the Adler–philosophy department fiasco, for example, the senate passed a motion requiring that all recommendations for appointment made by the president have the approval of the department and those of the department the approval of the president before being sent to the board of trustees. Further, the senate formed a committee on university policy, composed of two faculty members from each of the five divisions and one from each of the professional schools.[4]

In contrast, when the faculty's academic freedom was threatened from outside the university during his tenure, Hutchins' response was unequivocally protective. Arguing in 1931 that the only proper question to be raised about a professor was "his competence in his field," he informed the American Association of University Professors that any compromise of this position would surely erode academic freedom.[5] Moreover, he acted on this belief every time a trustee of the university complained about professors who criticized corporate management practices or conservative politics. His certainty about the inviolability of academic freedom was such that he did not anticipate the extent of the crisis the university faced when one of Chicago's powerful merchants complained about the teaching of communism in the university's social sciences introductory course.

In 1935 Charles R. Walgreen of the Walgreen Drug Stores family accused the university of betraying the public trust by using subversive materials in Social Sciences I. His niece, Lucille Norton, was a student in the course until Walgreen withdrew her from the college after hearing her description of the class and the required reading, including a work by Karl Marx. He wrote Hutchins an angry letter in April claiming that Norton had been exposed to "Communistic influences" and suggested a public meeting to discuss the issue.[6] Hutchins refused. He informed Walgreen that the university would not respond until he supplied evidence to support his contentions.[7] Dean Brumbaugh of the college and Social Sciences I faculty members tried to correct Walgreen's misperceptions but were unsuccessful.[8]

Apparently, assuming that if he ignored Walgreen he would go away or, alternatively, that his accusations were too preposterous to be considered credible, Hutchins did little to respond further. Walgreen requested the state senate to investigate the university. As a result, the Illinois senate initiated its examination of public allegations of "subversive communistic teachings and ideas" that posed a threat to the United States and the state of Illinois.[9]

The investigation took the university by surprise. A few weeks earlier trustees privately had expressed their dissatisfaction with Hutchins' "flippancy" around many of Chicago's leading citizens and businessmen. He assumed, one trustee suggested, that "academic freedom argue[d] its own case." His "take it or leave it" attitude, along with his well-known "wisecracking," had alienated "many substantial friends of the University."[10] Coupled with the persistent efforts of one Senator Baker to have the tax exemptions of the state's universities denied when professors expressed radical views, Hutchins' difficulties with the trustees and minimal response to Walgreen placed the university in a vulnerable position.

Hutchins faced a twofold task: rallying the trustees in defense of the university and restraining his impulse to treat the investigating senators with contempt. That he managed to do so was a measure of his desire to protect the faculty and of the loyalty and support of chairman of the board Harold Swift and the legal counsel of trustee Laird Bell, who reputedly offered the university a hundred dollars for each wisecrack Hutchins did not make.[11] During the hearing conducted by the Illinois senate committee in May and June of 1935, Swift testified to the integrity and the capitalist interests of the trustees as well as the scholarly distinction of the university's faculty. He denied any communist or subversive teaching on campus.[12]

In addition to Walgreen's initial charges, the committee responded to questions from the Hearst press about student groups, speakers on the campus, and professors' off-campus associations. In answer to Bell's challenge to control his tongue, Hutchins informed the committee that the only communism at the university was in books. The syllabus for the Social Sciences I course contained a wide variety of books discussing "different views of the subject" of communism and other economic, social, and political theories. Repudiating the committee's charges against the faculty, he gave vent to his contempt for the committee in only one instance, suggesting that the university's accusers were "ignorant, malicious, deluded, or misinformed."[13] In the end, the committee found no support for Walgreen's charges but requested that the university continue to conform with the state's sedition act.

Hutchins' fearless defense of the faculty to the senate committee represents one facet of his belief in academic freedom. An equally telling, yet different, aspect of his policy stance is evident in his 1934–35 annual report to the trustees. The modern university, he suggested, "aims to develop education and to advance knowledge." The achievement of those purposes was directly related to the extent of the university's freedom to pursue them. Because the university was "first of all a group of professors," how well it provided a haven for these individuals "specially qualified to pursue the truth" was entrusted to the board of trustees. Unlike the employees of a corporation, the faculty was "not working for the trustees; the trustees [were] working for the faculty."[14]

The president's function was to represent the trustees and the faculty. He was required to interpret the work of each to the other and of both to the outside world. He met his duties to the trustees by preventing the faculty from squandering the university's resources. He had the responsibility of enlightening the trustees about the university so that they would not interfere with education and scholarship, despite the embarrassment (barring illegal or incompetent behavior) professors might cause board members in the larger community. Finally, and most important, the president, with the deans and department chairs, was the arbiter of professorial competence.

This issue of professorial competence was especially crucial, Hutchins argued, at a time when all new appointments to the university were temporary. Instituted only because the university's investments and ability to raise additional funds were at the mercy of the Depression, the policy was dangerous if the president, deans, or chairs considered anything other than scholarship and teaching, personality only as it affected their exercise, comparative quality of scholarship within the academic discipline, and sufficient funds to support research in the academic field. Whatever political or personal differences responsible officers of the university might have with untenured faculty members, decisions about reappointment should not be affected by them.[15]

After the state's charges were dropped, Hutchins still had to contend with the trustees' displeasure over negative public opinion, which was partly responsible for the avidity with which the Hearst press and the Illinois senate pursued Walgreen's allegations. He invited his former Yale classmate William Benton to conduct a survey of local public opinion of the university and to devise strategies to improve it. The end of such work was to enhance recruitment to the college, regenerate fund-raising among alumni and Chicago businessmen, and better protect the university from further investigations.

Benton had been a dynamic and tireless entrepreneurial partner in the Benton & Bowles advertising agency. He had made a million dollars in the advertising business and was searching for more meaningful employment, involving some form of public service. He agreed to conduct the survey. The trustees appreciated his report and recommendations, one of which was to advise Hutchins to limit his public speaking to educational matters.[16] Hutchins wanted Benton to continue working for the university and persuaded him to become a half-time vice-president in 1937. Until he left in 1946 to serve the Truman administration as assistant secretary of state, he worked on enhancing the university's public image and extending Hutchins' educational ideas and other aspects of the university's work into the Chicago and national community.

He developed the University of Chicago Round Table educational radio program. He acquired and oversaw the revising of the *Encyclopaedia Britannica.* He initiated and encouraged the related publication of *Great Books of the Western World,* the fifty-four-volume collection based on Hutchins' and Adler's general honors lists and course. He fostered the production of educational films for use at the university and other institutions. In short, Benton accomplished much in the way of extending to the larger community some of the university's intellectual work.

One of Benton's major accomplishments in the months following the Walgreen controversy was to set up a meeting between Walgreen and Hutchins when he discovered that Walgreen regretted his role in the investigation. Hutchins and Walgreen began to meet regularly for lunch. In 1937, as reparation to the university, Walgreen donated $550,000 for the establishment of the Walgreen Foundation for the Study of American Institutions.[17] Hutchins had warned Walgreen earlier that he would pay for his insult to the University of Chicago. With Benton's assistance, his prediction came true.

A major problem was developing at the university in the middle 1930s that Benton could not resolve for Hutchins. It was a problem that represented another side to Hutchins' attitude about academic freedom: the extent of faculty power to shape the university's intellectual work through appointment and promotion of faculty members.[18] In 1936 Hutchins advised the trustees that the temporary appointment policy was a dangerous one, justified only because of the Depression. In fact, he had expressed skepticism of the policy of granting tenure early in his presidency. By supporting incompetent professors on permanent tenure, he thought, universities debased the salaries of competent professors and encouraged mediocrity. He would have preferred to see academic tenure restricted to protecting academic freedom rather than the jobs of the incompetent.[19] After the Walgreen affair, he decided he was "in favor of permanent tenure, with all its drawbacks, as by far the lesser of two evils."[20]

It is not entirely clear how his position on tenure affected the university's statutory tenure policy beginning in January of 1931. But on the basis of financial considerations, the university decided to maintain permanent tenure only for those faculty members who already had it. Others—instructors, assistant professors, associate professors, and new faculty—would be appointed for fixed terms. In the 1934–35 academic year, 99.2 percent of all appointments made were for one year and only one person was appointed to permanent tenure.[21] This state of affairs contrasts sharply with the growth and relatively stable distribution of faculty by rank throughout the university in the prior three decades.[22] It was a policy only a minority of private universities adopted. According to a report by the American Association of University Professors, in the 1930s the practice of one-year appointments was most prevalent in public institutions and least prevalent in private, nondenominational institutions.[23]

Other Depression measures included efforts to maintain faculty salaries at 1929 levels. Mandatory retirement at sixty-five years was enforced, and many distinguished faculty members left. Their positions were not always filled with new appointments. Instruction during the fourth quarter and in the extension division became regular departmental activities with no extra compensation as had been offered in the past. Administrative salaries were reduced by 10 to 20 percent. Finally, in 1932–33, some faculty salaries were reduced 10 to 20 percent because of continued financial losses, despite the retirement policy and the tenure policy, but were restored by 1935.[24]

In his 1934–35 report to the board of trustees, Hutchins reviewed the need for appointments to department chairs (four in 1934–35 and an additional twenty in the next five years) and listed the twenty-one departments that in his estimation did not require immediate attention.[25] His report was a plea to the trustees to consider raising salaries for all professors, not only those dispensable few who were being recruited by other institutions. He suggested terminating the temporary appointment practice "as soon as the budget" was "balanced," as there were 787 members of the faculty in such positions.[26] Appointments to full professorship with tenure were reinstituted on the basis of the president's recommendation in 1936–37, and the allowable time for a temporary appointment grew to three years from one. Then, in 1937–38, Hutchins instructed deans to recommend deserving candidates for appointments of more than a year.[27]

His ongoing difficulties with the faculty regarding appointment policies were not helped by such statements as "If we cannot find a good man we should not appoint anybody" and "Good men should be appointed within limits of the funds available whenever they can be found, without particular reference to the needs of specific departments."[28] His definition of a "good man" was part of the problem; he only rarely articulated what exactly that meant. But his repeated urging to search internationally suggests that American scholars often failed to meet his criteria of excellence. International renown seemed to be one basis of judgment. Moreover, he did not always agree with the assessments of members of the departments.

Departments were under tremendous stress trying to meet undergraduate, masters', and doctoral level program needs with the limited faculty members they had. Under these conditions, Hutchins' tenure policy coupled with his resistance to departmental suggestions and refusal to acknowledge their needs, his failure on a few occasions to consult with departments, and his ongoing attempts to redefine the mission of the university was interpreted as a threat to departmental self-definition and autonomy.

A case in point was the history department. From the beginning Hutchins had the support of William E. Dodd, who worked in 1931 to "allay the fears" of the faculty members upset with Hutchins' behavior toward the philosophy department.[29] But Dodd was called to Germany as ambassador during the Roosevelt presidency. And the history department was struggling internally with its self-definition in light of the reorganization of the university. The problem was whether the department belonged in the division of the social sciences or the division of the humanities. After a few long, difficult department meetings, it was agreed to place part of the faculty in each division and to offer courses in both divisions and undergraduate majors in one or the other.[30]

Bernadotte E. Schmitt was chair of the department from 1933 to 1936, and he shared Dodd's faith in Hutchins' judgment during his chairmanship, though by the early 1940s he was "disillusioned" with Hutchins' leadership.[31] Hutchins' report to the trustees of 1933–34 listed history as one of the twenty-one strong departments needing no further resources. Yet Schmitt's correspondence with Hutchins in 1933 and 1934 was a litany of pleas for the recruitment of additional faculty members to replace retiring faculty and reduce the teaching load of overburdened members of the department. All his requests were denied for lack of funds.[32] In 1934 Hutchins discussed with Schmitt ways Schmitt could shift the teaching responsibilities in the department without hiring anyone and still allow research time to a few members of the department.[33]

The department was in part a victim of Hutchins' belief that history was not in itself a discipline. Departmental conflicts that arose often centered on whether individuals agreed with Hutchins' ideas about teaching and scholarship.[34] Hutchins described his conception of what academic history should be in a 1933 convocation speech. He thought university historians should "transmit to the student, not a confused list of places, dates, and names, but some understanding of the nature and schemes of history," in order to make its facts "intelligible."[35] He informed the board of trustees in 1935 that historians in the department were engaged in "pseudohistory," trying to be scientists when they should be maintaining standards of historical scholarship.[36]

His assessment showed a fundamental lack of understanding of what historical research and argument involved. One only has to examine the work of the department's historians in the 1930s to see that they were engaged in significant studies of people and institutions, as well as social and intellectual movements. By 1937 Andrew C. McLaughlin had completed his *Constitutional History of the United States*. Dodd had published studies of Woodrow Wilson's peace efforts. Louis Gottschalk was examining Lafayette and eighteenth- and early nineteenth-century liberalism. Marcus Jurnegan was working on American immigration and the working classes during the colonial period. Schmitt was studying American neutrality from 1914 to 1917. Avery O. Craven was writing about the South and West during the Civil War. J. F. Rippy was working on revolutionary movements in Latin America. William T. Hutchinson, having completed his biography of Cyrus McCormick, was at work on a monograph on veterans in the public domain. Greek and Roman representative government was the focus of Jake Larsen's research. Bessie Pierce's research area was urban history, and her primary focus was the city of Chicago. Other work included Marshall Knappen's in English Puritanism, Samuel Halperin's on church and state in Italy, Harley McNair's on China and international relations, Herrlee Creel's in early Chinese history, and Samuel Harper's on Russian political institutions and Soviet international relations.[37]

Hutchins' judgment not only was intellectually problematic for the history department but also was supported by policy that exiled history from the college-level general offerings in the late 1930s and limited departmental history courses to upper division and graduate students. The result of this policy was to deny students exposure to the methodological, analytical, and interpretive problems of historical scholarship unless they decided to pursue the study of history for professional purposes.[38] A Committee on History had been organized in 1933 to locate and coordinate all the courses in the university that used historical methods and content. Ronald S. Crane, a strong Hutchins backer in the early 1930s (though his position changed by the early 1940s) and temporary head of the Committee on History, reputedly circulated a letter suggesting that the history department be abolished because nearly all the other departments offered some study of history.[39]

The history department responded to these criticisms by asserting that history was not merely a method, as Crane reportedly held, but rather a discipline that contributed to the construction of syntheses of man as a social being. The challenge Hutchins proffered had a positive effect on the department because the faculty members engaged in an ongoing critical examination of the department's activities. But there also were negative effects because the challenge was not merely an intellectual issue. Faculty morale was strongly affected by the fear that the department would be reduced or abolished.[40] This fear developed in the early 1930s as a result of perceptions of Hutchins' attitude and seemed to be confirmed by the administration's slow response to requests for faculty appointments and promotions. It continued into the 1940s as a result of a variety of disputes over curriculum and distribution of research support within the division of the humanities.

In the case of appointments and promotions, an examination of those made in history from 1929 to 1950 shows that the history department was required continually to fight for both. Deaths, resignations, and retirements of departmental faculty in the 1930s did not necessarily lead to replacements. Some faculty members went on half-time appointments. Chauncey Boucher, for example, was dean of the college in the early 1930s. James H. Breasted was head of the Oriental Institute during the period. John U. Nef and John T. McNeill had joint appointments in economics and the Divinity School, respectively, leaving less than half of their time for the history department.[41]

In some cases, promotions occurred fairly consistently with the chair's recommendation. Louis Gottschalk joined the faculty in 1927 and became a full professor in 1935. William T. Hutchinson joined as an instructor in 1924, was promoted to associate professor in 1931, and finally, in 1940, was made full professor. He waited patiently for the last promotion because he was one of the few faculty members who received a three-year appointment and a salary raise in 1936, which assured him of the administration's support.[42]

The relationship between Hutchins and the department was also manifest in the appointments and promotions that the department heads championed and that Hutchins or his deans did not approve. One finds, for example, faculty members like Bessie Pierce, appointed instructor in 1929, and Jake Larsen, appointed associate professor in 1930, waiting more than a dozen years for full professorships. Or in the case of Eugene Anderson, appointed instructor in 1925, a promotion to assistant professor in 1932 was not followed by any further promotion before he resigned in 1936. Similarly, Marshall Knappen, appointed instructor in 1927, received a promotion to assistant professor in 1930 but no subsequent promotion before his resignation in 1939.

Samuel W. Halperin was appointed instructor in 1930 but had received no promotion by 1940. He wrote in desperation to Hutchins, noting the department's unanimous recommendation of his promotion in the previous two years, saying he was willing to take the promotion with no accompanying salary increase if the university's financial condition was the factor precluding his advancement.[43] He received his assistant professorship then, promotion to associate in 1944, and finally a full professorship in 1949.

Louis Gottshalk, who had succeeded Schmitt to the chair in 1936, resigned from that post in 1942. He advised his successor, William T. Hutchinson (1942–50), to consult with the dean of the social sciences division (Robert Redfield, 1934–46; Ralph Tyler, 1946–53) about which candidates had the most chance of salary or rank increases before going to Hutchins with recommendations. Once recommended, Gottschalk advised, the candidate should continue to be endorsed in the succeeding years if the central administration refused the promotion.[44] However much he followed this advice, Hutchinson encountered problems throughout the 1940s whenever he suggested a promotion or an appointment.

These problems did not arise because of Hutchinson's relationship with either Redfield or Tyler. Hutchinson thought that Redfield was "a square shooter" with respect to matters of appointment and promotion. When Tyler became dean, Hutchinson was skeptical. He thought Tyler was "100% pro-Hutchins" and overly preoccupied with the education department, of which he had been chair. In retrospect, though, he thought Tyler had been "calm, impartial, energetic, and wise" throughout his tenure.[45] Rather, the problems arose because of Hutchins' unwillingness to accede to the department's wishes with respect to faculty.

In 1943, for example, Edgar Wind, an art historian in the humanities division, complained to Hutchins about the unwieldy power that Richard McKeon held. He was not only dean of the division but also professor of Greek and of philosophy, acting chair of the Latin department, and member of a number of committees in the division. Moreover, the acting chairs of three departments in the division were on probation, their terms to be assessed by the dean.[46] Because of the deterioration of Wind's relationship with McKeon, Redfield requested that the history department take him in. The department refused, unwilling to antagonize McKeon, and instead submitted a list of historians for the administration to consider for appointment to the department.[47] This same list was submitted a year later, with no action by the administration.[48]

Perhaps Hutchins' most damaging tactical response to history department requests was to reduce or delay appointments. When Marcus Jurnegan resigned in 1937, the department asked for an equivalent full professorial appointment in colonial history to replace him. Hutchins talked them down to a lesser appointment and then provided funds for an instructorship.[49] The department had lost not only Jurnegan but also Dodd and McLaughlin, three of its most distinguished members. Of the full-time appointments made in the 1940s, one was before 1945 and the others were between 1946 and 1949. Walter Johnson was appointed instructor in 1940. He advanced to assistant in 1943. In 1948, the second year Hutchinson recommended him for advancement, he rose to associate professor (a promotion Hutchins initially refused) and, in 1951, after Hutchins left and a year after he became chair of the department, Johnson was promoted to a full professorship.[50] The other appointments included one full professorship in European history (Hans Rothfels), one associate professorship in Asian history (Earl Pritchard), and assistant professorships in English history (Alan Simpson), classics (Carl Roebuck), modern Far Eastern history (Donald Lach), and American Western history (W. Turrentine Jackson).

In 1945 Hutchins antagonized the department by trying to appoint a man the faculty did not want. His choice was someone he had been suggesting for two years and whom the department had steadily refused. Supporting him in 1945 were deans Redfield and McKeon. Members of the department were so divided over the appointment and so upset with Hutchins' heavy-handed maneuvering that at least one member, Schmitt, threatened to resign.[51] The appointment was not made over the department's objections, but coupled with Hutchins' steady refusal to appoint or promote many of the department's choices, the dispute further damaged morale.

In 1947 one promotion was approved and two were denied. The two denied were men who had last received promotions seven years before. In addition, Harley McNair died. The department lacked a Far Eastern and a Russian historian, a situation that added to the faculty's discouragement. As Hutchinson recalled in 1947, in fifteen years the department had shrunk from a healthy twenty-five members with at least five distinguished scholars to nineteen members. These nineteen did not "average as high in distinction." Moreover, the number of history majors had increased by 42 percent.[52]

By 1950 the outlook was "grim." Hutchinson was uncertain which had the more devastating effect—the Depression or Hutchins. "Time and again," he remembered, when the department corresponded with the central administration and Hutchins about candidates, responses were "slow in coming or absent altogether." Denying the integrity of the department's assessment of curricular needs, Hutchins complained that the faculty overly stressed fields and periods rather than excellent scholarship. He granted the department visiting or temporary, in lieu of tenurable, appointments or, by contrast, pressured members to accept the administration's preferences. In addition to this kind of treatment under Hutchins' administration, of the fifteen social sciences division projects requesting administration support in 1945, the seven in history were rejected.[53]

Similar problems with the political science department have been explored elsewhere.[54] In that case, Hutchins and Charles E. Merriam communicated regularly. In fact, Merriam worked with Hutchins and Walgreen to establish the Walgreen lecture series in the aftermath of the investigation. Yet the department lost a number of scholars because Hutchins refused to promote them at the faculty's request. Barry Karl has noted that Hutchins accused Merriam of building a department full of "monuments to his passing whims."[55] Frederick L. Schuman, a former Merriam student, was promoted to assistant professor in 1932. When he was offered a full professorship and substantial salary raise by Williams College, Hutchins countered with an associate professorship and a lesser salary raise. Schuman went to Williams.[56]

Harold D. Lasswell and Harold F. Gosnell, promoted to associate professorships in 1932, were denied the advancements to full professorships the department recommended for them. According to one account, Hutchins did not find Lasswell's studies, using Freudian and sociological theory to examine politics, government, and propaganda, worthy of the university's support. He vetoed Lasswell's promotion in 1938.[57] Lasswell resigned and pursued a distinguished career in political science at the New School for Social Research and at Yale University. Gosnell stayed at the university until 1942, but finding no assurance from Hutchins that the university would recognize the quality of his empirical research in *Negro Politicians: The Rise of Negro Politics in Chicago* (1935) or *Machine Politics: Chicago Model* (1937), he resigned to work in government.[58]

Jerome Kerwin finally was given a full professorship in 1943, twenty years after his initial appointment to an instructorship. Kerwin had been a member of the social science curriculum committee in the college and had devoted much of his time in the 1930s to college activities. Perhaps Hutchins' reluctance in Kerwin's regard was related to Hutchins' dissatisfaction with the committee's work. Interestingly, Kerwin was most concerned in 1943 that the political science department maintain a strong emphasis on political theory through the "close examination of great writers" throughout history, in addition to its emphasis on political parties, public administration, and public law.[59] According to one of his colleagues, his promotion occurred "over the reluctance and opposition of the administration," though who opposed it is not clear.[60]

Yet, in 1948, when chairman of the department Leonard White requested the appointment of Leo Strauss to fill a chair in political theory, Hutchins eventually endorsed his choice. White's case was strengthened by the recommendations of two colleagues from Cambridge University.[61] Seeking other opinions, Hutchins advised Ernest C. Colwell, who had become president when Hutchins became chancellor in 1946, to solicit the opinions of three people as to Strauss' suitability: Mortimer Adler, Edward Levi, and Richard McKeon. Levi knew nothing of Strauss, but McKeon and Adler returned strong recommendations for appointment.[62] The difference was not simply the positive international and local opinions. Rather, the nature of Strauss' work appealed to Hutchins. As a classical political theorist, Strauss' teaching in the great books represented the kind of scholarship Hutchins could readily support in the political science department.

In his history of the sociology department of the University of Chicago, Martin Bulmer suggests that Hutchins had no measurable effect on its relative decline in the 1930s.[63] He argues instead that the lack of cohesive leadership guiding departmental treatment of methodological and substantive sociological problems, and the caliber of the graduate students, contributed to the department's transition from a school to a group of faculty members.[64] Whether Hutchins could have slowed or reversed the process is difficult to assess. Indeed, the official correspondence suggests good relations with William F. Ogburn, the department's foremost proponent of quantitative statistical research.[65] But by the 1940s there were telling signs of tension between the administration and the department.

Ogburn, for example, wrote a short paper entitled "On Power and Publicity" in which he suggested that a president's publicity carried little persuasive influence over the faculty. Perhaps the trustees could be influenced by the media's coverage of a president's activities, but the effect on faculty was less direct. Yet, when the president's fund-raising capabilities increased, so did his power in relation to the faculty within the university structure. Moreover, in what could well have been a veiled reference to Hutchins' public statements, Ogburn asserted that "spectacular" or "shocking" statements were "not very conducive to power."[66]

Another instance involved Louis Wirth, who had worked with Harry Gideonse in the 1930s to ensure that the social science courses for the college would not contain only books from the Hutchins-Adler list. When Adler presented a paper called "Systematic Social Science" at the university, Wirth was a primary respondent. He called Adler to task on his lack of concern for the relationship between social science research and society or social conditions. Rather, Adler's concern had been with scientific methodology and Aristotelian logic. Wirth kept a vigil over Adler's pronouncements and Hutchins' public statements.[67]

Hutchins asked Beardsley Ruml whether the university should take the opportunity "to lose" Wirth to Brooklyn College in 1939, an indication of his own opinion.[68] It is not clear which bothered Hutchins about Wirth: his scholarship in the sociology of knowledge, public planning, and race relations; his public activities as a consultant on urban affairs and unemployment; or his concerns with the president's use of power within the university. Wirth wrote to Hutchins in 1946 that friends had heard Hutchins at a dinner party "say that the I.Q. of the Sociology Department was very low." Hutchins had "no recollection of this alleged conversation."[69] Whatever the truth of the matter, Wirth was neither surprised nor dismayed by the statement itself, only by its public nature. At the very least such incidents indicate faculty members' apprehensions about Hutchins' activities.

Hutchins' effect on the humanities departments is more difficult to discern. After the philosophy department fiasco in 1930–31, the division as a whole was wary of Hutchins. When Gordon Laing expressed his intention to resign as dean of the division, the division's committee on policy made a motion expressing the "hope" that Hutchins would consult with a committee of the division before appointing a replacement.[70] Despite his having been a Hutchins choice for philosophy in 1930, Richard P. McKeon was invited to a visiting professorship in Greek in 1934 because Ronald S. Crane respected his work; he acceded to a full professorship at the request of the Greek department in 1935. With the concurrence of the divisional committee, Hutchins appointed him dean of humanities in 1935. The philosophy department agreed to his appointment as professor of philosophy in 1937.

Hutchins apparently left major decisions regarding the humanities departments to McKeon. That four departments in particular were allowed to decline must have been by agreement between the president and the dean. New Testament studies had three full professors in 1928–29 and none by 1938–39. English, where Ronald S. Crane initially had been a Hutchins supporter, lost six full, two assistant, and two associate professorial positions and one instructorship in the same period. Yet, with senior faculty members Crane, Robert Morss Lovett, John M. Manley, and George W. Sherburn, the department's reputation as a strong center of scholarship was assured in the 1930s. In addition, Crane respected McKeon's intellect and encouraged faculty members' use of Aristotle to develop methods of literary criticism. The difficulty of finding faculty was complicated by the requirement that appointments be approved by the dean of humanities (McKeon) and the chairs of the education and English departments.[71]

Romance languages, of which William A. Nitze was chair, gained two full professorships and one instructorship but lost an assistant professorship. In 1940 Hayward Keniston, one of the university's "pillars of strength" and professor of Spanish language and literature, was offered a position at the University of Michigan.[72] It was rumored that Keniston seriously considered the offer because he resented "dictation" by Hutchins of departmental appointments.[73] Nitze informed Hutchins that, if he let Keniston go, it would be an "irreparable loss to the University." Hutchins wrote "no answer" across the top of the letter, and Keniston left the university.[74]

In the case of the philosophy department, the correspondence indicates that Hutchins actively supported Ames' search for new faculty members to replace the five who resigned in 1931.[75] But in the end, only three full professors were recruited in the 1930s: Rudolf Carnap, whom Hutchins appointed reluctantly because he had doubts about the value of logical positivism for philosophy; Werner Jaeger, jointly in Greek and philosophy, who left for Harvard in 1939; and McKeon.[76] One assistant professor, Charles Hartshorne, joined the department in the 1930s. There were no promotions from 1931 to 1938.[77] Charles W. Morris, whom Hutchins had been required to invite as associate professor to appease the faculty in 1931, was not promoted for seventeen years. Charner Perry re-

Isaac Thompson Hutchins, Hutchins' great-grandfather (Berea College Archives).

The Reverend Robert Grosvenor Hutchins, Hutchins' paternal grandfather (Berea College Archives).

Hutchins' paternal grandmother, Harriet Palmer James Hutchins, Oberlin, Ohio, ca. 1886 (Berea College Archives).

Hutchins' maternal grandparents, Captain Maynard Hale Murch and Lucy Stephenson Murch, Cleveland, Ohio (Berea College Archives).

Hutchins' Uncle Francis Sessions Hutchins, in whose law firm Hutchins worked, 1925 (Berea College Archives).

The Reverend William James Hutchins, 1907, Brooklyn, New York (Berea College Archives).

Anna Laura Murch Hutchins in the Catskill Mountains with (left to right) *Francis Stephenson Hutchins, Robert Maynard Hutchins, and William Grosvenor Hutchins, 1903, Stamford, New York (Berea College Archives).*

Will and Anna Hutchins, ca. 1920, Oberlin, Ohio (Berea College Archives).

Robert Hutchins shortly before the family moved to Oberlin, 1907, Brooklyn, New York (Berea College Archives).

With what appears to be an Oberlin tennis team, Robert (third from left) *and William* (second from right) *Hutchins sporting mustaches like their father's, ca. 1915 (Berea College Archives).*

Robert Hutchins on a camping trip, ca. 1919 (Berea College Archives).

Robert Hutchins on his return from service in Italy with the U.S. Army Ambulance Corps, 1919 (Berea College Archives).

Hutchins, secretary to the Yale Corporation, at work in his office, 1923 (Berea College Archives).

Maude Phelps McVeigh Hutchins, shortly after enrolling in the Yale School of Fine Arts, 1923 (Berea College Archives).

Maude with Franja Hutchins, ca. 1926 (Berea College Archives).

Robert with Franja, ca. 1926 (Berea College Archives).

Robert Hutchins, just before assuming the presidency of the University of Chicago, 1929 (University of Chicago Archives).

Maude Hutchins, 1929 (Joseph A. Stone, University of Chicago Archives).

Inaugural Procession along the Midway, University of Chicago, 1929 (University of Chicago Archives).

Induction of Hutchins (in lectern at right) *as president of the university, Rockefeller Chapel, 1929 (University of Chicago Archives).*

Hutchins, during inaugural festivities, with honorary degree recipients William James Hutchins (left) *and Martin Ryerson (Underwood & Underwood, University of Chicago Archives).*

Hutchins (third from left) *with, from left, James Rowland Angell of Yale, President Scott of Northwestern University, and Harold H. Swift, president of the board of trustees of the University of Chicago, during the inauguration (Underwood & Underwood, University of Chicago Archives).*

In a rare photograph with his family, Hutchins celebrating Joanna Hutchins' birthday with (left to right) *Maude, Joanna, and Franja, ca. 1938 (Berea College Archives).*

Harold Swift (left) *with Maude and Robert Hutchins at Lakeside, his retreat on Lake Michigan, ca. 1931 (Berea College Archives).*

Robert Hutchins with unidentified guests in the president's office at the university; portraits of (left to right) *Harry Pratt Judson, William Rainey Harper, and Martin Ryerson hang on the wall (University of Chicago Archives).*

Mortimer Jerome Adler (University of Chicago Archives).

Robert and Maude Hutchins (center) *greeting students at the president's reception for freshmen in Ida Noyes Clubhouse, June 1938 (Paul H. Wagner, University of Chicago Archives).*

Hutchins conferring with Frederic C. Woodward (center) *and William Benton, ca. 1937 (Paul A. Wagner, University of Chicago Archives).*

Hutchins with unidentified student during Freshmen Week, October 1943 (University of Chicago Archives).

Hutchins speaking on the University of Chicago Round Table radio program about the issue of universal military training in peacetime, November 1944 (University of Chicago Archives).

Vesta and Robert Hutchins at a university reception, 1949 (University of Chicago Archives).

Vesta and Robert Hutchins with Barbara, at the chancellor's house (Stephen Lewellyn, University of Chicago Archives).

Vesta and Robert Hutchins at a farewell dinner for the chancellor, December 1951 (Stephen Lewellyn, University of Chicago Archives).

Vesta and Robert Hutchins signing autographs at the students' farewell dinner for the Hutchinses, 1951 (Stephen Lewellyn, University of Chicago Archives).

Robert and Vesta Hutchins with Lawrence and Mrs. Kimpton shortly before Kimpton assumed the presidency, December 1951 (Stephen Lewellyn, University of Chicago Archives).

William Benton (left), *Hutchins* (center), *and Mortimer Adler, with the set of the Encyclopaedia Britannica's Great Books of the Western World intended for Queen Elizabeth II of Great Britain, 1952 (University of Chicago Archives).*

Hutchins (left) *with Paul Hoffman* (center) *and William Benton at an Encyclopaedia Britannica dinner, 1952 (University of Chicago Archives).*

Robert Hutchins in 1956, after the Fund for the Republic's problems with public relations had eased (University of Chicago Archives).

Robert Hutchins (left) *with Paul Hoffman at the Ford Foundation in Pasadena, ca. early 1950s (University of Chicago Archives, William Benton Papers).*

Center for the Study of Democratic Institutions on Eucalyptus Hill in Santa Barbara, California (University of California at Santa Barbara Library, Department of Special Collections, Center for the Study of Democratic Institutions Archives).

Center conference room, with Hutchins at left, Harry Ashmore on his left, and Rexford Tugwell fifth from Hutchins' left (University of California at Santa Barbara Library, Department of Special Collections, Center for the Study of Democratic Institutions Archives).

Vesta and Robert Hutchins at the Center, ca. early 1970s (University of California at Santa Barbara Library, Department of Special Collections, Center for the Study of Democratic Institutions Archives).

Robert Hutchins on the Center terrace (University of California at Santa Barbara Library, Department of Special Collections, Center for the Study of Democratic Institutions Archives).

mained an assistant professor from 1933 to 1945 and an associate professor from 1945 to 1951, finally achieving a full professorship after Hutchins left the university. A. C. Benjamin remained assistant professor from 1932 to 1943 and associate from 1943 to 1945, when he left to take an endowed professorship and to chair the department at the University of Missouri.

Hutchins' pattern of inaction on appointments is particularly evident in the philosophy department's lack of leadership after Ames' retirement from the chairmanship in 1935. From 1935 to 1940, despite complaints by the humanities division's committee on policy, the philosophy department had no chair.[78] The department, with the concurrence of Frederick J. E. Woodbridge of Columbia University, recommended Charles W. Morris.[79] Ignoring the recommendations, McKeon appointed Charner Perry as secretary of the department and managed its affairs himself. In 1940 Perry was made acting chair and finally, eight years later, after McKeon was no longer dean, he became chairman of the department. McKeon reasoned that the department should know the candidate well and be associated with him long enough to be able to make a "sound judgment" about his ability to improve department morale.[80]

The department's thirteen-year wait for a chairman was not solely attributable to McKeon. He could not have stalled that long if Hutchins had not agreed with his rationale. The explanation for why Hutchins supported McKeon's management of the division is twofold. First, Hutchins had a great deal of respect for McKeon's intellect, as did many in the division, whatever their feelings about his administrative decisions.[81] Second, Hutchins knew he had in McKeon a strong supporter for many of his hopes for the university, from cohesive undergraduate humanities courses to his and Adler's long-held dream of an Institute for Philosophical Studies.

McKeon worked assiduously to bring the humanities faculty together on course work and common intellectual endeavors.[82] The Organization, Interpretation, and Integration course in the college was one major result. Committees on aesthetics, linguistics, and other topics explored relationships among the different disciplines. McKeon went so far as to remove the Committee on the Liberal Arts from the division and resign from it in order to protect these other efforts within the division.

The Institute for Philosophical Studies idea stayed alive in Hutchins' and Adler's minds, but remained only an idea throughout Hutchins' presidency. Adler again proposed it in 1934 and suggested that $50,000 per year would adequately support the institute's work, which would be separate from the philosophy department. Adler thought the institute could perform a cultural synthesis for the modern world similar to "the Greek and the Medieval" but more thoroughgoing than "the scientifically oriented synthesis built around Galileo, Descartes, and Newton."[83] Hutchins continued to entertain the idea throughout the middle and late 1930s.[84] And in 1948 McKeon ventured his own plan, which bore some resemblance to Adler's and was geared toward attracting Rockefeller Foundation support.

The difference between McKeon's large plans for the projected institute and the philosophy department's long list of real needs based on years of neglect is notable. The institute, he thought, could be a place for world-class philosophers to rehabilitate "philosophic speculation" for analyzing the theoretical issues underlying "the key concepts and the key problems of our time."[85] The philosophy department, by contrast, saw its mission as preserving and disseminating basic philosophical ideas and their history, critically analyzing contemporary theory in all disciplines, and "enriching the tradition" by developing and clarifying "fundamental ideas."[86] In order to do this, members thought, more than four full-time faculty members would be needed to satisfy the department's teaching and scholarship needs. It is quite likely that Hutchins supported McKeon's delaying tactics, despite the cost to the department, because he hoped one day to bypass the department and establish an institute under the auspices of the university.

This suggestion appears plausible upon examination of one philosophy department member's assessment of Hutchins' character after working with him for almost twenty years. As T. V. Smith, who "loved Hutchins . . . as a president and courageous leader," recalled, "Hutchins was a most exceptional man." But he also was "off-sided." Of Hutchins' ideas, Smith noted, "when he made up his mind, it would be dogmatic and adamant." He rarely admitted that he did not know the answer to a question. Though "generous" and "compassionate," he "could learn little or nothing from other men."[87] Hutchins had committed his support to Adler's ideas in the early months of his presidency. Unless the department's goals fit with his own conceptions of philosophical work, he withheld support and encouragement for the department as it was.[88]

There were departments that remained strong or grew in stature under Hutchins' presidency. In the case of anthropology, the department had three respected scholars when Hutchins arrived in 1929, two of whom stayed throughout most of his tenure. Edward Sapir, Fay-Cooper Cole, and

Robert Redfield began building the department even before it separated from sociology in 1929. The department was small in the 1930s. After Sapir departed for Yale in 1931, Redfield and Cole were joined by Manuel Andrade, Arthur Radcliffe-Brown (who went to Oxford in 1937), and Lloyd Warner (appointed jointly to sociology and anthropology). Some instructors were added, but most appointments in the 1930s were as research associates, temporary and nonprofessorial, and determination of these was left to the senior members of the department. Hutchins had a high regard for Cole and especially for Redfield.[89]

Redfield had been a student of Robert E. Park and brought a sociological orientation to his studies of cultures. He succeeded Ruml as dean of the social sciences and was extraordinarily successful in maintaining cross-disciplinary cooperation among departments in the division.[90] He believed in Hutchins' ideas about a general education for undergraduates but strongly disagreed with some of Hutchins' ideas about the conduct of scholarly research.[91] Yet their mutual respect far outweighed any intellectual disagreements. Small as the department was, it maintained its prestige during Redfield's tenure on the faculty.

The department of education was a similar case in point. Hutchins had a longstanding respect for Charles Hubbard Judd, who had chaired the department from John Dewey's departure, through the abolition of the School of Education and the establishment of the department solely for research and the training of graduate students in 1931, until his retirement in 1938.[92] When Judd retired, Hutchins recruited Judd's former student Ralph W. Tyler from Ohio State University to chair the department and improve the comprehensive examinations used in the college.

Hutchins' choice of Tyler was interesting for intellectual and practical reasons. Hutchins had acquired from Adler an early contempt for progressive ideas about education.[93] Tyler's research and teaching were strongly rooted in his interpretation of John Dewey's ideas and the tradition of progressivism in education. Curiously, Hutchins had never read Dewey's work for himself. Instead, he relied on secondhand interpretations by Adler and others. His one intellectual exchange with Dewey in the pages of the *Social Frontier* indicated that he fundamentally disagreed with Dewey's philosophical and educational ideas.[94] Tyler, in retrospect, has marveled at Hutchins' broad-mindedness in the instance of his appointment. Contrary to Smith's description of Hutchins' inability to learn from others, Tyler has claimed that, under his tutelage, Hutchins began to read Dewey and to "realize his misconceptions about . . . Dewey." After that, Hutchins made "no more attacks on Dewey," and his criticism of progressive educators distinguished the followers of Dewey from the man himself.[95]

Tyler and Hutchins' mutual respect ensured two important results. Redfield resigned as dean of social sciences in 1946. With the concurrence of the divisional faculty, Hutchins appointed Tyler as acting dean for two years and then dean. In that position Tyler was able to protect the education department. The department remained intact throughout the 1930s and 1940s. In 1931 the department had twenty-one members ranking from assistant to full professor, as opposed to history's nineteen and economics' fourteen.[96] A steady supply of instructors and assistant, associate, and full professors was added in the 1930s.[97]

Tyler began with a clear mission for the department that went beyond its prior emphasis on psychology, administration, and teaching methods. It involved working with all departments and divisions within the university to solve educational problems, from determining the content of education at different levels to defining the significance of that content.[98] Moreover, despite prejudicial reaction, he achieved for the department the appointment of Allison Davis, who became one of the few black faculty members at the university. He also acquired financing for Davis' research on the "acculturation of colored peoples."[99]

The healthy growth of the economics department during Hutchins' presidency has been well documented elsewhere.[100] Again, as with anthropology and education, this growth can be attributed to a strong group of researchers and mutual respect between Hutchins and key members of the department. In this particular case, John U. Nef, Frank H. Knight (with whom Hutchins carried on a persistent but friendly argument), and Paul H. Douglas were economists upon whom Hutchins usually could count for support.[101] When the faculty received a memorandum about establishing in writing departmental practices in curriculum development, staff meetings, budget design, promotions, and so on, Nef objected to such codification if it was intended to impinge on the president's power. The president, he noted, had never encroached on the department's prerogatives.[102]

One finds in the correspondence a rich collection of communications between the president's office and the department, covering such issues as faculty recruitment and the overall future direction of the department. Mary B. Gilson, a member of the faculty, informed Hutchins how difficult it was for her to participate fully in the intellectual life of the university because women were excluded from the Quadrangle Club, where male faculty members met, and generally were not invited to participate in conferences. Within a few weeks she was asked to speak at one meeting and invited to attend a conference on economics.[103]

In the 1930s there was one exception to the cooperation between the president's office and the department. Hutchins' continued refusal from 1936 to 1938 to promote Harry D. Gideonse angered department members, brought criticism from alumni, and resulted in Gideonse's departure from the university in 1938. This controversy was critical in the faculty's perception of his administration. Gideonse (with Louis Wirth and Jerome Kerwin) had been instrumental in developing the social science courses for the college. He deliberately had worked to ensure that social sciences faculty, rather than Hutchins or Adler, would have the final say on the books included in the syllabus.[104]

When the department voted unanimously to grant him tenure and a full professorship, Hutchins refused to promote him, despite the support of the acting dean of the college, A. J. Brumbaugh. In their letter of protest department members reminded Hutchins that, when Gideonse was appointed associate professor in 1930, the terms of the agreement were that he would devote most of his time to teaching in the college and that research would not be the criterion of his promotion. Gideonse, they noted, had fulfilled the terms of the agreement, devoting nearly all his time to lecturing, curriculum development, in-house publishing, and committee work in the college. Moreover, the department argued, he was an outstanding teacher. Finally, they cautioned Hutchins against basing his judgment of Gideonse's competence on his intellectual disagreements with Gideonse.[105]

Those disputes were public. Gideonse's series of lectures *The Higher Learning in a Democracy* was not simply a clarification of the distinction between Hutchins' ideal great books program as set forth in his *Higher Learning in America* (1936) and the University's actual program. It was also an argument supporting the validity of empirical research within the university. He criticized Hutchins' choice of metaphysics, "nourished by Scholasticism," as the central discipline of the university's search for truth. It was incompatible, he argued, with the modern university's more democratic reliance on science as the framework for disinterested, rational inquiry into "the multiplicity of modern paths to significant insight" in all of the disciplines.[106]

Hutchins was sufficiently disturbed by Gideonse's critique to ask

Mortimer Adler and Richard McKeon to analyze it for him.[107] In the process of denying promotion and tenure to Gideonse in 1936, he consulted McKeon about the economics department's letter supporting Gideonse; McKeon's recommendations were "chiefly negative."[108] When Gideonse was offered a full professorship in economics at Barnard College in New York, Hutchins refused to match the offer, claiming that the dean of the college (Brumbaugh) and the dean of the social sciences division (Redfield) did not support the promotion.[109] Whether or not that was true, Gideonse believed the issue was one of intellectual differences rather than competence, because William T. Hutchinson was offered (and refused) a full professorship to assume Gideonse's duties in the college.[110] Gideonse went to New York and a year later was appointed president of Brooklyn College.

What do these cases illustrate about Hutchins' relationship to the faculty? In the case of the history department, Hutchins did not think the discipline stood on its own. The department's status and power were limited by its location in two divisions, one of which was controlled by McKeon. In the case of political science, Hutchins disagreed with the department members' scholarly focus and refused to act on promotions. Hutchins' guarded relations with Wirth and his fundamental agreement with Adler's assessment of the discipline of sociology led to little action to promote the department's wishes, until Edward Shils joined the department in the late 1930s and the Committee on Social Thought in the 1940s. Hutchins' complete disregard for the quality of the philosophy faculty's work and judgment left the department without a chair, hence a strong advocate, for thirteen years.

By contrast, education, anthropology, and economics were strong departments, with faculty members widely respected in academia. Were that the only factor in their favor, they might have suffered as some of the other departments did. But these departments had institutional protection, born out of Hutchins' relationships with key people who were in positions that significantly enabled them to influence the scholarship and personnel in the departments: first Judd and then Tyler, chair of education and later dean of the division of social sciences; Redfield, member of a small, but strong, department, as well as dean of the division of social sciences; and Nef, who remained loyal to Hutchins throughout his tenure; Knight, whose intellectual disagreements were tempered by respect for Hutchins (and for whom Hutchins had a sincere liking); and Douglas, whose stature was unquestioned.

There is no doubt that Hutchins appointed people to faculty positions with whom he had fundamental disagreements. Rudolph Carnap is a case in point. Hutchins was no advocate of positivism, but Carnap's appointment was a coup for Hutchins and the university. Ralph Tyler is another example. Tyler's progressive ideas, his commitment to empirical research, and his understanding of social science scholarship made him an unlikely choice for Hutchins. Nevertheless, Hutchins recruited him. Redfield is a further example. His grasp of and adherence to empirical social science were strong. Hutchins left Tyler and Redfield relatively free to shape their departments and divisions. But these social scientists, and Nef can be included here, also shared fundamental agreements with Hutchins about culture, and like him, favored a general, common program in undergraduate education. So, too, did McKeon, whose battles with Hutchins in the 1940s did not entice Hutchins to interfere with McKeon's management of the humanities division and departments.

As Hutchins explained to Adler in 1937, "Being an educational philosopher and running an educational institution are often two incompatible occupations." No matter how duty-bound he felt to state and restate "eternal truths," many of his actions had to be dictated by the need to get "practical results," best reached by arriving at "approximations of eternal truths." Practical results required the appointment not of ideal persons to positions of power but of the best real persons he could find, for the "good" of the university.[111] But this prudence did not extend to accepting the judgment of departmental faculty in history, philosophy, political science, or, in the case of Gideonse, economics.

Some of these people may well not have been superior candidates. But whatever their actual merits, Hutchins' own lack of clarity about what constituted "the best" and his repeated refusals to acknowledge assessments by departments left many faculty members angry and mistrustful of his decisions. Wirth commented in 1938 that there was just cause to make a list of faculty members whose departments' recommendations were "either ignored or overruled by the administration." This action, he suggested, would "dispel the fiction that the democratic processes still prevail" at the university under Hutchins' leadership.[112]

Hutchins' differences of opinion with departments over quality of scholarship and personnel must be viewed within the context of the history of the university. Under Ernest W. Burton, who encouraged strong departments, Max Mason, who also supported the research culture of the university, and acting president Frederic Woodward, the years from 1923 to 1929 had been halcyon years for faculty power, particularly for the sciences and social sciences, but also for history and other humanities disciplines. The Laura Spelman Rockefeller Memorial's support of the Local Community Research Committee for joint research projects was exemplary of that power in the 1920s. Hutchins' behavior, in contrast, restricted departmental autonomy and supplied inadequate leadership in its stead for those departments most negatively affected by his actions.

In the end, these problems of appointment and promotion undercut Hutchins' efforts to redefine the mission of the university. Because they repeatedly had been overruled or ignored, many department members viewed with suspicion every public statement Hutchins made and every administrative change he suggested. By relying on the deans far more than on department chairs and members for assessments of merit, Hutchins neglected to build trust or communication between himself and a significant body of the faculty.

CHAPTER 9 *At Odds with the Faculty: The Mission of the University*

TO ARTICULATE HIS GOALS for the University, Hutchins explained his actions in terms of institutional imperative, institutional survival, and, in the 1940s, moral necessity. The preacher's son could not call on divine law to support his administrative decisions, but moral necessity served his purposes in that era of rising fascism, world war, and then atomic power and destruction, much as economic necessity had sufficed in the 1930s. Hutchins was not a man to question his own convictions. He wrestled instead with how a modern university ought to be led. Much as the college initially had served as a laboratory for his developing theories, so did the university for his developing ideas about the administration of scholarship.

The record of his administration of faculty appointments, promotions, and tenure, which he explained in part as Depression measures, brought the university under investigation by the American Association of University Professors (AAUP) in the late 1930s. In the end, he interpreted the investigation as a personal affront to his integrity. The debate about his proposals for administering the university came to a head in the early 1940s when he presented the faculty senate and board of trustees with a fundamentally revised blueprint for administering power and control over educational policy, for decisions about faculty, and for defining the mission of the university. When the faculty rebelled, the university entered a period of crisis. The compromise reached gave him better defined powers over educational policy and the title of chancellor of the university, but left everyone bruised.

From the appointment of Mortimer Adler to the philosophy department to the controversies over the college and the ongoing antagonism from many on the faculty, no one at the University of Chicago held a neutral opinion of Hutchins. And because the university neighborhood still bore the characteristics of a small town, comments and behavior that might have passed unnoticed in a larger institution escalated to major proportions in the community. Any public statement from Hutchins was sure to arouse someone's ire. His relations with the faculty have to be viewed with that caveat in mind. Nevertheless, his administrative style was not to consult the faculty but to rely on the deans for advice. Much to many faculty members' dismay, by the 1940s the deans were in agreement with many of his educational and administrative ideas about the organization and mission of the university.

Hutchins' action (or inaction) over personnel decisions was not the only factor contributing to faculty members' suspicion of his administration. He published *The Higher Learning in America* in 1936, in which he argued for the centrality of metaphysics in the university's work. He suggested that knowledge was not best generated by forming a theory and testing it against the data or, conversely, using empirical research to generate theory. Instead, the principles of a field of academic knowledge should first be determined and ordered in importance, preferably by metaphysicians in communication with other scholars.[1] The implication was that one group of scholars would make judgments about the importance of the work of all other scholars in the university. This suggestion was threatening because the president's closest friend on campus was not only a self-proclaimed philosopher but also a severe critic of the claims to validity (and authority) of the social sciences in the university.[2]

The social science scholars at the University of Chicago, for instance, were concerned with processes–social, political, historical, intellectual, cultural. Louis Wirth studied group action and interaction in an urban context to gain a better understanding of urban life and, ultimately, of modern man. Harold Lasswell focused on the development and shaping of political values, using Freudian theory and social theory to inform his work. Harold Gosnell studied political behavior and political relations between groups. William T. Hutchinson, Louis Gottschalk, Bessie Pierce, and their colleagues were concerned with a variety of processes occurring within particular time periods and contexts. Charles Morris' and Charner Perry's work was strongly influenced by pragmatism and its place in American philosophy. And Redfield and his colleagues analyzed cultural processes in many different contexts.

Redfield, responding to Hutchins' argument that the formulation of principles should precede empirical investigation, captured the difference in conceptions of scholarship between the scholars and the president. Intellectual activity, he suggested, proceeded neither from "the most recent observations to first principles" nor from "first principles to . . . recent observations." Rather, scholars engaged in research experienced "a constant interaction between principles (concepts) and empirical data."[3] The concepts Redfield described were not derived logically from metaphysical postulates but from the formulations that took their meaning from the theoretical work of the discipline.

University of Chicago scholars were inescapably conscious of the explosion of knowledge accompanying the expansion and development of the modern university in the twentieth century. They daily were challenged by the problem of keeping up with work in their own fields. As the disciplinary and interdisciplinary cooperative work of the Local Community Research Committee of the 1920s and early 1930s shows, they saw a clear relationship between the growing complexity of modern society and the knowledge necessary for understanding and managing it.[4]

By contrast, Hutchins concluded that the work of the modern university ought to focus on the principled construction of theory, primarily through the use of reason, to determine the significance and guide the exploration of research problems. His belief represented an antiprogressive, scholastic need to construct or locate a structure of knowledge that would unify the theoretical work of the university, unpolluted by the demands of the practical world. His Aristotelian emphasis on metaphysics delineated an institutional model that, in theory, was clean, rational, and easily discerned and explained. Hutchins did not attempt a complicated, messy struggle with the fundamental epistemological issues and methodological problems in developing knowledge of the modern world, with all of its contradictions, ambiguities, and unpredictable and evolving results. Instead, he settled on metaphysics or philosophy to order the disciplines in the ideal university he presented in *The Higher Learning in America.*

Many reviewers of *The Higher Learning* noted that Hutchins displayed an eloquent perception of the problems of the modern university, even as they disagreed with his proposed solutions.[5] His suggestion that too many policies were guided by "the love of money," including the university's accommodation of practices to the wishes of donors, students, and state legislatures instead of its own self-defined mission, was recognizable to anyone involved with higher education.[6] The tension he articulated between the research and teaching functions of the university was equally familiar. He described the problem of determining the intellectual mission of the university in a democratic capitalist society, where educational attainment correlated with social and economic opportunity. Overemphasis on professional and vocational training in light of this context, he thought, might well lead to a consequent undervaluing of intellectual development, though that speculation was not supported with evidence. Finally, he described the disciplinary isolation and fragmentation resulting from both the pressure for professional studies and the growth of new knowledge that developed out of scholars' research interests and the needs of modern society.

Hutchins' perception of the modern university was marked in 1936 with an inability to construct complex institutional approaches to solving the problems he so eloquently framed, at least in part because his analysis of them lacked deep and extensive engagement. Rather, his analysis was framed in his ongoing discussions with Adler. Interestingly, there were echoes of Oberlin College in his proposals, which is one of the keys to why Adler's ideas held such appeal for Hutchins. Agreement about what was fundamental and significant, shared beliefs about truth, and even the need to locate or create a unified structure of knowledge were implicit in his *Higher Learning,* and framed his educational experience in the evangelical and progressive culture of Oberlin. But his proposals ran directly counter to the ethos and diversity of experience guiding the scholarly work and teaching of many of the faculty of the University of Chicago.

The faculty were understandably suspicious of his effort to impose unity by using metaphysics to "restore" intellectual integrity to, and eliminate the "disorder" of, the work of the university. Metaphysics, he proposed, would establish a "hierarchy of truths" to indicate "which are fundamental and which subsidiary, which significant and which not." Metaphysics, a secular substitute for the theology of the medieval university, would have subordinate to it the empirically oriented work of the sciences and social sciences and would pervade the whole of the university. Scholarship based on empirical research would be encouraged only insofar as one could proceed from metaphysical "first principles to whatever recent observations were significant in understanding them." Unless professors were concerned with "fundamental problems" in metaphysics, natural sciences, humanities, or social sciences, their research ought to be consigned to technical institutes rather than universities proper.[7]

Faculty members at the University of Chicago found his orderly design to be drastically at odds with their own conceptions of their work. It showed little tolerance for uncertainty and no understanding of the ways research actually proceeded in any of the academic disciplines in the modern university. They were quite fearful that Hutchins would use this plan to guide his decisions about appointment and promotion, the relationship between graduate and undergraduate education, and other factors affecting the distribution of resources in the university. The faculty's reaction to the establishment of the Committee on the Liberal Arts and the appointments of Adler's friends Arthur Rubin, Scott Buchanan, and Stringfellow Barr to the committee within the humanities division (using private money that Hutchins had raised for the purpose) was a measure of this fear.

When the announcement was made about the formation of the committee in the spring of 1936, the senate committee on policy and personnel and the humanities division faculty requested that any appointments anywhere in the university outside departments or schools that were recommended by the president be approved by the divisional faculty and that any recommended by the faculty be subject to approval by the president.[8] All recommendations for appointment to divisions, the college, or the university at large, in other words, would be counterbalanced by the approval of either the president or the corresponding faculty, depending on where the recommendation originated.

A few months later, the humanities division passed a resolution reaffirming the function of its committee on policy: to discuss and formulate with the university administration all matters of curriculum "as are by statute placed within the final control of this Faculty."[9] As McKeon pointed out to Hutchins in the spring of 1937, the Committee on the Liberal Arts, although technically located in the division and focused on "inquiries into the nature and division of Humanistic studies," actually was more general in purpose. Further, it was composed mostly of people outside the division's staff.[10] In the end, the humanities division's committee on policy supported McKeon's decision to resign from the Committee on the Liberal Arts, to remove it from the division, and to place it under the purview of the president's office. The strength of the faculty's suspicions was such that McKeon announced the decision to the senate rather than risk further controversy by consulting the senate's committee on policy about the decision.[11]

Disturbed by the faculty reaction to *The Higher Learning* and the Committee on the Liberal Arts, Hutchins consulted with Adler. Adler advised him that much of his argument about philosophy in *The Higher Learning* had been misunderstood not only by the Chicago faculty but also by other university faculty members. Adler suggested that Hutchins make a clear distinction between science and philosophy, or "knowledge and wisdom," in his speech at the annual trustees' dinner for the faculty in 1937.[12]

Hutchins followed his advice. He stated that, while all knowledge "develops from experience by reflection," scientific knowledge depends on directed observations under controlled conditions. He was less clear on exactly what philosophical knowledge was: "knowledge" that "extends the boundaries" of "reflections about ordinary experience" by inquiring into the principles guiding all behavior. He attempted to convince the faculty that his argument about the place of philosophy in the university was less threatening than they thought. Of the fifteen new appointments for the 1937–38 academic year, twelve were in the natural sciences. "We all have a philosophy or metaphysics, whether we know it or not," he told them. The issue was not "that we should all have the same views on basic questions" or "that we should agree on what questions are basic." Instead, the faculty should "have a common acquaintance with ideas that can seriously pretend to be basic," which would provide for "the ideal of a university [that] is an understood diversity."[13]

As Adler later wrote him, the speech did not reassure the faculty and, unless Hutchins devoted more time to developing a clear argument about the role of philosophy in the intellectual life of the modern university and stated unequivocally which philosophy or metaphysics he avowed, "everyone" would be left "with the suspicion" that Hutchins meant "Aristotelianism or something like it."[14] Whether the faculty was truly suspicious that Hutchins planned to impose a particular system of belief on the university is unclear. What is clear is that the faculty suspected him of wanting to impose his standards and values on the intellectual life of the University of Chicago without consulting them.

The tenor of his speeches and books, his close relationship with Adler, and the pattern of his behavior with respect to appointments and promotions in combination were enough of a threat for the faculty to request an investigation of the appointment and promotion practices of the university. The American Association of University Professors agreed that a committee chosen by the University of Chicago chapter should conduct the investigation. Two reports resulted in 1938, one exploring academic tenure and the other the organization of departments. Each made recommendations for changing policies and practices to protect the faculty's decision-making power with respect to educational policy within the university.

The report of the committee on academic tenure showed the members' perceptions of problems in the delegation of power and control among the actors: the president, the deans, and the department chairs and members. The "conflict of authority" the committee found was attributed to a range of factors, including "vagueness" of standards in evaluating staff, particularly when the president and departments disagreed.[15] This conclusion was not unmerited, as one discussion between Redfield and Hutchins about a candidate reveals. Redfield had highly recommended a candidate for sociology and, in the end, accepted Hutchins' judgment against the candidate, but did not understand it. Hutchins suggested the man was "a thoroughly conventional boy on the make" who had produced "large volumes of . . . inferior stuff," was likely to offer "no leadership and no new ideas," and would probably "go along with the Division in an uncritical fashion."[16] Hutchins did not reveal why he thought the person's work "inferior." But in his president's report to the trustees in 1937, he explained that he had not been making appointments "unless it was necessary" or unless a candidate "was distinguished or promised to be."[17]

The committee on tenure explored the historical context of the faculty's concern about the president's power. The appointment of Adler to philosophy and the attempt to bring in Buchanan inspired the election of policy committees in some of the divisions. The president's ultimate power of appointment to the divisions, the college, and the university at large increased his control, whether or not he chose to exercise it. Finally, the freedom to debate educational policy issues and ideas within the university was threatened if the president attempted to translate his particular ideas into policy through faculty appointments while the policies were still under debate, an obvious allusion to the Committee on the Liberal Arts.

The committee found startling results of the Depression measure to suspend new tenured appointments in 1931. The overall picture of faculty ranking changed markedly in the 1930s. From 1929 to 1930, full professorships increased by just over 10 percent while instructorships and research associate positions increased by 54 percent. By 1936–37, three-fifths of the faculty were "on the probationary level of the youngest recruits."[18] Accordingly, the committee recommended increasing the proportion of tenured appointments to ensure a better balance of power between the faculty and the president in debates over educational policy.

Other recommendations included explicit recognition within the university statutes of the faculty's responsibility to participate in appointment, promotion, and termination decisions; a method of reviewing such cases in which differences between the faculty and the president could not be resolved; resumption of the practice of annual publication of appointments, promotions, and terminations (which had been discontinued because of the cost); protection of the faculty from repeated short-term appointments; and clear, well-formulated standards for promotion, tenure, and termination, to be used in all cases and to be explained to every faculty member judged by them. The committee on departmental organization recommended more systematic procedures for assessing candidates for appointment and promotion within all departments, based on its findings that procedures within departments ranged from systematic, recorded practices to casual conversations about the decisions.[19]

Hutchins' response to both reports was indicative of his unwillingness, or inability, to view the faculty as his colleagues in determining the mission of the university. He found a number of "objectionable" statements in the report, recommendations that he thought "impossible" to act on, and contrary perceptions of the history of the university and his activities as president.[20] He presented the reports, as requested, to the faculty senate, which voted to ask the senate committee on university policy to investigate the questions. But he informed the trustees that the tenure report was "disingenuous and inaccurate" while the departmental organization report was "insignificant." Moreover, he found none of the recommendations of either report "worth adopting."[21]

Hutchins took this opportunity to explore some of the problems he perceived in the organization of the university. The faculty, he noted, was "in sole control of education." The president had no jurisdiction over student admissions, curriculum, examinations, or degrees. The senate was too large to manage policy efficiently, and the senate committee on university policy, far from being representative of the whole faculty, operated on a "ward basis," protecting divisional interests. Because university faculties were "notoriously hostile to change," any reforms the president hoped to introduce were limited by his ability "to persuade the faculty to accept his view of persons and policies."[22] Despite his seeming responsibility, the president's only real power was the privilege of persuasion.

This power extended to the appointment of deans and chairs, recommendations of faculty appointments, and budgetary and salary decisions. But in practice, he argued, all those decisions were made in consultation with the deans, chairs, and faculty members. The president was most able to persuade when conditions of financial stability allowed for expansion of faculty, departments, and schools in the university. However, even if the university had the ability to expand, he did not recommend such a course. Rather, "the problem of the University of Chicago [was] one of integration," improving what it had, making sense of its programs, eliminating "entangling alliances," and reducing the number of courses, faculty, departments, and schools.[23]

Hutchins' perception of the role of the president in relation to the faculty and of the needs of the university in 1938 was markedly at odds with the faculty's. As the AAUP report and the senate's vote to investigate its findings indicate, members of the faculty thought that they were best equipped to determine educational policies and to shape the organization of scholarship at the University of Chicago. Vested interest alone did not lead them to believe that this was the case. Their ongoing responsibilities for teaching their disciplines, their intimate contact with the problems of research, and their understanding of the continual expansion of knowledge in each academic discipline informed their vision of the university and its responsibilities to students, faculty, and the larger community.

By contrast, Hutchins perceived the president as the one person in the institution who was able to see "the university as a whole." The growth of American universities in the twentieth century made it impossible for members of the faculty to know them whole or to "pass intelligently on the problems of any part" of them. The traditional organization of the university may be "ineffective" as a result of expansion over the previous forty years. "The problem," Hutchins ventured, was how to protect the faculty's academic freedom "and at the same time eliminate or minimize mediocrity and advance an educational program." Because the board of trustees had "protected the faculty admirably" during the Depression, Hutchins found "the problems of eliminating mediocrity and getting something done" to be "much more pressing than that of protecting the faculty."[24]

In 1939 Hutchins presented anew his vision of the university's mission, placing it in the context of the rise of nazism and fascism in Europe. It would be "inadequate" simply to specify the university as "a place of education and research," or a community of scholars, without determining the ends of these activities or clarifying the significance of each scholar's work in relation to others'. "The pursuit of knowledge for its own sake" did not suffice if academic knowledge continued to be sought along narrow lines of specialization. Rather, the university "should symbolize the highest powers of man," manifest in human reason and will. Rationality, the characteristic by which humans were distinguished from animals, ought to determine the standards of "education, research, and university policy." The organization of the university should reflect this rationality, because democracy, unlike fascism or Marxism, rested on a belief in the power of reason and assumed that the exercise of reason and will would enlighten and discipline communities to achieve the common good.[25]

The two subcommittees of the senate committee on university policy met with Hutchins throughout 1939. In 1939 the committee on departmental organization presented a number of recommendations for modifying the statutes to require more systematic procedures in divisions, departments, and schools. A survey taken by the committee indicated that a majority of the faculty who responded favored more participatory practices than the statutes allowed in decision-making processes involving the appointments of deans and chairs and in the determination of educational policies in committees, divisions, and departments. A significant portion of the faculty surveyed agreed with Hutchins' practice of consulting departments about appointments (though the statutes did not require such consultation), and additional respondents thought the practice should be more specifically defined.[26]

In 1940 the committee on tenure submitted recommendations for modifying the statutes in two notable ways. The first was to clarify the procedure for the appointment of deans, including the election of a committee to consult with the faculty and the president, to make a list of candidates, and to confer with the president about his list before nominating a candidate to the board of trustees for a five-year term. The second modification was a procedure for making appointments and promotions, including no more than four one-year appointments for instructors, two three-year appointments for assistant professors, and indefinite tenure for associate and full professors.[27] The senate voted to recommend the changes to the trustees, and in July of 1940 the trustees approved them.[28]

With the United States' entry into the war in 1941, the faculty rallied behind Hutchins' call for the university to devote whatever was necessary to the cause.[29] But when he submitted a plan to the trustees for an administrative reorganization and continued to proffer a mission for the university with which the faculty could not agree, the conflict became more heated than any in the 1930s.

He offered two alternative proposals, based on the problems he had outlined in his annual report of 1939. Both were premised on his view that the authority of the president was "slight and his responsibility great." The first suggested the president's responsibilities should be reduced, his title changed to chairman of the faculty, and his administrative duties dispersed among faculty members.[30] The first proposal did not figure in subsequent discussions, presumably because, however logical Hutchins found it, the trustees and faculty considered it impractical. The second proposal, which he developed on his own but revised in consultation with the deans and administrative officers, suggested thoroughly overhauling the statutes to redistribute power and responsibility for the administration of teaching and scholarship.[31]

Increasing the president's "authority commensurate with his responsibility," Hutchins thought, could be accomplished by giving him control over "the educational and scholarly work of the University, its course of study, publications, appointments to its faculty, and all other matters relating" to education and research. By contrast, a reduced (from fifteen members to five), elected senate committee would advise the president on university policy. The remaining senate members' power would be limited to stating their lack of confidence in the president if they found his policies unacceptable, which would then require the president to offer his resignation to the board. The board of trustees would be compelled to accept it in the event that a two-thirds majority of the senate so voted in two consecutive meetings. The board also would have to examine the situation whenever 5 percent of the faculty asked the trustees to remove the president. Deans were to be appointed by the president on the advice of an elected faculty committee and were to be subject to the same rules of resignation as the president.[32]

The trustees agreed to Hutchins' request for the senate to elect a committee of seven to consult with a committee of board members on the proposals. The board's committee on instruction and research was headed by Laird Bell. Bell had informed Hutchins that he found the second proposal flawed. Hutchins not only was unrealistic to expect "academic men of the highest calibre" to accede to sacrificing "a measure of autonomy in their departments and schools" but also was subjecting himself "to the charge that" he was "seeking dictatorial powers" by not offering more checks and balances.[33]

The faculty's committee on academic reorganization included Leonard D. White (political science), Fay-Cooper Cole (anthropology), Ernst W. Puttkammer (law), Paul C. Hodges (medicine), and others, some of the most respected members of the faculty, none of whom was considered a particular ally of Hutchins. Neither committee agreed with Hutchins' alternatives for organizing the university. The board committee rejected an alternative proposal by the senate committee, and both committees agreed in 1944 to continue to work on a plan acceptable to the president and the faculty.

The discussions might well have proceeded in this orderly fashion had Hutchins not fanned the flames with additional proposals to the board and numerous speeches in support of them. In *Education for Freedom* (1943), for example, he argued that the preservation of democracy required the cultivation of free minds, disciplined by reason through exposure to the liberal arts and the great books. The construction of the good life and the good society depended on universities' offering study and research in metaphysics, ethics, and politics "to determine the good and the order of goods." Of all systems of government, only democracy had as its end "the good for man." The war had plunged the world into a "great moral, intellectual, and spiritual crisis." The university's responsibility was to supply Americans with "the moral courage, the intellectual clarity, and the spiritual elevation" to "uphold them in this critical hour." Pioneering "on the new frontiers of research" was an obvious means of doing so, but, more important, the university could provide "candid and intrepid thinking about fundamental issues" to "formulate, to clarify, to vitalize the ideals which should animate mankind."[34]

In January of 1944 he informed the faculty that "the purpose of the University is nothing less than to procure a moral, intellectual, and spiritual revolution throughout the world" by reversing "the whole scale of values by which our society lives." A practical step in this direction would be to create "a democratic and effective academic community." This could be accomplished by abolishing "the farce of academic rank," which guaranteed "division and disappointment in the faculty." Another means was to place all faculty members on a full-time basis, raise their salaries, and require that all outside earnings be turned over to the university. In addition, professors should be paid what they needed in order to live, but relative salaries within the university should be determined by such needs as the size of one's family. Finally, he suggested that to fulfill this role the university might have to establish an Institute of Liberal Studies to educate teachers of the liberal arts and award them Ph.D.'s. Those scholars trained in research could receive, instead, doctorates of science or of letters.[35]

Hutchins' formal proposals for reorganization and his speeches about the aims of the university and how they might be reached would probably have inspired some debate within the faculty, but not necessarily the controversy that arose in 1944. Like the investigation of appointment and tenure practices, the 1944 faculty memorial to the board of trustees was fueled by Hutchins' behavior. Redistributing power in the university or abolishing rank or establishing the institute without consulting the faculty looked like more than mere possibilities, particularly when the trustees decided in early 1944 (without consulting the faculty senate) to raise salaries and require that faculty members return to the university their outside earnings.

The memorial controversy began with an exchange of letters between Hutchins and an informal group of six faculty members, Jacob Viner, Ronald S. Crane, Avery O. Craven, E. J. Kraus, Sewall Wright, and Frank H. Knight. These six burghers, as they were called, had grown increasingly disturbed with Hutchins' pronouncements in light of his past record, his reorganization plan, and the policy changes that had occurred as a result of his actions. They expressed frank reservations about a "crusade" that seemed to require the faculty to adhere "to a particular analysis of what is wrong with the world" and then "to a particular hierarchy of moral and intellectual values" with "a philosophically unified program of academic studies."[36] They also requested that no changes in program or degrees occur without senate deliberation and vote. Hutchins assured them that he had no intention of violating the statutes. Despite the power the statutes had accorded him to recommend to the board the founding of any new school without the approval of the senate, he reminded them, he had not done so.[37]

Viner and his colleagues thought Hutchins was not really addressing their concerns about committing the university to a particular doctrine in view of his proposal to increase the president's powers and decrease the faculty's.[38] In response, Hutchins contended that he planned to proceed, as he had in the past, outlining his "general program" to the faculty and taking steps toward its "realization" whenever it seemed "wise" to do so. "Where it is judicious to consult the faculty," he promised, "it will be consulted."[39] Not surprisingly, the six burghers did not find Hutchins' terse response reassuring. At the request of the senate committee on policy a few weeks later, Hutchins stated his views on the reorganization. He described his proposals and volunteered to hold them "in abeyance" and engage in a cooperative effort with the faculty to arrive at a more "democratic and efficient" means of administering the university.[40]

By then, though, Viner and Crane had circulated among members of the faculty a memorial, signed by 120 members. The memorial stated that the signers welcomed change to enliven the organization of the university and recognized the obligation of the university to participate in moral, intellectual, and spiritual improvement of the modern world. But they balked at allowing anyone (for example, an administrator) not experienced in teaching and research to determine degree requirements or programs. And they objected to any particular ideological commitment on the part of the whole university to the pursuit of these activities. In effect, the memorial asked the board of trustees to assure the senate and the faculty "that the University will not be officially committed to any 'purpose' which would tend to subordinate, in reality or in appearance, its essential activities and programs, and the free choice of principles and methods of research and teaching, to any particular formulation of moral, social, philosophical, or scientific values."[41]

After much discussion, the senate voted to request Hutchins to transmit the memorial to the board, on the understanding that the vote in no way implied "raising a question of confidence in the President."[42] In response, Wilber Katz (of the Law School) and John Nef circulated a petition in support of Hutchins' record of protecting academic freedom and his courageous leadership of the university, and received the signatures of seventy-six members of the faculty.[43] The trustees accepted the memorial, acknowledging the "misunderstandings" that had arisen, but reiterated the university's and the president's commitment to academic freedom, the board's confidence in the president, and the need for developing better means of cooperation between faculty, board, and president.[44]

In July, Hutchins issued a statement called "The Organization and Purpose of the University" in an effort to clarify his reorganization proposals, to show the consistency of his thinking over the previous fifteen years, and, once again, to defend his stand on the purpose of the modern university.[45] The controversy and its resolution left him discouraged, almost bitter. He could not understand the criticisms of his presidency that the senate committee members raised in meetings, including the suggestion that his statements dismayed the faculty, that he had not promoted scientific research, and that he did not collaborate enough with faculty on appointments and promotion. In the fall, he offered to resign to assist in implementing the new organization but withdrew the offer when board members protested.[46]

In December the trustee committee on instruction and research, in consultation with the senate committee on academic reorganization, presented the board with its recommendations. To provide for the presentation of views and, at the same time, encourage the consideration of programs and policies that would best use the university's resources, the trustees offered a number of suggestions. These included enlarging the senate to incorporate all full-time faculty in residence for at least three years; electing a forty-member senate council to deliberate with members of the administration on educational matters and to take action on them;

establishing a seven-member executive committee of this council to confer with the president; holding regular meetings of both groups with the president; and instituting presidential veto power over council actions, with provisions for the council to resubmit the action and the board to make a final ruling if the president and council could not agree.[47] This last provision was used in the case of the B.A. degree in the college in 1946 and worked well to balance the power of the president with the power of the faculty.

Upon reflection, one might argue that the memorial was an extreme and unfounded response to Hutchins' speeches and proposals. Certainly those faculty members who most consistently supported him made this argument at the time.[48] Ralph Tyler, for example, has stated that Hutchins encouraged Tyler's educational ideas and programs, provided his arguments for them were reasonable, and that he presented all his proposals to the deans for discussion and advice prior to making them public.[49] Yet, according to a Rockefeller Foundation official who spoke with Robert Redfield in April 1944, Redfield's assessment of the controversy suggested that Hutchins had no understanding of politics or of irrational motives. He expressed his ideas "in a way best calculated to evoke opposition." Redfield agreed with Hutchins' ends but found his methods objectionable.[50]

Louis Wirth, on the other hand, noted at the time the flaws in Hutchins' premise that the university's organization prior to 1944 hobbled institutional change. Curricular experiments laying the groundwork for the new plan for the college had been carried out by departmental faculty members across disciplines in the late 1920s. The work of its departments and commitment to modern scholarship, he argued, had placed the university among the preeminent research institutions in the United States. Finally, Hutchins' claim that only the president could see the university as a whole was overblown. The expansion of knowledge, reflected in the university's "widespread fields of investigation" and in the demands of training future leaders, required strong departments with chairs knowledgeable about their fields and a president who devoted "his efforts to the creation of an environment which will encourage and reward creative scholarship, research, and teaching."[51]

One member of the faculty, with whom Hutchins previously had fairly good relations, appears to have been both victim and perpetrator in this struggle. Richard McKeon, in pursuit of his own program in the division of the humanities, had undermined a number of departments by not appointing strong chairs and by refusing to approve departmental choices for appointments and promotions. Hutchins respected McKeon's intellect and his contributions to the college program and past support of his own ideas. But he had strong reservations about his judgment in choosing faculty (particularly Antonio Borgese in romance languages and Rudolph Carnap in philosophy) and department chairs. He believed that McKeon had betrayed him in 1944 by "participating in the organization of a clique against him."[52]

The faculty memorial, he thought, resulted because McKeon encouraged Ronald Crane to pursue it. Rather than confronting Hutchins in deans' meetings about the administrative reorganization and the Institute of Liberal Studies idea, McKeon had given "aid and comfort . . . to those who were out to thwart [Hutchins'] hopes and plans." Hutchins preferred that McKeon "fight [him] hard to [his] face or in Deans' meetings but accept the decision without rancor."[53]

Whether McKeon or anyone else could have altered fundamentally Hutchins' perception of himself as the moral and intellectual leader of the University of Chicago is a moot question. McKeon apparently thought he could not within the forum of the deans' meetings with the president. Clarence Faust remembered that it was difficult to summon the courage to disagree with Hutchins but that he usually received support when he did.[54] A more accurate measure of the faculty's skepticism of his power is the senate election of its committee on university policy. Every member elected from the divisions in November of 1944 had opposed Hutchins.[55]

Arguing that the administration of the university had grown more complex during his presidency, Hutchins proposed to the board a new position, that of chancellor of the university. The board created the Office of Central Administration (OCA), consisting of the chancellor, chief executive officer of the university; the president, educational administrator of the university to share responsibility with the chancellor; vice-president and dean of the faculties; vice-president in charge of business affairs; vice-president in charge of development; and assistant to the chancellor. Deliberately emulating corporate organization, the OCA represented a top-heavy administrative structure, as Hutchins told the faculty, in part to enable "direct communication between the faculty and the chief executive."[56] Ironically, though, matters of faculty concern, including recommendations for appointments and promotion and departmental budgets, were handled first by other officers, in effect creating a thicker layer of administration between Hutchins and the faculty.

In 1949 Hutchins again was called to protect the faculty's academic freedom from outsiders. As other historians and social scientists have shown, the period from the late 1940s into the 1950s was a time of trial for American universities.[57] Students and faculty members on campuses across the country continued to engage in political activity, including campus Communist clubs after World War II. Colleges and universities increased suppression of such activity on their campuses, particularly after the Truman administration created the federal loyalty-security program to ensure no subversive activities among government employees and began to prosecute known leaders of the Communist party under the Smith Act. State legislatures also formed committees and commissions to investigate what they believed to be subversive activities. Illinois named its investigative unit the Broyles Commission after its leading member.

Organized in 1947, the Broyles Commission covertly sought signs of seditious activity on campuses throughout the state. In 1949 the commission introduced a set of bills to deal more explicitly with offending parties. The bills contained provisions requiring loyalty oaths by teachers and other public employees and denying employment to anyone affiliated with Communist organizations or Communist front organizations, or with any agency threatening the overthrow of the government.[58] Angered that the bills were to be considered at a little publicized meeting of the legislature, University of Chicago and Roosevelt College students and other concerned individuals held a noisy protest on the day the bills were introduced in Springfield, Illinois. The protest was taken to the streets of Springfield and grew into a civil rights demonstration, with black and white students integrating a segregated lunch counter in a local drugstore.[59]

The following day, the Illinois House of Representatives authorized the commission to initiate a public investigation of the University of Chicago and Roosevelt College. The hearings took place in April and May of 1949. Hutchins made the opening statement for the university. Protesting against any policy of repression of ideas, he informed the commission that it was highly unlikely that the capitalist businessmen who made up the board of trustees would sanction subversive activities on the campus. Defending the faculty as "one of the most distinguished in the world," he argued that it was possible to protest fascism and racism without "desiring to subvert the government." The students, he suggested, possessed inalienable rights "as American citizens to protest against pending legislation" that they disapproved. They may have been "impolite," he noted, but "rudeness and Redness are not the same."[60]

Hutchins not only courageously defended the First Amendment

rights of faculty and students in the university but also reminded the questioner of proper legal procedure. To the delight of those who heard his testimony, he skillfully demonstrated the absurdity of the proceedings. Questioned about an emeritus professor of the Medical School, Maud Slye, Hutchins explained that her research had involved using mice in the study of cancer. Pressed about her various affiliations with organizations and her continuing pension from the university, Hutchins avowed that her associations on campus were confined to mice. When asked if she had not perhaps engaged in "indoctrination by example," Hutchins' incredulous response, "Of mice?" brought down the house.[61]

In his closing statement to the commission, Hutchins informed the members that "the University does not subscribe to the doctrine of guilt by association . . . the University believes that if a man is to be punished he should be punished for what he does and not for what he has belonged to or for those with whom he has associated." Unable to resist using the stand as a pulpit, and perhaps thinking that he could appeal to their Christianity, he reminded the commission "of the words of scripture: 'He consorted with publicans and sinners, therefore He is guilty.' "[62] In the end, with two dissensions, the commission recommended a variety of actions to control subversive activities on campuses but had so little evidence of such activities that the legislature refused to vote more money to the commission and Governor Adlai Stevenson vetoed the bills.

Hutchins' defense of the university constitutes "perhaps the most signal deliverance on the principles of academic freedom" made to a political investigating body, according to Robert M. MacIver.[63] Although an apparently conservative position on First Amendment rights, much like his position in 1927 on the Sacco-Vanzetti case with respect to guilt by association, this stand appeared radical in the context of the late 1940s. Ellen Schrecker's penetrating study of the era illustrates how American universities' acquiescence to state and federal pressure to institute loyalty oaths (at the University of California, for example) or to fire faculty members who were Communists or former Communists (at the University of Washington, for example) set the stage for purging faculty members for their political beliefs from institutions all over the country in the 1950s. Hutchins' stand set a different precedent for the state of Illinois and the University of Chicago.[64]

How can Hutchins' vigorous defense of academic freedom from public assault be explained in light of his persistent refusal to cooperate with the faculty in their efforts to define the educational and research mission of the University of Chicago? As many who knew or worked under Hutchins noted, he seemed in many ways unsuited to lead a modern university.[65] Despite his impressive bearing, his urbanity, and his astonishingly quick mind, he simply did not deal well with the University of Chicago and its complicated milieu. He chose instead to crusade for a vision of a unified intellectual community, modeled on the idealized and simplistic notion of Greek and medieval intellectual life to which Adler had introduced him in the early 1930s and that he reconstructed out of his own ordered interpretation of the great books.

His frustration at his inability to communicate this vision and at the faculty's refusal to share it is evident in an essay he entitled "The Administrator." Having "no way to win," since every decision he made would be bound to raise someone's ire, the administrator should continue to manifest "courage, fortitude, justice and prudence." He suggested that a lack of courage and fortitude, for example, would be evident if an administrator appointed "committees to advise him" about appointments rather than taking responsibility for the decisions himself. Finally, it was the administrator's responsibility to be a "troublemaker." He had to "accept a special responsibility for the discovery, clarification, definition, and proclamation" of the university's aims, to "get others to join him in the search," to promote "a continuous discussion of the mission and destiny of the institution," and to order the means to achieve that end.[66]

The faculty's perception of Hutchins was fraught with ambivalence. James Webber Linn, who loved and admired Hutchins, urged him in 1938 to explain clearly to the faculty how his educational ideas and programs related to the processes of tenure, appointment, and promotion at the university. If he did not, he was bound to be misinterpreted.[67] George K. K. Link, the professor of botany who had headed the AAUP tenure committee, had advised Hutchins to initiate contact with faculty members, to discuss their work and ideas with them, rather than simply to urge them to come to the president's office to talk with him.[68]

William T. Hutchinson thought that Hutchins should have proposed "*definite* goals" and "methods" to the faculty, using tact and bringing the members of the senate into his confidence, during the memorial controversy. After attending a Hutchins oration in 1948, Hutchinson observed, "He is magical as a speaker, even if one doesn't agree with him." A few years later, he concluded that Hutchins was "fundamentally a preacher-evangelist, who, however compelling in his appearance, thought, and speech, can never even imagine that he may be in error on any issue of importance."[69] T. V. Smith concurred in this estimation. When Hutchins made up his mind, Smith recalled, he was "incautious and . . . arrogant." By surrounding himself with "a coterie of men" equally unwilling to admit their ignorance on any topic, Hutchins increased the difficulty of communicating with him.[70]

The problem was compounded by those very qualities about which James Rowland Angell had warned the trustees in 1929. Hutchins' was a cool and distant personality, particularly with those whom he did not know well or trust. Partly a product of his position—his privacy in that close community was guarded—and partly a product of his personality, the distance was difficult to breach for those who did not know him well. Moreover, it was shaded, in their perceptions, by his public persona—forceful, confident, full of conviction, occasionally arrogant and impatient.

If Hutchins had held social gatherings beyond the annual New Year's tea at the president's house or had lunched more often at the Quadrangle Club, there might have been greater opportunity for the kind of casual conversation necessary to close the distance. But Maude Hutchins made it very plain when she arrived in 1929 that she would not serve as a hostess to the faculty, except at the annual New Year's tea. This decision was intended to protect her professional and personal life; given the demands on Hutchins and the public nature of their lives, it is understandable. And he supported her in this effort to shield their family. However, she began in the middle 1930s to protest Hutchins' frequent university engagements, talking to alumni, meeting with faculty members, lunching downtown with individual trustees, and attending trustee functions, particularly in the evenings and on weekends.

Her attitude became increasingly demanding and abrasive. The scrutiny of the university community probably exacerbated her problems. She was outspoken in her opinions, and her quick tongue often offended trustees and faculty members with whom the Hutchinses socialized.[71] One year she humiliated her daughter Franja and appalled the community by adorning their annual Christmas card with a nude line drawing of her.[72] She made it plain that she had no interest in enhancing Hutchins' social relationships with faculty, administrators, or Chicago's captains of industry. In the end, her behavior severely restricted his ability to mingle casually in the university community.

Despite these problems, her beauty, wit, and intelligence continued to captivate Hutchins. When she began to have attacks of nerves that, she contended, required extended stays in one of the university hospitals, he left the children with a babysitter and shared steak and wine dinners with her in the hospital.[73] When she requested summer trips to Europe to spend time with him away from the university, he accompanied her, trying to conduct whatever business he could abroad, often leaving the children with his parents or with their nanny at Harold Swift's estate on Lake Michigan. When she traveled to Florida or, more often, to Arizona in the winter and spring to rest, he spent a week or two with her. The Committee on the Liberal Arts controversy broke while he was in Arizona in the spring of 1936.

In the early 1940s Maude's obsession with him and her unpredictable behavior in public increased. The strain within the family also grew: Franja, Joanna, and Clarissa (born in 1942) were required to stay quiet and amuse themselves when Maude demanded their father's attention.[74] Hutchins faced confrontations and threats nearly every time he tried to leave the house, sometimes so vehement that he asked others to substitute at meetings and speaking engagements for him.[75]

Whether Maude Hutchins' behavior can be attributed to the stress of maintaining a career and an identity in an era when women were expected to devote themselves to family and good works in the community is impossible to know.[76] The early deaths of her parents and an unhappy childhood spent in wealthy relatives' homes, combined with a tendency toward self-involvement, probably played some role in her behavior. Whatever the causes—and they no doubt were complicated—by 1946, Hutchins was no longer able to tolerate the disruption to his work and to their daughters that Maude's behavior caused. He took a nine-month leave of absence from the university, working at the *Encyclopaedia Britannica* office in Chicago's Loop and keeping more domestic hours. By then it was too late. One morning in April of 1947, he arose early, dressed, wrote a note to Maude explaining that he was leaving her, and never saw her again.[77] As he informed his mother and father, he saw "no hope" for rebuilding the marriage.[78]

The following year Maude Hutchins filed for divorce on grounds of desertion. Hutchins agreed to her alimony and child support demands, and she received custody of Joanna and Clarissa. The divorce was final in July of 1948. Trustee James H. Douglas convinced Maude to vacate the chancellor's house sometime later, and she moved to Southport, Connecticut, to live for fourteen months with William and Helen Benton before she bought her own house.[79]

In May of 1949, in the presence of his mother and his daughter Franja and his new stepdaughter Barbara, and with his father officiating, Hutchins married his secretary and editorial assistant at *Encyclopaedia Britannica,* Vesta Sutton Orlick. Her daughter Barbara was Clarissa Hutchins' age and took Hutchins' name as her own. Vesta Hutchins made Robert Hutchins' comfort and happiness her primary concern. She enjoyed her new role as the chancellor's wife and welcomed the duty of entertaining people from the university. For the first time in years, Hutchins experienced domestic tranquillity.

With respect to his relations with the faculty, the freedom that accompanied this peace came too late. Since 1929 he had allowed the power of his convictions to interfere with his ability to hear what the faculty told him throughout his presidency. The curriculum was their responsibility; their scholarship and expertise informed their teaching. Assessment of the quality of scholarship in specific academic disciplines had to begin in consultation with them. John Dale Russell of the education department informed him in 1939 that curriculum policy belonged with the faculty, for they determined the success or failure of curricular programs.[80] In 1944, even those powerful faculty members who admired him, including Ronald S. Crane and Frank H. Knight, opposed his efforts to gain more control over their locus of expertise: teaching and scholarship.

When Hutchins presented his ideas about re-creating the modern university in *The Higher Learning* and when Adler interpreted Hutchins' thinking in his "God and the Professors" four years later, the two men completely ignored the political implications of such reordering of scholarly work and teaching. The disputes over power and control of the curriculum and over faculty appointments in departments from the beginning of his presidency were recurring instances in which Hutchins attempted to impose his own preferences on the faculty. He refused to acknowledge the legitimacy of department faculty members' scholarship in history, political science, philosophy, and, judging by his refusal to move on appointments, other disciplines as well.

In many of these instances, he denied faculty members the authority they felt they were most qualified to assume. Hutchins had instructed a freshman social science course at Yale for a year, in 1924–25, and he had dabbled in social science literature for a few years in the Law School. He had little experience with humanities disciplines, except as a student and in his great books reading. In short, he never had conducted research or taught beyond an introductory level in the very disciplines about which he was making judgments. In more than a few cases departmental faculty members found him ignoring their recommendations, expertise, and advice. But beyond that, he persisted in proffering, in different guises, his own model for organizing their work. The effort to load the philosophy department in 1930, his discussions about the Institute of Philosophical Studies in 1933, his Committee on the Liberal Arts in 1936, and his descriptions of the Institute of Liberal Studies in 1944 were variations on the same theme.

At the heart of Hutchins' problems with the faculty was his treatment of them as "employees" and the university as his "instrument."[81] With his new marriage and the easing of the tension of past battles, he began appearing at the Quadrangle Club, "trying more than ever before to be 'one of the boys,' " as one observer noted in 1949.[82] He delivered his last speech to the trustees' dinner for the faculties with humility and emotion, according the same observer, something the faculty had rarely, if ever, seen from him.[83] But by that time he had decided to leave the university.

With a naive arrogance in the beginning and a stubborn conviction of the righteousness of his own judgment as time passed, Hutchins had used his presidency to undermine the strong role faculty members had assumed in the 1920s in the shaping of their academic disciplines and departments. Enlarging on Adler's ideas about the centrality of philosophy in providing an intellectual synthesis for the modern world, Hutchins used his presidency as a bully pulpit for redefining the mission of the university. In 1936 that mission included a narrow delineation of its educational and scholarly functions to protect the quality of its theoretical work. By the early 1940s that mission had broadened—to use this theoretical work to effect a moral, spiritual, and intellectual revolution in the modern world.

The fact that Hutchins, the preacher's son raised with Protestant evangelical convictions, assumed his leadership responsibility in this way is not surprising. But in doing so, he lost the opportunity to collaborate with the faculty in policymaking and in developing a vision of the University of Chicago that they might have shared.

CHAPTER 10 *Leavetaking*

THE CONTINUAL OPPOSITION of faculty members to his ideas about the organization of teaching and scholarship began to wear on Hutchins by the late 1930s. His ongoing efforts to educate the trustees and to raise money for the university became less challenging and more of a chore. Yet, Hutchins achieved notable successes at the University of Chicago. Changes in the Law School curriculum and staffing practices, creating an intense intellectual and interdisciplinary environment, were a direct result of Hutchins' encouragement and support. The Committee on Social Thought and other interdisciplinary committees were outstanding innovations that breached the traditional barriers between departments in the university. Loyal backing from a significant core of faculty members and support from the board enabled him to establish these committees. The development of the School of Medicine and disaffiliation with the Rush College of Medicine ensured that medical research and teaching would be conducted in the biological sciences division. This encouraged biological sciences to flourish during his presidency. But these enterprises engaged his attention only until they were operating; others took responsibility for sustaining them.

In the 1940s he increasingly turned his attention to problems outside the university, including adult education in the great books, freedom of the press, and world peace. He entertained a number of possible career changes but did not pursue them until he was offered an associate directorship of the Ford Foundation in 1950. Unable to resist the lure of the money and power to establish programs he had been unable to initiate at the University of Chicago, he officially left the university in 1951 to become a philanthropic foundation executive.

In 1939 Hutchins had to admit to the trustees of the University of Chicago that the chances of receiving further financial support from the Rockefeller Foundation were small. A $3 million gift in 1936 had been a Depression-related, one-time donation to replace term grants from the General Education Board. However, the university budget was still showing disparities between income and expenses, particularly in the Medical School and clinics and in the general divisions of the university. He foresaw the need for a fiftieth anniversary funding-raising campaign to supply the university with the $1.2 million per year over ten years necessary to maintain "its present position."[1] He thought, erroneously, that the Rockefeller Foundation might make a contribution to this effort to raise endowment funds.[2] In the event that enough money were not raised, the board ought to consider using capital funds (5 percent of $16 million annually until the total amount was "consumed") that the Rockefeller Foundation and the General Education Board earlier had provided without restrictions on use.[3]

The fiftieth anniversary campaign was not an easy one for Hutchins. He eliminated intercollegiate football just as the campaign began in 1939. The team had become more legendary for its losses than its wins, and the university under Hutchins was unwilling to sacrifice academic standards to recruit and pay for a better team. Hutchins was able to gain support from the board for the move, but the public was less sanguine about the issue. It is difficult to know the effect of the decision on alumni, but the total contribution of 15,000 alumni (one-third of the university's graduates) to the fund drive reached $520,000 by October of 1941.[4] The average donation was $34.

Hutchins relied extensively on board members to assuage angry alumni throughout his presidency. His protests against the actions of the Chicago school board in 1933, the accusations of Walgreen in 1935, and his occasionally supercilious attitude toward some of the members of the "State Street oligarchy," as John Gunther labeled Chicago's leading businessmen, repeatedly required mitigation by Harold Swift and Laird Bell and other trustees who supported his decisions.[5]

Laird Bell, in fact, was instrumental in convincing the other board members to relinquish the university's off-campus Rush Medical College in favor of maintaining the School of Medicine.[6] The Medical School (now called the Pritzker School of Medicine) was fully staffed by physicians who also were members of the biological sciences division, reflecting the model of medical education that Abraham Flexner had outlined in his 1910 report for the Carnegie Foundation for the Advancement of Teaching and that the Rockefeller Foundation had supported for many years at the university.[7] In 1941 Bell presented the argument that resolved the issue of medical education at the university by transferring Rush to the University of Illinois, something Hutchins had been unable to accomplish by his own efforts. A faculty member credited Hutchins with a "passive acquiescence and magnificent remoteness" that allowed a "splendid Faculty" to assemble in the Medical School and biological sciences division.[8]

In the end, Hutchins raised over $9 million of the hoped-for $12 million for the endowment by the October celebration of the fiftieth anniversary.[9] Edward Levi, a longstanding Hutchins friend and admirer and president of the University from 1968 to 1975, has noted that Hutchins did not do all he could have to raise money for the university.[10] Indeed, in 1949 the trustees notified the faculty that the budget deficit was so extreme that expenditures across the whole university were to be reduced by 6 percent.[11]

Hutchins had begun to tire of the duties of the presidency in the late 1930s. He informed his father and his friend Mortimer Adler of his ennui with the board of trustees, the faculty, and the city of Chicago.[12] His father commiserated with him, remarking that "the lifting of funds from the pockets of the impious is a sorrowful task," but urged him to persist because his moral commitments and ideals warranted his continued leadership of the university.[13] Adler, in contrast, encouraged Hutchins to search for a position that would allow him to act on his educational ideals. Hutchins at that point was seeking as the most appealing alternatives the chancellorship of the City College of New York and an associate justiceship on the Supreme Court.[14]

The chancellorship was never offered to him. But the associate justiceship, which he dearly wanted, remained a possibility for some time. Throughout the 1930s he had gone back and forth between Chicago and Warm Springs, Georgia, to talk with Franklin D. Roosevelt about a variety of positions, from a Cabinet position to head of the Securities and Exchange Commission (SEC). Only the SEC position finally materialized, and Hutchins refused the offer, although he agreed to serve as public representative on the New York Stock Exchange for a brief period until he realized that the extent of reform he foresaw for that body was not shared by other board members. The Supreme Court associate justiceship went, in the end, to Hutchins' good friend William O. Douglas, who had been the first head of the SEC and a loyal Roosevelt supporter. Hutchins simply was unwilling (and possibly unable) to cultivate the kinds of relationships with politicians that would have been required to secure an acceptable position in the city that his father called "the cage of unclean beasts."[15]

Such was the extent of the press coverage of Hutchins in these years, sometimes with stories that ran for days on whether or not he had been offered a position and whether or not he would take it, that the faculty occasionally was moved to make its own timely statements on national issues. When Hutchins declared his opposition to United States involvement in World War II in early 1941, for example, the faculty coincidentally circulated a petition supporting the lend-lease bill. The press and many observers interpreted this petition as a rebuttal of Hutchins' speeches critical of Roosevelt's preparedness statements.[16]

Hutchins' opposition to preparedness was rooted in a fear that it would arouse the kind of hysteria that had accompanied United States participation in World War I, destroying First Amendment freedoms and reallocating funds that should be used at home to fight poverty, racism, and other forms of oppression.[17] Despite his abandonment of this argument by December 7, 1941, it destroyed whatever might have been Hutchins' future in politics. As a result, his charisma with the press became a less formidable challenge to the faculty in the 1940s.

Hutchins' successes at the University of Chicago reflected his ongoing interest in cross-disciplinary ventures. These included a curricular reorganization in the Law School and the establishment of interdisciplinary committees, most notably the Committee on Human Development and the Committee on Social Thought. The new curriculum and staffing practices in the Law School occurred with little opposition, in part because the law faculty supported the plans and in part because the Law School was sufficiently removed from the research culture and teaching concerns of the divisional faculty. The two committees encountered some opposition precisely because they offered the means to bypass the normal appointment and curriculum procedures in the divisions. Nevertheless there was enough faculty support to make them as much a part of the university's identity as the divisional reorganization of 1931.

True to the spirit of his efforts to raise standards at the Yale Law School, Hutchins began at the University of Chicago by appointing Harry Bigelow as dean in 1929. One of his first acts was to support Bigelow's desire to boost entrance requirements, admitting only those in the upper one-third of their college classes unless the dean chose to make an exception.[18] One unfortunate result was a 20 percent drop in enrollment and a $34,000 drop in tuition income in the second year of the Depression.[19] The tuition was raised to $125 per quarter the following year, despite protests by students that the raise denied "equal opportunity" to poor students, and then lowered to $100 per quarter for first-year students.[20] Clearly, Hutchins' hope of maintaining quality was sustained by limiting access through tuition raises intended to compensate for lack of applicants.

Hutchins and Bigelow agreed upon nearly all appointments made to the Law School. An offer of a position to William O. Douglas, who accepted, then refused in order to continue his research at Yale, was one such agreement. Others included Hutchins' unsuccessful efforts to recruit Felix Frankfurter from Harvard and Charles E. Clark from Yale.[21] Adler's shift from the philosophy department to the Law School was another. This move was crucial to the later curricular changes that occurred.

Adler and Malcolm Sharpe, a member of the law faculty who earlier had taught in Alexander Meiklejohn's Experimental College, in 1933 designed a prelaw honors course called Law 201. In 1934 they organized the yearlong course with three tutors (William Gorman, James Martin, and Adler's old friend Arthur Rubin), who later worked on the Committee on the Liberal Arts. Adler and Sharpe introduced their prelaw students to grammar, rhetoric, logic, and mathematics in the first part, and great books lectures and discussions in the second part of the year.[22]

Hutchins' interest at Yale in a legal education that primarily sought to increase students' understanding of real social conditions and problems became transformed at the University of Chicago into support for a legal education that incorporated a wide exploration of principles of law. This shift understandably occurred during the same period that he was reading the great books with Adler. Adler's prelaw course was exemplary of the kind of reform he and Hutchins would have liked to bring about throughout the university. In conjunction with the later curricular changes offering cross-disciplinary study, the course was meant to ground students in the habit of asking important and principled questions of legal theory.

Law faculty member William Crosskey, for example, sent Hutchins a memorandum in 1936 declaring that good law could be measured by how closely its effects matched society's desires. Hutchins wrote in the margins "no morals" and responded in a note by quoting from book IV of Plato's *Republic* on the difference between the necessary and the good and by commenting that simply living with "the beast" (in the social world) did not teach this difference.[23]

Apparently satisfied with the experiment of having a philosopher on the law faculty, in 1934 the Law School began inviting faculty members from such academic disciplines as history, home economics and economics, anthropology, psychology, sociology, and political science to teach law students.[24] Hutchins approved this method of appointment. In 1937 a new curriculum, designed by a committee headed by Wilber Katz, was instituted to reflect this cross-disciplinary approach to the law. Arguing that judges, lawyers, and legislators faced problems that were "basically economic and social," the program required four years of study for University of Chicago college graduates and three years for graduates of other institutions.[25]

Students in the first year were required to take Edward Levi's course on legal methods and materials. Levi had read the great books in one of Adler's honors classes and believed that the introduction to the study of law ought to include nonlegal materials, the development of critical perspectives on the law and on social policy, and the formation of value judgments about the ends of law. A course on ethics required in the third year was also designed to raise these issues for the more experienced law student.[26] In addition, courses were required in economic theory, economic organization, family relations, political theory and government, crime as a social and legal problem, and historical methods in economic, legal, and social history.

Hutchins' explicit endorsement of the program enabled the younger faculty members, headed by Wilber Katz, who became dean in 1939, to introduce the curricular changes. Adler's permanent appointment to the law faculty in 1937 ensured one strong advocate on the faculty, but unlike Hutchins' experience in the divisions of the university, a majority of the law faculty supported the reforms. The program continued until 1949, when it was reduced to three years while maintaining its cross-disciplinary nature. Shortly after joining the faculty, Edward Levi, in the context of a spirited conversation about legal education, argued aggressively with Hutchins for additional stenographic assistance in the Law School. Hutchins provided the funds and continued to encourage Levi's work. Levi's appointment as dean in 1950, despite anti-Semitic objections from the community, affirmed Hutchins' support of the program. Levi considered Hutchins a kind of model–"one of the great persons" that he knew.[27]

The Committee on Human Development was another cross-disciplinary program Hutchins supported. The idea originated out of the Committee on Child Development, chaired by Frank Freeman in the department of education and financed initially by the Rockefeller Foundation. Ralph Tyler, head of the department when Freeman resigned from the university, suggested that the committee explore development across the life span, a highly innovative approach to psychology and education in 1939. Building on the original plan of bringing together people with different academic and professional orientations, Tyler invited biologists, psychologists, educators, pediatricians, nutritionists, sociologists, and anthropologists to join the committee. He had Hutchins' encouragement for the interdisciplinary venture and for recruiting Robert Havighurst to the university to join the department and head the committee.[28]

The Committee on Human Development undertook a number of community studies during Hutchins' presidency. Publications based on research on human development in Quincy and Morris, Illinois, were results of its work.[29] In addition, scholars whose interests did not fit with particular departments' self-conceptions were able to pursue research interests through the committee. The sociologist David Riesman was one such faculty member in the college who worked with the committee before leaving for Harvard.

The Committee on Social Thought was the brainchild of John U. Nef. In contrast to his role with the Committee on Human Development, Hutchins was closely involved from the beginning in the planning and design of the Committee on Social Thought. Like many of the men who aligned their interests with Hutchins', Nef had been "struck" early in Hutchins' presidency with his "great physical charm" and was "drawn to him as an intellectual force." The two men shared a concern with the role of culture in education and with combining academic disciplinary perspectives. In the early 1940s Hutchins and Nef began to invite others, including Robert Redfield, Frank H. Knight, Joseph Schwab, and Ralph Tyler, who were interested in the relationships between values, culture, education, and the production of knowledge to discreet lunches at the Shoreland Hotel near the University.[30] These preliminary discussions of the committee were held secretly to avoid raising the rancor of the divisional faculty before the organizers brought their plan to fruition.

The group's discussions reflected some of the telling distinctions between Hutchins' and his colleagues' assumptions about the role of scholars in determining truth. Hutchins and Nef, for example, argued that knowledge of human reason stems from a belief that it exists. One could only determine truth, Hutchins thought, by faith in human reason, "which must come to him by Grace."[31] This intuitive or a priori knowledge formed the basis for moral behavior, freedom, responsibility, and respect for human dignity. In contrast, Redfield and Knight doubted the authority of such intuitive knowledge. Without empirical verification, relying only on intuition or religious revelation opened the door to claims of absolute truth or to intellectual stagnation. They were more interested in how communities create, revise, reconstruct, and judge truths over time and in particular social and cultural contexts.[32]

In 1942 the committee was established by the board of trustees. Initially called the Committee on Civilization, its name was changed for pragmatic reasons. Thinking that it ought to be located in the division of the social sciences, where Redfield was dean, and Nef, Tyler, and Knight were powerful faculty members, Hutchins appropriately renamed it the Committee on Social Thought. With official sanction, Nef and the others ceased worrying that the work on the committee might be subverted by protest from faculty members critical of Hutchins' innovations. Wilber Katz of the Law School joined the committee, furthering its cross-disciplinary nature and solidifying its university-wide position. Redfield served as chairman from 1942 to 1946, and Nef succeeded him, holding the position until 1964 and providing significant funding for the committee's operation from his first wife's (Elinor Castle Nef) estate.

The committee's work was unique in the university. Nef initially compiled a list of relevant courses offered by other departments and slowly developed a cross-disciplinary curriculum for master's and doctoral students studying through the committee. His view of the links between intellectual culture and the arts were more expansive than Hutchins', but whatever differences they had over policy and personnel, Hutchins supported Nef's curricular innovations. Nef invited numerous lecturers in the arts, philosophy, theology, and other disciplines to the campus. After the war, the committee began adding its own faculty members, among them Daniel Boorstin in history, Edward Shils in sociology, Frederick von Hayek in economics, and others in philosophy, music, and aesthetics, many of whom had been denied a faculty position by traditional departments at the university.[33]

Unlike the college program, the Committee on Social Thought survived Hutchins' presidency. In part, that survival can be attributed to its independence and its financial support from Nef. In addition, the committee was not an essential component in the educational offerings of the university, whatever its ultimate intellectual contributions to the community. The tuition of its students did not support a significant portion of the graduate program. The faculty it recruited tended to be luminaries in their fields. Departments could welcome them or ignore them as they chose. At the same time, the existence of the committee provided the university with a certain caché—unusual interdisciplinary opportunities in graduate education and in cultural contributions to the community—without seriously threatening the structure and process of undergraduate education and graduate education and research. And in the years after Hutchins left, a number of other such committees were established, following the interdisciplinary precedent of the Committee on Social Thought.

In a sense, the committee represents a paradox of Hutchins' leadership of the university. Anyone less sure of the righteousness of his convictions about the importance of the Committee on Social Thought might have been powerless to buck the protest that seemed to arise every time Hutchins tried to bypass departments. Yet the same convictions worked against Hutchins when he attempted to tamper with what was central to the university's mission—scholarship and the education of undergraduates. The problem was not so much one of the range of curricular offerings the university extended. Rather, it was one of power and control over the central mission of the university.

When the United States was attacked by the Japanese at Pearl Harbor on December 7, 1941, Hutchins' attempts to determine the mission of the University and faculty opposition to those attempts entered a brief period of quiescence. Ironically, Hutchins' actions as president reaffirmed and strengthened the university's mission in the postwar period as a leader in the sciences. Calling it "an instrumentality of total war," Hutchins turned the university to the war effort.[34] Military training was instituted on campus along with military studies. William Benton was sent to Washington, D.C., to confer with government officials and to volunteer the university's scientists and laboratories for military research.[35]

Arthur Holly Compton, a physicist at the University of Chicago, had directed atomic research projects at Columbia, Princeton, Harvard, the University of Chicago, and the University of California at Berkeley. He had been trying to determine the best location among these universities for the Manhattan Project, which involved building the radioactive pile that would be needed to test the feasibility of setting off a nuclear chain reaction. With Hutchins' approval, he located the Metallurgical Project (the code name) at the University of Chicago. To carry out the project, he brought to the university some of the most eminent physicists in the country: Harold C. Urey, Enrico Fermi, Leo Szilard, and many others. Working under the squash courts on the campus in 1942, they built the pile that resulted in the first self-sustaining nuclear reaction to release atomic energy.[36]

While Hutchins' approval of the project was necessary for its completion, he had little to do with actually bringing it about and very little to do with the scientists on campus. Most of them moved to the Argonne Laboratory outside of Chicago to continue to explore atomic energy or to Los

Alamos, New Mexico, to build the bombs that would later be dropped on the cities of Hiroshima and Nagasaki. This prospect of dropping the bomb near the war's end drew some of the scientists back to the University of Chicago and to Hutchins.

Leo Szilard had been concerned about the possible uses of the bomb as early as 1943. Szilard, Walter Bartky, and Urey approached Hutchins in 1945 seeking a way to convince President Truman that dropping the bomb on a city was not necessary to end the war.[37] Hutchins helped them set up a meeting with James F. Byrnes, who was about to become Truman's secretary of state. They proposed a demonstration bombing of a deserted island instead of destroying an inhabited area. When they were unsuccessful in this mission, the scientists requested that Hutchins sponsor a conference to examine the long-term social and political implications of atomic energy. The university held the conference in 1945.

In addition, Hutchins authorized an allocation of $10,000 from special educational funds to help the scientists organize the Atomic Scientists of Chicago, Inc. The group's purpose was to educate the public and the Congress about the need to establish civilian rather than military control of the development of atomic energy. They began publishing a journal, *Bulletin of the Atomic Scientists,* and organized community efforts to influence public policy. Hutchins and many others testified in support of their cause.[38] The result was the Atomic Energy Commission, a body that was intended to regulate research and development of atomic energy in the public interest, as distinct from the interests of the military.

The publicity such a campaign brought to the university was not unwelcome. Hutchins claimed a certain moral imperative in the university's involvement. He later recalled that members of the community were shocked after the bombs were dropped and, to assuage their "guilt," were open to ways "to repair the damage."[39] When the war was over, Hutchins announced the establishment of three new institutes to conduct research on the peaceful uses of atomic energy. In addition to providing an opportunity to contribute more positively to atomic research, the institutes were a means for Hutchins to rebuild the scientific community at the university.

As Edward Shils has noted, the "real" University of Chicago was composed (in addition to the stellar social scientists and humanists) of such dedicated scientists as Michelson, Millikan, and Loeb, who were responsible for the university's reputation in the physical sciences.[40] The establishment of the Institute of Nuclear Studies, the Institute of Metals, and the Institute of Radiobiology furthered the restoration of the physical and biological sciences during Hutchins' presidency. Enrico Fermi joined the physics department, and Harold C. Urey joined the chemistry department. Both men conducted research through the Institute of Nuclear Studies.

Hutchins perceived the institutes as a way to protect such research from control by industry or the military. Though federal and private industry funds contributed to the institutes' financial support, their primary work was intended to advance knowledge rather than to develop military and industrial applications of nuclear energy. The knowledge advanced by the institutes was to be as accessible as any other basic scientific research. The university also joined a consortium of universities and research institutes in overseeing the new Argonne National Laboratory outside Chicago, established to conduct applied research and overseen by the Atomic Energy Commission.[41] These arrangements enabled the university to use a variety of resources to rebuild its reputation in the sciences. Hutchins' ability to retain the scientists and to work with the biological and physical sciences divisions after the war to establish the institutes not only enhanced the university's reputation but also "stimulated research in borderline fields," unencumbered by departmental "barriers."[42] The Max Planck Institute and the Fermi Institute continue such research today.

The Law School curriculum, the interdisciplinary committees, and the rebuilding of the sciences at the university were notable and enduring successes of Hutchins' leadership and testaments to his ongoing commitment to cross-disciplinary intellectual activity. Admittedly, they were largely set apart, by virtue of their organization and functions, from the mainstream educational activities taking place in the departments and divisions. And Hutchins' role in these endeavors diminished significantly or ended shortly after they were established and assumed the character of the people who ran them. But they all had an enduring influence in perpetuating structures within the university to enable cross-disciplinary study and teaching long after Hutchins left.

Having rejected, or been denied access to, political opportunities commensurate with his reputation and acceptable to his self-definition, and tired of the university battles, Hutchins was open to other kinds of public roles. In the 1940s he participated in three of these, each one enabling him to maintain a kind of academic purity, protected by his affiliation with the university from the "unclean beasts" and the posturing required to succeed in the political world. The *Encyclopaedia Britannica*'s (EB) *Great Books of the Western World,* the Commission on the Freedom of the Press, and the Committee to Frame a World Constitution each represented the opportunity to explore big issues: the preservation and dissemination of particular cultural values, the responsibilities of the press in a democratic society, and world peace and world government. The details of Hutchins' involvement in these endeavors have been explored more fully elsewhere.[43] What is notable about them for understanding Hutchins' relationship with the modern university is manifest in the pattern of his leadership, the ways he outlined the tasks of the groups he led, and the products of each group's work.

The EB's great books project, for example, grew out of the reading groups Adler had established in the university's extension division and out of the university's acquisition of the EB as a joint venture with William Benton.[44] Benton was a member of the Fat Men's Great Books Class for Chicago businessmen. Thirty men and their wives met biweekly at the University Club in the Loop to discuss the books with Hutchins, Adler, and other group leaders, including Milton Mayer, who worked in the university's public relations office, and Arthur Rubin, Adler's friend. Benton was frustrated when he could not find some of the books on the reading list. He suggested to Hutchins that the university and EB consider publishing a set of the books to be used with the extension classes and the other groups that had formed in the Chicago area or to be used by individuals as an autodidactic tool.

Hutchins' initial response was negative. He thought the reading program required discussion groups. Publishing a set of books did not guarantee that people would become educated by them. Adler, on the other hand, relished the notion of producing an index to guide readers to particular ideas as they were treated in the texts in the set. With Hutchins' and Benton's approval, Adler embarked on his Syntopicon project, which was slated to take two years and cost $60,000 but which actually took seven years and cost $1 million.[45]

Hutchins' responsibility was to organize and administer the editorial advisory board for the set of books. His pattern of administration grew partly out of the nature of the project and partly out of his preferred way of leading. His first task was to recruit the advisers. From the university faculty he drew Clarence Faust, Joseph Schwab, and Mortimer Adler, who shared his views about the liberal arts and culture. In addition, he appointed Scott Buchanan, Stringfellow Barr, Mark Van Doren, and John Erskine from the Columbia University and People's Institute programs. Alexander Meiklejohn also served on the board for a time. On one hand, this group was composed of men who had worked with the books in a variety of formal settings. On the other, it reflected an extraordinarily parochial group of men, all academics bent on protecting and disseminating a particular canon of texts and singularly uninterested in evaluating the educational outcomes of the program. They simply assumed its merits.

Originally, the set was to include introductory essays for each volume to explain the contents to new readers and reintroduce the writings to the already initiated. The protracted discussions and arguments among members of the advisory board, particularly among Adler and others, and the construction of Adler's Syntopicon so inflated the cost of the set that these educational tools had to be dropped. This meant that the only interpretations to which readers were exposed were Hutchins' introductory essay in volume 1 and Adler's two-volume idea index.[46]

As in the case of the philosophy department in the early 1930s, the Committee on the Liberal Arts in the middle 1930s, and, not incidently, his own marital problems, Hutchins seemed unable to address the personal disagreements that arose in connection with the project. He had little skill in negotiating between hurt parties or in dealing directly with others' criticisms of his conduct and, in fact, tended to shy away from situations that could not be handled through rational discussion or tidy resolutions based on clear ethical or moral positions.[47] He had a low tolerance for ambiguity. In the case of selecting works for inclusion in the set, judgments of merit often involved taste rather than distinct rational standards.

An outline of his ideal great books program for adults is a good example of his ambivalence about the project. He informed his principal advisers, Adler, Buchanan, and Barr, that the best way to teach the books was with the "tutorials, public lectures, and communal support" that the St. John's program offered. For adults, the equivalent setting would be a facsimile of the Danish folk high school or "full-time, residential centers." In the absence of such an educational utopia, the set of books ought to reveal to adults the flaws of learning in biweekly discussion groups or by reading on one's own and constantly dealing with the interruptions of everyday life. Initially, these readers should seek to join discussion groups of the kind Adler was organizing. Then, the readers should be moved to demand ongoing opportunities for residential adult education programs. In short, the set should create in adults a desire for a liberal education modeled on the St. John's College program, with some adjustments made for adult needs.[48]

Adler proselytized the discussion program all over the country in the early 1940s. In consequence, the extension program grew too large for the University of Chicago to manage. In 1946 the EB formed the Great Books Foundation to finance training sessions for group leaders, creating, Hutchins and Benton hoped, what would be a ready market for the set of books when it was published.[49] Hutchins' interest was not in financial profit, although he was concerned about covering the costs of producing the set. Rather, he wanted American adults to seek a liberal education through the books. He predicted that eventually 15 million adults could be reached through the groups and the set.[50]

In the end, 15 million American adults did not want to become liberally educated through the discussion groups or the set itself. By 1953, according to one study, 100,000 adults had attended at least one discussion and 20,000 were currently enrolled in Great Books Foundation programs offered in libraries, churches, and homes.[51] This was a significant accomplishment, a measure of Hutchins' and Adler's public relations acumen, backed by EB funds, and of the desire for the kind of cultural experience they advertised.[52] The set, entitled *Great Books of the Western World,* was published in fifty-four volumes in 1952, without the prefatory essays originally intended to draw adults into the program. In 1953 only 138 sets were sold.[53] Hutchins reorganized the marketing of the sets. By 1962, a total of 150,000 had been sold and by 1977 nearly 1 million had been sold.[54] These figures, of course, do not provide information on how many buyers actually read the books.

Hutchins' introductory volume, *The Great Conversation,* argues that "the emergence of democracy as an ideal" could be traced to liberal education beginning with the Greeks.[55] The selections in the set, he argued, embodied some of the most significant thinking the Western cultural tradition had to offer. Dwight Macdonald found Hutchins' claims "pompous," smacking of "Madison Avenue cant." Rather than present the books to make them accessible, he argued, Hutchins and Adler had attempted to "fix the canon of the Sacred Texts." Their choices reflected "the religion of culture that appeals to the American academic mentality."[56] Another reviewer found Hutchins' remarks "dogmatic" and "haughty," and his criticism of American education out of place in a volume intended to inspire the average reader to explore the following fifty-three volumes.[57]

Even Jacques Barzun, who was enthusiastic about "the enterprise as a whole," thought the choices of texts betrayed "a high-minded axe-grinding in the direction of intellectualism."[58]

In light of Hutchins' goals for the set, these criticisms are ironic. For a collection meant to appeal to a broad range of adults (Hutchins mentioned the importance of liberal education for workers in his introductory volume), the narrow, parochial, and overly academic nature of the choices reveals fundamental flaws in Hutchins' administration of the advisory board and in his conception of how to introduce readers in nonformal settings to the books. The compromises within the group and, in the end, his determination of what was best to include framed the choices.

His work with the Commission on the Freedom of the Press presents a similar case. Hutchins was persuaded by his Yale classmate Henry Luce to undertake a critical examination of the press beginning in 1943. He agreed, despite his skepticism of "the policies" of Luce's magazines, because Luce promised him control over the project, including placing the funds for the commission under the administration of the University of Chicago.[59] Once again, Hutchins organized a group of academic experts to examine the problem and determine the final product.[60] He did not invite members of the press to sit with the commission because representation from every branch of the press (radio, magazine publishing, newspapers, and movies) would have made the group "unwieldy."[61]

The commission began its work with a shared set of premises. They reflected a characteristically thorough outline Mortimer Adler, who was not a member of the commission, had sent to Hutchins before their first meeting. Adler covered "principles to be agreed upon," how to categorize "the problem," "questions to be investigated," and "methods of investigation."[62] Hutchins more simply suggested that the commission should "attempt to define freedom of the press, to state what the values are which it attempts to secure, to indicate the areas of failure or danger, and to propose practical measures to remedy" the problems. No research should take place, he thought, "until the commission knows what it wants to find out."[63]

In 1947, after hearing testimony and collecting memoranda from members of the press, industry, government, and private agencies concerned with the press and civil liberties, the commission published its reports.[64] The reports covered a variety of topics, from international mass communications issues, to radio, to First Amendment responsibilities, to the movie industry.[65] Hutchins was primarily responsible for editorial supervision of all the volumes. The summary volume, which was officially edited by Robert D. Leigh, was completed in a final series of drafts by Hutchins. Entitled *A Free and Responsible Press,* the report described the various media, how they were organized, and their costs. It presented an argument for the press' responsibility to educate the public in a democratic society and analyzed and criticized its performance of that function. Finally, it made a number of recommendations for how the press might fulfill the responsibilities the commission had outlined.[66]

Briefly, the commission suggested that the press, with a few exceptions, was failing to live up to its responsibilities to inform the public fully about daily events, to represent accurately all segments of society, and to govern itself in the execution of these duties. The press was protected by the First Amendment. But, because Americans were dependent upon all the media of mass communication to make informed decisions about public affairs, this freedom could not be ensured if the press continued to fail to meet these needs of society. Its many recommendations included constitutional guarantees protecting radio and motion pictures, better regulation of press monopolies, nonprofit ventures in media, experimental programs sponsored by the media, improved training in journalism (including liberal education), and an independent agency to assess press performance. In its most controversial suggestion, the commission suggested that the government consider establishing its own agency of mass communication if private agencies failed to fulfill their responsibilities to inform the public.

The report was received positively by Walter Lippmann, A. J. Liebling, and the *New York Times.*[67] Henry Luce was "disappointed."[68] The "visceral" reactions by the American Society of Newspaper Editors, who were furious with Hutchins and the report, are partially responsible for the lack of policy responses.[69] A press council to engage in ongoing, systematic criticism of the press' performance never materialized. The key to this failure is in the makeup of the commission. Not a single member of the press participated in determining the problem to be examined or in writing the final reports. Much as the critics of the great books venture found fault with the narrow academic slant of Hutchins' advisory board, the critics of the press report resented a group of scholars informing them of their duties.

Beyond that problem, the reports received little coverage in the press, other than in the trade periodicals and brief mention in *Time* and *Fortune* and a few newspaper columns. Hutchins' goal of stirring public debate and educating the public to press problems remained largely unfulfilled.[70] His inclusion of academic experts may well have been an effort to ensure that the report would be taken seriously, but it did not address the issue of public perceptions of press performance. Nor were members of the general public included in the process of assessing or making recommendations about press performance or press responsibilities.

In short, the Hutchins Commission recommendations were rejected or ignored by many members of the press. The reports were unavailable to members of the public unless they deliberately sought them. While historians of the media have suggested that the reports of the commission represent "the most cogent single body of criticism of the press," little came of those reports in terms of actual reforms of the mass media problems they addressed.[71] Hutchins' message had only successfully reached the already converted.

Hutchins' initiation into the problems of world peace bore similarities to his other 1940s ventures. The Committee to Frame a World Constitution was composed of a group of academic experts who were concerned about the dangers of atomic energy.[72] Not a grass roots reform movement, like the atomic scientists' coalition of citizens, scientists, and politicians, the committee met at the University of Chicago in relative isolation from 1945 to 1947. It produced a journal, *Common Cause,* edited by Antonio Borgese, professor of Italian at the University of Chicago, and Elisabeth Mann Borgese, his wife. The journal published monthly issues from 1947 to 1951. It served as a forum for discussions of world government and international peace.[73]

The constitution that resulted from the committee's efforts was entitled "A Proposal to History" and published in the March 1948 issue of *Common Cause.*[74] It resembled the United States Constitution in its provisions for the branches of government and the distribution of powers. The proposal suggested that national boundaries be abolished and that political divisions be based on regional interests. Human civil rights and liberties were to be protected, and all people were to have access to education. An idealized version of social democratic government on an international scale, the proposal reflected Hutchins' clear-cut moral and ethical concerns and a naive perception of world politics.[75]

If Hutchins' intention was to influence significantly public officials' thinking through the committee's constitution, *Common Cause,* or his numerous speeches on world peace, he failed miserably. The parochialism of the committee, all Western academic intellectuals in a world with a predominantly Eastern population, and the naiveté of the proposal, notwithstanding its appealing idealism, did not help him. The strong moral persuasion in his speeches no doubt moved his listeners, but whether they were moved to action is difficult to know.[76] Additionally, the political climate of the times worked against his efforts. According to one poll, the American people supported a strong United Nations in the postwar period, but the Cold War effectively subdued numerous world peace groups and limited the reach of their publications.[77] American officials were concerned with strengthening the United Nations, not with world government.

As initial ventures into the public policy arena, Hutchins' great books set, his Commission on the Freedom of the Press, and his Committee to Frame a World Constitution were tentative. How many ears the substance of these activities reached and how many minds they changed is impossible to know. Ellen Condliffe Lagemann, in her study of the Carnegie Corporation, has described the ways the corporation began to use commissioned studies to try to influence public policy in the 1940s.[78] Hutchins' efforts resemble this technique, but without the effects that the corporation had.

The Great Books of the Western World, for example, was an effort to promote good taste as defined by cultural elites and, at the same time, sell it to the American public while educating the public to want it. The Commission on the Freedom of the Press represented the gathering of a panel of experts, but their work was primarily directed to theoretical issues of press responsibility and relied on public hearings and the members' own deliberations rather than the exhaustive social science research more likely to influence policy.[79] The Committee to Frame a World Constitution was another handpicked group of academic experts, but, as their document indicates, their expertise tended to lie in the areas of philosophy and law rather than in any real acquaintance with global politics.

These ventures are important for understanding Hutchins and his relationship to the university. He found very congenial the process of gathering together groups of intelligent and well-informed men to discuss significant problems and to explore the flaws in democratic institutions. In the case of the set of books, it was the education of adults by default, accomplishing what colleges seemed uninterested in doing. In the case of the commission, it was the media's responsibility as educators. In the case of the committee, it was constitutional law and world peace in the atomic age. More important to Hutchins than exposing flaws was devising recommendations to remedy them.

The process was more controllable than his battles with the faculty at the university, and the ends were more suited to his manner of getting things done. Even if the discussions became heated or if everyone did not in the end agree completely about the product, a product resulted. It included a statement of principles, an exploration of the theoretical problem, some attention to real conditions, and recommendations for how to create the conditions necessary to meet the statement of principles.

There was little of the uncertainty of empirical investigation here, of reformulating the problem in light of the evidence uncovered, of incorporating tolerance for multiple explanations or a variety of interpretations. The products of these efforts were more like sermons—reminding people that they ought to care about learning, the press, and world peace and suggesting what they might do to live up to the principles that ought to shape these activities and issues. After Hutchins left the University of Chicago to work in the philanthropic foundation world, he continued to seek similar kinds of forums of experts conducting similar kinds of studies, mostly involving discussion and recommendations intended to formulate principles for guiding conduct in the public sphere.

Hutchins exhibited extraordinary talents, intelligence, and eloquence as president and chancellor of the University of Chicago. He was a strong leader and a clear articulator of principled conduct for the institution, particularly when academic freedom was threatened. But leadership of such an institution required a careful balancing of the needs of different constituents within the constraints of real conditions—the Depression for the first ten years of his presidency and the war in the later years—as well as within one's family life and one's convictions. By the end of his twenty-two years at the university, one or the other of those demands had tipped the balance at any given time and had made all areas of his life difficult.

Because he tended not to change his mind once he arrived at a conclusion, and because he relied on a small group of advisers, some wise and well informed, others apparently not, his basic positions on university scholarship and teaching did not change between 1936 and 1951. Nor did he understand what moved the faculty of the university any better at the end than he had at the beginning. Ultimately, he grew tired of the battles that grew out of the fundamental misunderstandings that he himself had generated and perpetuated.

When Paul Hoffman invited him to become an associate director of the Ford Foundation in late 1950, he accepted the position. No doubt the prospect of dealing with the university's growing deficit, the need to reduce the size of the faculty, and the continuing responsibility of raising money figured in his decision to leave. Then, too, the opportunity to work on the cultural and educational problems that were important to him without having to raise money or meet every week with trustees or administer the huge bureaucracy the university had become was appealing.[80] As he informed his father, he might have been in "the wrong job." Much of the administration of the institution no longer interested him, and he was opposed to some of the work, including the atomic bomb research. He thought he could accomplish more in education at the Ford Foundation than he could at the University of Chicago.[81]

In spite of all the battles at the university, members of the faculty were sorry that he was leaving. There was a brief movement to try to dissuade him. However difficult he was to live with, his efforts to change the mission of the university, his protection of the college, the innovations of the interdisciplinary committees, and his defense of academic freedom had revitalized the discussion of education and redefined the unique ethos of the University of Chicago.[82] And however dissonant his vision was with the research culture of the University of Chicago, at least he had a vision. As numerous faculty members have noted, no matter how much they disagreed with him over issues of policy, personnel, and basic philosophy, his insistence on discussions of substance profoundly affected their perceptions of academic work.[83]

It is ironic that Hutchins' most touching farewell was directed to the students. Aside from his honors classes, convocation and commencement speeches, and occasional visits to student groups, he had had little to do with them in his twenty-two years at the university. Yet he had inspired them and they, in turn, had "been the inspiration of [his] life" and certainly of his efforts to reorient the educational agenda of the University of Chicago. They were symbols "of the rising generation and the hopes of mankind." Because he thought that "our mission here on earth is to change our environment, not adjust ourselves to it," which was a reflection of the function of education at Oberlin College, Hutchins' attempts to redefine the mission of the University of Chicago were also intended to shape future generations differently from past generations.[84]

This is certainly the role of an educator. Yet the noncollaborative way he carried out his mission was a major flaw in Hutchins' presidency of the University of Chicago. He had little real understanding of the life of scholarship that characterized the university and treated the aims of many of the faculty as "wrongheaded."[85] These were the people most directly responsible for shaping future generations, and they were acting on their conceptions of education within a modern university. By not joining with them and attending to the context of their work in the process of establishing his leadership and the vision guiding it, by turning instead to Mortimer Adler and relying on the judgment of so many who agreed with him, Hutchins made himself less powerful and influential in acting on his ideas.

There is no doubt that Hutchins' presence at the university left an ineradicable mark, a means of participating in scholarship across disciplines and departments, and an ethos of intellectual rigor that has continued to shape the institution. But that ethos is not precisely the one he set out to create. The resistance to his ideal intellectual community and the dissolution of many of his innovations were disappointments that moved him to continue to experiment with ways to implement them elsewhere for the remainder of his life.

PART THREE *A Prince in Exile, 1951–77*

In a perceptive essay, Edward Shils aptly characterized Hutchins as "a prince in exile" in his post-Chicago years.[1] *The description is fitting because Hutchins spent the years from 1951 to 1977 seeking a perfect institutional form in which to conduct intellectual work. The modern university had fallen far short of the mark, he thought. He proceeded to devote his energy, administrative expertise, and intellect to creating the conditions and the institution that would satisfy his own vision.*

From 1951 to 1954, he was an associate director of the Ford Foundation. His principal accomplishments included encouraging investment in the technology needed to develop educational television and the organization of intercultural publishing ventures to support UNESCO*'s efforts to foster international cultural exchange. He established three semi- or wholly independent funds, each based on the educational interests that had grown out of his presidency at the University of Chicago and his friendship with Mortimer Adler. By 1953 he had so antagonized key members of the board of directors of the foundation with his inconoclasm and independence that he was forced to look for another job. And two of the funds, the Fund for the Advancement of Education and the Fund for Adult Education eventually were absorbed into the foundation.*

From 1954 until his death in 1977, Hutchins was president of the Fund for the Republic, the only independent fund the Ford Foundation financed. He oversaw the fund's grant making to civil liberties and civil rights projects and programs. Not satisfied with financing others' programs, which he saw as short-term approaches to these problems, he shifted the fund's direction. In 1959 he reorganized the fund's operations into the Center for the Study of Democratic Institutions. Located in the hills of Santa Barbara, California, the center was a residential facility for the study, discussion, and clarification of democratic ideas and institutions.

The center was the closest Hutchins ever came to achieving the intellectual community he had sought since the early years of his presidency of the University of Chicago. An elegant, distanced aerie that welcomed visiting experts, sponsored discussions, and published them, it was defined wholly by his leadership. At the same time, the resident fellows, all chosen by Hutchins, were bound to organize the work of the center around particular topics upon which the whole group agreed. In the end, Hutchins proved no more able to deal with the different needs, desires, and interests of this group than he had been with the faculty of the University of Chicago.

His leadership was crucial to continue the discussions and convocations on politics and law, education, social problems, ecological issues, and world peace with the energy and sumptuousness of the center's earlier years. When Hutchins died in 1977, the center lost its independent status and was moved to the campus of the University of California at Santa Barbara. In 1987 the center was closed.

CHAPTER 11 *Financing Ideas*

HUTCHINS ACCEPTED the associate directorship of the Ford Foundation because he thought he could create with Ford money centers of knowledge that would also be models of education. His Ford Foundation dreams arose directly out of his failures at the University of Chicago. They were meant to counter all that he found problematic with the modern university: excess specialization, fragmentation of formal knowledge, vocationalism, and subordination of intellectual ends to practical or public demands.

His approach to his work in the 1950s, first at the foundation and later at the Fund for the Republic, was patterned on his strategy with the *Great Books* advisory board, the Commission on the Freedom of the Press, and the Committee to Frame a World Constitution. Guided by the progressive notion that experts were needed to solve public problems, Hutchins gathered together groups of elites to frame the problems upon which the Ford Foundation and the Fund for the Republic would focus. In this case, though, Hutchins did not merely recommend. He had authorization of the foundation to provide the funds to finance the programs to address the problems.

Not surprisingly, Hutchins encountered difficulties at the foundation and at the Fund for the Republic similar to those he had encountered at the university. He had conflicts with the board of directors. His assumption that the board would support his positions simply because they were right bordered on arrogance. His single-minded determination to develop programs that embodied his ideals and his inability to communicate well with directors over incidents involving policy were recurring issues in his participation in the philanthropic foundation world.

Yet the same qualities that had inspired many of Hutchins' colleagues at the university also inspired his fellow staff and board members at the foundation and the fund. The strength of his convictions, the power of his oratory, the simple and clear expression of his moral commitments all contributed to his ability to gather around him people who felt that they shared his vision–of education, law and politics, and world peace. In effect, their respect for him ultimately helped to shield him from board members who did not have his courage or convictions or simply did not like his leadership style, right-wing politicians and media people who would have liked to silence him, and staff members who had similar goals but differed about the means.

Paul Hoffman was a college dropout who had worked his way up to the presidency of the Studebaker Corporation. He had served as Harry Truman's Economic Administration coordinator, implementing the Marshall Plan in postwar Europe. He was on the board of trustees of the University of Chicago. He also was a prominent Republican. When Henry Ford II needed someone to become president of the Ford Foundation, he asked William Benton to approach Paul Hoffman about taking the job. The foundation was the recipient of 90 percent of the Ford family's nonvoting stock holdings in the Ford Motor Company, worth over $2 billion. By transferring the stock to the foundation the family was able legally to retain control over the company without having to sell the stock to pay inheritance taxes from the Edsel and Henry Ford estates. This action transformed the beneficiary from a small, local philanthropy into a major philanthropic organization, the wealthiest in the history of foundations.[1]

In 1948 Ford had financed a study that was to determine the direction of the foundation's grant making. It was conducted by H. Rowan Gaither, Jr., an attorney who had helped design the RAND Corporation. After consulting with academic experts and public officials and leaders, Gaither delineated the five general areas of focus for the foundation. They were "the establishment of peace," "the strengthening of democracy," "the strengthening of the economy," "education in a democratic society," and "individual behavior and human relations."[2] Attracted by the scope of the project and the vast resources of the foundation, Hoffman told Benton that he would take the presidency on condition that Benton could persuade Hutchins to be an associate director and that Ford would agree to the arrangement.

Hutchins was intrigued by the prospect. He critically reviewed the Gaither report for Hoffman, suggesting that the greatest advancements in education and science had occurred with the establishment of "models and centers." Supporting models, whether universities or other institutions, was preferable to the typical foundation tactic, which was to support projects or individual scholars, Hutchins argued. The foundation had too much money to disburse to proceed that way. Unless Hoffman was willing to acquire a top-heavy administration composed of the expertise necessary to choose among a wide variety of individual projects, the foundation ought to consider financing "model colleges of liberal arts" and "model programs of adult education" as well as "model secondary school systems." Moreover, the foundation should not duplicate other agencies' efforts. Instead, it should provide additional funds to those, like the Institute of International Education and the Guggenheim Foundation, already supporting international exchanges or to existing universities, whose managers could determine what would be financed.[3] Clearly, higher education was to become a major area of Ford Foundation giving.[4]

Whatever doubts Hutchins had about the rectitude of serving as a foundation executive were mitigated by the fact that his father had become an adviser to the Danforth Foundation in 1940 when he left Berea College. Such a choice did not necessarily lead to corruption. Using foundation funds, Hutchins could begin to address the dilemma of American education, and far more quickly than he could if he were to stay at the University of Chicago.[5] This dilemma was manifested, on one hand, by rationalizing universal education as a means of providing "political equality and justice" and, on the other, by not equipping Americans with the ability to criticize media propaganda that offered "power and success" as preferable alternatives to the "wisdom and goodness" necessary to perpetuate a politically active, just society.[6]

In this time of expanded international aid, when the United States was exporting material goods and skills to developing countries, Americans were obligated also to export democratic values and a respect for learning. "Justice, peace, freedom and order" could only be maintained "by the exercise of intelligence" among citizens. "A republic," Hutchins suggested, was "really a common educational life in process." Every political decision in a republic was a product of education, since, by its very nature, republican government existed by the consent of the governed.[7] The abundant resources of the newly reorganized Ford Foundation enabled Hutchins to act on these beliefs.

Hoffman set an additional condition for Ford—locating the foundation's main office in Pasadena, California, where Hoffman's family resided. Hutchins was pleased to settle in California. He and Vesta and Barbara Hutchins lived in the wealthy suburb of San Marino, and his other daughters visited frequently.[8] The remaining foundation officers also moved to Pasadena. They included H. Rowan Gaither, Chester C. Davis, who had headed the Agriculture Adjustment Administration in the 1930s, and Milton Katz, professor of law at Harvard and Hoffman's assistant with the Marshall Plan. In the beginning of 1951 they formulated plans for allocating the vast amounts of capital the foundation was required to spend to maintain its tax-exempt status. With Hoffman and Hutchins, these officers spent $186 million between 1951 and 1954.[9]

Hutchins devised a strategy to allocate the money without creating a top-heavy management at the foundation's headquarters. His areas of administration were peace and education. Rather than financing separate projects, he suggested that the foundation create two funds to choose what would be supported and to disburse the money. A third, the East European Fund, to assist Iron Curtain refugees, was Hoffman's responsibility. The remaining officers oversaw the other international programs, including refugee relief, war relief in Germany, and agricultural extension in India and Pakistan. Hutchins also was accountable for Intercultural Publications, Inc., headed by James Laughlin, to educate other countries about American literature and art; the American Friends Service Committee's peace programs; and scholar exchanges with the universities of Berlin and Frankfurt.[10]

Of interest here are the two funds Hutchins initiated. Early in 1951, the directors established the Fund for Adult Education and the Fund for the Advancement of Education. Creation of the two funds allowed Hutchins the money and power to act on educational problems he had outlined in his books and addresses in the 1930s and 1940s. The directors also approved the presidents Hutchins chose to lead the funds. Both C. Scott Fletcher, head of the former, and Clarence Faust, head of the latter, were committed to Hutchins' "views, theories, practices, ideas, ideals, etc.," Hutchins informed his parents. Moreover, the "majority" of members of the separate boards of the two funds were "chosen with the same qualifications in mind."[11]

The Fund for Adult Education reflected Hutchins' concern for the kind of education that would absorb adults' leisure time. Fletcher had been a salesman with the Studebaker Corporation until he joined the Encyclopaedia Britannica organization to manage EB Films, one of its divisions. He agreed with Hutchins that the areas to target included radio, television, and community-based discussion programs. The Fund for Adult Education provided much of the initial financing for educational television stations and for programming, often through such groups as the National Association of Educational Broadcasters. Fletcher and the fund played a significant role in pressuring the Federal Communications Commission to reserve channels for public television.[12] In addition, grants were made to adult education organizations, including the Adult Education Association, the American Foundation for Political Education, and the Great Books Foundation. The fund financed development of pamphlets, books, films, and other study aids for community-based education groups.

In all, the Fund for Adult Education received $25 million by the fall of 1955, and an additional $3.5 million per year from 1955 to 1960, before it was dissolved. Its major criterion for supporting programs was that they contribute to the "liberal education of adults" outside established institutions.[13] In addition to supporting discussion programs and publishing materials on the great books and international relations, the fund conducted surveys of needs, it coordinated adult education activities, and it gave scholarships for study of that field and the mass media. To further the development of high-quality programming, the fund invested in the Television-Radio Workshop. The most notable results of this venture were "Omnibus," aired on Sunday afternoons for a number of years, and experiments in children's television, after the Television-Radio Workshop was transferred from the fund to the foundation itself.

The Fund for the Advancement of Education bore the mark of Hutchins and Clarence Faust. Alvin Eurich was the vice-president of this fund. Eurich had known Faust in college in Iowa and had risen through the ranks of higher education administration to the vice-presidency of Stanford University and then to the first presidency of the State University of New York. The fund's major interest was formal higher education. Many members of the board of directors had been faculty members or administrators in higher educational institutions. Some were business executives interested in education. The remainder were from the fields of law, journalism, government, and publishing. Ralph Bunche, Walter Lippmann, Barry Bingham, Walter Paepcke, Owen J. Roberts, and Mrs. Douglas Horton were among the first group of directors.[14]

Many of them agreed with Hutchins' ideas about education, and the grants the fund made reflected this agreement. His ideas about education had not changed much since *The Higher Learning in America* had been published. His criticisms were virtually the same, reflecting little depth or complexity in his portrayal of education in a democratic society, with but one exception. He briefly addressed a central problem John Dewey had confronted more than fifty years earlier: "The problem of making work significant in an industrial, mechanized economy." By 1953, two years after the fund had been established, he suggested the university was a place where diversity of opinion, ideas, and points of view, particularly over practical, political, and economic matters, ought to be respected. Debate was necessary if a society wanted to avoid the tyranny of conformity, intolerance, and indoctrination. But in order to ensure that controversial topics were addressed wisely by university people, the university must rest at the apex of an educational system that emphasized communication skills ("reading, writing, and figuring") in the initial ten years and taught history, geography, great literature, foreign languages, the arts, music, and science. Only after such an education would students be prepared to enter the university. From the first year in school through the collegiate years, all courses in these disciplinary areas ought to be prescribed, Hutchins thought. Only then could a democratic republic rest assured that its citizens were well educated and progressing toward wisdom.[15] Clearly, he still did not understand that one of the fundamental problems of the college at the University of Chicago was the fully prescribed program for a diverse pool of students in an era marked by enormous increases in the production of knowledge.

The Fund for the Advancement of Education focused on formal education. A grant was made to study the effects of racial segregation in southern school systems, which resulted in Harry Ashmore's *The Negro and the Schools,* published in 1954. The Southern Education Reporting Service, also supported by the fund, was a resource for school districts to use in devising remedies to respond to the *Brown* decision. Grants to historically black colleges and to experimental teacher education programs in these colleges were further efforts to enhance educational opportunities for African-Americans. A program to finance scholarships for early entrance to college directly reflected a concern Hutchins and Faust shared. A grant to help support a joint graduate program among southern California liberal arts colleges bore the mark of Hutchins' interest in better-articulated relationships between undergraduate and graduate programs.

Two areas of grant giving by the fund were very close to Hutchins' heart. One provided $565,000 to establish in 1952 the Institute for Philosophical Research. The institute was Mortimer Adler's dream. The money was to finance his effort to clarify Western thought and philosophy, with a focus on education.[16] Rather than his projected Summa Dialectica, however, his work resulted in a two-volume study of freedom. Adler had conducted a seminar on freedom for the board of the Ford Foundation at Hutchins' invitation, but the directors apparently were uninterested in having Adler educate them. When Hutchins prepared to invite him for another such gathering, Hoffman suggested that the board might have had enough instruction from Adler.

Alone, Hutchins would not have been able to provide the money for Adler. Faust was impressed with Adler's plans, as were some of the members of the fund's board, including Lippmann and Roberts. Others, including Frank Abrams of Standard Oil, were not, but Faust prevailed. In the end, the board members were all disappointed in the results and Adler received a terminal grant of $75,000.[17] At that point, Hutchins was about to exit his position with the foundation and was powerless to grant Adler more Ford money. Adler's institute received further funding elsewhere and eventually assumed partial responsibility for revising the *Encyclopaedia Britannica.*

Teaching and teacher education was the other area of the fund's activity. An alarming teacher shortage, becoming evident in the 1950s as children born in the postwar period began entering public schools, moved the fund to devise a number of ways to treat it. Faust and Hutchins had long agreed that the best education for teachers was a liberal education. A grants program for high school and college teacher sabbaticals, and another for teacher aides, absorbed some of the fund's money. But the Arkansas program received the most notice. All the state's teachers' colleges participated in an experiment in which future teachers received no methods courses in their four college years. These years were devoted solely to liberal arts study. The fund then financed a fifth year for those who planned to teach so that they could receive the pedagogical training they needed.

Some institutions participated voluntarily in the fund's fifth-year experiment by adding a master of arts in teaching (M.A.T.) program and using fund grants to pay the fifth year's tuition. They tended already to offer a liberal education. Harvard University, Goucher College, Temple, Yale, and other institutions participated. The idea had come from a program that had existed at Harvard since the 1930s. Faust had developed the plan in discussions with Abraham Flexner and Francis Keppel, dean of the Harvard Graduate School of Education.[18] But the program obviously carried the mark of Hutchins and the former dean of the college at the University of Chicago. Beyond these elite members of the higher education establishment, Hutchins and Faust did not attempt to include a wider group of educators in the process of conception or implementation.

As a historian of the fund has noted, the opposition to the Arkansas program was extensive. Professional educators thought that the design reflected little knowledge of the problems of schools and ignored the extensive pedagogical training future teachers needed if they were to perform successfully in the classroom. Critics claimed that the program was elitist in nature, because teachers would have to delay entering the profession and earning an income for another year. With the teacher shortage of the early 1950s, it was also impractical. In addition, there was no provision for research on the effectiveness of the plan in comparison to existing teacher education programs.[19] The fund merely asserted the superiority of the approach, much as Hutchins had made similar assertions about liberal education at the University of Chicago.

The hostility from professional associations and other colleges of education was intense. The Arkansas program folded after a few years because the teachers and administrators lost confidence in the efficacy of the approach. Had Faust and his board consulted with professional educators, members of teacher organizations, and classroom teachers, the results might have been different.[20] Relying on a narrowly defined group of experts and on a conception of education divorced from the realities of teachers' lives meant that a significant opportunity for Hutchins to create a model to increase the foundation's effectiveness was lost. Though many institutions continue to offer a fifth-year option (without the support of foundation funds), the predominant method of training teachers continues to be undergraduate programs.

The Fund for the Advancement of Education was absorbed into the Ford Foundation in 1967. During its sixteen-year existence it spent nearly $71 million on education, over $26.6 million on teacher education, and over $22.39 million on the improvement of education, including teacher aide training, educational television, and other programs.[21] While much of this investment undoubtedly improved education for the many who benefited from the grants and programs, there is little to indicate that Hutchins' characteristic views on education left a mark.

By late 1952, Hutchins was in trouble with the Ford Foundation's board. A number of board members had begun to resent the fact that half of the foundation's disbursements were going to the funds and various other programs he oversaw. Donald David, of the Harvard Business School, wondered why his favorite causes could not be financed if Hutchins' were.[22] A number of the funds' staff and board members were Hutchins' former colleagues, and a number of grants were provided for his friends, another point of resentment.[23] In addition to the involvement of Faust, Fletcher, Adler, James Laughlin of Intercultural Publications, James Webb Young of the Television-Radio Workshop, James H. Douglas, Paepcke, and others who served on the board of the funds, the University of Chicago received Ford money for Robert Redfield to study, compare, and classify cultures. The Redfield project was to provide some theoretical understanding of cultural differences and similarities.[24] Laughlin's Intercultural Publications published magazines designed to enhance cultural understanding between the United States and European and Asian countries. Magazines on United States culture were to be distributed to other countries, and magazines on other cultures were to be distributed to United States schools and libraries.[25] Whatever the merits of the projects, the board perceived culture as another area over which Hutchins had control of foundation policy.[26]

Hutchins' problems were compounded by circumstances beyond his control. The early months had been full of hope and excitement for the kinds of projects the Ford Foundation could launch and sustain. But hope was not enough for Henry Ford II and the board of directors of the foundation. Ford was disturbed with Hutchins' and Hoffman's loose managerial style. They delegated much responsibility for program management to staff members in both the Pasadena and the New York offices. Hoffman was frequently absent from the offices during his first year, traveling abroad and throughout the United States. He decided in March of 1952 to take a leave of absence to work on Dwight Eisenhower's presidential campaign. The burden of managing the foundation's affairs fell on Hutchins' shoulders. His relationship with Henry Ford rapidly deteriorated, and this deterioration was compounded by the other board members' resentment of the extent of his power.[27]

Hutchins refused to engage in the tactful education of foundation board members, including Henry Ford, as he had at the University of Chicago with Harold Swift and others. His disdain for Ford money and power was obvious to all who worked at the foundation.[28] This disdain is not surprising. However much he had come to appreciate first-class treatment at the university, the comfort of his social status, and the ease of California life, Hutchins had been raised to hold in contempt the power that a man like Ford derived from his wealth and family connections. Beyond the personal animosity that existed between Hutchins and Henry Ford, Ford, Donald David, and other trustees had reservations about the particular focus of the two funds—liberal education as defined by Hutchins.[29]

Hutchins' response to these reservations was to reiterate the independent nature of the funds' relationship with the foundation and the need to preserve that independence. He noted that this did not mean that the funds could deviate from the original goals of the foundation. But the board retained control because it could refuse to continue providing appropriations whenever members thought the funds' activities did not accord with the purposes and policies for which the funds had received earlier appropriations.[30]

Hutchins was involved in the establishment of the foundation's third fund, which represented area II of the foundation's sphere of activity, the strengthening of democracy. Following Adler's August 1951 seminar for the directors on freedom, Hutchins and W. H. Ferry worked out the strategy for addressing area II.[31] Ferry was with the Earl Newsom agency as the public relations adviser to the foundation and Henry Ford's speech writer. He had graduated from Harvard, taught at Choate, and returned to Grosse Point, where his father had been president of the Packard Motor Company. Ferry had begun to deviate from the expectations of Grosse Point's upper crust when he became public relations director of the Congress of Industrial Organizations (CIO) Political Action Committee.[32]

Ferry and Hutchins were both iconoclasts. Their design of the Fund for the Republic was motivated by the activity of Senator Joseph McCarthy and the House Un-American Activities Committee (HUAC), growing fears of communist subversion and the media's exploitation of them, the prevalent use of loyalty oaths for numerous occupations, the expansion of the federal loyalty-security program, and a variety of civil rights abuses, including denial of voting rights, racial discrimination in housing, education, and employment, and other violations of the Fourteenth and Fifteenth Amendments.[33]

A number of detailed accounts of the development of the Fund for the Republic exist.[34] Of interest here is the way Hutchins transformed the original intention of the fund into an institution that closely resembled his model of intellectual work. Initially, Hutchins did not plan to become directly involved in the fund beyond establishing it and laying out a tentative program. He pushed Hoffman to gain the foundation directors' approval for financing it. Hoffman was successful in October of 1951, and the fund received a million-dollar initial allocation.

Hutchins began to work out some of the problems the fund would address, including the problems mentioned above, as well as the conditions of migrant workers, freedom of the press, governmental dishonesty, and the rights of conscientious objectors.[35] Study of or action on any one of these problems was potentially inflammatory in the early 1950s, and Hoffman and Ford agreed that the officers should carefully choose the fund's president and board. As president, Hoffman suggested Charles E. Wilson, a politically conservative former president of General Motors and member of the Ford Foundation board. Wilson took five months to turn down the position, and Ford decided to delay action on the fund until after the 1952 presidential election.[36]

In the fall and winter of 1952, Hutchins, by his own account, "hand-picked" the members of the fund's board, presumed to be people who could withstand any public pressure that might arise.[37] Hoffman and Ford gave final approval to Hutchins' choices. Hutchins was anxious to proceed. Shortly before the presidential election, he presented the board with a list of possible grantees who had come to the attention of officers of the foundation, and the suggested range of activities the fund might pursue.[38]

A temporary president was chosen at the board's first meeting in December 1952. David Freeman was a lawyer and member of the Ford Foundation staff. In February the fund's board requested that the foundation provide a lump sum grant in order to protect itself from the opposition and hostility that were sure to arise as a result of the fund's activities in sensitive areas of civil rights and liberties. A grant of $15 million, including the original $1 million was made, with $2.8 million payable immediately and the balance upon request of the fund's board.[39] In May, Clifford P. Case, Republican congressman from New Jersey, accepted the presidency of the fund, to begin in September.

By early 1953, Paul Hoffman's relationship with Ford and the board had deteriorated. Ford was upset with Hoffman's management of the foundation and decided that the operations should be moved to New York. Hoffman resigned in March but was appointed chairman of the Fund for the Republic's board. Hutchins elected to remain in Pasadena. He and Vesta Hutchins, who had been diagnosed as having a weak heart, preferred California to New York for personal and health reasons, and Hutchins thought he could oversee his responsibilities just as well in Pasadena. By the summer of 1953, it was clear that many of the foundation's board members wanted Hutchins out.[40] But he refused to go without an adequate settlement.

He spent the succeeding months negotiating with the board. He wanted a position commensurate with his reputation, preferably one that paid him enough to cover his alimony to Maude Hutchins and his living expenses in California. Benton offered him a lifelong executive position with the EB, and the Ford Foundation offered him a part-time consultant position; but these were not satisfactory, in light of the prestige and power of his previous work.[41] In the same period, the Fund for the Republic attracted the attention of conservative congressman Brazilla Carroll Reece of Tennessee, who decided that the fund, Hutchins, and the Ford Foundation were protecting the "civil liberties of Communists" and ought to be investigated.[42] The foundation could not turn Hutchins out under the circumstances.

Since leaving Chicago, Hutchins had been exploring the possibility of establishing with Ford money an academy that would reflect his conception of the ideal intellectual community. In 1951 he raised the question with his fellow officers of where "intellectual illumination and sound practical advice" were going to come from in contemporary American life.[43] He chaired two gatherings through the Fund for the Advancement of Education in 1953, one in Princeton and one in London, to discuss the form such an academy would take and received endorsement for the idea from the participants.[44]

The academy's task would be to counter "the disintegration of the intellectual world." He thought it ought to include "the greatest minds of our time in all fields" who "could advance knowledge and perform the task of illumination by the joint consideration of the most important problems, speculative and practical." He suggested that the project might begin by gathering together "a small group of senior men" who could decide upon a problem for study and circulate in writing their research and thinking on particular aspects of the problem.[45]

The directors were agreeable to Hutchins' focusing on the academy and any other projects he wanted to pursue through the existing Fund for the Advancement of Education until they could concur on how his future should be settled.[46] In February he submitted a statement of his interests, which included the academy. He outlined some of the "basic issues" he thought needed the attention of "a group of the best minds of our time": organized labor, taxation, medical care costs, freedom of expression, and intellectual leadership in democratic societies "committed to mass education."[47] In the end, he got everything he wanted, but not because the directors of the Ford Foundation gave him the $10 million he thought it would cost to operate the academy for ten years.

In March of 1954, Case resigned from the Fund for the Republic to run for political office. The board of the fund decided that Hutchins should become the next president. Henry Ford was opposed to the idea, probably because he would have liked to rid the foundation completely of Hutchins. Two directors, Paul Hoffman and George N. Shuster, wanted

Hutchins to remain as a consultant to the fund. The majority prevailed, however, and Hutchins was appointed in April. With his appointment, the fund took a leap forward in its work in civil rights and civil liberties.

The fund had commissioned a number of projects under Freeman and Case that reflected Hutchins' early outline of possible program areas and set its course for the next few years. These included an American Bar Association study of constitutional violations of individual liberties by congressional investigating committees, a survey of public opinion about communism and civil liberties by Samuel A. Stouffer of Harvard, and a study of communism in the United States by Clinton Rossiter of Cornell. The American Friends Service Committee received support for its race relations program, as did the Southern Regional Council and the Carrie Chapman Catt Memorial Fund for community education programs. Although it had begun to address some of the disturbing problems of the era, including violations of civil rights and liberties, the board was impatient with the amount of time it was taking to get these projects under way and so was Hutchins.

As he later recalled, when he "innocently accepted the Presidency of the Fund for the Republic," he "overestimated the public knowledge of foundations and the way they work" and public familiarity with the Bill of Rights.[48] He was unprepared for the immense campaign against the fund by various congressional investigating committees and the right-wing press. He had testified before the Cox Committee in 1952 in defense of the Ford Foundation and had gained the respect of the chairman of the committee for his spirited and witty defense of the foundation's activities.[49] But that was before the fund began its activity. Under Hutchins, the pace and intensity of giving increased.

The fund provided increased support for community education programs in civil liberties and race relations and for projects investigating the treatment of Mexican migrant workers in the United States, the rights and liberties of Native Americans, racial discrimination in housing by real estate brokers in cahoots with lending agencies, and the extent and effects of blacklisting in the entertainment industry. As a result of McCarthy's attack on the Army, the fund financed a study by Samuel Stouffer of the effects on public opinion of televising the Army-McCarthy hearings. Adam Yarmolinsky, who later joined the fund's staff, began compiling a history of government loyalty-security cases.

By stepping up the fund's activities in these areas and calling into question federal and state laws that had allowed constitutional violations of civil rights and liberties, Hutchins and his board placed the fund in direct opposition to conservative, fundamentalist groups. The investigation of the fund by the Reece committee in 1953 and 1954 revealed the extent to which such right-wing groups were threatened by the modernist, liberal implications of the fund's work to preserve constitutional ideals and educate the American people about them.

Because of the strength of his convictions and his willingness to put himself in the line of fire to defend them (in the best Oberlin tradition), Hutchins was a good candidate to head the fund in the middle 1950s. But not long into his presidency, the board began to have reservations about the appropriateness of his behavior. No doubt some of the members' trepidation can be attributed to their personal fears about the vehemence of such critics as Fulton Lewis, Jr., Westbrook Pegler, George Sokolsky, the American Legion, and the Reece committee. Yet Hutchins' particular style of defense also raised serious questions about his ability to work with his staff and to keep his board members educated and informed about the fund's activities.

When he agreed to take the presidency, Hutchins asked W. H. Ferry to be his vice-president and to run the New York office of the fund. Ferry's strong commitment to civil rights and liberties and his willingness to face down the fund's critics induced him to leave the Newsom Agency and take the position. As he has recalled, some of his greatest difficulties in the first year had to do with Hutchins' management style. Hutchins requested that Ferry dismiss a couple of Case's staff members and provide them with severance pay. When these staff members did not like Ferry's terms, they appealed to Hutchins, who acceded to their demands, undercutting Ferry's authority and creating dissension in the office. In addition, Hutchins occasionally approved small grants knowing that Ferry had refused them, which led some grantees to bypass the New York office. But Ferry stayed on because he respected Hutchins and otherwise found it easy to work with him. The two men agreed on many issues of principle.[50] As staff member David Freeman recalled, Hutchins was a "terrific idea man" who was "good at delegating" responsibility and, for the most part, "tended to back people up" on policy issues.[51]

As manager of the New York office, Ferry was obliged to deal with members of the press. Although he always consulted Hutchins about the interviews beforehand, board members only read about them afterward. Ferry was known as an abrupt, often impatient and argumentative man, particularly when his sensibilities were offended. He had little tolerance for the questions and criticisms of Fulton Lewis, Jr., and others who designated themselves as watchdogs of the fund. Unfortunately, the directors viewed this arrangement with Ferry as damaging to the fund. They thought Hutchins ought to establish better rapport with the press to protect the fund's work. He, in contrast, thought Ferry's "dedication, drive, persistence, imagination, and courage" were necessary to the fund's effectiveness.[52]

Hutchins compounded matters when he delivered a speech on the Reece committee early in 1955, shortly after it folded operations without finding any wrongdoing by the fund, Hutchins, or the Ford Foundation.[53] Claiming that he spoke only for himself and not for the fund, he accused the committee of a "wild and squalid" effort to excoriate foundations by "exploit[ing]" public concerns "about communism and subversion." From the beginning, he told the National Press Club, the investigation was "a fraud." The committee's premises represented a highly selective and self-serving interpretation of constitutional rights, he thought.[54] Throughout 1955 the fund continued to suffer from repeated accusations by its critics. Speeches like this by Hutchins, however justified in spirit, threatened to hamper the board's ability to finance the investigations of abuses and to educate the public about them.

Hutchins informed the board in September that he had authorized Ferry to hire Amos Landman, a man who had pleaded the Fifth Amendment before HUAC, to assist in the New York office. Ferry hired Landman in part to test director Erwin Griswold's commitment to the arguments he had made in his *Fifth Amendment Today* about the importance of protecting employees from being fired for any reason other than incompetence.[55] Informed after the fact, board members, particularly Griswold, were furious. One, Arthur Dean, resigned. Hutchins determined to repair the public image of the fund and assuage board members' fears about further harassment by agreeing to a press conference in November. Unfortunately for his purposes, when questioned, he admitted that he would be willing to "hire a communist" if qualified for the job and if he (Hutchins) were in a position to supervise him.[56]

Taken together, these and other actions that drew criticism brought Hutchins into confrontation with members of his board. In early November, at the board's request, Hutchins submitted a review of the program's compliance with the original intentions of the fund. According to Ferry, the Ford Foundation was pressuring the Fund's board, citing the directors' prerogative to demand return of the grant if the fund was not complying with its original mandate.[57]

Hutchins informed the directors that, by the very nature of its mission, the fund was liable to be attacked. He suggested that the board might profit in its effort to deal with these attacks by meeting for longer periods to explore the full implications of each grant. Further, some additions to the staff to better facilitate public relations might help. But it was clear that Hutchins expected the full backing of the board for each project the fund supported and every action undertaken by the fund's staff, no matter how controversial. Because the fund was "trying to help save the Republic," it was crucial for the board to exhibit "steadfastness" in resistance to public criticism.[58]

In December he agreed to appear on "Meet the Press" to respond to questions about the fund, but the interviewers interrogated him about whether he would hire a Communist. Rather than drawing on his dry humor or witty store of quips, Hutchins grew sullen on the air, leaving an impression that disturbed even his friends and supporters. The fund received word that its tax-exempt status was under investigation by the Internal Revenue Service and by Chairman Francis E. Walter of HUAC. For four board members particularly, the issue was not the controversial nature of the fund's projects but Hutchins' management of the fund under the intense scrutiny of the press and of public officials on the political right. They requested Hutchins' resignation.[59]

Erwin Griswold, the trustee who initiated the request, noted that Hutchins' defense of the fund's work asserted, rather than explained, the merits of the fund's activities. His "provocative" and "dramatic" public responses to criticism had evoked "strong reactions," increasing opposition and misunderstanding instead of persuading others of the importance of defending civil liberties and civil rights.[60]

Clearly, Hutchins was not trying to make enemies for the fund. But this kind of concern about his influence on the fund's future shows a pattern similar to the one about which James R. Angell and the University of Chicago trustees had complained: the attitude he projected of arrogance, impatience, and superior morality and intelligence. When he thought he was right, he simply could not understand why others failed to agree with his position or why they criticized his tactics. The moral correctness of the position, he seemed to think, ought to draw support. But his board, like many foundation boards of the period, was composed mostly of white male businessmen who, however strongly they valued civil rights and liberties, were not accustomed to having their names and reputations associated with unpopular causes and dragged through the press.[61] This was a reality Hutchins had trouble grasping.

In response to Griswold's and the other directors' demand that he resign, Hutchins provided the board with a plan for reorganizing the fund's operations. He agreed to relocate all the fund's operations in New York, to move Ferry from dealing with the press to overseeing programs, and to put David Freeman, a more tactful man than Ferry, in charge of administering the office. He suggested hiring a public relations expert. He clarified the fund's relationship to its grantees, one that refrained from controlling projects after a grant was made. He defended the rapidity with which the program had moved under his presidency by recalling that the directors themselves had been impatient with the fund's progress before he arrived. And he reminded the board that the fund had to stand by the principles, embodied in the Constitution, that it was pledged to defend, including the First and Fifth Amendments.[62] He was willing to make changes in his managerial style but was unwilling to compromise on his beliefs. As Ferry later recalled, Hutchins was confident that the board ultimately would support him, because he was right.[63]

A special January meeting of the directors resulted in approval of Hutchins' reorganization "on a trial basis."[64] Shortly afterward, the Hutchinses moved to New York, where Barbara enrolled in the Chapin School, Joanna already held a job, and Clarissa, who was in school in Andover, Massachusetts, would be close enough for weekend visits. With his family settled, Hutchins made the other changes he had promised. Frank K. Kelly, a former Senate aide and more recently an executive at the Stephen Fitzgerald public relations agency, began to repair the fund's image. He made contact with all his friends and colleagues in the media and developed a four-page newsletter called the *Bulletin* that was sent to one hundred thousand people on the fund's mailing list. He persuaded Hutchins and trustee Elmo Roper to agree to allow the American Broadcasting Company to televise a thirteen-week series featuring celebrities who would talk about "Survival and Freedom," to be hosted by Mike Wallace.[65]

Kelly's efforts began to show results almost immediately. The IRS investigation was quietly halted, and the Walter committee eventually withdrew. When John Cogley's *Report on Blacklisting* was published and he was called before HUAC to testify about his informants, sympathy for Cogley and the fund had already been generated by Kelly's public relations work.[66] And Hutchins' more prudent administration regenerated some of the board support he had lost in 1955.

By 1956 the fund had allocated $5,414,201. Nearly one-third of the money had been spent to improve race relations in the South, another third to stimulate local community discussions about civil liberties, and the remainder on commissioned studies of minorities, communism, and loyalty-security cases. Over $1 million had been used for administrative expenses, an excessive amount for this purpose. But much of it covered the legal assistance and public relations expenses necessary to defend the fund.[67]

Throughout 1956, Hutchins pressed the board to consider reorienting the fund's mission, in part because he found in the fund's troubles and in the continuing legacy of Joseph McCarthy's campaign disturbing evidence of the need for wider public education on the principles of American democracy. He hoped to transform the activities from active grant making in a variety of areas to a centralized, coherent study and discussion program focusing on particular problems. The proposal was not unlike the kind of proposition he had made in *The Higher Learning in America* about the redirecting of intellectual work in the university or his ongoing dream of an Institute of Philosophical Studies.

Whereas the organizing principles of his 1930s and 1940s schemes were predicted on the subordination of all scholarly endeavors to the study of philosophy, the guiding ideas of his 1956 plan were based on the notion that responsible political behavior by Americans required a group of experts to clarify for them the basic ideas and ideals of democracy. He had exchanged for a scholastic philosophy a political theory as the intellectual center of his ideas.[68] By the end of 1956 it was obvious that Hutchins had been successful. The gradual attrition of staff and board members opposed to his plans, and the loyalty of staff and board members who believed in him contributed to the realization of his hopes for an academy-like enterprise.

Members of the board had begun to rethink the fund's activities in early 1956. Roger Lapham, for example, thought the fund should focus its grant making where it might be most effective. One benefit of this plan would be to reduce the overhead costs that had been created by the large staff necessary to oversee projects in the fund's areas of giving, areas in which other foundations had not operated. Lapham thought the most important area of civil rights and liberties was racial desegregation. Getting "the country to accept" the *Brown* decision and apply it broadly would be "well worth" the fund's remaining assets.[69] This was the last serious effort by a board member to take the initiative in suggesting the direction of the fund. Throughout 1956 the board members who disagreed with Hutchins' basic issues program engaged in resistance rather than initiation.

At the May meeting of the board, for example, Hutchins proposed using a portion of the fund's budget to establish an institute or council for the study of freedom. The council would be composed of "qualified, compatible men" of differing viewpoints and professional backgrounds. They would gather full-time for part of the year "to work out the concepts basic to freedom" and "arrive at common convictions in spite of profound philosophical differences." They would study, read, and discuss, and produce reports, papers, and books. The institute would be "something like a university," but there would be no students, classes, or degrees. The ultimate educational goal would be to clarify civil liberties issues for the American people.[70] He hoped "to show a pluralistic society how it can reach unanimous devotion to justice and freedom."[71]

The board granted him $25,000 to gather together a group of experts to hold seminars on the proposal. He held meetings in Chicago, Princeton, and New York, consulting an impressive group of academics, theologians, and publishers, among them some of his colleagues from Chicago, including Mortimer Adler, Robert Redfield,and Richard McKeon.[72] As a result of these meetings, he proposed to the board in October that the members consider providing more money for organizing the program, which would represent the primary work of the fund and, at the same time, continue some of the earlier kinds of projects. He thought, for example, that the group could treat race relations issues by putting them "outside the realm of acrimonious controversy" with a theoretical consideration of the problem and conducting "factual" studies of blacks and of racism. A long-term commitment of the fund to this kind of program, the gathering of prominent people in various fields to study and discuss "practical" problems in light of basic democratic ideals, would do more for the country than scattered giving or short-term commitment to such a project.[73] And Hutchins himself would have more control over the direction and outcome.

Not everyone at the fund agreed. Three directors resigned in 1956, two of them over disagreements with Hutchins.[74] Three who supported Hutchins were added. Harry S. Ashmore, Pulitzer Prize–winning editor of the Little Rock *Gazette,* had been a director but had taken a leave of absence. Alicia Patterson, newspaper publisher, and Bruce Catton, historian, also joined the board. Two incumbents, Griswold and Lapham, continued to disagree with Hutchins. Two staff members who were against the plan presented an alternative proposal for the November meeting of the board. Adam Yarmolinsky and David Freeman were committed to the diverse perspectives that produced the commissioned studies of race relations and civil liberties issues and to the local, community-based educational efforts of the Carrie Chapman Catt Memorial Fund and the Southern Regional Council. They thought clarification of civil liberties and civil rights issues would more likely occur through publication of the studies to be used by those making public policy and through local discussion of them by ordinary people in their communities.[75]

The board decided in November to support Hutchins' program. The trustees appropriated an additional $20,000 for him to develop the proposal. At the same meeting the board assigned funds to ongoing programs favored by Freeman, Yarmolinsky, Griswold, and Lapham.[76] By February of 1957, Hutchins had presented the board with three initial areas of investigation—the corporation, the military, and the church—for which the program received $100,000. Three more areas were in preparation—the union, the mass media, and voluntary associations. The emphasis of the study group was to be on how each of these agencies restricted or enhanced individual freedom. He received an additional $125,000 in November of 1957.[77]

By the end of 1957, Lapham had resigned and Griswold was the only remaining board member who disagreed with Hutchins. He and Hutchins had attended Oberlin, where Griswold was Francis Hutchins' classmate and Will Hutchins' student. Despite this history, they had never been comfortable with each other.[78] But this dispute over the direction of the fund cannot be attributed solely to their personal history. Hutchins clearly sought to use the fund to establish his ideal intellectual community. If the ideas were clear enough, people would be persuaded to adopt them. Griswold wanted to see the fund continue as a grant-making agency, financing studies that could be used to inform public policy and financing other institutions or agencies, like the Southern Regional Council, that were equipped to educate the public. Freeman and Yarmolinsky had similar views.[79] They resigned in 1957. Griswold followed them within the year.

Somehow, Lapham, O'Brian, Zellerbach, Griswold, Freeman, and Yarmolinsky simply were not swayed by the Hutchins charm. Their conception of the fund's mission was so well defined and their belief in institutionally directed education so strong that Hutchins could not persuade them to think differently about it. But for the remaining staff and board members Hutchins' leadership was unquestioned. The single-mindedness of his ideas and the repetitiveness of his discussion of them notwithstanding, even to those who did not agree with him, his "personality and style" sometimes made him "seem larger than life."[80]

Hutchins used the $225,000 basic issues allocation to assemble a group of consultants to examine the six basic issues areas in light of the ideas embodied in the Declaration of Independence and the Constitution. He called upon such luminaries as Adolph A. Berle, Jr., former secretary of state, Eugene Burdick, political scientist at the University of California at Berkeley, Eric Goldman, historian at Princeton, Clark Kerr, chancellor of the University of California, John Courtney Murray, Jesuit theologian, Reinhold Niebuhr, theologian at Union Theological Seminary, Isidor Rabi, Nobel physicist at Columbia University, and his old friends Walter Millis, military historian and Yale classmate, Scott Buchanan, Robert Redfield, and Henry Luce.[81]

This kind of assemblage was his dream. As president of the University of Chicago, he had never been able to bring together such a group to engage in intense intellectual discussions of a particular topic of his choosing, except on a short-term basis as with the Commission on the Freedom of the Press. In addition, he had never had such control of the content and direction of the discussions. He requested a memorandum from Leonard W. Levy, legal historian, on "the original meanings of the First Amendment's clauses" for one session. After research in primary legal materials, Levy concluded that the framers intended clear separation of church and state, but according to the record, suppressed free speech with latitudinarian seditious libel laws from 1776 to 1791. Hutchins, who did not like the latter conclusion, exercised control by telling Levy he would publish only part of his work.[82]

The consultants met seven times from May of 1957 to May of 1958. Their research and discussions resulted in four pamphlets: *Individual Freedom and the Common Defense,* by Walter Millis, *Economic Power and the Free Society,* by Adolph A. Berle, Jr., *Unions and Union Leaders of Their Own Choosing,* by Clark Kerr, and *The Corporation and the Republic,* by Scott Buchanan, all published by the fund. But by the end of that year of meetings, it was clear that Hutchins was not happy with the results.

Illness prevented regular attendance by Niebuhr, Luce, Rabi, and Redfield. To Hutchins' great sorrow, Redfield lost his battle against leukemia and died in 1958. The consultants who were able to attend regularly did not function well together. Preeminent in their fields, they tended to state and defend their positions as if they were debating each other instead of engaging in discussion that would result in the agreement about principles that Hutchins sought.[83] Staff members thought Hutchins ought to take a lead in focusing the discussions.[84] And Scott Buchanan thought too many members of the group acted like "primadonna [sic] pundits."[85]

Hutchins did not think the problem with the group's discussions was his fault or theirs. Rather, the way the program was organized made it less effective than it might be. He informed the board that the solution was to make a long-term, well-financed commitment. He recommended allocating $4.5 million of the fund's assets to the basic issues program. The remaining $1 million would finance any outstanding projects in other areas for three years.[86] The board agreed to support the program for three years.[87] In late 1958, Hutchins invited his friend William O. Douglas to become a consultant and help the group focus on legal and constitutional problems.[88] But when only five consultants attended the March 1959 meeting, it was clear to the staff and consultants that the group had not lived up to anyone's expectations.[89]

Hutchins informed the board at the May 1959 meeting that the consultants' group had failed. Knowing that the directors supported him, he persuaded them that the problem with the program was not its fundamental conception but that part-time participation in discussions was difficult for the caliber of participant the fund desired. In contemplating a residential program for the fund, Hutchins had explored the possibility of moving its activities away from New York.

He and Vesta owned a piece of land in Santa Barbara, California, to which they planned to retire. When his wife urged him to think about relocating the fund there, he asked a friend to investigate the available real estate. On finding an old, reasonably priced estate up in the hills in Montecito and acquiring a donation adequate to cover the cost of remodeling the house, Hutchins decided to put the whole proposition before the board. At the May 20 meeting, the directors voted unanimously to rename the program the Center for the Study of Democratic Institutions and to move the fund's operations to California.[90]

The failure of the basic issues program of the fund can be seen in at least two ways. It reflected Hutchins' typical short-term commitment to the innovations he devised. The Law School program at Yale and the Committee on the Liberal Arts at Chicago had benefited from his energy and lively rhetoric. These also were efforts to create an intellectual community that would serve as an alternative to existing programs, but Hutchins exhibited little sustained engagement with them. More significant, he showed even less interest in questioning or changing his fundamental approach to dealing with the personalities, conflicts, and behaviors of the members of these groups. The basic issues program can be seen as the failure of Hutchins to understand how to handle complicated group dynamics in a sustained way. Its demise suggests, too, that there were flaws in his attempt to show that the discussion by elites of pressing practical problems in light of political ideals was more beneficial to the larger society than financing local community discussion programs.

On one hand, Hutchins described the earlier grant-making program as a futile effort to put out the fires of controversy without examining the fundamental ideas that ought to inform rational discussion of them.[91] On the other hand, the academy idea, he argued, would be a more effective means of public education because great minds could define the problems and the terms of discussion in the rational way that was necessary. Unfortunately, there were no other foundations in 1958 waiting in the wings to address the problems of civil liberties and civil rights once the fund abandoned them. Eventually, others stepped in, but in those crucial years after the *Brown* decision and before desegregation remedies were in place in most states, communities were on their own.[92]

Hutchins' commitment to the idea of the academy inspired the remaining board members and staff. The goal of repairing the intellectual and cultural life the modern university had helped to fragment was far more appealing to Hutchins and his board than research on public policy issues and support of popular educational programs. They all moved to California in 1959 to seek the utopian intellectual community he hoped to create.

CHAPTER 12 *Problems in Utopia*

THE CENTER FOR THE STUDY OF DEMOCRATIC INSTITUTIONS was a kind of utopia for Hutchins. His envisioned academy, the center was an alternative university established to consider political problems, clarify ends and means, and enlighten the larger society. It had no students, no classes, and no obligations to publish. There was no specialization. Center participants were to work together on the problems chosen for examination and discussion. They studied, using the library at the University of California at Santa Barbara, they conducted research, they attended colloquia, and they welcomed visiting scholars.

If Hutchins could have established his imagined academy anywhere, he should have been able to do it there. Set in the sun-dappled, eucalyptus-covered hills, with a broad view of the Pacific, in an old marble-floored villa wrapped around a courtyard, it could have been mistaken for paradise. But it never succeeded as a viable alternative to, nor as a haven from, the modern university. The reasons for this failure are understandable. As inspiring as Hutchins' idea and ideals were, he did not have a rich textural view of the world.

The rigidity of his ideas was compounded by his human frailty. He had little skill in negotiating conflicts in personal relationships, a significant component of any intellectual activity involving cooperation. That lack of skill had undone many of the other cooperative endeavors he had attempted. Further, he had little tolerance for uncertainty or diversity. Despite his wit and appreciation for irony, his was not a playful intellect, and not until the late 1960s did his thinking about his major preoccupation, education, exhibit growth and wisdom.

The center's demise occurred because Hutchins was so much a part of its definition that when his health failed, there was not enough of a commitment to the idea on which it was based to sustain it. The idea itself reflected little understanding of the real needs and desires that moved the "best minds" he continually sought to gather together. He set the center in contradistinction to the university, increasingly the source of the scholarship that influenced public policy, and apart from the general public, for whom it was clarifying the basic issues underlying public policies. By doing so,

Hutchins effectively left the center's constituents with little rationale for continuing to support the institution without his leadership.

"El Parthenon," Hutchins' nickname for the center, reflected his grand dreams and elegant tastes. Early every morning the tall, distinguished president, wearing his perennial blue suede shoes and bow tie, drew his silver Jaguar up to the decaying white stucco main house on the forty-acre estate.[1] The formal gardens, tennis courts, and empty swimming pool remained unused and untended. And the distant, elevated location, with views of the sea and the mountains, served as a metaphor for Hutchins' clear preference for removed, rational discussion of politics, law, and education.

Hutchins invited a number of his associates from the Fund for the Republic staff and the basic issues consultants to join him in Santa Barbara, but philosopher Scott Buchanan was the only nonstaff person to move immediately with him into the center's new offices. Buchanan's job included helping to shape the discussions that would be the central activity of the center's program. He was to teach the participants the arts of discussion to counter the desultory results of the basic issues program.[2] Until his death in 1968, he was Hutchins' closest and most influential colleague at the center.

W. H. Ferry was reluctant to go, despite Hutchins' insistent invitation. As he later recalled, he perceived the center as a chance for Hutchins to make a new start, choosing people for the expertise and scholarly capability most suitable to the center's mission.[3] But Ferry finally agreed to make the move, as did fellow staff members Frank Kelly and Hallock Hoffman, and consultant John Cogley. Eventually, more staff members and consultants joined the center under the auspices of a variety of projects and financing schemes that helped keep the organization financially afloat.

Several accounts of the center's history exist.[4] For the purposes of understanding how Hutchins translated his relationship with the modern university into his leadership of the center, an extensively detailed account of every center activity, crisis, and participant is unnecessary. Rather, what is of interest here is the way some of these activities, crises, and participants were treated by Hutchins in his effort to secure his academy. One of his early decisions, for example, was to try to avoid the academic proclivity for specialization. This resulted in the recruitment to the center of a number of journalists, including Harry Ashmore and Donald McDonald (of the Marquette School of Journalism), and in Hutchins' expectation that all staff members would participate in center discussions.

A brief overview of the center's history is in order. For the first decade,

Hutchins continued the basic issues program. Harry Ashmore joined the center in October of 1959. He agreed to work half-time with Frank Kelly on the media study, which was part of the basic issues program. The Benton Foundation, established by William Benton to study the media, covered Ashmore's salary. The remainder of Ashmore's time in the first year was spent on free-lance projects of his own. He became Hutchins' confidant after Buchanan died.

Hallock Hoffman, formerly of the American Friends Service Committee (and Paul Hoffman's son), focused on the political process. Cogley continued his study of religious institutions. Walter Millis elected to remain in New York to proceed with his work on the military. Paul Jacobs, who had been working with Clark Kerr on the trade union study, remained in Berkeley with Kerr to carry that project forward. By the late 1960s this group produced a number of pamphlets, reports, and papers that were distributed to libraries, individuals, and schools as part of the center's growing publications program.

The center's operations were expensive. Hutchins' interest in bringing together "the best minds" to ponder the problems the consultants studied resulted in gatherings with numerous luminaries, including Isadore Rabi, Reinhold Niebuhr, John Courtney Murray, William O. Douglas, who joined the board, Lewis Mumford, Robert F. Kennedy, Gunnar Myrdal, Walter P. Reuther, Thurgood Marshall, and many others, a reflection of Hutchins' drawing power and the center's hopes for wide-ranging influence. It became clear to Hutchins that the $4 million remaining in the fund's budget would not cover the costs of running the center on the scale he desired. In 1960 Hutchins, William Benton, and the rest of the *Encyclopaedia Britannica* (EB) board decided that the EB needed thorough revision in time for its two-hundredth anniversary in 1968. Rather than rely on an already busy University of Chicago faculty to carry out the revisions, Benton, who controlled the voting stock, turned to the center.

Hutchins agreed to the plan and asked Harry Ashmore to serve as editor-in-chief of the project, drawing on the expertise of the center's consultants and board of directors. This agreement covered Ashmore's expanded salary and operating expenses of $750,000 per year until 1964. The financing enabled Hutchins to add to the group of consultants and broaden the basic issues program. Because the planned revision included a topical reorganization of the EB, Ashmore proposed a series of "roof articles" to experiment with this new approach. The roof articles focused on "scientific, social, political, educational, economic, and cultural institutions and processes" and their effects on "ordinary" people's daily lives.[5] This design was intended to contrast with typical academic categories.

The broad purview of the EB project allowed Cogley, for example, to propose another area of study for the center, the "American Character." He recruited Paul Jacobs and Michael Harrington, both of whom had worked on the blacklisting study, and Donald McDonald. He hosted a four-day conference in Washington, D.C., increasing the center's visibility, and published a number of pamphlets on the consultants' findings. Michael Harrington's *The Other America* (1962), credited with raising Americans' consciousness of poverty, was based on his research and was written at the center. And McDonald joined the center's staff after finishing his work on the ethics of the press as his "American Character" assignment.

Benton grew impatient with the progress of the EB revisions. In 1964 he moved the operation to Chicago and offered Mortimer Adler a lifetime contract to oversee the mammoth task under the auspices of his Institute for Philosophical Research. Hutchins, of course, continued to be connected with the project as chairman of the board of editors, a position he had held since the EB had been acquired by Benton and the University of Chicago. But the center lost the annual infusion of money that had helped expand its operations. The roof articles were published in 1968 as *Britannica Perspectives* to celebrate EB's two-hundredth anniversary. Adler's version of the completed revisions was published in 1974.

A further search for funds shaped other center activities. The Parvin Foundation, formed by hotel owner Albert B. Parvin, William O. Douglas, and Hutchins, was designed to explore one of Douglas' concerns, the role of law in restoring order in Third World countries that were throwing off the yoke of colonialism. The center participated in the Parvin Foundation's work by offering staff support and conducting dialogues and conferences with visiting dignitaries from Latin America and with international relations scholars and public officials from the United States. Douglas' involvement with the center continued until his retirement from the Supreme Court in 1975, following his stroke. He was chairman of the board and participant in conferences, offering his experience on the Court to the center discussions.[6]

The cost of running the center in the style Hutchins preferred was over a million dollars a year. Further attempts to raise money were conditioned by his hesitation to seek local support. He wanted to protect the center's agenda from control by any donors, and he thought local donors would likely take a proprietorial interest in the center's topics of study. But in the end, the schedule was continually shaped by the activities he pursued in search of funds. A founding members' program brought in some money, and various public relations events, such as a sixty-fifth birthday celebration for Hutchins, added to the center's budget. The Ford Foundation in 1962 turned down requests by the center's directors for a $15 million endowment grant, then for $16.4 million for a ten-year continuation grant, and finally a request from Hutchins for a $10 million endowment.[7]

Hutchins once again was soliciting funds from private individuals, a task he thought he was free of upon leaving the university. Holding symposia for wealthy prospects became one aspect of the center's activities. As Ashmore notes, Hutchins used his public relations expertise to bring together impressive groups of intellectuals and public figures, who would hold substantive discussions on various topics, such as the future of democracy, sponsor elaborate dinners, and solicit donations.[8] The efforts were not overwhelmingly successful, but Hutchins had come to realize that he could raise no money without personal contact with donors.

In 1965 the center held a convocation in New York to celebrate Pope John XXIII's Pacem in Terris encyclical by bringing together world leaders to discuss world peace. Three more such convocations were held, one in Geneva in 1967, where the war in Vietnam was the focus, and two in Washington, D.C., in 1973 and 1975. These convocations served multiple purposes. They succeeded in providing a forum for discussions of peace by political leaders. They also increased the center's public visibility and brought in some funds. And they generated continued media coverage of Hutchins' activities.

The center's financial difficulties began to ease in 1964 when Hutchins met Chester F. Carlson, the inventor of the Xerox process. Carlson had been Linus Pauling's student at the California Institute of Technology. When Pauling was ready to retire, Carlson financed his fellowship at the center and began making sizable donations to the center's operations, first with the convocations and then with the expansion of communications. He joined the board of directors. By 1966 the center was stable financially, and in 1967, with a Carlson matching grant, it started publishing the *Center Magazine,* which was the forum for the center's papers and dialogues. By 1969 subscriptions had reached one hundred thousand and were covering nearly half the center's operating costs. Carlson died suddenly in 1968. He left the center a major bequest that, combined with his other grants since 1964, totaled over $7 million in Xerox stock and cash grants.

Beyond the public relations activities and the convocations, the center's daily activities continued. With the growth in funds by the middle 1960s Hutchins added a number of resident consultants—or fellows, as they came to be called—raising the total to twenty-five by the late 1960s. He hoped to improve the quality of the center's primary daily activity—the dialogue. The dialogue was premised on his academy proposal to the Ford Foundation in 1953: a group of the best minds, focused on a particular issue, pursuing individual study, then gathering together regularly to discuss it. But by 1969, after soliciting ideas from the fellows for ways to improve the discussions and their participation, he decided the program needed major revisions. Carlson's bequest enabled him to proceed.

He fired a number of the fellows, including Ferry and Hoffman. Ferry was especially bitter; he had joined Hutchins in California in 1959 only reluctantly. On the basis of conversations with Hutchins, he was under the impression that all the fellows had tenure with the center. He sued the center, but settled his severance payment out of court. Seven fellows remained, and five others were added on a less than full-time basis. In 1970 Hutchins' health began to deteriorate. Heart and cancer surgery enabled him to continue at the center, but he pushed the directors to search for a successor so that he could retire from administrative duties. Ashmore became acting president in the interim.

In 1974 the directors appointed Malcolm Moos, retiring president of the University of Minnesota and a friend of one of the remaining fellows, Harvey Wheeler. Moos managed to alienate a critical core of board members and fellows with his plan for redesigning the center's program and was asked to resign in 1975, at which point Hutchins was reappointed president. Relying heavily on Ashmore, Hutchins reorganized the center once more. Hutchins lost one of his most loyal board members, Jubal R. Parten, in the ensuing conflict over the center's future. The fellows became associates. Ralph Tyler opened a center office in Chicago to continue the dialogues and to capitalize on the proximity of a core group of intellectuals residing at or visiting the university. Ironically, this was the very same university that had inspired Hutchins to seek an alternative means of organizing an intellectual community.

The center began selling its Santa Barbara land to cover severance agreements with the former fellows. After Hutchins' death, many of the directors resigned and the office was moved to the campus of the University of California at Santa Barbara, where a scaled-down program of dialogues continued. A succession of presidents who lacked Hutchins' charisma, resources, and singular vision could not prevent the center from closing in 1987.

When the center was founded in 1959, its goal was to identify and clarify the basic issues and widen the circles of discussion about them. Hutchins' primary focus was clarifying the issues. Widening the circles of discussion ensued as the center sought financial support and occurred in a number of ways in addition to the convocations. Florence Mischel was appointed in the middle 1960s to direct the audiotape program and, from the recorded sessions of previous years, to create and catalog the cassettes. They were sent upon request to individuals, organizations, schools and colleges, and libraries. The publications program grew, with pamphlets based on the dialogues and bulletins about center activities. It reached its most sophisticated level with the *Center Magazine,* edited by John Cogley.

Identifying the topics of research and discussion occurred out of the original basic issues program and in line with the interests of the group of fellows at any given point in time. But particular themes recurred. The role of technology in a democracy; the responsibilities of the media; the activities of and ideas behind various social and political movements, including the civil rights movement, the women's movement, the student movement, and the antiwar movement; world peace and international relations; and economics and economic policy in a democracy were among the issued studied and discussed.

Particular projects were supported. Rexford Guy Tugwell became a fellow and spent years at the center redesigning the United States Constitution to take account of changes in modern life the authors had not foreseen. The fellows conducted discussions of his ongoing drafts as they were written.[9] Elisabeth Mann Borgese moved from the EB editorial board to the center. The one female fellow at the center, she translated her earlier work at the University of Chicago on the world constitution into proposed laws to protect the seas. She held international convocations and introduced her proposals to the United Nations.[10]

Hutchins' areas of interest were politics, law, and education. Every center project was examined for its political implications, as part of its basic charter. In the early years, Hutchins pursued symposia that explored political ideas and ideals. In "The Two Faces of Federalism," for example, he articulated the tension between individual citizens' rights and liberties, protected by restrictions on the power of government, and community needs for government intervention and regulation. Arguing that law was educative insofar as it reflected the use of reason to determine the common good, he claimed that a system of laws could not protect freedom if it was based on standards of technical expertise and efficiency rather than on the political deliberations of citizens. The participating fellows discussed the paper by exploring the powers of government in relation to free speech, social institutions, the legal profession, and corporations.[11] The dialogue represented Hutchins' hopes for the center's future activities—the joint exploration of the problems of modern democracy from a variety of intellectual perspectives.

Hutchins sponsored dialogues about law by inviting legal scholars to the center to discuss the Constitution and First Amendment issues. In one case, Harry Kalven from the University of Chicago Law School and Alexander Meiklejohn spent July of 1964 at the center. They presented their work to the fellows. Buchanan, who also presented a paper, oversaw the conference while Hutchins was on vacation. He considered it "one of the best months" the center had ever had because the participants "stuck to a topic" such as free speech and self-government and allowed "running discussion" to continue, without striving for the kind of closure or agreement Hutchins sought when he led discussions.[12]

Hutchins' own contributions to the discussions on law ranged from examinations of Supreme Court decisions to discourses on natural law. He wrote essays arguing that freedom to dissent was essential to the protection of minority opinions.[13] This position was an enduring theme from his Oberlin past, his protection of academic freedom at the University of Chicago, and his decisions as president of the Fund for the Republic. Hutchins sponsored discussions about natural law in part because he found in the philosophical debate the basis for a "normative jurisprudence" that affirmed "a difference between good and evil and an obligation to do one and avoid the other." Moreover, natural law was "universal," because it was "binding on all men."[14]

From this position he presented an eloquent series of criticisms of the Nixon administration's definition of law and order and of the decisions of the Burger Court as opposed to the Warren Court in the early 1970s. Potential violations of civil liberties in Nixon's legislative agenda disturbed Hutchins. "The poor and the black" were the people whose liberties suffered while the real problems of criminal justice, including overcrowded prisons, an inefficient court system, and poor treatment facilities for drug addicts and alcoholics, remained underfinanced.[15]

As troubling for Hutchins as Nixon's legislative program was his plan to reorient the Supreme Court from the Warren Court's effort to "establish national standards" for enforcing the Bill of Rights and the Fourteenth Amendment to an interpretation of the Constitution based on "strict construction" of its meaning. Although there were clear virtues to judicial restraint, Hutchins argued, it ought to be viewed within "the American hierarchy of values." The "different perspectives" of the justices framed their interpretation of the Constitution; therefore, choosing them was the most "important task" of the president.[16]

Just as his work on legal issues remained theoretical, so did his work in education. The center held a conference on the university in America in Los Angeles in 1966. Participants included Eric Ashby, Jacques Barzun, Clarence Faust, J. William Fulbright, Walter Lippmann, Rosemary Park, and other notables. Hutchins' paper suggested that the university was too closely linked to the demands of the larger society and had become a "service station," when what the United States needed was "an autonomous thinking community" to "fashion the mind of the age."[17]

His work in education culminated with the publication in 1968 of *The Learning Society,* a book that reflects a growing understanding of the complexity of education in a modern, democratic society. This growth was due largely to the time Hutchins had to read, to draft and redraft his ideas, to subject them to the discussions of the fellows, and to reflect on the wide range of thinking about politics and education of the center's many visitors.[18] Placing schooling squarely in the context of the larger community and in the relation of schooling to the changing family, the economy, and the mass media, Hutchins incorporated the themes explored by center fellows to make an argument for lifelong, ongoing education for all members of society.[19]

His willingness to deal theoretically with the complexity of educating all members of society expanded in the succeeding years. The center sponsored the symposium "Ghetto Education" in 1968 including Robert F. Kennedy, Kenneth B. Clark, Oscar Lewis, and Neil V. Sullivan, all of whom had participated in or had studied the process of desegregation to provide equal opportunities for schooling for minority children.[20] Hutchins published an article exploring the need to address social and economic conditions that discriminated against poor children and placed them at a disadvantage when measured against children with educational and economic advantages.

Educational standards, he wrote, "no matter how 'scientific', are culturally derived." Because of the role of the school in determining children's future participation in American society, the schools had an obligation to abolish the tracking system, in which children are grouped according to their performance on standardized tests, because it served as "a means of perpetuating poverty and racial discrimination."[21]

From 1969 to the early 1970s, he explored with the fellows and visitors a constitution of public education. Combining his examination of Supreme Court decisions with his concerns for justice and enriched understanding of the social conditions of schooling, Hutchins developed an argument about the relationship between the Constitution and public education. According to the provisions in the Bill of Rights and the Fourteenth Amendment, he suggested, state responsibilities included protecting teachers' rights to foster free inquiry and open debate, developing equitable financing of all schools, offering compensatory programs, and achieving racial balance in schools.[22]

In a passionate argument to preserve the public schools against such proposals as the voucher system (providing tax vouchers for parents to use for private schools of their choice) or deschooling (eliminating public schools altogether), Hutchins claimed that "every child must be given the chance to become the kind of citizen the First Amendment demands." That responsibility must not be left to parents but assumed by the community through the schools. It was a public commitment, he argued, and the schools' first object "must be to equip the student with the tools of learning," then "to open new worlds to the young," and, finally, "to get the young to understand their cultural heritage."[23] The political health of a community was directly related to the health of its schools. In a heterogeneous society, integrating schools was a means of transcending the "cultural boundaries" of neighborhoods. Culturally diverse classrooms could lead future citizens "to the recognition of the gaps in one's own culture, of the merits of another, of the need for change in oneself, and of the possibility of accommodation to others."[24]

The principles underlying such arguments and Hutchins' contributions to the discussions about politics, law, and education at the center represent the kind of commitment that elicited support for center projects. But in real life, in confrontation with the heterogeneous groups he discussed in the abstract and with the passions moving them, he was far less comfortable. This discomfort was due partially to the need to control the dialogue. By choosing participants in center forums, Hutchins could define their general character. And he most often chose people of his own class, race, gender, and level of education. There were exceptions but not many. In addition, Hutchins was not moved to address immediate problems, as the demise of the early fund programs indicated. He preferred some distance and abstraction, the underlying issues rather than the manifestations of them, as if they could effectively be considered separately.

The center held four kinds of dialogue, and each kind was used to educate. The most central was the daily discussion that took place every morning at eleven in the center's conference room. Hutchins rang the bell in the courtyard, and the fellows and staff would leave their reading, writing, and other work to gather around the table to discuss a paper that was on the basic issues agenda. Intended to focus the members of the intellectual community Hutchins determined to create and sustain, these dialogues were the only obligation of center staff members. Anyone in residence was expected to attend.

Two other forms of discussion took place away from the center. Those held in Los Angeles, New York, and Washington, for example, were designed to demonstrate the center's purpose and to feature discussants who would attract other participants and an audience. They were held away from the center to make participation more convenient for the notable speakers. But they also were able to draw press coverage, ongoing donors, and donations. Some of the "American Character" talks were held at a high school in Beverly Hills, and people paid admission for them. Another form of discussion was the convocation. The Pacem in Terris convocations were on the grandest scale of such gatherings, but smaller meetings also took place. A convocation in New York celebrating the tenth anniversary of the Fund for the Republic at the Americana Hotel that included guest speakers Admiral Hyman Rickover, Attorney General Robert F. Kennedy, Secretary of Labor Willard Wirtz, FCC Chairman Newton Minow, and others was such a gathering.[25]

The first three kinds of discussion session tended to be fairly sanitary means of public education. They took place either with center visitors and resident fellows and staff members or before an audience that was there to be educated. The participants often came from similar class backgrounds or occupational levels. They were predominantly men and mostly white. There were exceptions: Rosemary Park, for example, and Thurgood Marshall. But most were public leaders or professionals from the academic world. In the case of the center discussions, invited visitors could attend the dialogues, or people could read about them in pamphlets or the *Center Magazine*. Again, a controlled distance could be maintained.

A fourth kind of discussion that took place at the center involved either outsiders who were invited to participate or center fellows who chose to study and write about less powerful groups in American society. When the groups participating or being studied were students, minorities from community-based organizations, or women, Hutchins was least comfortable. Such discussions with ordinary people were not the kinds of discussions he sought. They were difficult to control, and their outcomes did not necessarily lead to the unity in diversity Hutchins proffered as the center's goal. Despite his abstract arguments about justice, law as community educational device, and the responsibilities of communities to educate everyone for participation in the political conversation, he felt little personal responsibility to involve himself directly in these activities.

Student activists, for example, met at the center in August of 1967 to consider the university in society. Representatives from various student groups including the Student Non-violent Coordinating Committee participated with fellows in discussions about the kinds of education universities should provide, the kinds of political action students could pursue, and relationships of power in universities.[26] Hutchins was not comfortable with the provocative and antagonistic statements of students and was skeptical of the passion they exhibited.[27] For a brief period, the center had a junior fellows program, which Hutchins disbanded because he found it detracted from the center's main purpose—the fellows' study and discussion—and because students would not take instruction.[28]

In the case of women, there was never an actual gathering at the center, but Irving Laucks, a retired chemist, made a donation to the center to finance conferences on race relations, poverty, and peace. The money slated for peace was intended to pay for a staff position at the center and another at the fund's New York office. Both appointees were members of Women Strike for Peace, a feminist group that advocated unilateral disarmament. Neither woman played a large role in the center's ongoing operations, and Hutchins paid little attention to feminist perspectives on world peace.[29] Donald McDonald decided in 1972 to publish in the *Center Magazine* his interpretation of the women's movement.[30] The following issue included the critical responses of numerous women who preferred to speak for themselves or who complained that the center virtually ignored the concerns of women.[31] In the end, the center convened neither discussions, conferences, nor any other typical center forum to address the issue of women in American society.

Ferry and Steve Allen, another participant in center activities, were interested in minority and race relations issues. They organized conferences, inviting black and Hispanic community leaders to discuss their concerns. As Ferry later recalled, Hutchins was unfailingly courteous but "terribly ill-at-ease" with the minority groups about whose rights he wrote. He was affable at lunch with the guests but left quickly afterwards. He could deal with the ideas, Ferry noted, but not with the people themselves or with their direct involvement in framing the discussion. Holding such conferences interested some of the fellows because they thought it important to begin to "disentangle" some of these issues with the leaders of minority communities, but Hutchins was "physically" uncomfortable with people from minority groups who lacked extensive formal education.[32]

Beyond class differences, Hutchins' discomfort reflected his desire to remain removed from the emotional aspects of such discussions at the center. Another manifestation of this desire was evident when, during the center's one period of relative financial security, 1969, Hutchins chose to reorganize it. No one ever doubted his central leadership role, least of all the fellows and board members. But this curiously inept reorganization process gave him further control over the personnel and the program by eliminating those who differed with him. Rather than confronting the disagreements and dealing directly with their emotional and intellectual ramifications, Hutchins excised them.

Since 1960, he had been urging the fellows to make the center's work "more systematic and coherent."[33] He appointed Ferry to oversee this process, but as Scott Buchanan noted two years later, the group "disintegrated" whenever Hutchins was away. When Hutchins asked Buchanan to lead the group, Buchanan suggested that the center become self-governing.[34] Hutchins' frustration continued into the middle 1960s. One visitor recommended that the center separate the academic program from the conferences for donors and reorganize on a quarterly basis, designing seminars around particular topics upon which everyone would focus throughout the quarter.[35]

The problem of organization was exacerbated by the manner in which fellows had come to the center throughout the 1960s. As Ferry had warned Hutchins in the beginning, the staff and fellows should be selected with great care. Instead, Hutchins had taken people in haphazardly, as money for projects had been donated. When the projects ended, he kept them on out of loyalty and the hope that they would each contribute a generalist's perspective to the discussions.[36] The fellows did not necessarily agree on the center's central mission, nor did they completely understand it. And Hutchins' refusal to take a more definitive leadership role, at the same time that it was obvious to all involved that the center would not exist without him, made the situation untenable.

Compounding the difficulties, Hutchins was in his sixties and thinking about retiring from administrative work. The house he and Vesta had built on their land in Santa Barbara burned to the ground in 1964, but Vesta immediately began rebuilding it and the Hutchinses were planning to retire in Santa Barbara, where Hutchins could continue his scholarly work at the center when he chose. He wanted to leave the center with a stable form of governance and sufficient funds to continue to operate.

In 1966 and 1967 the fellows participated in an ongoing discussion of methods of governance. They could not agree on how power should be allocated or decisions made. As Ashmore noted at the time, the fellows were concerned with titles and status.[37] This preoccupation was a clear indication of their lack of security with the organization as it stood. Moreover, they could not decide upon a new program to replace the basic issues program as the focus of their research and discussions. In late 1966, Hutchins asked John R. Seeley, a sociologist and former dean at Brandeis University, to act as dean of the fellows. But other fellows disagreed with Seeley's plans for the direction of the program or refused to acknowledge his role as academic leader.[38]

These disputes had begun to wear on Hutchins, and he did not know how to reconcile all the fellows' needs and desires with his original conception of the academy.[39] In 1968 came the death of Buchanan, upon whom Hutchins had so often relied for counsel. Hutchins then turned increasing responsibility for administration over to Ashmore, whose "heavy hand" in carrying out the unpleasant tasks of administration disturbed some of the fellows and extended his distance from them.[40]

Tension between the focused, cooperative examination and discussion of basic issues Hutchins desired and his inability to deal decisively with the fellows came to a head with the center's reorganization and was manifest in the actual process itself. Rather than take full responsibility for reorganizing the group and the employment decisions reorganizing entailed, Hutchins followed an old monastic practice, in which he selected the first fellow, who, with him, selected the third, and so on. He chose Harvey Wheeler as the first fellow who would remain at the center. Wheeler had taught political science at a number of universities, been a consultant to the basic issues program of the fund, joined the center as part of the EB project in 1961, and coauthored *Fail-Safe* with Eugene Burdick.

Hutchins and Wheeler together were to choose the third fellow, but Wheeler decided no one at the center was suitable. He asked Hutchins to canvass for the best scholars in the Western world and refused to name anyone else, leaving the remaining fellows uncertain about their futures. Finally, Hutchins insisted that they move forward, and they agreed on Rexford Tugwell. Hutchins, Wheeler, and Tugwell chose Ashmore, then Cogley, to carry on administrative and publications duties, respectively. These five men chose Harvey Wilkinson on the basis of his "devotion" to the center's "purposes" and "proven creativity and productivity."[41] Elisabeth Borgese was the final fellow chosen. The remaining fellows—except for Frank Kelly, who kept his position as vice-president, and the publications personnel—left the center.

Ferry, who had worked with Hutchins for eighteen years, was out of the country at the time, completely unaware of the reorganization. He learned about it on his return. Hutchins preferred to send him a letter rather than to tell him in person about the decisions made. In successive notes, he suggested that Ferry leave immediately, and accept a year's salary and some compensation for a second year. Leaving without delay should make any "agony or chaos" as "brief as possible," he felt.[42] Within a few months, Hutchins notified a director that the center was "working better than it ever did," because "the removal of a good deal of deadweight" had made meetings "more effective."[43]

Shortly after the reorganization Hutchins claimed that one major problem had been that fellows had other interests besides the center and its program. Ferry's and Seeley's concerns with minorities and students were examples of this distraction.[44] Further, the kinds of people the center required were rare: "masters of their disciplines and at the same time philosophers."[45] But personnel problems were not the only factor that had kept the center from functioning the way Hutchins imagined it could. After another, more protracted search new associate fellows were added in the summer of 1969. Representing a variety of disciplines and countries, most of these new fellows acted as consultants to the center, visiting for specific periods of time. Two, Alexander Comfort, the biologist whose royalties from *The Joy of Sex* were to cover his salary and relieve him from British taxes because they were assigned through a tax-exempt institution, and Lord Ritchie-Calder, former professor of international relations at the

University of Edinburgh, moved to Santa Barbara and became full fellows.[46] The others remained associates because they were unwilling to join the center on a full-time basis.[47]

Despite the reorganization and the board's decision to grant the fellows complete control of the academic program, the center continued to be plagued with difficulties. Debates among the fellows about how the center should be organized persisted into the middle 1970s.[48] This problem of attracting fellows, creating a constitution to govern the center, and determining the focus of the program were compounded by Hutchins' illnesses. He had open-heart surgery in 1970, cancer surgery in 1970 and again in 1971, and a hernia operation in 1972.

While the center searched for a successor to Hutchins, the board appointed Ashmore president of the fund and center. Hutchins remained responsible for the academic program. At that point, Ashmore's legal power was commensurate with Hutchins': he was on the board of directors, president of the center, and a senior fellow, an arrangement that other senior fellows resented.[49] Hutchins asked Norton Ginsburg, a University of Chicago college graduate and professor of geography, to become dean of the academic program. Ginsburg worked with Borgese on her law of the seas project and, according to Ashmore, was successful with the fellows and the program.[50]

Finally, at the end of 1973, the directors chose Hutchins' successor, Malcolm Moos, slated to retire from the presidency of the University of Minnesota in June of 1974. Moos and Harvey Wheeler had taught at the Johns Hopkins University early in their academic careers, and director Jubal R. Parten made the arrangements necessary to bring Moos to the center. Hutchins, at seventy-five, was able seriously to contemplate retirement. He and Vesta had hoped to travel after Moos took the presidency, but they remained in Santa Barbara because of Vesta's heart condition.

Almost immediately there were problems with Moos and his plans for the center. He was hesitant about honoring prior commitments to programs with the already small center budget. When Ginsburg extended his resignation as a matter of form, Moos accepted it. Moos' suggestion that the remaining fellows and staff also resign angered some of the board members, who demanded that Ashmore be appointed vice-president to counterbalance Moos.[51] Working through Harvey Wheeler until June, Moos managed to alienate most of the fellows and staff and a significant portion of the board. He informed the directors a few months before he arrived at the center that he hoped to carry forward Hutchins' idea of the academy as an alternative to the modern university but that "it would be something like a Rockefeller University for humanities" with "a small group of students" and "a very distinguished faculty."[52] Moos' idea was supported enthusiastically by some directors, including Parten.

Hutchins ceased working in his recently established cottage office on the center grounds when Moos arrived and worked, instead, at home for a number of months. In the summer and fall of 1974, Moos spent a great deal of time away from the center, largely unsuccessfully trying to raise money for his plan. He placed Wheeler in charge of the academic program. The mood of the center fellows deteriorated rapidly. Wheeler wanted to retire all of the fellows and begin anew. Hutchins was besieged by fellows' and directors' complaints about the Moos-Wheeler administration.

Finally, in the spring of 1975, Hutchins and a majority of the other board members realized that the severance payments to the fellows would require more than the fund's liquid assets. To continue operating without substantially increasing financial support would leave the fellows with nothing. Moos resigned with a hefty severance agreement. Hutchins resumed the presidency, and all the fellows resigned, except for Comfort, whose agreement to share royalties from *The Joy of Sex* was the subject of a lawsuit. Parten was the only remaining original fund director, aside from Eleanor Stevenson. He resigned from the board because he was angry with Hutchins about the Moos debacle and the disposition of the fund's assets.

Land was sold in order to cover severance payments. The center's operations were reduced. A center office was established in Chicago, paid for by one of the directors and run by Norton Ginsburg. Ralph Tyler commuted from California to organize the program. He drew upon the faculty of the University of Chicago as part-time participants in the dialogues he held. He recorded the dialogues and distributed the tapes through the center's audiotaping program. Many of the dialogues featured in the *Center Magazine* between fall of 1975 and spring of 1977 took place in Chicago.[53] Hutchins, Borgese, and Ashmore remained in Santa Barbara with McDonald, who ran the *Center Magazine.*

"Pale and gaunt," Hutchins continued to work at the center. He oversaw a "leaner program" with visitors and part-time participants.[54] Three faculty members from the Santa Barbara campus, including historian Otis L. Graham, became regular contributors. With these men, William Gorman (who had gone to St. John's College from the Committee on the Liberal Arts and had worked with Adler and at the center since his Chicago years), Joseph Schwab, Clifton Fadiman, who had retired in the area, a few other local people, Borgese, Ashmore, and Tugwell participating, Hutchins' dialogue sessions reflected a curious mix of many of his earlier enterprises.

Hutchins had corresponded with his old friend Thornton Wilder all through the center's tenuous and secure times until Wilder's death in 1976. As Ashmore has noted, Hutchins never admitted to Wilder, with whom he shared his most personal concerns, that he ever had any doubts about the "soundness" of the idea behind the center.[55] Until his final illness and death in May of 1977, he wrote about education, law, and peace and saw Vesta through the open-heart surgery that rewarded her renewed health.

Hutchins published an essay in early 1977 that cast back to his Oberlin experience, in which "the most important word" in one's vocabulary "was 'ought.' " The "real questions" humans faced, "what should we do, why should we do these things?" were not the fare of modern universities, he wrote. Information and technique were more highly valued than knowledge in most educational institutions. Despite recent decisions by the Supreme Court that relied on the equal protection clause of the Fourteenth Amendment, there was no indication that lawyers ever encountered a discussion of the meaning of equality before they arrived at law school. More than ever, he argued, Americans needed "the interpenetration of the political community and the intellectual community" that provided the Greeks with the "mastery of the whole," "grasp of principles," "critical standards," and "comprehension" that "extended their influence" to the modern world.[56]

This was his goal for the center dialogues. In his last two years, without the indecision and divisiveness of the earlier years and with far fewer participants, Hutchins finally felt that he was closer than he ever had been to reaching it.[57] That he was never able to attain it can be attributed to all the problems explored here. Hutchins' discomfort with the emotional and nonrational elements of a community was one problem. Without clearer guidance, in the form of administrative procedures or strenuous efforts to mediate disputes, Hutchins' ongoing expectation that the fellows would eventually sort out their differences was naive or, worse, irresponsible. Those fellows who sought an alternative direction in the program—Ferry, for example—were dismissed. Those who tried to create coherence and received little support from Hutchins—Seeley, for example—also were expelled.

As one disillusioned fellow has noted, Hutchins did not choose the center's participants carefully. He surrounded himself with people who agreed with his ultimate goals and who would perform unpleasant tasks for him. This tendency was compounded by his perception of himself as one "of a small group of very good minds."[58] After Buchanan died, it is doubtful Hutchins believed that anyone at the center, with the possible exception of Tugwell, possessed intellectual powers equal to his own, however equably he treated the fellows socially. The subject of Hutchins' arrogance recurs in his colleagues' commentary throughout his career, from the Yale Law School to the University of Chicago to the Ford Foundation to the fund and the center.

Another problem was created by the emphasis Hutchins continued to place on a particular kind of discussion: clean, with some kind of agreement at the end, "working toward perfection," in one participant's memory, as opposed to a running discussion, where the ends were unknown and undetermined, but "insight" was the goal.[59] The choice to foster the participation of elites in the discussion rather than the individuals and groups Hutchins thought might eventually receive the benefits may well have limited the influence of the center's work and reinforced its appearance of distance and rarefaction.

Finally, the idiosyncratic nature of Hutchins' vision was such that few of the great minds he sought were willing to reside permanently at the center. And the inextricable linking of the vision with the man made it virtually impossible for the center vigorously to continue without him. The Moos presidency was one example of this problem. Another was the appointment of Maurice Mitchell after Hutchins' death. Unable to find donors, including board members, willing to support the center without Hutchins, Mitchell made an arrangement with the University of California at Santa Barbara to move the center's office there and to sell the estate in Montecito to provide operating funds for its remaining years. Then he resigned. Again, one finds here echoes of the failure of the Yale Law school systematically to continue its alliance with the Institute of Human Relations, or the University of Chicago college to survive intact, after Hutchins left those institutions.

In the end, though, these factors alone are inadequate to explain Hutchins' failure to achieve his goal. To understand fully the fundamental flaws of Hutchins' academy idea in the real world of the late twentieth century, one has to look to other kinds of intellectual communities that were created in the same period to serve as complements or alternatives to the university, and that survived their originators.[60] The design and aims of the center were somewhere between those of two other institutions that were established in the early 1950s, the Aspen Institute and the Center for the Advanced Study of the Behavioral Sciences (CASBS).

The Aspen Institute was formed with a commitment to education far more directed and firm than Hutchins' indirect educational interests.[61] Hutchins himself was involved in its planning stages with his friend Walter Paepcke. Like the center, the institute had a powerful founder in Paepcke; but a succession of strong leaders followed, and the institute reflected their different proclivities.

The institute's early operations were financed by Paepcke, who also was its first president, and by its trustee, benefactor, and president after Paepcke's death, Robert O. Anderson. Anderson, an alumnus of the Hutchins-Adler great books seminar and the University of Chicago, was founder of the Atlantic-Richfield Oil Company. He expanded the institute's offerings from those of the Paepcke years and managed to do so without alienating the staff and board members and other supporters of the institute's activities.

The institute was in a location far more remote than Santa Barbara. Yet, beginning with the Goethe bicentennial celebration in 1949, it continued to attract notable speakers, teachers, and participants. The executive seminars, which were designed and conducted by Mortimer Adler to introduce business executives to the great books, were an early and ongoing educational feature. But these two-week seminars for the privileged were not the sole function of the institute.

A variety of activities broadened the range of participants in the institute. Most occurred during the summer months in Aspen. The programs dealt with wide-ranging humanistic interests, including the arts and scientific concerns of a general nature, including technology and ecology. There were conferences on design, on photography, on the role of science in society, and on climatology. There were seminars for biology teachers and an institute at which physicists could spend sabbatical months. Like the center, the institute welcomed visiting scholars and short-term conference participants. But unlike the center, there was a local opera house, an orchestra, a music school, art exhibitions, and an athletic program. People were drawn to Aspen for the intellectual stimulation of the conferences and seminars, but the directors and presidents through the years were acutely conscious of the participants' other needs.

In another, fundamental way Aspen was different from the center. Beyond the value of the diversity of its offerings to attract participants was the value of its variety to attract funds. The Aspen Society of Fellows, not unlike the founding members program at the center, provided some ongoing support from individuals. But the institute successfully solicited money from the National Science Foundation, the Ford Foundation (Alvin Eurich and Joseph Slater, both at one time foundation officers, also served as presidents of the institute), the Benton Foundation, the Rockefeller Brothers Fund, the Danforth Foundation, and others. It was able to establish strong links with other organizations and agencies that had resources that could be shared, including the United Nations, the Salk Institute, the International Institute for Environmental Affairs, and the World Bank. Where Hutchins shunned such links for fear they would control the center's agenda, the institute's presidents sought them because they knew the institute could not offer a rich program and survive otherwise.

More than a list of organizations, these agencies represent the Aspen Institute's ability to connect with money and power and to sustain those connections in its efforts to educate participants and influence public policy. Hutchins had been able to make contact with political and academic leaders for the various center activities, but his singular enterprise was too idiosyncratic to appeal to the wide range of support and cooperation the institute managed to attract and sustain. In Hutchins' stubborn adherence to a unique idea lies one source of the center's demise.

The CASBS, too, bore some similarities to the center, but its fundamental mission, like the institute's, was very different. The CASBS had been established by the Ford Foundation to address area V of its agenda, the human and behavioral sciences. Located near the Stanford University campus, the CASBS was headed by Ralph Tyler, who was assisted by Preston Cutler, Hutchins' former secretary at the University of Chicago. The aim of the CASBS reflected Tyler's profound understanding of the way scholars preferred to work. His goal was to provide an environment where scholars could grow. They were invited to the CASBS for the length of their sabbaticals from their home universities and colleges. There on a hill above Stanford University, they were offered private office space, secretarial assistance, access to the university library, and any other amenities within reason that would allow them to work on their projects. In addition, the fellows invited to the CASBS tended to be doing work of high quality and to be respected in their fields. The attraction of possible encounters with other serious scholars was strong.

According to Cutler, Tyler hoped there would be interaction between scholars while they were in residence at Stanford, and he sought an atmosphere in which they could produce scholarship; but the ends of each scholar's endeavor were self-determined.[62] Because there was no particular institutional voice at the CASBS requiring that scholars work cooperatively on a problem, there was a great deal of freedom to work at one's own pace and to choose one's interactions. Alternatively, unlike the center, scholars were not asked to spend the remainder of their working lives at the CASBS. As Tyler has noted, academics wanted short periods away from their institutions and their students, but needed interaction with students over the long term.[63] Tyler understood that need, whereas Hutchins saw students as a distraction.

The institute and the CASBS did not have the grand and lofty goals of the center, but they survived in late twentieth-century America where the center did not. Rather than posing themselves as clear, contrary alternatives to the modern university, they were organized to complement existing institutions and the structure of people's lives. The seminars at the institute, whether in Aspen or at its other offices, did not demand the allegiance of the staff or the complete disruption of participants' work. The CASBS was acutely attentive to the ways scholars, whose working lives were situated in modern universities, wanted and needed to carry on their research and writing. In the end, by placing the center so at odds with academic life, and with the organization of modern higher educational institutions and the needs of their constituents, Hutchins unknowingly guaranteed its demise.

That said, it is important to reexamine what the center did accomplish, because such a perusal addresses the core of Hutchins' ability to change the ways people thought about things. As one colleague remembers, "There was something about Hutchins that was bigger than anything he ever did."[64] It was a quality of moral uprightness, self-assurance, that was best conveyed through his oratory and writing, but was also acutely apparent in his appearance and bearing. One participant during the final years, Otis L. Graham, argues that no other organization in those two decades matched the range of topics and the reach of the center's social criticism. Its national membership, discussion groups, and continued ability to attract participants and press coverage to the four Pacem in Terris convocations all reflect these characteristics.[65] But this ability was not primarily the center's. It was Hutchins'.

The range of topics and the rigor with which they were explored can be credited to the many participants in the center's dialogues. But the administrative and financial core of the center's operations rested with Hutchins. The uniqueness of the center's mission, clarifying basic issues and promoting dialogue, were intrinsic to Hutchins' conception of the model intellectual community and bore a resemblance to his experiences at Oberlin, the Yale Law School, and the great books discussion groups. This focus on cooperative dialogue over the long term meant the center was unable to retain most of the scholars it sought. But among those who completed work under the center's auspices there is an almost uniform gratitude for the center's accomplishments.

The process of clarifying issues, for example, whether in the shorter conferences or longer sessions that could last a month, combined interesting, and often, but not always, powerful people. The ongoing nature of the daily dialogues resulted in numerous insights and accumulated understandings that no splashy convocation or brief encounter could produce.[66] They exhibited the characteristics of a good, longstanding seminar. Because the center provided the appropriate setting, participants could join in the formal dialogues and continue them in less formal conversations over lunch, dinner, and on into the evening. These "series of exchanges" created deeper, more enriching and "productive" discussions of the issues.[67]

Such outcomes were precisely Hutchins' aim. That they could not be sustained in the majority of the sessions or throughout the center's history is as much attributable to his educational leadership as are those sessions that were successful by his own rigorous standards. It is not enough to argue, as some have, that the lack of money, the bickering among inappropriately chosen colleagues, and the disinterest of the larger public led to the center's demise.[68] It is important, instead, to look at Hutchins' fundamental conception of the center's mission and the ways he chose to act on it, to learn from his educational labors.

The Center for the Study of Democratic Institutions was able under Hutchins' leadership to point to remarkably persistent political and educational problems in the modern democracy of the late twentieth-century United States. They are problems that are not ever likely to be completely resolved. But under the center's auspices they were scrutinized in ongoing discussions by people working across the boundaries of academic disciplines. These explorations may continue to hold clues for thinking about the issues. As Michael Harrington has noted, Hutchins' faith in the dialogue, in the process of learning from speaking and, most important, from listening, needs to be translated so that all citizens "at the grass roots" can participate.[69] Rather than focus on the "best minds" in the creation of the dialogue, what is needed is to develop centers for all citizens to participate in informed discussions about public problems. This was Hutchins' ultimate aim.

E P I L O G U E

ROBERT HUTCHINS' MAJOR ACCOMPLISHMENT was the "clarity of vision" he offered to the institutions and the colleagues with whom he worked.[1] In reflecting upon this life, some definite parallels emerge. Isaac Thompson Hutchins speaking publicly and using his newspaper column to try to shape the values, attitudes, and sensibilities of the citizens of West Killingly, Connecticut, was not unlike Hutchins using his oratorical skills and essays to shape the values, attitudes, and sensibilities of the community at the University of Chicago. Instead of his great-grandfather's, grandfather's, and father's Bible, he used the great books to suggest means for binding together the community and seeking the beliefs that would guide it.

The assumptions behind the endeavors of these different Hutchinses also are not dissimilar. The people of rural West Killingly in the early nineteenth century more likely shared the beliefs Isaac Hutchins proselytized, making his mission far less difficult than his great grandson's. But the assumption that a single system of values and beliefs, embodied in a particular text or set of texts, could contain and transmit a single common culture can be found in these men's work.

A connection can be found, too, between Hutchins' singular model of undergraduate education and his exceptional conception of intellectual work. While both served as ideals toward which institutions could strive, their exceptionality left them deeply flawed. These models were not well suited to the realities of the modern world and its institutions, making it impossible for them to survive intact without Hutchins; they had no internal continuity to sustain them. In addition, their small constituencies indicate that their reach was not great, at least not for periods long enough to build a strong following.

Interestingly, Hutchins' Puritan ancestors seemed to have had a clearer grasp of the need both to hold to strong principles and to deal pragmatically with the real world. There was no halfway covenant in the prescribed curriculum of the college of the University of Chicago or in the design Hutchins imposed on the Center for the Study of Democratic Institutions. Indeed, his father wrote him praising an essay he had written on the ideal legal education and calling him a "Prophet," but noting that, for young law students trying to finish school and support themselves and their families, "the dust of the Actual is pretty thick and heavy."[2]

Hutchins spent his life arguing for the best institutional model for education. But it is obvious in his early criticisms of Dewey and his later commentaries on pragmatism that he had little tolerance for uncertainty, for plural truths, for the need to weigh evidence in thinking about ends. More than that, his analyses created caricatures of pragmatists' ideas and of the practices of educational institutions.[3] As a result, his own arguments became caricatures, descriptions of worst cases, rather than grounded, reflective criticisms.[4] As Edward Shils has recalled, Hutchins believed that, once stated, principles "could serve as direct and unambiguous guides to conduct."[5] For this reason, he was never moved to question his own assumptions about the existence of a single common culture or about the obligation and the means to initiate the young into it.

One might wonder why Hutchins persisted in seeking his perfect form of intellectual work despite its incongruity with the real world and the intense opposition he encountered. In "The Administrator," he made plain his perception of his life work—the commitment to pursue "a continuous discussion of the mission and destiny of the institution."[6] Provoking discussion by defining the end according to an ideal was a powerful device of his leadership. But he had a narrow apprehension of the sources of wisdom and goodness. His father, in contrast, had a far wider view. Will Hutchins mentioned once that, as much as he admired Robert Hutchins' arguments in *Education for Freedom,* he could not help but wonder if one "should not seek wisdom and goodness in a little mountain woman." Reminding his son of the role of humility in human endeavor, he noted that "there is an old word that The meek will He guide in judgment, and the meek will He teach His way."[7]

A more inclusive view, applied to intellectual work, was exemplified in a report introduced by Harvard's faculty. James Bryant Conant, president of Harvard during the same period Hutchins was at the University of Chicago, had asked the faculty to reexamine Harvard's undergraduate program; the report was the result. *General Education in a Free Society* (1945) was a collaborative effort, marked by conflict as well as agreement, by the faculty and the president to make a case for general education in an undergraduate program. The purpose of this form of education, the Harvard group argued, was to offer "preparation for life in the broad sense of completeness as a human being."[8] Acknowledging the difficulty of formulating the program in an age of tremendous expansion of knowledge, of enormous growth in the educational system, and of increasing social complexity, Conant and the Harvard faculty made clear that these were not issues to be ignored. Rather, they were difficulties to be addressed squarely by any educational plan.

Much as Hutchins finally began to situate his conceptions of liberal education within the full educational system and modern society in his *Learning Society* in 1968, the Harvard committee noted that all these institutions had to be seen as part of a larger whole. When one part of the system failed students, the entire system needed to be examined. The challenge for the United States approaching mid-century was to create a system "as fair to the fast as to the slow," meeting "the separate needs of each" while fostering "that fellow feeling between human being and human being which is the deepest root of democracy." Contrary to Hutchins' repeated assertion that education should be the same at any time in any place to mirror the common characteristics of human nature, the Harvard committee presented a plan for general education that acknowledged that, even if common standards exist, "there is no single form of instruction that can reach all equally."[9] Interestingly, Hutchins' colleague Ralph Tyler perceived the need for this diversity in approach to learning, apparent in his work in the college at the University of Chicago, and to conducting scholarship, obvious in his design for the Center for the Advanced Study of the Behavioral Sciences.

As Tyler and others who worked with Hutchins have made clear, there was a positive side to Hutchins' principled idealism, which in excess had proved so detrimental to the continuity of his institutional innovations. This positive side is reflected in the high standards he set at the University of Chicago. Preston Cutler credited Hutchins with creating an atmosphere in which everyone around him was moved to do his best work, because it was expected of him.[10] Faculty members who often opposed him, including Leonard White, as well as those who shared some of his goals, including Charles E. Merriam and Clarence Faust, were quick to remark that his standards of excellence had the most lasting of all his influences on the institution.[11] Students at the university in the years after he left have remarked that these standards continue to be part of the ethos of the college.[12]

The intellectual climate his standards created within the college influenced the undergraduate program in other ways in the decades after he left. The interdisciplinary commitment has remained in various reforms introduced since the Hutchins years, even if the precise curriculum itself no longer survives. Moreover, the Hutchins college program was compelling enough that a number of collegiate institutions, including Shimer College, Notre Dame, and others, incorporated all or parts of it in their undergraduate programs.

Hutchins left another kind of mark on the university, the interest in reaching across disciplinary boundaries. It was a concern that moved him at Yale and that shaped his subsequent activities after he left the university. But at the University of Chicago, an institution characterized by powerful department chairs who built their domains by competing for faculty and resources and protecting their own, he persuaded people to view their work within divisions of knowledge and to seek cooperation outside their departments and divisions.

Over the years since he left the university, interdisciplinary bodies like the Committee on Social Thought have thrived and multiplied. Some combine social sciences and humanities disciplines; some combine physical and biological sciences; some—the Committee on the Analysis of Ideas and the Study of Methods, for example—combine sciences, social sciences, and humanities. Some have the power to grant degrees; others simply offer programs that can be pursued. All are staffed largely by professors tenured in departments but who share interdisciplinary interests, and all receive support from the institution. The divisional structure Hutchins initiated, and the resources he provided to committees, established a unique and innovative tradition for the university that still flourishes.[13]

Clark Kerr has called Hutchins "the last of the giants" to rule American universities.[14] He had a vision of the goal of the institution and strove mightily to change fundamentally the mission of the University of Chicago. However contrary his goals and methods in relation to the faculty's, he did have a vision, a characteristic in short supply among leaders of institutions, who too often are driven not by ideas but by budgetary considerations.

Shils described Hutchins as a "man of honor" who "tried to live up to his convictions."[15] It was for this reason that, in the end, the faculty of the University of Chicago did not want him to leave and the board of the Fund for the Republic continued to support his utopian quest. And it is for this reason that educators who did not agree with all he promulgated could appreciate that "his words make a difference in the practical world."[16]

The same strength of belief that so antagonized the divisional faculty of the University of Chicago and Erwin Griswold at the Fund for the Republic also fueled Hutchins' fearless protection of academic freedom. This occurred in the late 1940s and early 1950s, an era when most other university presidents were collapsing their defenses. The power of his vision and the strength of his convictions make his stand on academic freedom and his challenge to examine and reexamine the ends of educational institutions his most lasting legacies.

APPENDIX *Enrollment at the University of Chicago*

Table 1. Entering Classes by Geographic Origin and Gender and by Residence while Attending College (%)

	1932		1937		1940	
	MALE	FEMALE	MALE	FEMALE	MALE	FEMALE
Geographic Origin:						
Chicago area	N/A		64.21	68.22	67.49	74.22
Mean	68.1		65.66		70.44	
Illinois*	N/A		4.74	6.07	5.19	3.83
Mean	4.83		5.22		4.59	
North Central†	N/A		12.37	10.28	11.75	12.89
Mean	13.95		11.62		12.25	
Other U.S.	N/A		18.16	14.49	15.85	10.80
Mean	14.36		16.84		13.32	
Foreign	N/A		.79	.93	1.64	.70
Mean	.14		.84		1.23	
Residence:						
At home	62.7	64.5	57.37	57.94	59.29	62.02
Mean	63.5		57.58		60.49	
Not at home	34.9	31.6	40.26	40.19	38.25	36.59
Mean	33.5		40.23		37.52	
Unknown	2.4	3.9	2.37	1.87	2.46	1.39
Mean	3.0		2.19		1.99	
N	416	307	380	214	366	287
Total *N*	723		594		653	

*Not including Chicago.
†Indiana, Iowa, Michigan, Minnesota, Ohio, Wisconsin.
Sources: W. F. Cramer to Emery T. Filbey, March 24, 1933, box 67, folder 7, "Statistics of the Freshman Class Entering Autumn Quarter, 1937" and "Statistics of the Freshman Class Entering Autumn Quarter, 1940," box 77, folder 1, Presidents' Papers, 1925–45, University of Chicago Special Collections.

Table 2. Entering Classes by Race and Gender (%)

	1932		1937		1940	
	MALE	FEMALE	MALE	FEMALE	MALE	FEMALE
Gentile	71.7	73.3	72.63	71.50	77.32	79.09
Mean	72.3		72.22		78.10*	
Jewish	26.2	25.7	26.58	27.10	21.31	20.21
Mean	26.0		26.77		20.83*	
Negro	1.9	.7	.53	1.40	.55	.70
Mean	1.4		.84		.61*	
Other†	.2	.3	.26	0	.82	0
Mean	.3		.17		.46	
N	416	307	380	214	366	287
Total *N*	723		594		653	

*The entering class of 1939 was 81% Gentile, 18.22% Jewish, and .47% Negro; it appears to have been the low point for racial heterogeneity in the classes of the 1930s.
†Not consistently described; probably of Asian and Asian-American origin.
Source: W. F. Cramer to Emery T. Filbey, March 24, 1933, box 67, folder 7, "Statistics of the Freshmen Class entering Autumn Quarter, 1937," and "Statistics of the Freshman Class Entering Autumn Quarter, 1940," box 77, folder 1, Presidents' Papers, 1925–45, University of Chicago Special Collections.

Table 3. Entering Classes by Parents' Educational Attainment (%)

	1932		1937		1940	
	FATHER	MOTHER	FATHER	MOTHER	FATHER	MOTHER
Did not finish high school	40.6	40.9	37.20	41.08	27.57	31.85
High school graduate*	19.8	29.0	17.85	27.95	23.74	32.77
Some college	9.8	13.3	9.43	11.11	10.42	15.01
College graduate	28.3	14.4	34.68	17.51	36.91	18.53
Unknown	1.4	2.4	.84	2.36	1.38	1.84
Total *N*	723		594		653	

*No college.
Sources: W. F. Cramer to Emery T. Filbey, March 24, 1933, box 67, folder 7, "Statistics of the Freshman Class Entering Autumn Quarter, 1937," and "Statistics of the Freshman Class Entering Autumn Quarter, 1940," box 77, folder 1, Presidents' Papers, 1925–45, University of Chicago Special Collections.

Table 4. Entering Classes by Source of Financial Support and by Gender (%)

	1932		1937		1940	
	MALE	FEMALE	MALE	FEMALE	MALE	FEMALE
Fully self-supporting	3.1	2.3	3.16	3.27	4.64	5.92
Mean	2.8		3.2		5.21	
Partly self-supporting	42.5	18.2	43.42	30.84	41.53	26.48
Mean	32.2		38.89		34.92	
Full private support	54.4	79.3	52.63	64.95	53.28	67.25
Mean	65.0		57.07		59.42	
Not known	N/A		.79	.93	.55	.35
Mean	N/A		.84		.46	
N	416	307	380	214	366	287
Total *N*	723		594		653	

Sources: W. F. Cramer to Emery T. Filbey, March 24, 1933, box 67, folder 7, "Statistics of the Freshman Class Entering Autumn Quarter, 1937," and "Statistics of the Freshman Class Entering Autumn Quarter, 1940," box 77, folder 1, Presidents' Papers, 1925–45, University of Chicago Special Collections.

Table 5. Entering Classes by High School Class Rank and by Gender (%)

	1932		1937		1940	
	MALE	FEMALE	MALE	FEMALE	MALE	FEMALE
First in class	7.4	6.8	11.58*	17.29*	13.12*	14.28*
Mean	7.2		13.63*		13.63*	
Top one-tenth	39.4	41.0	42.63	51.87	39.89	41.11
Mean	40.1		45.96		40.43	
Remaining top one-third	28.6	33.5	28.69	30.37	30.87	28.57
Mean	30.8		29.29		29.87	
Honor society member	27.4	30.9	N/A		N/A	
Mean	28.9		N/A		N/A	
Total *N*	723		594		653	

*First and second in class.

Sources: W. F. Cramer to Emery T. Filbey, March 24, 1933, box 67, folder 7, "Statistics of the Freshman Class Entering Autumn, 1937," and "Statistics of the Freshman Class Entering Autumn, 1940," box 77, folder 1, Presidents' Papers, 1924-45, University of Chicago Special Collections.

N O T E S

ABBREVIATIONS

ABF-UC	Archival Biographical Files, University of Chicago, Joseph Regenstein Library
BCA	Berea College Archives
C	Columbia University, Butler Library
CEC-YU	Charles E. Clark Papers, Yale University Library, Manuscripts and Archives
CEM-UC	Charles E. Merriam Papers, University of Chicago, Joseph Regenstein Library
CHJ-UC	Charles H. Judd Papers, University of Chicago, Joseph Regenstein Library
COHC	Oral History Collection, Columbia University, Butler Library
CSDI-UCSB	Center for the Study of Democratic Institutions Files, University of California at Santa Barbara Library, Special Collections
DCA	Dartmouth College Archives
DCR-UC	Dean of the College Records, University of Chicago, Joseph Regenstein Library
FFA	Ford Foundation Archives
FHK-UC	Frank H. Knight Papers, University of Chicago, Joseph Regenstein Library
FR-PUL	Fund for the Republic Papers, Princeton University, Mudd Library
FSH-BCA	Francis Stephenson Hutchins Papers, Berea College Archives
GEB, RAC	General Education Board Files, Rockefeller Archive Center
IHR-YU	Institute of Human Relations Files, Yale University Library, Manuscripts and Archives
IPR	Institute for Philosophical Research
HCK-PP-OCA	Henry Churchill King, Presidents' Papers, Oberlin College Archives
HHS-UC	Harold H. Swift Papers, University of Chicago, Joseph Regenstein Library
HU	Harvard University, Houghton Library

JRA-PR-YU James Rowland Angell, Presidential Records, Yale University Library, Manuscripts and Archives

JUN-UC John U. Nef Papers, University of Chicago, Joseph Regenstein Library

LG-UC Louis Gottschalk Papers, University of Chicago, Joseph Regenstein Library

LOO-OCA Logan Omer Osborn Papers, Oberlin College Archives

LSRM, RAC Laura Spelman Rockefeller Memorial Files, Rockefeller Archive Center

LW-UC Louis Wirth Papers, University of Chicago, Joseph Regenstein Library

MJA-IPR Mortimer J. Adler Files, Institute for Philosophical Research

OCA Oberlin College Archives

OVP-UC Office of the Vice-President Papers, University of Chicago, Joseph Regenstein Library

PP, UC President's Papers, University of Chicago, Joseph Regenstein Library

PUL Princeton University, Mudd Library

RAC Rockefeller Archive Center

RFA, RAC Rockefeller Foundation Archives, Rockefeller Archive Center

RMH-UC Robert M. Hutchins Papers, University of Chicago, Joseph Regenstein Library

RMH(A)-UC Robert M. Hutchins Papers, Addenda, University of Chicago, Joseph Regenstein Library

RMH(AU)-UC Robert M. Hutchins Papers, Unprocessed Addenda, University of Chicago, Joseph Regenstein Library

RR-UC Robert Redfield Papers, University of Chicago, Joseph Regenstein Library

SB-HU Scott Buchanan Papers, Harvard University, Houghton Library

SR-YU Secretarial Records, Yale University Library, Manuscripts and Archives

UC University of Chicago, Joseph Regenstein Library

UCSB University of California at Santa Barbara Library, Special Collections

WB-UC William Benton Papers, University of Chicago, Joseph Regenstein Library

WHF-DCA	W. H. Ferry Papers, Dartmouth College Archives
WJH-BCA	William James Hutchins Papers, Berea College Archives
WTH-UC	William T. Hutchinson Papers, University of Chicago, Joseph Regenstein Library
YU	Yale University Library, Manuscripts and Archives

PREFACE

1. Edmund Morgan, *The Puritan Dilemma: The Story of John Winthrop* (Boston: Little, Brown & Company, 1958), xii.

2. Robert M. Hutchins, *Freedom, Education, and the Fund: Essays and Addresses, 1946–1956* (New York: Meridian Books, 1956), 15.

CHAPTER ONE

1. Horace Bushnell, *Christian Nurture* (New York: Charles Scribner's Sons, 1916 [1861]); Washington Gladden, *Applied Christianity: Moral Aspects of Social Questions* (Boston: Houghton Mifflin Company, 1886).

2. Lawrence A. Cremin, *American Education: The Metropolitan Experience, 1876–1980* (New York: Harper & Row, 1988), chaps. 1 and 2; Robert M. Crunden, *Ministers of Reform: Progressives' Achievement in American Civilization, 1889–1920* (Urbana: University of Illinois Press, 1984 [1982]).

3. Fannie C. Hutchins to Robert M. Hutchins (RMH), n.d., Box 3, Folder 8, RMH-UC.

4. Speech, February 5, 1862, and other materials, WJH-BCA.

5. Journal of Isaac T. Hutchins, WHJ-BCA.

6. Robert Grosvenor Hutchins Journal 1, 1855, WJH-BCA.

7. Robert Grosvenor Hutchins, miscellaneous notes, n.d., WJH-BCA; Crunden, *Ministers of Reform.*

8. Milton Mayer, "Hutchins of Chicago, Part I," *Harper's Magazine* 178 (1939): 344–45.

9. Clipping in Isaac T. Hutchins' journal, WJH-BCA.

10. Isaac T. Hutchins to Fannie and Gracie (to be read to Will and Grosvenor), July 26, 1879, WJH-BCA.

11. *Los Angeles Tribune,* January 16, 1890, copy, WJH-BCA.

12. *General Catalogue of Oberlin College, 1833–1908* (Oberlin: Oberlin College, 1909), Int. 78, 500–501; "Fannie C. Hutchins, M.D.," Box 70, Folder 2, RMH(A)-UC; Interview with Francis S. Hutchins, January 8, 1986.

13. John Barnard, *From Evangelicalism to Progressivism at Oberlin College, 1866–1917* (Columbus: Ohio State University Press, 1969), is my principal source on Oberlin's history; chap. 2, for quote. Others will be so noted.

14. Registrar's Office, Oberlin College, Students' Grades, Book XI, 136, OCA; Florence M. Snell to Will Hutchins, August 27, 1890, WJH-BCA; Will Hutchins notebook, and C. B. Martin to Will Hutchins, February 23, 1891, WJH-BCA; Robert Grosvenor Hutchins to Henry Churchill King, May 15, 1907, Box 40, HCK-PP-OCA.

15. Office of the Secretary, Student and Desk Cards, OCA.

16. Will Hutchins to Anna L. Murch, April 22, 1896, WJH-BCA; William R. Hutchison, *The Modernist Impulse in American Protestantism* (Cambridge, Mass.: Harvard University Press, 1976).

17. "Wm. J. Hutchins Reexamined," *New York Times,* June 3, 1896, 5.

18. "In Memoriam" (Maynard H. Murch), WJH-BCA; Maynard H. Murch, Jr., to Mother, September 10, 1920, WJH-BCA.

19. Arthur C. Cole, *A Hundred Years of Mount Holyoke College: The Evolution of an Educational Ideal* (New Haven: Yale University Press, 1940), chap. 6; Registrar's Office, Oberlin College Student Grades, Box XVII, 319, OCA. *General Catalogue of Oberlin College,* 700. I found no indication in the Hutchins papers at Berea College as to why she finished at Mount Holyoke rather than Oberlin. See also Jane Hunter, *The Gospel of Gentility: American Women Missionaries in Turn-of-the-Century China* (New Haven: Yale University Press, 1984).

20. Interview with Francis S. Hutchins, January 8, 1986; correspondence in WJH-BCA.

21. "They Reared a University President," *St. Louis Star-Times,* January 4, 1950, 29; Interview with Francis S. Hutchins, January 8, 1986; Elisabeth S. Peck, "Remarks," *Berea Citizen,* March 31, 1960, 4.

22. Robert M. Hutchins, "Your Guest or Honor," in *Significant Addresses Delivered in Connection with the Retirement of Dr. William J. Hutchins as President of Berea College* (Berea: Berea College Press, 1939), 22–24.

23. *A Decade of Progress in the Bedford Presbyterian Church, Brooklyn, New York, 1894–1904* (Brooklyn, New York: Bedford Church, June 1, 1904). See Cremin, *American Education: The Metropolitan Experience,* 72–75, on the institutional church.

24. Will Hutchins to Henry Churchill King, April 15, 1903, Box 40, HCK-PP-OCA; Will Hutchins, "Walk and Not Faint," 1907, and "Church and Society," March 17, 1901, WJH-BCA.

25. Will Hutchins, Sermon, January 19, 1896; "The Sabbath School," September 26, 1896; "Children's Sermon," 1907; WJH-BCA.

26. Will Hutchins, "City's Shame Our Personal Sin," November 31, 1901; "Caesar and Childhood," November 25, 1904; and "Colored Work," November 6, 1901; WJH-BCA.

27. Will Hutchins to Henry Churchill King, April 2, 1907, Box 40, HCK-PP-OCA.

28. Robert G. Hutchins to Will Hutchins, telegram, April 15, 1907, WJH-BCA.

29. Billy Holmes to Will Hutchins, April 23, 1907, WJH-BCA, on WJH's reasoning.

30. Will Hutchins to "My Beloved People," May 7, 1907, WJH-BCA.

31. Will Hutchins to Henry Churchill King, September 13, 1912, Box 40, HCK-PP-OCA.

32. Will Hutchins to Henry Churchill King, November 6, 1908, Box 40, HCK-PP-OCA. W. E. Bigglestone, "Oberlin College and the Negro Student, 1865–1940," *Journal of Negro History* 56 (1971): 198–219, on racial problems at Oberlin.

33. Francis Brown to Will Hutchins, April 7, 1911, WJH-BCA.

34. Will Hutchins, "Religious Conversation," January 24, 1913, WJH-BCA.

35. Will Hutchins, "The Religious Life of Oberlin Students," February 21, 1916, WJH-BCA; RMH, "The Next Fifteen Years," *University of Chicago Magazine* 36 (April 1944): 8–11.

36. In WJH-BCA.

37. Oberlin Academy, Student Grades, Book 108, 47, and Oberlin College, *The Annual Catalogue, 1914–1915,* 281–87.

38. Bigglestone, "Oberlin College and the Negro Student."

39. Robert Samuel Fletcher, *A History of Oberlin College: From Its Foundation through the Civil War,* 2 vols. (Oberlin: Oberlin College, 1943).

40. RMH, *Freedom, Education, and the Fund: Essays and Addresses, 1946–1956* (New York: Meridian Books, 1956), 14.

41. Quoted in Lawrence A. Cremin, *American Education: The National Experience, 1783–1876* (New York: Harper & Row, 1980), 43; Fletcher, *A History of Oberlin College,* vol. 1.

42. George E. Peterson, *The New England College in the Age of the University* (Amherst: Amherst College Press, 1964); see also Thomas Le Duc, *Piety and Intellect at Amherst College, 1865–1912* (New York: Columbia University Press, 1946).

43. Donald M. Love, *Henry Churchill King of Oberlin* (New Haven: Yale University Press, 1956).

44. Louise L. Stevenson, *Scholarly Means to Evangelical Ends: The New Haven*

Scholars and the Transformation of Higher Learning in America, 1830–1890 (Baltimore: Johns Hopkins University Press, 1986).

45. Robert G. Hutchins to Henry Churchill King, May 15, 1907, Box 40, HCK-PP-OCA.

46. Kemper Fullerton to Will Hutchins, September 25, 1910, WJH-BCA.

47. Interview with Francis S. Hutchins, January 8, 1986.

48. Reported in the *Cleveland Plain Dealer* by John Barden, July 6, 1977, 3B, and James B. Flanagan, "Further Particulars," August 4, 1977, 7B.

49. William Grosvenor Hutchins to Milton Mayer, September 17, 1972, Box 1a, FSH-BCA.

50. Henry Churchill King to Will Hutchins, June 27, 1916, Box 40, HCK-PP-OCA.

51. Box 20, Folder 99, Goodrich Row, Pew 2, OCA.

52. RMH to E. S. Brace, March 27, 1929, Box 3, Folder 2, RMH-UC.

53. *Oberlin Review,* October 29, 1915, on students.

54. Quoted in Barnard, *From Evangelicalism,* 122.

55. *Oberlin Review,* February 14, 1915, February 4, 1916, September 26, 1916, October 27, 1916, April 20, 1917.

56. *Oberlin Review,* November 12, 1915.

57. *Oberlin Review,* March 17, 1916.

58. RMH, "Your Guest of Honor," 22.

59. William G. Hutchins to Milton Mayer, September 17, 1972.

60. RMH, notes from Bible class, WJH-BCA.

61. RMH, *No Friendly Voice* (Chicago: University of Chicago Press, 1936), 93.

62. Students' Grades, Book XXX, 150, OCA; Oberlin College, *The Annual Catalogue for 1916–1917.*

63. RMH, *No Friendly Voice,* 93.

64. RMH, *No Friendly Voice,* 87–94.

65. W. F. Bohn to Charles W. Flint, April 4, 1928, William Eugene Mosher file, Student Records, OCA.

66. *New York Times,* June 2, 1945, Mosher file, Student Records, OCA.

67. Linda Simon, *Thornton Wilder: His World* (Garden City, N.Y.: Doubleday & Company, 1979); Gilbert A. Harrison, *The Enthusiast: A Life of Thornton Wilder* (New Haven, Ct.: Tichnor & Fields, 1983).

68. Interview with Francis S. Hutchins, January 8, 1986.

69. Reuben Holden, *Yale in China: The Mainland, 1901–1951* (New Haven: Yale in China Association, 1964).

70. Elisabeth S. Peck, *Berea's First Century, 1855–1955* (Lexington: University Press of Kentucky, 1955), and Jerome W. Hughes, *Six Berea College Presidents: Tradition and Progress* (Berea: Berea College, 1984), are my sources on Berea's history.

71. William J. Hutchins, *Children's Code of Morals* (Washington, D.C.: National Institute for Moral Instruction, 1919); *The Preacher's Ideals and Inspirations* (New York: Fleming H. Revell Company, 1917); *The Religious Experience of Israel* (New York: Association Press, 1919).

CHAPTER TWO

1. *Oberlin Review,* February 13, 1917, 1, 3.

2. David M. Kennedy, *Over Here: The First World War and American Society* (New York: Oxford University Press, 1980).

3. Donald M. Love, *Henry Churchill King of Oberlin* (New Haven: Yale University Press, 1956), 203–7.

4. *Oberlin Review,* April 18, 1917, and May 15, 1917.

5. William J. Hutchins, "Oberlin Ambulance Corps Address," June 1917, WJH-BCA.

6. Will Hutchins to Anna Hutchins, September 22, 1917, and to Father, September 14, 1917, WJH-BCA.

7. Will Hutchins to Father, September 14, 1917.

8. Will Hutchins to Bobs, September 21, 1917, WJH-BCA.

9. Dorothy Wright Osborn to Ella Parmenter, May 29, 1965, Alumni and Development Office Records, Logan Omer Osborn file, OCA. See also Harry S. Ashmore, *Unseasonable Truths: The Life of Robert Maynard Hutchins* (Boston: Little, Brown & Company, 1989), 16–24.

10. William G. Hutchins to Milton Mayer, September 17, 1972, Box 1a, FSH-BCA.

11. William G. Hutchins to Milton Mayer, September 17, 1972.

12. RMH, "Trees Grew in Brooklyn," *Center Magazine* 1 (November 1968): 18.

13. *Oberlin Review,* February 22, 1918, 1.

14. *Oberlin Review,* May 14, 1918; and Donald MacGregor, "Good News for W. J. Hutchins: He Wins a $5,000 Prize," *American Magazine* 80 (April 1918): 25–27.

15. Interview with Francis S. Hutchins, January 8, 1986.

16. Charles M. Bakewell, *The Story of the American Red Cross in Italy* (New

York: Macmillan Company, 1920); Young Men's Christian Association (YMCA), *Service with Fighting Men: An Account of the Young Men's Christian Association in the World War,* 2 vols. (New York: Association Press, 1922).

17. Letters in WJH-BCA.

18. Will Hutchins to My Dear Boys, September 4, 1918, WJH-BCA.

19. Logan Omer Osborn diary, 1918–19, Box 1, Folder 6, LOO-OCA; letters from Italy, WJH-BCA; ditties in Box 1, Folder 5, LOO-OCA.

20. *Camp Crane News,* January 4, 1919, 2, OCA.

21. RMH to Father and Mother and Francis, October 23, 1918; RMH to People, October 25, 1918; RMH to Family, October 26, 1918; WJH-BCA.

22. RMH to Father and Mother and Francis, November 17, 1918, WJH-BCA.

23. RMH to Father, March 25, 1919, WJH-BCA. *Oberlin Review,* December 18, 1918, 1, 5.

24. RMH to Family, November 3, 1918, WJH-BCA.

25. RMH to Father, March 25, 1919, WJH-BCA.

26. Karl F. Geiser to RMH, May 6, 1929, Box 3, Folder 7, RMH-UC.

27. Storer B. Lunt to Irwin Ross, January 30, 1956, Box 2, FR-PUL. All quotes from this collection used with permission of Princeton University Libraries.

28. Francis Sessions Hutchins to Will Hutchins, April 28, 1919, WJH-BCA.

29. Will Hutchins to RMH, June 23, 1919, WJH-BCA.

30. George Wilson Pierson, *Yale: College and University, 1871–1937,* 2 vols. (New Haven: Yale University Press, 1952 and 1955), and Brooks Mather Kelley, *Yale: A History* (New Haven: Yale University Press, 1974), are my principal sources on Yale's history. Others will be so noted.

31. Helen Lefkowitz Horowitz, *Campus Life: Undergraduate Cultures from the End of the Eighteenth Century to the Present* (Chicago: University of Chicago Press, 1987), and Henry Seidel Canby, *American Memoir* (Boston: Houghton Mifflin Company, 1947), 143–59.

32. RMH to Father and Mother, February 1, ca. 1920 (n.d.), WJH-BCA; Yale College, *The Course of Study in Yale College and in Particular the Prospectus of Courses, 1920–1921* (New Haven: Yale College, 1920).

33. Charles E. Clark to Cleburne L. Farr, July 13, 1956, Box 8, Folder 105, CEC-YU.

34. Lunt to Ross, January 30, 1956.

35. W. A. Swanberg, *Luce and His Empire* (New York: Charles Scribner's Sons, 1972), and Sydney S. Hyman, *The Lives of William Benton* (Chicago: University of Chicago Press, 1969).

36. *Yale Alumni Weekly* 30 (April 15, 1921): 751; *Yale Alumni Weekly* 29 (May 7, 1920): 760, and (May 28, 1920): 838.

37. Clark to Farr, July 13, 1956; and Lunt to Ross, January 30, 1956.

38. Clark to Farr, July 13, 1956.

39. Benton, quoted in Hyman, *The Lives of William Benton,* 69–70.

40. William G. Hutchins to Milton Mayer, September 17, 1972.

41. RMH, "With the Undergraduates," *Yale Alumni Weekly* 30 (March 4, 1921): 586; (March 18, 1921): 640.

42. RMH, "Undergraduate Affairs," *Yale Alumni Weekly* 30 (April 15, 1921): 751.

43. RMH to Stokes, May 6, 1921, Box 66, Folder 8878, SR-YU.

44. Lunt to Ross, January 30, 1956.

45. Clark to Farr, July 13, 1956.

46. Interview with Francis S. Hutchins, January 8, 1986.

47. Clark to Farr, July 13, 1956.

48. Clark to Farr, July 13, 1956, and Lunt to Ross, January 30, 1956.

49. RMH, "Class of 1921," Box 33, RMH(AU)-UC.

50. RMH, "Our Contemporary Ancestors," Box 33, RMH(AU)-UC.

51. Arthur Twining Hadley, "The Baccalaureate Sermon," *Yale Alumni Weekly* 30 (July 8, 1921): 1115, 1116.

52. George W. Pierson, *The Education of American Leaders: Comparative Contributions of U.S. Colleges and Universities* (New York: Frederick A. Praeger, 1969).

53. George Wilson Pierson, *A Yale Book of Numbers: Historical Statistics of the College and University, 1701–1976* (New Haven: Yale University Press, 1983), 491, on the class of 1923; the trend had continued for a number of years. Hyman, *The Lives of William Benton,* 72–73, on the class of 1921.

54. RMH to Mother and Father, Sunday ca. 1921 (n.d.), WJH-BCA.

55. RMH to James R. Angell, October 19, 1922, Box 106, Folder 1079, JRA-PR-YU.

56. RMH to Mother and Father, January 4, 1919 (should read 1920), WJH-BCA (emphasis his).

57. Francis Sessions Hutchins to Will Hutchins, January 5, 1920, WJH-BCA.

58. Francis Sessions Hutchins to Will Hutchins, February 26, 1921, WJH-BCA.

59. Will Hutchins to RMH, January 8, 1920, WJH-BCA.

60. RMH to Storer B. Lunt, March 5, 1923, Box 2, Folder 8, RMH-UC.

61. RMH to Bill Hutchins, February 9, 1923, Box 1, Folder 30, RMH-UC.

62. RMH, "Trees Grew in Brooklyn," 18.

63. William G. Hutchins to Milton Mayer, September 17, 1972.

64. George Parmley Day to James R. Angell, October 6, 1922, and Angell to Day, October 6, 1922, Box 106, Folder 1079, JRA-PR-YU.

65. RMH to Angell, October 19, 1922.

66. "Robert Maynard Hutchins, Secretary of Yale University," Box 1, Folder 29, RMH-UC.

67. RMH, "Class of '96 Dinner," January 27, 1923, Box 19, Folder 1, RMH-UC.

68. Papers and notes, Box 26, Folder 2, RMH-UC.

69. RMH to Angell, March 6, 1926, Box 106, Folder 1079, JRA-PR-YU.

70. Marsha Graham Synnott, *The Half-Opened Door: Discrimination and Admissions at Harvard, Yale, and Princeton, 1900–1970* (Westport, CT.: Greenwood Press, 1979), 125–59; Dan A. Oren, *Joining the Club: A History of Jews and Yale* (New Haven: Yale University Press, 1985). See Harold S. Wechsler, *The Qualified Student: A History of Selective College Admission in America* (New York: John H. Wiley & Sons, 1977), on other institutions engaging in the practice.

71. In Box 8, Folder 11, RMH(A)-UC.

72. Pierson, *Yale: The University College, 1921–1937* (1955), vol. 2 of *Yale: College and University,* 20.

73. Pierson, *Yale,* vol. 2, and Reuben A. Holden, *Profiles and Portraits of Yale University Presidents* (Freeport, Me.: Bond Wheelwright Company, 1968), 107–17.

74. Clark to Farr, July 13, 1956.

75. Pierson, *Yale,* vol. 2, and James Rowland Angell, *American Education: Addresses & Articles* (New Haven: Yale University Press, 1937).

76. Pierson, *Yale,* vol. 2, 256–59, and 508–12.

77. Quoted in Pierson, *Yale,* vol. 2, 24.

CHAPTER THREE

1. John Henry Schlegel, "American Legal Realism and Empirical Social Science: From the Yale Experience," *Buffalo Law Review* 28 (1979): 459–586, and Laura Kalman, *Legal Realism at Yale, 1927–1960* (Chapel Hill: University of North Carolina Press, 1986), on Yale's history, unless noted.

2. Yale University Law School, Faculty Governing Board and Board of Permanent Officers' Minutes (hereinafter, simply Faculty Minutes), March 17, 1924, YU.

3. Charles E. Clark to Cleburne L. Farr, July 13, 1956, Box 8, Folder 105, CEC-YU.

4. RMH and Charles E. Clark, "The Real Party in Interest," *Yale Law Journal* 34 (1925): 259–76; "Comment: Modern Views of the Election of Remedies," *Yale Law Journal* 34 (1925): 665–70.

5. Benjamin N. Cardozo, *The Nature of the Judicial Process* (New Haven: Yale University Press, 1921).

6. Jerold S. Auerbach, *Unequal Justice: Lawyers and Social Change in Modern America* (New York: Oxford University Press, 1976); Robert Stevens, *Law School: Legal Education in America from the 1850s to the 1980s* (Chapel Hill: University of North Carolina Press, 1983); John W. Johnson, *American Legal Culture, 1908–1940* (Westport, Ct.: Greenwood Press, 1981); and William Twining, *Karl Llewellyn and the Legal Realist Movement* (Norman: University of Oklahoma Press, 1985 [1973]).

7. Stevens, *Law School,* 112–23.

8. Kalman, *Legal Realism at Yale,* 98–102, on Corbin and Hohfeld; Twining, *Karl Llewellyn,* 37–40, on Cook.

9. John Henry Schlegel, "American Legal Realism and Empirical Social Science: The Singular Case of Underhill Moore," *Buffalo Law Review* 29 (1980): 204–13, on Columbia.

10. Gerald Lawrence Fetner, "Counsel to the Situation: The Lawyer as Social Engineer, 1900–1945" (Ph.D. thesis, Brown University, 1973), 58.

11. David E. Ingersoll, "American Legal Realism and Sociological Jurisprudence: The Methodological Roots of a Science of Law," *Journal of the History of the Behavioral Sciences* 17 (1981): 490–503; Lawrence M. Friedman, *A History of American Law* (rev. ed.; New York: Simon & Schuster, 1985), 627.

12. Ellen Condliffe Lagemann, *The Politics of Knowledge: The Carnegie Corporation, Philanthropy, and Public Policy* (Middletown: Wesleyan University Press, 1989), chap. 4; Johnson, *American Culture,* 58–61, 67–68.

13. Kalman, *Legal Realism at Yale,* 28–31, 35–38.

14. Interview with Thomas I. Emerson, June 21, 1988.

15. James Rowland Angell, in *A History of Psychology in Autobiography,* vol. 3, ed. Carl Murchison, 3 vols. (New York: Russell & Russell, 1961 [1930]), 26.

16. Corbin to Angell, February 5, 1924, Box 119, Folder 1229, JRA-PR-YU.

17. Faculty Minutes, January 9, 1924, YU.

18. "Plan for Honors Courses in the Yale School of Law and for Graduate Work in Procedure," n.d. (ca. January 1926), Box 2, Folder 3, RMH-UC, submitted January 21, 1926, Faculty Minutes, YU.

19. "Plan for Honors Courses," n.d. (ca. January 1926).

20. RMH to Llewellyn, May 7, 1926, Box 2, Folder 6, RMH-UC.

21. RMH to Llewellyn, May 7, May 11, May 17, May 14, and May 21, 1926, on faculty objections; Llewellyn to RMH, May 6, 1926, noting that Corbin would not agree to "terms purely of competitive necessity"; Box 2, Folder 6, RMH-UC.

22. RMH to Llewellyn, May 7 and 14, 1926, Box 2, Folder 6, RMH-UC.

23. Faculty Minutes, December 4, 1926, YU.

24. Faculty Minutes, March 5 and 11 (for quote), and March 26, 1926, YU.

25. RMH (and Charles E. Clark), "A Program of Research in the Administration of the Law," n.d. (ca. 1926), Box 2, Folder 5, RMH-UC.

26. RMH and Clark, "A Program of Research in the Administration of the Law," n.d. (ca. 1926).

27. Schlegel, "Yale," 462–63.

28. Kalman, *Legal Realism at Yale,* 35–38.

29. Yale University, *Catalogue of the Law School, 1926–1927* (1926).

30. Interview with Thomas I. Emerson, June 21, 1988.

31. Thomas W. Swan to Angell, February 1, 1927, Box 121, Folder 1247, JRA-PR-YU; Faculty Minutes, January 12, 1927, YU.

32. Faculty Minutes, January 28, 1927; Corporation Records, February 12, 1927; YU.

33. RMH to Bill (Hutchins), February 4, 1927, Box 1, Folder 30, RMH-UC.

34. Faculty Minutes, February 17, 1927, YU.

35. John H. Wigmore to Angell, April 1, 1927, Box 121, Folder 1247, JRA-PR-YU.

36. Felix Frankfurter, *The Case of Sacco and Vanzetti: A Critical Analysis for Lawyers and Laymen* (Boston: Little Brown & Company, 1929 [1927]).

37. RMH, "Cross-Examination to Impeach," *Yale Law Journal* 36 (1927): 388, 390.

38. Auerbach, *Unequal Justice,* 144–49.

39. Taft to Angell, May 1, 1927, Box 119, Folder 1231, JRA-PR-YU.

40. Stetson to Angell, May 3, 1927, Box 119, Folder 1231, JRA-PR-YU.

41. Angell to RMH, May 3, 1927, Box 119, Folder 1231, JRA-PR-YU.

42. Angell to Wickliffe Rose, July 3, and November 4, 1926, GEB, Series 1, Subseries 4, 2200d (GEB 1:4), Box 636, Folder 6673, RAC.

43. Angell to Ruml, December 1, 1926, LSRM, Series 3 (LSRM, 3), Box 79, Folder 830, RAC.

44. Martin Bulmer and Joan Bulmer, "Philanthropy and Social Science in the 1920s: Beardsley Ruml and the Laura Spelman Rockefeller Memorial, 1922–29," *Minerva* 19 (1981): 347–407.

45. LKF (Frank), memorandum of interview, January 15, 1927, LSRM, 3, Box 79, Folder 830, RAC.

46. LKF (Frank), memorandum, February 4, 1927, LSRM, 3, Box 79, Folder 830, RAC.

47. RMH to Frank, March 2, 1927, LSRM, 3, Box 79, Folder 830, RAC.

48. Quoted in RMH, "Memorandum in re Proposals of the Law School to the Laura Spelman Rockefeller Memorial," December 7, 1927, Box 122, Folder 1255, JRA-PR-YU; Frank to RMH, March 3, 1927, LSRM, 3, Box 79, Folder 830, RAC.

49. William R. Vance to Angell, April 15, 1927, Box 121, Folder 1247, JRA-PR-YU.

50. Vance to Angell, April 15, 1927.

51. Report of the Committee on the Selection of the Dean, in Faculty Minutes (inserted between May 31, 1927, and October 7, 1927), YU. Clark to Farr, July 13, 1956, and interview with Thomas I. Emerson, June 21, 1988.

52. Faculty Minutes, May 26, 1927, and May 31, 1927; Corporation Records, December 10, 1927; YU.

53. RMH and Slesinger, "Some Observations on the Law of Evidence [S.O.L.E.]: Spontaneous Exclamations," *Columbia Law Review* 28 (1928): 432–40.

54. RMH and Slesinger, "S.O.L.E.: Memory," *Harvard Law Review* 41 (1928): 860–73.

55. RMH and Slesinger, "S.O.L.E.: The Competency of Witnesses," *Yale Law Journal* 37 (1928): 1017–28.

56. RMH and Slesinger, "S.O.L.E.—Consciousness of Guilt," *University of Pennsylvania Law Review* 77 (1929): 725–40; "S.O.L.E.—State of Mind to Prove an Act," *Yale Law Journal* 38 (1929): 283–98; "S.O.L.E.: State of Mind in Issue," *Columbia Law Review* 29 (1929): 147–57; "S.O.L.E.: Family Relations," *Minnesota Law Review* 13 (1929): 675–86.

57. Schlegel, "Yale," 482.

58. Conversation with John H. Schlegel, September 18, 1988.

59. Kalman, *Legal Realism at Yale,* 110–13; RMH to Angell, May 24, 1928, and Angell to RMH, June 1, 1928, Box 119, Folder 1232, JRA-PR-YU.

60. RMH to Angell, June 8, 1928, Box 119, Folder 1232, JRA-PR-YU, and RMH to Vance, July 21, 1928, Law School, Office of the Dean files, Box 88, Folder 361, YU.

61. RMH to Edmund E. Day, December 9, 1927; RMH to Day, January 11, 1928; Ruml to Angell, February 27, 1928; LSRM, 3, Box 79, Folder 830, RAC.

62. Angell to Edwin Embree, October 20, 1926, RFA, Record Group 1.1, Series 200 (RG1.1, 200), Box 67, Folder 804, RAC.

63. Brooks Mather Kelley, *Yale: A History* (New Haven: Yale University Press, 1974), 380–81; Abraham Flexner, *Medical Education in the United States and Canada* (Carnegie Foundation for the Advancement of Teaching, bulletin 4, 1910).

64. Ruml to Angell, October 5, 1928, LSRM, 3, Box 79, Folder 826, RAC; "It may be recalled . . . ," n.d. (ca. spring 1928), Box 122, Folder 1261, JRA-PR-YU.

65. "A Program for an Institute of Human Relations at Yale University," May 20, 1928, LSRM, 3, Box 79, Folder 826, RAC.

66. "More than a year has elapsed," October 1928, Box 114, Folder 1161, and RMH to Angell, December 3, 1928, Box 122, Folder 1261; JRA-PR-YU.

67. Faculty Minutes, February 23, 1928, and Corporation Records, March 10, 1928, YU.

68. RMH to Angell, April 4, and April 13, 1928, Box 122, Folder 1261, JRA-PR-YU.

69. Charles H. Sherrill to Angell, November 27, 1928, Box 119, Folder 1232, JRA-PR-YU; Corporation Records, December 8, 1928, YU.

70. RMH to Angell, December 3, 1928.

71. Angell to RMH, December 5, 1928, Box 122, Folder 1261; Sherrill to Angell, November 27, 1928; JRA-PR-YU.

72. Angell to George E. Vincent, October 24, 1928, GEB, 1:4, Box 636, Folder 6673, RAC.

73. RMH to Day, October 25, 1928, LSRM, 3, Box 79, Folder 826, RAC.

74. Day to RMH, November 3, 1928, LSRM, 3, Box 79, Folder 826, RAC.

75. RMH to Day, November 9, 1928, LSRM, 3, Box 79, Folder 826, RAC.

76. Rockefeller Foundation Minutes, January 22, 1929, Box 114, Folder 1161, JRA-PR-YU.

77. Frank to RMH, December 18, 1928, LSRM, 3, Box 79, Folder 826, RAC.

78. "Family Situations and Treatment of Delinquency and Crime," n.d. (ca. 1928); RMH to Frank, December 20, 1928; LSRM, 3, Box 79, Folder 826, RAC.

79. "Human Relations Section: Yale Law School" RFA, RG1.1, 200, Box 67, Folder 804, RAC.

80. Rockefeller Foundation Minutes, January 3, 1929, RFA, RG1.1, 200, Box 67, Folder 804, RAC; Rockefeller Foundation Minutes, January 22, 1929, Box 114, Folder 1161, JRA-PR-YU.

81. William D. Healy and Augusta F. Bronner, *New Light on Delinquency and Its Treatment: Results of a Research Conducted for the Institute of Human Relations* (New Haven: Yale University Press, 1936); they credited Hutchins with inspiring the project.

82. J. G. Morawski, "Organizing Knowledge and Behavior at Yale's Institute of Human Relations," *Isis* 77 (1986): 219–46; Mark A. May, "A Retrospective View of the Institute of Human Relations at Yale," *Behavior Science Notes* 6 (1971): 141–72.

83. RMH, *Report of the Dean, 1928–1929,* 5–6, and "Human Relations Section."

84. Schlegel, "Yale," 491–586; Kalman, *Legal Realism at Yale,* 115–44; Clark to RMH, November 6, and December 23, 1929, Box 35, Folder 6, RMH(A)-UC.

85. Clark to Angell, December 29, 1936, Box 120, Folder 1242, JRA-PR-YU.

86. Copy of resolution in Box 3, Folder 22, RMH-UC.

87. William O. Douglas, *Go East, Young Man: The Early Years* (New York: Dell, 1974), 167.

88. Schlegel, "Yale," 489–90.

89. RMH, "Legal Research in West Virginia," *West Virginia Law Quarterly* 35 (1929): 115, and Douglas, *Go East, Young Man,* 165–66.

90. RMH, "Memorandum in re Proposals of the Law School to the Laura Spelman Rockefeller Memorial."

91. RMH, "The Law School Tomorrow," *North American Review* 225 (February 1928): 12.

92. Abraham Flexner, *Abraham Flexner: An Autobiography* (New York: Simon & Schuster, 1960), 210–13; and RMH to Flexner, October 25, 1927, Flexner to RMH, October 26, 1927, and RMH to Flexner, November 4, 1927, GEB, 1:4, Box 636, Folder 6673, RAC.

PART TWO

1. Reubin Frodin, "Bibliography of Robert M. Hutchins, 1925–1950," *Journal of General Education* 4 (1950): 303–24, and addendum in Box 17, Folder 10, RMH-UC.

CHAPTER FOUR

1. Helen Lefkowitz Horowitz, *Culture & the City: Cultural Philanthropy in Chicago from the 1880s to 1917* (Lexington: University Press of Kentucky, 1976); and Kathleen D. McCarthy, *Noblesse Oblige: Charity & Cultural Philanthropy in Chicago, 1849–1929* (Chicago: University of Chicago Press, 1982); Edward Shils,

"The University, the City, and the World: Chicago," in *The University and the City: From Medieval Origins to the Present,* ed. Thomas Bender (New York: Oxford University Press, 1988), 210–30.

2. Steven J. Diner, *A City and Its Universities: Public Policy in Chicago, 1892–1919* (Chapel Hill: University of North Carolina Press, 1980); Shils, "The University."

3. James Sloan Allen, *The Romance of Commerce and Culture: Capitalism, Modernism, and the Chicago-Aspen Crusade for Cultural Reform* (Chicago: University of Chicago Press, 1983), 78–79.

4. Swift to Charles W. Gilkey (of the Divinity School and chair of the search committee), December 28, 1928, and Swift memorandum "Re. R. M. Hutchins," December 29–30, 1928, Box 38, Folder 11, HHS-UC. Benjamin McArthur, "A Gamble on Youth: Robert M. Hutchins, the University of Chicago and the Politics of Presidential Selection," *History of Education Quarterly* 30 (1990): 161–86, for a lively and engaging description of the selection process.

5. Embree to Swift, March 16, 1929, Box 38, Folder 11, HHS-UC.

6. Richard J. Storr, *Harper's University: The Beginnings* (Chicago: University of Chicago Press, 1966), Thomas W. Goodspeed, *The Story of the University of Chicago, 1890–1925* (Chicago: University of Chicago Press, 1925), and Diner, *A City,* 14–18.

7. Laurence R. Veysey, *The Emergence of the American University* (Chicago: University of Chicago Press, 1965).

8. Embree to Swift, March 16, 1929.

9. Storr, *Harper's University;* William Michael Murphy and D. J. R. Bruckner, eds., *The Idea of the University of Chicago: Selections from the Papers of the First Eight Chief Executives of the University of Chicago from 1891 to 1975* (Chicago: University of Chicago Press, 1976).

10. Barry D. Karl, *Charles E. Merriam and the Study of Politics* (Chicago: University of Chicago Press, 1974), 156–61.

11. Swift to Ted Donnelley, March 28, 1929, Box 38, Folder 11, HHS-UC.

12. Embree to Swift, March 16, 1929.

13. Embree to Vincent, April 4, 1929, RFA, RG1.1, 216, Box 1, Folder 1, RAC.

14. Vincent to Swift, April 12, 1929, Box 38, Folder 11, HHS-UC.

15. Swift to Ernest E. Quantrell, April 9, 1929, and to Donnelley, April 9, 1929, Box 38, Folder 11, HHS-UC.

16. Quantrell to Swift, April 12, 1929, Box 38, Folder 11, HHS-UC.

17. "Report of E. E. Quantrell" to Swift, April 16, 1929; and Angell to Swift, April 16, 1929; Box 38, Folder 11, HHS-UC.

18. Donnelley to Swift, April 4, 1929, Box 38, Folder 11, HHS-UC.

19. Karl, *Charles E. Merriam,* 161.

20. Storr, *Harper's University,* 332–68. Conversations with Dan Meyer on the distinction between Harper's wish to control university affairs and his laissez-faire attitude toward faculty who found outside support for their work.

21. RMH to William F. Ogburn, April 30, 1929, Box 3, Folder 15, RMH-UC.

22. Martin Bulmer, *The Chicago School of Sociology: Institutionalization, Diversity, and the Rise of Sociological Research* (Chicago: University of Chicago Press, 1984); Darnell Rucker, *The Chicago Pragmatists* (Minneapolis: University of Minnesota Press, 1969); Karl, *Charles E. Merriam;* and Shils, "The University."

23. Bulmer, *The Chicago School of Sociology,* chap. 3, for these developments.

24. William James, "The Chicago School," *Psychological Bulletin* 1 (July 5, 1904): 1–5.

25. William T. Hutchinson, "The Department of History in Retrospect," 1956, Box 17, Folder 8, WTH-UC.

26. On Ruml, Martin Bulmer, "The Early Institutional Establishment of Social Science Research: The Local Community Research Committee at the University of Chicago, 1923–1930," *Minerva* 18 (1980): 51–110, and "Philanthropy and Social Science in the 1920s: Beardsley Ruml and the Laura Spelman Rockefeller Memorial, 1922–1929," *Minerva* 19 (1981): 347–407, and chap. 8, *The Chicago School of Sociology.* See also Roger L. Geiger, *To Advance Knowledge: The Growth of American Research Universities, 1900–1940* (New York: Oxford University Press, 1986), chaps. 4 and 5.

27. Conversations with Dan Meyer and Barry D. Karl on the implications of this development for Hutchins' subsequent relations with the faculty.

28. Karl, *Charles E. Merriam,* 164.

29. N. G. Annan "The Intellectual Aristocracy," in *Studies in Social History,* ed. J. H. Plumb (London: Longmans Green, 1955).

30. Daniel Boorstin, "Universities in the Republic of Letters," *Perspectives in American History* 1 (1967): 374.

31. "Report of the Committee on the Presidency," April 17, 1929, Box 38, Folder 11, HHS-UC.

32. Swift to Donnelley, April 9, 1929.

33. Box 3, RMH-UC.

34. Boxes 48 and 49, HHS-UC. His initial salary at the university was $25,000.

35. Interview with Elizabeth (Nitze) Paepcke, February 16, 1989. "Mrs. Hutchins Carves Out Her Career in Art," *Chicago Daily News,* May 4, 1929; "The Midway's Versatile First Lady," *Chicago Sunday Tribune* (copy), ABF-UC.

36. Edward Shils, "Robert Maynard Hutchins," *American Scholar* 59 (1990): 211.

37. *University Record* (n.s.) 16 (January, 1930): 11.

38. Ibid., 26–30.

39. Ibid., 30.

40. Ibid., 36.

41. Ibid., 38.

42. Swift to Frederic Woodward, May 10, 1929, Box 135, Folder 7, HHS-UC. Swift to Ernest D. Burton, December 1, 1924, and Edith Foster Flint, Marion Talbot, and Elizabeth Wallace to Swift and Burton, n.d. (ca. 1924); Box 136, Folder 21, HHS-UC, on the lack of representation of women throughout the university.

43. RMH to Karl Llewellyn, April 29, 1929; Llewellyn to RMH, April 26, 1929, Box 3, Folder 12; Jerome N. Frank to RMH, June 14, 1929, Box 3, Folder 6; RMH-UC.

44. Woodward to RMH, May 15, 1929, Box 70, Folder 12, RMH(A)-UC.

45. "President Hutchins's First Convocation Address," *University Record* (n.s.) 15 (1929): 119, 122, 123.

46. RMH, "Memorandum on Graduate Study," December 9, 1929, Box 11, Folder 1, CHJ-UC; "Convocation," *University Record* (n.s.) 16 (1930): 158–63.

47. George E. Vincent's diary excerpt, October 14, 1929, RFA, RG1.1, 216, Box 1, Folder 1, RAC.

48. *Annual Report of the General Education Board, 1928–1929* (New York: General Education Board, 1930), 9–12; Roger L. Geiger, *To Advance Knowledge,* 141, on the dismay.

49. George E. Vincent's diary excerpt, October 14, 1929.

50. *Annual Report of the General Education Board, 1929–1930* (New York: General Education Board, 1931), 11, and RMH, "Address to the First Midwinter Assembly of the Alumni," *University Record* (n.s.) 16 (1930): 90.

51. Charles H. Judd to RMH, August 21, 1930, Box 102, Folder 4, PP, 1925–1945, UC.

52. RMH to Trevor Arnett, January 17, 1931, RFA, RG1.1, 216, Box 1, Folder 4, RAC, and *Annual Report of the General Education Board, 1930–1931* (New York: General Education Board, 1932), 6–8.

53. Raymond B. Fosdick, *The Story of the Rockefeller Foundation* (New York: Harper & Brothers, 1952), 207.

CHAPTER FIVE

1. Mortimer J. Adler, *Philosopher at Large: An Intellectual Autobiography* (New York: Macmillan, 1977), 109 ff. His account is corroborated in their correspondence: RMH to Adler, July 15, 1927; Adler to RMH, July 19, 1927; RMH to Adler, July 21, 1927; RMH to Adler, July 29, 1927; MJA-IPR.

2. Adler, *Philosopher,* on his biography.

3. RMH, "Literacy Is Not Enough or The Autobiography of an Uneducated Man," in *Co-operative Effort in Schools to Improve Reading,* ed. William S. Gray (Chicago: Supplementary Educational Monographs, no. 56, September 1942), 12–17.

4. Adler, *Philosopher,* and Amy Apfel Kass, "Radical Conservatives for a Liberal Education" (Ph.D. thesis, Johns Hopkins University, 1973), for a detailed account of these friends and their activities.

5. Adler to RMH, August 10, 1927; RMH to Adler, September 2 and 9, 1927; MJA-IPR.

6. RMH to Adler, September 2 and 9, 1927; Adler to RMH, Sunday, n.d. (ca. January 1928), MJA-IPR.

7. Adler to RMH, September 17, 1927, MJA-IPR.

8. Adler to RMH, Monday the 27th, n.d. (ca. May 1929), Box 4, Folder 2, RMH-UC.

9. Adler, *Philosopher,* 117–19.

10. Adler to RMH, Saturday, n.d. (ca. December 1929), and Tuesday, n.d. (ca. January 1930), Box 4, Folder 2, RMH-UC.

11. Adler to RMH, Saturday, n.d. (ca. December 1929), and Sunday, n.d. (ca. December 1929), Box 4, Folder 2, RMH-UC.

12. Adler to RMH, Tuesday, n.d. (ca. January 1930). On Meiklejohn and the Experimental College, see G. C. Sellery, *Some Ferments at Wisconsin, 1901–1947: Memories and Reflections* (Madison: University of Wisconsin Press, 1960), 9–34, and Cynthia Stokes Brown, ed., *Alexander Meiklejohn: Teacher of Freedom* (Berkeley, Calif.: Meiklejohn Civil Liberties Institute, 1981).

13. Tufts to RMH, October 28, 1929, Box 106, Folder 14, PP, 1925–45, UC.

14. "A Statement from the Department of Philosophy," n.d. (ca. March 1931), Box 106, Folder 14, PP, 1925–45, UC.

15. Adler, *Philosopher,* 48.

16. RMH to Adler, March 25, 1930, Box 4, Folder 1, RMH-UC.

17. Adler to RMH, December 13, 1929; Tufts to Adler, December 11, 1929; Box 4, Folder 2 and 4, RMH-UC.

18. Mortimer J. Adler and Jerome Michael, *Crime, Law, and Social Science* (New York: Harcourt, Brace, & Company, 1933).

19. Adler to RMH, Tuesday, n.d. (ca. January 1930).

20. Adler to RMH, April 8, 1930, Box 4, Folder 2, RMH-UC.

21. Adler to RMH, Wednesday, n.d. (ca. spring 1930), MJA-IPR.

22. Adler to RMH, n.d. (ca. 1933), Box 4, Folder 2, RMH-UC.

23. Adler to RMH, Monday the 27th, n.d. (ca. May 1929).

24. Adler to RMH, Tuesday, n.d. (ca. January 1930).

25. RMH to Adler, July 6, 1929, MJA-IPR.

26. Adler, *Philosopher,* 134.

27. Adler to RMH, Tuesday evening, n.d. (ca. spring 1930); Wednesday, n.d. (ca. spring 1930); MJA-IPR.

28. Adler to RMH, Wednesday, n.d. (ca. spring 1930). In Adler, *Philosopher,* 134, he suggests that he expressed these (or similar) opinions in public.

29. Darnell Rucker, *The Chicago Pragmatists* (Minneapolis: University of Minnesota Press, 1969), and Charles Morris, *The Pragmatic Movement in American Philosophy* (New York: George Braziller, 1970), 174–91.

30. "A Statement from the Department of Philosophy."

31. "A Statement from the Department of Philosophy."

32. RMH to Adler, January 30, 1930, February 14, 1930, March 10, 1930, Box 4, Folder 1; and Adler to RMH, November 15, 1929, "Monday," n.d. (ca. February 1930), Box 4, Folder 2; RMH-UC.

33. G. H. Mead to Frederic Woodward, November 1, 1930, Box 106, Folder 14, PP, 1925–45, UC.

34. "A Statement from the Department of Philosophy."

35. Rucker, *The Chicago Pragmatists,* 25–26, and Adler, *Philosopher,* 145–48, for accounts of the dispute and its results.

36. George H. Mead, E. A. Burtt, and Arthur E. Murphy to the committee on educational policy of the humanities division, Box 106, Folder 4, PP, 1925–45, UC.

37. T. V. Smith to Frederic Woodward, March 4, 1931; see also T. V. Smith to RMH, March 21, 1931; Box 106, Folder 14, PP, 1925–45, UC.

38. "The Reminiscences of Robert M. Hutchins," November 1968, COHC.

39. Edward Shils, "Presidents and Professors in American University Government," *Minerva* 8 (1970): 440.

40. Mortimer Adler, "Robert M. Hutchins, 1899–1971," *Center Magazine* 11 (September/October 1977): 27.

41. Adler to RMH, Sunday, n.d. (ca. December 1929); RMH to Adler, March 25, 1930; and Adler, *Philosopher,* 129–33.

42. Adler to RMH, Tuesday evening, n.d. (ca. spring 1930).

43. RMH to Adler, July 24, 1930 (Homer, Aeschylus, the Old Testament, Herodotus), and August 8, 1930 (Aristophanes, Thucydides), MJA-IPR.

44. RMH to Adler, July 2, 1931, Box 4, Folder 1, RMH-UC.

45. Letter from Elizabeth H. Paepcke, February 25, 1989.

46. Adler, "Great Books, Democracy, and Truth," *Educational Studies* 19 (1988): 296.

47. Edward Shils, "Robert Maynard Hutchins," *American Scholar* 59 (1990): 217; Adler, *Philosopher,* 138; J. D. Hess, "Teaching Ideas in College Classes," *College Board Review,* fall 1987, 19–21, 33.

48. RMH, *No Friendly Voice* (Chicago: University of Chicago Press, 1936), 4.

49. Interview with Mortimer Adler, May 25, 1985.

50. RMH, "The Administrator," in *The Works of the Mind,* ed. Robert Heywood (Chicago: University of Chicago Press, 1947), 135–56.

51. RMH to Father, November 5, 1931, WJH-BCA. See also "Sees Hunger in Chicago," *New York Times,* February 4, 1932, 14.

52. Commission of Inquiry into National Policy in International Economic Relations, *International Economic Relations* (Minneapolis: University of Minnesota Press, 1934); and RMH, "The Future of World Trade," *Economic Forum* 3 (1935): 133–48.

53. RMH, "Drive the School Board Out!" and "Who Ordered Cuts in Schools?" *British American* [Chicago] 45 (July 22, 1933): 6; "Public Education vs. Political Jobbery," *Chicago Herald Examiner,* July 21, 1933. Julia Wrigley, *Class Politics and Public Schools: Chicago, 1900–1950* (New Brunswick: Rutgers University Press, 1982), 210–36, describes the cutbacks and political response.

54. RMH, "Education as a National Asset and Responsibility," delivered over NBC Radio, February 12, 1933, Box 19, Folder 8, RMH-UC; "The School Tax Problem," *New York Times,* October 30, 1932, VIII, 5; "Education Post in Cabinet Urged," *New York Times,* October 31, 1933, 4.

55. RMH, "A Democratic Platform," June 27, 1932, Box 19, Folder 8, RMH-UC.

56. RMH, *No Friendly Voice,* 4.

57. RMH, *No Friendly Voice,* 9.

58. See the *Social Frontier* 3 (1936–37): John Dewey, "Rationality in Education," 71–73; "President Hutchins's Proposals to Remake Higher Education,"

103–4; "The Higher Learning in America," 167–69; RMH, "Grammar, Rhetoric, and Mr. Dewey," 137–39; and Edward A. Purcell, Jr., *The Crisis of Democratic Theory: Scientific Naturalism & the Problem of Value* (Lexington: University Press of Kentucky, 1973).

59. RMH, *The Higher Learning in America* (New Haven: Yale University Press, 1936), 63, 67.

60. Warren I. Sussman, "The Thirties," in *The Development of an American Culture,* ed. Stanley Coben and Lorman Ratner (Englewood Cliffs, N.J.: Prentice-Hall, 1970), 179–218.

61. RMH, *Report of the President to the Board of Trustees, 1930–34,* 30, UC.

62. Russell Thomas, *The Search for a Common Learning: General Education, 1800–1960* (New York: McGraw-Hill, 1962); Frederick Rudolph, *Curriculum: A History of the American Undergraduate Course of Study since 1636* (San Francisco: Jossey-Bass, 1977); Daniel Bell, *The Reforming of General Education: The Columbia College Experience in Its National Setting* (New York: Columbia University Press, 1966); and R. Freeman Butts, *The College Charts Its Course: Historical Conceptions and Current Proposals* (New York: McGraw-Hill, 1939).

63. Adler to RMH, n.d. (ca. 1933), Box 4, Folder 2, RMH-UC. Adler to RMH, March 26, 1937, Box 1, Folder 11, RMH(A)-UC; Adler to RMH, January 17, 1944, Box 4, Folder 2, RMH-UC. Adler to RMH, August 23, 1936, and Adler to RMH, June 25, 1937, MJA-IPR. RMH to Adler, August 6, 1934, and RMH to Adler, n.d. (ca. summer 1936), MJA-IPR.

64. RMH to Adler, August 16, 1938, MJA-IPR.

CHAPTER SIX

1. RMH, *Report of the President to the Board of Trustees, 1930–1934* (February 1, 1935), 2, UC.

2. The sequence of events indicates the administrative problems were Hutchins' major concern. See also Geoff Cox to Dan Meyer, October 13, 1987, ABF-UC.

3. RMH, "Inaugural Address," *University Record* (n.s.) 16 (January 1930): 8–14. RMH to Roger Burlingame, November 1, 1960, Box 8, RMH(AU)-UC, on Ruml.

4. See Paula S. Fass, *The Damned and the Beautiful: American Youth in the 1920's* (New York: Oxford University Press, 1977); Helen Lefkowitz Horowitz, *Campus Life: American Undergraduate Cultures from the End of the Eighteenth Century to the Present* (Chicago: University of Chicago Press, 1987); David O. Levine, *The American College and the Culture of Aspiration, 1915–1940* (Ithaca: Cornell University Press, 1986).

5. Floyd W. Reeves, W. E. Peik, and John Dale Russell, *Instructional Problems in the University,* vol. 4 of *The University of Chicago Survey,* ed. Floyd W. Reeves et al. (Chicago: University of Chicago Press, 1933), 3–22, for a detailed account of these changes in the undergraduate program before 1931.

6. Reuben Frodin, "Very Simple, but Thoroughgoing," in *The Idea and Practicing of General Education: An Account of the College of the University of Chicago,* ed. F. Champion Ward (Chicago: University of Chicago Press, 1950), 25–99, is my principal source on the college's history. See also Chauncey Samuel Boucher, *The Chicago College Plan* (Chicago: University of Chicago Press, 1935). Other sources will be noted.

7. "The University Senate" (statutes), Box 18, Folder 11, PP, 1940–46, UC.

8. RMH, "Inaugural Address."

9. RMH, *Report of the President, 1929–1930,* UC; *Annual Report of the General Education Board, 1928–1929* (New York: General Education Board, 1930), 10–13.

10. R. Freeman Butts, *The College Charts Its Course: Historical Conceptions and Current Proposals* (New York: McGraw-Hill, 1939), 274–78.

11. *Annual Report of the General Education Board, 1929–1930* (1931), 12–16.

12. Russell Thomas, *The Search for a Common Learning: General Education, 1800–1960* (New York: McGraw-Hill, 1962), chap. 4.

13. Butts, *The College Charts Its Course,* chap. 21.

14. William Summerscales, *Affirmation and Dissent: Columbia's Response to the Crisis of World War I* (New York: Teachers College Press, 1970), chap. 5; Daniel Bell, *The Reforming of General Education: The Columbia College Experience in Its National Setting* (New York: Columbia University Press, 1966).

15. RMH to Adler, May 6, 1930, Box 1, Folder 11, RMH(A)-UC; Adler to RMH, Tuesday evening, n.d. (ca. spring 1930) MJA-IPR.

16. Harold S. Wechsler, *The Qualified Student: A History of Selective College Admission in America* (New York: John Wiley & Sons, 1977), 223.

17. Frederick Rudolph, *Curriculum: A History of the American Undergraduate Course of Study since 1636* (San Francisco: Jossey-Bass, 1977), has informed all of these descriptions: 276–77, on Meiklejohn; Alexander Meiklejohn, *The Experimental College* (New York: Harper & Brothers, 1932); G. C. Sellery, *Some Ferments at Wisconsin, 1901–1947: Memories and Reflections* (Madison: University of Wisconsin Press, 1960), 9–34; Cynthia Stokes Brown, ed., *Alexander Meiklejohn: Teacher of Freedom* (Berkeley, Calif.: Meiklejohn Civil Liberties Institute, 1981), 1–35.

18. Scott Buchanan, *Poetry and Mathematics* (Philadelphia: J. B. Lippincott Company, 1962 [1929]); Amy Apfel Kass, "Radical Conservatives for a Liberal Ed-

ucation" (Ph.D. thesis, Johns Hopkins University, 1973), 129–35; Gerald Grant and David Riesman, *The Perpetual Dream: Reform and Experiment in the American College* (Chicago: University of Chicago Press, 1978), 40–76.

19. Lotus D. Coffman, *The State University, Its Work and Problems: A Selection from Addresses Delivered between 1921 and 1933* (Minneapolis: University of Minnesota Press, 1934); James Gray, *The University of Minnesota, 1851–1951* (Minneapolis: University of Minnesota Press, 1951); Rudolph, *Curriculum;* and Lawrence A. Cremin, *The Transformation of the School: Progressivism in American Education, 1876–1957* (New York: Alfred A. Knopf, 1961), 313–18.

20. Colin B. Burke, "The Expansion of American Higher Education," in Konrad H. Jarausch, ed., *The Transformation of Higher Learning, 1860–1930: Expansion, Diversification, Social Opening, and Professionalization in England, Germany, Russia, and the United States* (Chicago: University of Chicago Press, 1983), 108, 116.

21. *Annual Report of the General Education Board, 1930–1931* (1932), 6–8; RMH, *Report of the President, 1930–1934,* 36, UC.

22. Floyd W. Reeves et al., *The University of Chicago Survey.*

23. Mortimer J. Adler, *Philosopher at Large: An Intellectual Autobiography* (New York: Free Press, 1977), 143–45.

24. Book lists, Box 19, Folder 8, PP, 1925–45, UC.

25. RMH, "The Essentials of a College Curriculum," n.d. (ca. 1931), Box 19, Folder 8 (an early version), and "Report of the College Curriculum Committee," n.d. (ca. January 9, 1931), Box 19, Folder 9, PP, 1925–45, UC; Boucher, *The Chicago College Plan.*

26. H. I. Brock, "The College Claims to Recall an Ideal," *New York Times,* June 15, 1930, IV, 4–5, 20; "Chicago Remakes Its University," *Literary Digest* 107 (December 27, 1930): 16; "The New Chicago Plan," *School and Society* 33 (April 18, 1931): 536–37.

27. Bruce A. Kimball, *Orators & Philosophers: A History of the Idea of Liberal Education* (New York: Teachers College Press, 1987), 195.

28. Boucher, *The Chicago College Plan,* chaps. 3 and 7.

29. Boucher to Woodward, October 11, 1929; D. H. S. to RMH, October 15, 1929, Box 23, Folder 2, PP, 1925–45, UC.

30. RMH to A. J. Brumbaugh, May 7, 1936, Box 19, Folder 4, PP, 1925–45, UC, for example.

31. Minutes of the Divisional Committee, Division of the Biological Sciences, June 4, 1931, Box 109, Folder 3, PP, 1925–45, UC.

32. RMH, *Report of the President, 1935–1936,* 22, UC.

33. Adler, *Philosopher,* 163–66, and Edward A. Purcell, Jr., *The Crisis of Democratic Theory: Scientific Naturalism & the Problem of Value* (Lexington: University Press of Kentucky, 1973), 3–5, on the debate.

34. Taliaferro to RMH, March 28 and September 30, 1935, Box 109, Folder 4, PP, 1925–45, UC.

35. E. C. Miller to E. T. Filbey, February 25, 1938, Box 109, Folder 4, PP, 1925–45, UC.

36. Boucher, *The Chicago College Plan,* 209. There is surprisingly little evidence of written communication between the president's office and divisional faculty about the program. Perhaps Hutchins felt he was out of his league with the physicists and chemists. Or perhaps he simply was not as concerned with their contributions as he seems to have been with the social sciences and humanities faculty members'.

37. Wirth to Gideonse, July 28, 1938, and Gideonse to Wirth, August 6, 1938, Box 4, Folder 2, LW-UC.

38. Gideonse, "Report on the First Year of the Introductory Course in the Social Sciences," n.d. (ca. 1934), Box 110, Folder 1, PP, 1925–1945, UC.

39. Redfield to RMH, November 12, 1934, Box 110, Folder 1, PP, 1925–45, UC. Gideonse to Boucher, June 9, 1933, Box 6, Folder 8, DCR-UC, suggests that some senior faculty objections to the courses could be attributed to the boldness with which new plan students challenged professors' assumptions in the divisional courses.

40. Wirth to Gideonse, December 14, 1939, Box 4, Folder 2, LW-UC.

41. Marshall E. Dimock to Fay-Cooper Cole and C. C. Colby, February 4, 1938, on the purposes of the general courses, for example; Redfield to RMH, July 15, 1935, Box 110, Folder 1, PP, 1925–45, UC, and Box 11, Folders 10–12, LG-UC, for the lectures; RMH, *Report of the President, 1935–1936,* 22, and RMH to Ogburn, May 9, 1938, Box 108, Folder 10, PP, 1925–45, UC, on his impatience.

42. Crane to RMH, December 13, 1930, Box 103, Folder 6, and Crane to RMH, November 9, 1933, Box 103, Folder 7, PP, 1925–45, UC.

43. Adler, *Philosopher,* 160–61.

44. Laing to RMH, February 4, 1935, Box 109, Folder 6, PP, 1925–45, UC.

45. Adler to RMH, "Further Notes on the College and the Dean," n.d. (ca. 1935), Box 4, Folder 16, RMH-UC.

46. Frodin, "Very Simple," for a fuller description of the proposal; Boucher to RMH, November 25, 1932, Box 19, Folder 3, PP, 1925–45, UC.

47. RMH, *Report of the President, 1930–1934,* 4.

48. RMH, "What It Means to Go to College" (1935), in *No Friendly Voice* (Chicago: University of Chicago Press, 1936), 20, 23.

49. RMH, "President Tells of the University's Responsibilities" (speech at trustees' dinner for the faculties), *University Record* (n.s.) 19 (April 1933): 122.

50. RMH, *The Higher Learning in America* (New Haven: Yale University Press, 1936), 70, 85, 63.

51. John S. Brubacher and Willis Rudy, *Higher Education in Transition: An American History, 1636–1956* (New York: Harper & Brothers, 1958), 101–2, on the Yale Report; John Henry Newman, *The Idea of a University: Defined and Illustrated* (Oxford: Clarendon Press, 1976 [1852]); Thorsten Veblen, *The Higher Learning in America: A Memorandum of the Conduct of Universities by Businessmen* (New York: Sagamore Press, 1957 [1918]); the relationship of the book to Newman's and Veblen's is described in Benjamin McArthur, "Revisiting Hutchins and *The Higher Learning in America*," *History of Higher Education Annual* 7 (1987): 18–19.

52. John Dewey, "Rationality in Education," *Social Frontier* 3 (1936–37): 72, and "The Higher Learning in America," *Social Frontier* 3 (1936–37): 167. For further descriptions of the debate, see Brian Alair Cole, "Hutchins and His Critics, 1936–1953" (Ph.D. thesis, University of Maryland, 1976); Mary Ann Dzuback, "Robert M. Hutchins, 1899–1977: Portrait of an Educator" (Ph.D. thesis, Columbia University, 1987), 191–203; and McArthur, "Revisiting Hutchins," 20–22.

53. Louis Wirth to RMH, September 13, 1935; H. I. Schlesinger to RMH, September 9, 1935, Box 19, Folder 4, PP, 1925–45, UC.

54. RMH to A. J. Brumbaugh, May 7, 1936, Box 19, Folder 4, PP, 1925–45, UC.

55. Harry D. Gideonse, *The Higher Learning in a Democracy: A Reply to President Hutchins' Critique of the American University* (New York: Farrar & Rinehart, 1937), 15. See also Adler, *Philosopher,* 161, 169, 181–83.

56. H. F. McNair to A. J. Brumbaugh, November 26, 1935, Box 2, Folder 11, DCR-UC, on the history department's lack of interest in Barr.

57. Adler to RMH, n.d. (ca. 1935), "Further Notes on the College and Dean."

58. RMH, *Report of the President, 1935–1936,* 21.

59. RMH to Adler, August 21, 1936, MJA-IPR, and Adler to RMH, "Further Notes on the College and Dean."

60. See, for example, Adler, *Philosopher,* 173–77; Buchanan, "The Liberal Arts and the Great Books," in J.A. Lauwerys and N. Hans, eds., *The Year Book of Education, 1952* (London), 83–98; and Kass, "Radical Conservatives," 135–56. A

more detailed description of the committee is in Dzuback, "Robert M. Hutchins," 185–91.

61. McKeon to RMH, March 18, 1937, and March 19, 1937, Box 109, Folder 6, PP, 1925–45, UC.

62. See material in Box 127, Folders 5–8, and Box 128, Folder 1, RMH(A)-UC.

63. "The Subcommittee on the 'Ideal' Program," January 25, 1936, RMH to Brumbaugh, January 26, 1937, and other material in Box 19a, Folder 1, PP, 1925–45, UC; RMH, *Report of the President, 1935–1936,* 20–21.

64. Frodin, "Very Simple," for descriptions of the curriculum; see specific chapters in *The Idea and Practice of General Education* for more detail on divisional courses. See also Donald N. Levine, "Challenging Certain Myths about the 'Hutchins' College," *University of Chicago Magazine* 77 (winter 1985): 36–39, 51. Other sources will be noted.

65. A. J. Brumbaugh to RMH, July 10, 1944, Table V, Box 3, Folder 10, PP, 1940–46, UC: 118 in 1937–38; 246 in 1938–39 (freshmen and sophomores); 295 in 1939–40 (freshmen, sophomores, and juniors); 325 in 1940–41 (including all four years); 268 in 1941–42 (total).

66. A. J. Brumbaugh to RMH, October 29, 1940, Box 3, Folder 11, PP, 1940–46, UC.

67. Minutes, Executive Committee of the Division of the Social Sciences, November 13, 1939, Box 110, Folder 1, PP, 1925–45, UC, for example.

68. C. S. Boucher to Emery T. Filbey, April 8, 1932, Box 81, Folder 3, PP, 1925–45, UC; *Report of the President, 1938,* 22, UC; Filbey to RMH, May 4, 1943, Box 3, Folder 10, PP, 1940–46, UC.

69. Brumbaugh, "The In-Service Training of Staff Members in the Introductory General Courses and English 102 in the College Division," May 12, 1941, Box 3, Folder 10, PP, 1940–46, UC.

70. Minutes of the University Senate, April 9, 1942, Box 11, Folder 9, DCR-UC; Frodin, "Very Simple," 68, 95 (n. 123); and RMH, "The Reminiscences of Robert M. Hutchins," 96, COHC.

71. Faust to RMH, October 15, 1942, and other correspondence in Box 3, Folder 10; Joseph Schwab to RMH, December 5, 1945, and Russell Thomas to RMH, February 6, 1945, Box 3, Folder 9, PP, 1940–46, UC.

72. Thorough descriptions of all these courses and the reading lists can be found in Russell Thomas, "The Humanities," pp. 103–22; Milton B. Singer, "The Social Sciences," pp. 123–48; Joseph J. Schwab and Merle C. Coulter, "The Natural Sciences," pp. 149–98; Eugene P. Northrop, "Mathematics," pp. 199–203; Henry W. Sams, "Writing," pp. 204–11; William H. McNeill and William O'Meara, "In-

tegration," pp. 225–55; and other essays on courses, teaching, examinations, and advising, in Ward, ed., *The Idea and Practice of General Education.*

73. Minutes, Council of the University Senate, March 5, 1946, Box 4, Folder 8, DCR-UC.

74. Committee of the (Senate) Council, "Statement to the Board of Trustees by Members of the Committee of the Council," April 2, 1946, Box 144, Folder 18, HHS-UC.

75. Bell, *The Reforming of General Education,* 190–94.

CHAPTER SEVEN

1. Hayward Keniston to C. S. Boucher, January 17, 1933, Box 19, Folder 2, PP, 1925–45, UC.

2. Floyd W. Reeves and John Dale Russell, *Admission and Retention of University Students,* vol. 5 of *The University of Chicago Survey* (Chicago: University of Chicago Press, 1933), 26, 70.

3. RMH, *Report of the President to the Board of Trustees, 1930–34,* 36, UC.

4. William T. Hutchinson (WTH) journal, October 27 and November 1, 1932, Box 2, WTH-UC.

5. Louis Gottschalk to Avery O. Craven, February 12, 1934, Box 10, Folder 3, LG-UC.

6. "Report of an Evaluation of the College Program by Divisional Instructors," 1939, Box 9, Folder 13, DCR-UC.

7. Schlesinger to C. H. Faust, February 10, 1942, Box 21, Folder 11, DCR-UC.

8. Gerard to Alfred Emerson, February 12, 1942, Box 21, Folder 11, DCR-UC.

9. Moore to the College Committee on Policy and Personnel, February 18, 1942, Box 21, Folder 11, DCR-UC.

10. Minutes, Council of the University Senate, March 5, 1946, pp. 3, 6, and 7, Box 4, Folder 8, DCR-UC.

11. "Statement to the Board of Trustees by Members of the Committee of the Council," April 2, 1946, p. 5, Box 144, Folder 18, HHS-UC. This was the case with those studying languages, medicine, other sciences, and the social sciences requiring mathematics for statistical research.

12. "The College Proposal Arguments Pro and Con: The Issue," Box 144, Folder 18, HHS-UC.

13. Lawrence A. Cremin, *The Transformation of the School: Progressivism in American Education, 1876–1957* (New York: Alfred A. Knopf, 1961).

14. RMH, *The Higher Learning in America* (New Haven: Yale University Press, 1936), 66.

15. John Dewey, "Challenge to Liberal Thought," *Fortune* 30 (August 1944): 155–57 ff.; and "The Problem of the Liberal Arts College," *American Scholar* 13 (1944): 391–93.

16. Minutes, Council of the University Senate, March 5, 1946; Tyler to E. C. Colwell, March 27, 1946, Box 12, Folder 7, PP, 1945–50, UC; interview with Ralph Tyler, October 20, 1988. By 1948, Tyler was able to claim the following about University of Chicago college students' performance on the Graduate Record Examination: on the general examinations Chicago students scored higher on average than those from other institutions; on specialized examinations, 14% of Chicago students scored as high as the average of graduates of specialized studies in other institutions (University of Chicago B.A. students did not engage in specialized study); Tyler, "The Results of the Graduate Record Examination," November 17, 1948, Box 12, Folder 6, PP, 1925–45, UC.

17. College Faculty Minutes, December 8, 1948, Box 11, Folder 13, DCR-UC. Joseph Axelrod, Benjamin Bloom et al., *Teaching by Discussion in the College* (Chicago: College of the University of Chicago, January 1949).

18. Interviews with Ralph Tyler, October 20, 1985, and Joseph Schwab, August 10, 1984. See Henry W. Sams, "Supplementary Editorial Comment: The Hutchins College after the War," *Journal of General Education* 30 (1978–79): 59–64; Maurice Browning Cramer, "A Voice from the Hutchins College: A Pluralistic Interpretation of a Poem by Robert Browning," *Journal of General Education* 30 (1978–79): 10; Daniel Bell, *The Reforming of General Education: The Columbia College Experience in Its National Setting* (New York: Columbia University Press, 1966), 32; Earl McGrath to RMH, March 9, 1949, Box 135, Folder 7, HHS-UC.

19. Memorandum for Meeting of Members of the Central Administration with the Members of the Policy Committee and Administration of the College, February 17, 1947, Box 12, Folder 9, PP, 1945–50, UC; F.C. Ward to RMH, E. C. Colwell, and R. W. Harrison, August 31, 1949, Box 1, Folder 9, DCR-UC.

20. Minutes, Division of the Social Sciences, October 12, 1950, Box 34, Folder 8, PP, 1945–50, UC. The overall drop in enrollment in the university was 13.7%, 10.21% overall in the divisions, and 10.34% in the social science division alone.

21. University Senate, "Council Subcommittee on Student Enrollment," November 1952, Box 4, Folder 8, DCR-UC.

22. RMH, *Report of the President, 1939,* 23, UC.

23. Floyd W. Reeves and John Dale Russell, *The Alumni of the Colleges,* vol. 6 of *The University of Chicago Survey,* 10, Table 3; the exact percentage overall from

1893 to 1930 was 87.6% from the central states and 55.5% from Illinois. Both percentages rose in the 1920s to 88.3% and 58.5%, respectively.

24. William B. Benton, *The University of Chicago Public Relations* (1937), 165, UC.

25. The following statistics are for the freshman classes: 93.2% from the Midwest, 70.4% from Chicago, in 1931; 63.5% planned to live at home while attending in 1932; W. F. Cramer to Emery T. Filbey, March 24, 1933, "Chicago Plan Attracts Superior Students," Box 67, Folder 7, PP, 1925–45, UC.

26. The figures for freshmen entering in 1940 were 70.44% from the Midwest, 24.96% from outside of Illinois, and 60.49% planning to live at home; "Statistics of the Freshman Class Entering Autumn Quarter, 1940," Box 77, Folder 1, PP, 1925–45, UC.

27. Harold S. Wechsler, *The Qualified Student: A History of Selective College Admission in America* (New York: John Wiley & Sons, 1977), 230, 235 (n. 48); "Criticisms of the University Which May Tend to Explain the Decreasing Enrolment," n.d. (ca. 1937), Box 76, Folder 15, PP, 1925–45, UC; Benton, *The University of Chicago Public Relations,* 21.

28. Reeves and Russell, *The Alumni of the Colleges,* 15, Table 6; Cramer to Filbey, March 24, 1933, Table IV; "Statistics of the Freshman Class Entering Autumn Quarter, 1937," Table IV, and "Statistics of the Freshman Class Entering Autumn Quarter, 1940," Table IV, Box 77, Folder 1; PP, 1925–45, UC. The percentage of blacks admitted as freshmen at the University of Chicago in the 1930s was very small (despite perceptions of some critics of the university's admissions policies): 1.4% in 1932 (ten students), a low of .47% in 1939 (three students), and .61% in 1940 (four students).

29. Copy of statement, n.d. (ca. November 1937), Box 60, Folder 1, PP, 1925–45, UC. The studies were conducted by the Local Community Research Committee under Louis Wirth and Ernest Burgess.

30. See, for example, G. O. Fairweather to Woodward, August 10, 1937, to Professor Warner, August 26, 1937, and to RMH, November 17, 1937, Box 60, Folder 1, PP, 1925–45, UC, on the university's interests in the neighborhood and landlord status. See also Arnold R. Hirsch, *Making the Second Ghetto: Race and Housing in Chicago, 1940–1960* (Cambridge: Cambridge University Press, 1983).

31. RMH to William James Hutchins, September 22, 1937, WJH-BCA. See also Harry S. Ashmore, *Unseasonable Truths: The Life of Robert Maynard Hutchins* (Boston: Little, Brown & Company, 1989), 306–8.

32. Interview with Ralph Tyler, October 20, 1985. Davis joined the faculty in 1941.

33. In 1932–33, 50% of the total student body (graduate and undergraduate)

received aid; by 1938–39, 35% were receiving aid (3,499) and 47% of those were undergraduates; Chicago charged $325–50 in annual tuition fees (the total cost for those living in dormitories was approximately $1,014 per year); Northwestern charged $308 and the University of Illinois charged $80 in annual fees; Harvard, by contrast, charged $420 for a year's tuition; Office of the Registrar, "Students at the University of Chicago," 1939, Box 78, Folder 2, PP, 1925–45, UC. For a number of years in the early 1930s Hutchins maintained a scholarship fund for students by contributing the public speaking fees he earned; Box 139, Folder 5, RMH(A)-UC.

34. Committee of Racial Equality, *Discrimination at the University of Chicago,* n.d. (ca. 1943); E. C. Colwell to RMH, "Areas of Racial Discrimination at the University of Chicago," n.d. (ca. August 21, 1943); Stephen Corey to RMH, et al., June 2, 1943, on the Laboratory School teachers' vote to admit black children in 1944; Box 60, Folder 1, PP, 1925–45, UC.

35. W. E. B. DuBois, "As the Crow Flies," *Star & Amsterdam News,* May 29, 1943, copy in Box 60, Folder 1, PP, 1925–45, UC; Interview with Ralph Tyler, October 20, 1985.

36. Filbey to Munnecke, August 17, 1944, Box 60, Folder 1, PP, 1925–45, UC.

37. Statement by Wirth, n.d. (ca. December 15, 1937), Box 60, Folder 1, PP, 1925–45, UC.

38. RMH to Munnecke, August 26, 1944, Box 60, Folder 1, PP, 1925–45, UC; "Robert M. Hutchins Interviewed by George Dell," January 13, 1977, tape #G-44, CSDI-UCSB.

39. Munnecke to RMH, August 21, 1944, Box 60, Folder 1, PP, 1925–45, UC.

40. RMH to Munnecke, August 26, 1944.

41. Reeves and Russell, *The Alumni of the Colleges,* 8, Table 2, and 71, Table 27.

42. Cramer to Filbey, March 24, 1933. The occupations are not broken down into manual and managerial levels in such occupations as "manufacturing and industry" (22.1%), "transportation and communication" (3.7%), and "mining" (1.1%) in the way they are for the earlier period; 61.4% of the fathers were in clearly middle-class occupations.

43. Cramer to Filbey, March 24, 1933, on the 1932 figures, and "Statistics of the Freshman Class Entering Autumn Quarter, 1940."

44. Colin B. Burke, "The Expansion of American Higher Education," in *The Transformation of Higher Learning, 1860–1930: Expansion, Diversification, Social Opening, and Professionalization in England, Germany, Russia, and the United States,* ed. Konrad Jarausch (Chicago: University of Chicago Press, 1983), 111, puts the national male and female high school graduation rate roughly parallel to the college enrollment rate (of eighteen- to twenty-one-year-old whites) at 15%.

45. Reeves and Russell, *The Alumni of the Colleges,* 18, Table 7.

46. Cramer to Filbey, March 24, 1933.

47. "Statistics of the Freshman Class, 1937" and "Statistics of the Freshman Class, 1940."

48. RMH, *Report of the President, 1930–1934,* 31, UC; Benton, *The University of Chicago Public Relations,* 117–21; and Wechsler, *The Qualified Student,* 228–30.

49. Wechsler, *The Qualified Student,* 227–32. Rejection rates were 21.6% in 1931, 17.3% in 1932, 11.3% in 1933 (the lowest point they reached), 23% in 1937, and 25.6% in 1939 (the highest point): Office of the Registrar, "Students at the University of Chicago," 1939.

50. Cramer to Filbey, March 24, 1933; "Statistics of the Freshman Class, 1937" and "Statistics of the Freshman Class, 1940."

51. Office of the Registrar, "Students at the University of Chicago," 1939. The other quarter claimed a range of reasons, including closeness to home (7.7%), study in particular departments (5.5%), and family pressure (3.2%).

52. Reeves and Russell, *Alumni of the Colleges,* 1. The number of bachelor's degrees, 18,936, was not broken down by gender.

53. Lynn D. Gordon, *Gender and Higher Education in the Progressive Era* (New Haven: Yale University Press, 1990), chap. 3; and Barbara Miller Solomon, *In the Company of Educated Women* (New Haven: Yale University Press, 1985), 58, 72.

54. These and all the following figures are taken from Reeves and Russell, *Alumni of the Colleges,* for the 1893 to 1930 period; Cramer to Filbey, March 24, 1933; "Statistics of the Freshman Class, 1937" and "Statistics of the Freshman Class, 1940"; Office of the Registrar, "Students at the University of Chicago," 1939.

55. See, for example, Helen Lefkowitz Horowitz, *Campus Life: Undergraduate Cultures from the End of the Eighteenth Century to the Present* (Chicago: University of Chicago Press, 1987), 213–15.

56. David O. Levine, *The American College and the Culture of Aspiration, 1915–1940* (Ithaca: Cornell University Press, 1986), 185–209.

57. Wechsler, *The Qualified Student,* 215–36.

58. George Works to RMH, December 22, 1938, and other materials in Box 140, Folder 3, HHS-UC, document recruitment efforts.

59. Office of the Registrar, "Students at the University of Chicago," 1939. This was a sizable increase from the 34% of those accepted for the 1932 freshman class; Cramer to Filbey, March 24, 1933.

60. Reeves and Russell, *Admission and Retention of University Students,* vol. 5 of *The University of Chicago Survey,* 26.

61. Office of the Registrar, "Students at the University of Chicago," 1939.

62. Brumbaugh to RMH, October 14, 1937, Box 76, Folder 15, PP, 1925–45, UC.

63. C. F. Huth to RMH, October 20, 1937, Box 76, Folder 15, PP, 1925–45, UC. In addition to fears of comprehensive examinations, Huth mentioned poor relations between the university and local public schools and the length and expense of graduate studies, hence a loss of teachers in the master's program; lower tuition rates at Roosevelt Junior College and at the local Catholic universities, which drew off very able but financially strained students; and general confusion of the college program with Hutchins' ideas in *The Higher Learning*.

64. Office of the Registrar, "Students at the University of Chicago," 1939.

65. Office of the Dean of Students and University Examiner, "Criticisms of the University Which May Tend to Explain the Declining Enrollment," n.d. (ca. 1937); Brumbaugh to RMH, October 14, 1937; G. Works, "President Jessup . . . ," n.d. (ca. 1937); Box 76, Folder 15, PP, 1925–45, UC.

66. Seymour Martin Lipset and David Riesman, *Education and Politics at Harvard* (New York: McGraw-Hill, 1975), 305n, 317n.

67. G. Works, "President Jessup . . . "

68. C. H. Faust to John F. Moulds, April 5, 1944, Box 3, Folder 10, PP, 1940–46, UC.

69. Zens L. Smith to Emery T. Filbey, October 13, 1941; C. H. Faust to William Benton, March 1, 1943; A. J. Brumbaugh to RMH, July 10, 1944, Box 3, Folder 10; PP, 1940–46, UC.

70. Faust to RMH, October 15, 1942, Box 3, Folder 10, PP, 1940–46, UC.

71. Brumbaugh to RMH, July 10, 1944, Box 3, Folder 10, PP, 1940–46, UC.

72. Committee of the (Senate) Council, "Statement to the Board of Trustees," April 2, 1946, Box 144, Folder 18, HHS-UC.

73. "Degrees Conferred: The University of Chicago," n.d. (ca. 1956), Box 140, Folder 4, HHS-UC. The number of bachelor's degrees granted by the divisions and professional schools declined from 650 in 1942–43 to a low of 24 in 1952–53.

74. Lynn A. Williams, Jr., to E. C. Colwell, October 17, 1949, Box 1, Folder 2, DCR-UC.

75. Williams to Colwell, October 17, 1949.

76. Williams to Colwell, October 17, 1949; "Council Subcommittee on Student Enrollment," November, 1952, Box 4, Folder 8; DCR-UC.

77. Williams to Colwell, October 17, 1949; W. V. Morgenstern to Hutchins, Filbey, and Colwell, March 10, 1944, on the range of student activities, and Dorothy Dunaway to Brumbaugh, July 5, 1944, on parents' worries; Box 3, Folder 10, PP, 1940–46, UC.

78. Williams to Colwell, October 17, 1949.

79. F. C. Ward to RMH, E.C. Colwell, and R. W. Harrison, August 31, 1949, Box 1, Folder 9, DCR-UC. See also F. Champion Ward, "Requiem for the Hutchins College: Recalling an Experiment in General Education," *Change,* July/August, 1989, 25–33.

80. C. H. Faust to RMH, July 12, 1944, Box 3, Folder 10, PP, 1940–46, UC.

81. Aaron Sayvetz, a student in the 1930s and a faculty member later, "The Rational Revolutionary," *Journal of General Education* 30 (1978–79): 4; David S. Broder, "The Freedom That Education Built," *Washington Post,* May 18, 1977, A15. Interview with Mark Ashin, a freshman in 1937, February 17, 1989.

82. The attrition rate was lower in the middle 1940s than in the 1930s, quite possibly another indication of a high level of self-selection: 46.8% in 1943–44, 42.5% in 1944–45, and 38.2% in 1945–46. Students left for a variety of reasons including social maladjustment, prior plans, and financial problems; Frances L. Horler, Abstract of "Factors Related to Withdrawal from the College of the University of Chicago," n.d. (ca. February 8, 1950), Box 2, Folder 7, DCR-UC.

83. Don Levine and David Cummings to RMH, September 12, 1950, Box 12, Folder 5, PP, 1945–50, UC. The letter was signed by thirteen other students.

84. Levine and Cummings to RMH, September 12, 1950.

85. Lipset and Riesman, *Education and Politics at Harvard,* 317n.

86. L. A. Wilson to Lynn A. Williams, June 1, 1949, Box 1, Folder 9, DCR-UC. The exact figures given were 88.8% and 66.6%, respectively.

87. John R. Davey to F. C. Ward, "Treatment Accorded Graduates of the College Who Transfer to Other Schools," n.d. (ca. December 15, 1950), Box 2, Folder 5; "Council Subcommittee on Student Enrollment," November 1952; "Report of the Council Subcommittee on Enrollment," n.d. (ca. 1953), Box 4, Folder 10; DCR-UC.

88. Levine, *The American College;* Burke, "The Expansion of American Higher Education"; Wechsler, *The Qualified Student,* chap. 10.

89. Louis Graff, dean of admissions at St. John's College for a time, found many students interested in its fully prescribed program but few willing to commit to it for four years; letter from Louis Graff, March 7, 1989. The content of Chicago's program was different, but the element of prescription was not.

90. "Report of the Council Subcommittee on Enrollment," n.d. (ca. 1953).

91. "Council Subcommittee on Student Enrollment," November 1952.

92. Documents on recruitment in Box 1, Folder 9; Report of the Subcommittee on Admissions, College Faculty Minutes, May 26, 1949, Box 11, Folder 13; DCR-UC.

93. Alfred L. Putnam et al. to Harold Swift, May 16, 1953, and other materials in Box 144, Folder 11, HHS-UC.

94. James Sloan Allen, *The Romance of Commerce and Culture: Capitalism, Modernism, and the Chicago-Aspen Crusade for Cultural Reform* (Chicago: University of Chicago Press, 1983), and Sidney Hyman, *The Aspen Idea* (Norman: University of Oklahoma Press, 1975), on the festival and the institute.

95. Ward, "Branch Colleges," July 19, 1952; "Some Advantages of Establishing a Branch of the University of Chicago at Aspen, Colorado"; "Report of the Trustees Committee Appointed to Investigate the Proposal for Establishing a Branch of the University of Chicago College at Aspen, Colorado," February 21, 1953; Box 144, Folder 12, HHS-UC. See also Clarence Faust and F. Champion Ward, "Aspen College," *Journal of General Education* 30 (1978–79): 67–72.

96. Enrollment figures can be found in the following issues of the *Maroon:* September 24, 1954; September 30, 1955; September 28, 1956; October 5, 1957; October 3, 1958; October 2, 1959; and September 30, 1960; and in university press releases; both in UC. Letter from Maxine H. Sullivan, university registrar, July 6, 1990, with graduation rates.

97. The University of Chicago, *The College: Courses and Programs of Study, 1990–91,* lists these. I owe my understanding of the continuity of these curricular concerns to Ralph Nicholas, dean of the college.

98. RMH to William Benton, January 7, 1953; and RMH to Benton, February 16 and June 24, 1953, Box 100, Folder 3, WB-UC.

99. RMH to Adler, n.d. (ca. summer 1936), MJA-IPR.

100. Adler to RMH, August 11, 1937, and RMH to Adler, "Tuesday," n.d. (ca. August 1937), MJA-IPR.

101. Ralph Tyler, "Digest of Notes on Discussion between Mr. Filbey and Mr. Tyler on the Four-Year Experimental College," July 31, 1939, Box 19, Folder 4, PP, 1925–45, UC.

102. F. C. Ward to RMH, January 5, 1949, Box 12, Folder 6, PP, 1945–50, UC.

CHAPTER EIGHT

1. Barry D. Karl, *Charles E. Merriam and the Study of Politics* (Chicago: University of Chicago Press, 1974), 145.

2. Edward Shils, "Robert Maynard Hutchins," *American Scholar* 59 (1990): 211–13.

3. See Mary Ann Dzuback, "Robert M. Hutchins, 1899–1977: Portrait of an Educator" (Ph.D. thesis, Columbia University, 1987), 241–49, and Harry S.

Ashmore, *Unseasonable Truths: The Life of Robert Maynard Hutchins* (Boston: Little, Brown & Company, 1989), 193–99.

4. George K. K. Link, Percy H. Boynton, and Ernst Puttkammer, American Association of University Professors, University of Chicago Chapter, "Report of the Committee on Academic Tenure" (February 1938), Box 6, Folder 5, PP, 1925–45, UC (AAUP Report on Tenure).

5. RMH, *No Friendly Voice* (Chicago: University of Chicago Press, 1936), 149.

6. Walgreen to RMH, April 10, 1935, Box 191, Folder 5, HHS-UC.

7. RMH to Walgreen, April 13, 1935, Box 191, Folder 5, HHS-UC.

8. Brumbaugh to Harold Swift, April 13, 1935, Box 191, Folder 5, HHS-UC.

9. "State Senate Resolution, No. 33, State of Illinois," Box 190, Folder 3, HHS-UC.

10. James Stifler to Swift, summarizing and quoting the opinions of the following trustees: Harry B. Gear, William M. Blair, and Laird Bell, March 29, 1935, Box 49, Folder 6, HHS-UC.

11. Ashmore, *Unseasonable Truths,* 131.

12. Harold H. Swift, "Statement to the Illinois Senate Investigating Committee," May 13, 1935, Box 2, Folder 2, PP, 1925–45, UC.

13. RMH, "Teaching at the University," Box 2, Folder 2, PP, 1925–45, UC.

14. RMH, *Report of the President to the Board of Trustees, 1934–1935,* 12, 13, 14, UC.

15. RMH, *Report of the President, 1934–1935.*

16. William Benton, *The University of Chicago Public Relations* (1937), UC.

17. Sydney Hyman, *The Lives of William Benton* (Chicago: University of Chicago Press, 1969), is the most complete account of his activities. The Hutchins-Benton correspondence in the Benton Papers, Office of the Vice-President Papers, Hutchins Papers, and Presidents' Papers, 1925–45, all in UC, detail these activities. See also Dzuback, "Robert M. Hutchins," 236–38.

18. Walter P. Metzger, "The Academic Profession in the United States,"in *The Academic Profession: National, Institutional, and Disciplinary Settings,* ed. Burton R. Clark (Berkeley: University of California Press, 1987), 123–208, explores this tension in a national historical context.

19. RMH, "The Professor Pays" (1931), in RMH, *No Friendly Voice,* 150, 153.

20. RMH, "The Sheep Look Up" (1935), in *No Friendly Voice,* 121.

21. AAUP Report on Tenure, 15, UC.

22. Floyd W. Reeves, Ernest C. Miller, and John Dale Russell, *Trends in University Growth,* vol. 1 of *The University of Chicago Survey* (Chicago: University of Chicago Press, 1933), 114–36, and Floyd W. Reeves et al., *The University Faculty,* vol. 3 of *The University of Chicago Survey.*

23. Malcolm M. Willey, *Depression, Recovery, and Higher Education: A Report by Committee Y of the American Association of University Professors* (New York: McGraw-Hill, 1937), 80.

24. RMH, *Report of the President, 1930–1934,* 32, UC.

25. RMH, *Report of the President, 1934–1935* (1936), 23–27.

26. RMH, *Report of the President, 1934–1935,* 29.

27. "Conference with President Hutchins," July 18, 1938, Box 6, Folder 5, PP, 1925–45, UC.

28. RMH, *Report of the President, 1934–1935,* 28, 28–29.

29. Dodd to RMH, February 2, 1931, and March 10, 1931, Box 104, Folder 4, PP, 1925–45, UC.

30. William T. Hutchinson (WTH) journal, January 17 and 24, 1931, Box 2, WTH-UC; Memorandum from the History Department, January 20, 1931, and Woodward to deans Laing and Ruml, January 29, 1931, Box 104, Folder 4, PP, 1925–45, UC.

31. Schmitt to Hutchinson, June 11, 1944, Box 10, Folder 1, WTH-UC.

32. Schmitt to Filbey, August 25, 1931; Schmitt to RMH, February 17, 1933; Schmitt to Woodward, July 3, 1933; Woodward to Schmitt, July 13, 1933; Schmitt to Woodward, July 14, 1933; Woodward to Schmitt, July 20, 1933; Box 104, Folder 4, PP, 1925–45, UC.

33. RMH to Schmitt, November 1, 1934, Box 104, Folder 4, PP, 1925–45, UC.

34. William T. Hutchinson, "The Department of History in Retrospect," Box 17, Folder 8, WTH-UC.

35. RMH, *No Friendly Voice,* 31.

36. RMH, *Report of the President, 1934–1935,* 36.

37. Robert Redfield, "Status of Curriculum and Research in the Division of the Social Sciences," 1937, Box 110, Folder 1, PP, 1925–45, UC.

38. Bernadotte Schmitt to Laird Bell, January 23, 1942, copy in Box 7, Folder 9, PP, 1940–46, UC, complaining in retrospect about the results of the policy.

39. Hutchinson, "The Department of History in Retrospect," 43–44.

40. Avery O. Craven to Louis Gottschalk, March 20, 1934, Box 10, Folder 3, LG-UC, and WTH journal, April 29, 1938, and July 25, 1942.

41. Faculty Appointments, Faculty Promotions, and Faculty Resignations, 1930–37, Box 2, Folder 1:1, Presidents' Reports (Hutchins), UC. Unless otherwise noted these are my sources on appointments and promotions. Hutchinson, "The Department of History in Retrospect," Table C, on history.

42. WTH journal, May 10 and June 5, 1936, and January 18, 1939.

43. Halperin to RMH, March 9, 1940, Box 7, Folder 9, PP, 1940–46, UC.

44. Hutchinson, conversation on September 28, 1942, with Louis Gottschalk, Box 9, Folder 2, WTH-UC.

45. WTH journal, June 7, 1943, on Redfield, June 23, 1944, and May 12, 1953, on Tyler.

46. Statement in "Bill of Particulars" submitted by Edgar Wind to the Senate Committee on University Policy, ca. September 1944, Box 41, Folder 2, PP, 1945–50, UC.

47. WTH journal, October 26 and November 1, 1943.

48. Hutchinson to Tyler, January 19, 1945, Box 7, Folder 8, PP, 1940–46, UC.

49. WTH journal, January 11 and May 10, 1937.

50. RMH to Hutchinson, March 10, 1948, Box 18, Folder 26, PP, 1945–50, UC.

51. WTH journal, January 2, May 11, 15, 16, 17, July 27, 1945.

52. WTH journal, July 17, 1947.

53. Hutchinson, "The Department of History in Retrospect," 48, 49.

54. Barry D. Karl, *Charles E. Merriam,* and Martin Bulmer, *The Chicago School of Sociology: Institutionalization, Diversity, and the Rise of Sociological Research* (Chicago: University of Chicago Press, 1984).

55. Hutchins, quoted in Karl, *Charles E. Merriam,* 286.

56. RMH to Ennis H. Coale, February 16, 1937, and *Daily Maroon,* February 24, 1937, Box 107, Folder 10, PP, 1925–45, UC.

57. Bulmer, *The Chicago School of Sociology,* 204.

58. Ibid. and Karl, *Charles E. Merriam,* 286.

59. Kerwin to Leonard White, October 5, 1943, Box 13, Folder 2, PP, 1940–46, UC.

60. Simeon E. Leland to Kerwin, October 4, 1944, Box 13, Folder 2, PP, 1940–46, UC. Kerwin apparently thought Hutchins had a large influence on securing his promotion: Kerwin to RMH, June 14, 1943, Box 13, Folder 3, PP, 1940–46, UC.

61. White to Ralph Tyler, June 16, 1948; Michael Oakeshott to White, June 1,

1948, and Ernest Barker to White, June 2, 1948; Box 31, Folder 10, PP, 1945–50, UC.

62. RMH to Colwell, August 3, 1948; McKeon to Colwell, n.d. (ca. August 1948); Levi to Colwell, August 10, 1948; Adler (verbally) to Colwell, August 4, 1948; Box 31, Folder 10, PP, 1945–50, UC.

63. Bulmer, *The Chicago School of Sociology,* 205.

64. See also Edward Shils, *The Calling of Sociology and Other Essays on the Pursuit of Learning* (Chicago: University of Chicago Press, 1980), 215–20.

65. RMH to Ogburn, June 15, 1934, Box 108, Folder 10, PP, 1925–45, UC.

66. Ogburn, "On Power and Publicity," n.d. (ca. 1944 or 1945), Box 15, Folder 7, PP, 1940–46, UC.

67. Shils, "Robert Maynard Hutchins," 213.

68. RMH to Ruml, October 6, 1939, Box 155, Folder 4, RMH(A)-UC, and other letters on Wirth.

69. Wirth to RMH, February 25, 1946, Box 35, Folder 4, PP, 1945–50, UC. Hutchins' reply noted on same.

70. Laing to RMH, February 4, 1935, Box 109, Folder 6, PP, 1925–45, UC.

71. Elder Olson, "R. S. Crane," *American Scholar* 53 (1984): 232–38; Emery T. Filbey to Harold Swift, March 29, 1938, Box 81, Folder 8, PP, 1925–45, UC.

72. Nitze to RMH, March 10, 1940, Box 14, Folder 5, PP, 1940–46, UC.

73. WTH journal, March 13, 1940.

74. Nitze to RMH, March 12, 1940, Box 14, Folder 5, PP, 1940–46, UC.

75. In Box 106, Folder 14, PP, 1925–45, UC, and Box 134, Folder 17, HHS-UC.

76. RMH to McKeon, March 18, 1936, Box 109, Folder 6, PP, 1925–45, UC.

77. "Faculty Promotions," Box 2, Folder 1:1, Presidents' Reports (Hutchins), UC.

78. "Report of the Committee on Policy of the Division of the Humanities," 1938, Box 109, Folder 6, PP, 1925–45, UC.

79. G. J. Laing to RMH, January 7, 1935, and Woodbridge to Laing, January 2, 1935, Box 106, Folder 15, PP, 1925–45, UC. Woodbridge was referring to candidates from within the department.

80. McKeon to Perry, February 4, 1937, Box 109, Folder 6, PP, 1925–45, UC.

81. Elder Olson, "R. S. Crane," 235–36.

82. McKeon to RMH, March 18, 1937, and "Report of the Committee on Policy of the Division of the Humanities," 1938, Box 109, Folder 6, PP, 1925–45, UC.

83. Adler, "Institute of Philosophy," March 1, 1934, Box 106, Folder 14, PP, 1925–45, UC.

84. RMH to Adler, August 16, 1936, MJA-IPR.

85. McKeon to RMH, October 25, 1948, Box 30, Folder 20, PP, 1945–50, UC.

86. "Memorandum on the Functions and Needs of the Department of Philosophy of the University of Chicago," n.d. (1948) (presumably authored by Charner Perry), Box 30, Folder 20, PP, 1945–50, UC.

87. T. V. Smith, *A Non-existent Man: An Autobiography* (Austin: University of Texas Press, 1962), 231, 230, 232, 233, 234.

88. In a preliminary draft of RMH, *Report of the President, 1935–1936,* 9, he noted that he differed "with the Department of Economics about Mr. Gideonse, with the Political Science Department about Mr. White, and with the Philosophy Department about the entire staff," Presidents' Reports (Hutchins), Box 1, Folder 1:2, UC. The final draft substituted "about questions of personnel" (p. 6) for the specific names.

89. RMH, "Robert Redfield," delivered in 1958 at a memorial service for Redfield, CSDI-UCSB. This eulogy is borne out in their correspondence in the Hutchins and Presidents' Papers, UC. When Redfield wanted to recruit Clyde Kluckhohn, a respected anthropologist, Hutchins fully supported the effort: Redfield to Reuben Gustavson, January 23, 1946, Box 5, Folder 1, PP, 1945–50, UC. Kluckhohn elected to stay at Harvard.

90. See, for example, Redfield, "This memorandum . . . ," n.d. (ca. spring 1935); Redfield to RMH, July 15, 1936; "Status of Curriculum and Research in the Division of the Humanities," 1937.

91. See Redfield to RMH, September 30, 1936, Box 121, Folder 13, RMH(A)-UC.

92. On Judd's chairmanship, see Woodie T. White, "The Study of Education at the University of Chicago, 1892–1958" (Ph.D. thesis, University of Chicago, 1977), and Robert L. McCaul, "Charles Hubbard Judd, 1873–1946," *Education at Chicago* 3, no. 1 (1973): 12–17.

93. Adler to RMH, December 13, 1929, Box 4, Folder 2, RMH-UC, on the "goddam Deweyized bunk" Adler "so long abominated at Columbia," is but one example of his opinion. Hutchins referred to progressives with disdain in numerous speeches. Pertinent examples can be found in RMH, "The Sheep Look Up" (1935), in *No Friendly Voice,* 127–29, and in *The Higher Learning in America* (New Haven: Yale University Press, 1936), 70–71, 75.

94. Dewey, "Rationality in Education," *Social Frontier* 3 (1936–37): 71–73; "President Hutchins's Proposals to Remake Higher Education," in same, 103–4;

"The Higher Learning in America," in same, 167–69; RMH, "Grammar, Rhetoric, and Mr. Dewey," in same, 137–39.

95. Interview with Ralph Tyler, October 20, 1985. See also Ralph W. Tyler interviewed by Malca Chall, 1985, 1986, 1987, University of California at Berkeley, Regional Oral History Office, Bancroft Office (copy in UC). RMH, *Education for Freedom* (Baton Rouge: Louisiana State University Press, 1943), 32, 91, for an example of his reappraisal of Dewey.

96. Beardsley Ruml, "Need for Research Facilities, Division of the Social Sciences," December 1931, Box 109, Folder 10, PP, 1925–45, UC.

97. "Faculty Appointments," Box 2, Folder 1:1, Presidents' Reports (Hutchins), UC.

98. Tyler to RMH, December 4, 1937, Box 103, Folder 2, PP, 1925–45, UC.

99. Tyler to Redfield, December 22, 1943, Box 5, Folder 7, PP, 1940–46, UC, on Davis' budget needs. Interview with Ralph Tyler, October 20, 1985, on racial objections to the appointment.

100. Melvin W. Reder, "Chicago Economics: Permanence and Change," *Journal of Economic Literature* 20 (March 1982): 1–38; Paul A. Samuelson, "Economics in a Golden Age: A Personal Memoir," in *The Twentieth-Century Series: Studies in the Biography of Ideas,* ed. Gerald Holton (New York: W. W. Norton & Company, 1972 [1970]), 155–70, and "Jacob Viner, 1892–1970," *Journal of Political Economy* 80 (1972): 5–11; Bulmer, *The Chicago School of Sociology,* 204–5, 214.

101. On Nef: correspondence in Box 103, Folders 2–10, RMH(A)-UC; John U. Nef, *Search for Meaning: The Autobiography of a Nonconformist* (Washington, D.C.: Public Affairs Press, 1973), and Interview with John Nef, July 22, 1986. On Knight: correspondence in Box 59, Folders 5–10, FHK-UC, and in Box 80, Folder 1, RMH(A)-UC. On Douglas: Douglas to RMH, November 22, 1934, Box 102, Folder 2, PP, 1925–45, UC. See also Shils, "Robert Maynard Hutchins," 215–16, 221.

102. "Memorandum on Meeting of Professors, Department of Economics," April 27, 1938, and Nef to Henry Schultz, May 4, 1938, Box 102, Folder 3, PP, 1925–45, UC.

103. Gilson to RMH, March 18 and April 4, 1937, Box 102, Folder 3, PP, 1925–45, UC.

104. RMH to A. Brumbaugh, May 7, 1936, Box 19, Folder 4, PP, 1925–45, UC, on Gideonse's book list; Gideonse to Wirth, August 6, 1938, Box 4, Folder 2, LW-UC, alluding to the pressure they had felt from Hutchins.

105. H. A. Millis et al. to RMH, July 16, 1936, Box 60, Folder 15, FHK-UC.

106. Harry D. Gideonse, *The Higher Learning in a Democracy: A Reply to President Hutchins' Critique of the American University* (New York: Farrar & Rinehart, 1937), 10, 31.

107. Adler to RMH, June 25, 1937, MJA-IPR; McKeon to RMH, June 29, 1937, Box 60, Folder 11, RMH(A)-UC.

108. McKeon to RMH, July 29, 1936, Box 92, Folder 1, RMH(A)-UC.

109. RMH to Ernest F. Witte, June 18, 1938, Box 102, Folder 3, PP, 1925–45, UC.

110. Gideonse to Louis Wirth, n.d. (ca. 1938), Box 4, Folder 2, LW-UC. Gideonse also did not believe that Brumbaugh had not recommended him for promotion, calling it Hutchins' "old Dean story," or an effort to deflect blame (in same).

111. RMH to Adler, "Tuesday," n.d. (ca. August 1937), MJA-IPR.

112. Wirth to Gideonse, July 28, 1938, Box 4, Folder 2, LW-UC.

CHAPTER NINE

1. RMH, *The Higher Learning in America* (New Haven: Yale University Press), 99, 108.

2. Martin Bulmer, *The Chicago School of Sociology: Institutionalization, Diversity, and the Rise of Sociological Research* (Chicago: University of Chicago Press, 1984), 203, on Adler's seminar on a unified social science, presented to the social sciences division in 1933; "God and the Professors" (1940) in *Pragmatism and American Culture,* ed. Gail Kennedy (Boston: D. C. Heath & Company, 1950), 67–76, in which Adler accused professors of being positivists because they denied the equal validity of philosophy with empirical science for determining truth; and "The Crisis in Contemporary Education," *Social Frontier* 5 (1938–39): 140–45.

3. Redfield to RMH, September 30, 1936, Box 121, Folder 13, RMH(A)-UC, responding to RMH, "University Education," *Yale Review* 25 (1936): 665–82, published as chap. 4 in *The Higher Learning.*

4. T. V. Smith and Leonard D. White, eds., *Chicago: An Experiment in Social Science Research* (Chicago: University of Chicago Press, 1929); Leonard D. White, ed., *The New Social Science* (Chicago: University of Chicago Press, 1930); Louis Wirth, ed., *Eleven Twenty-Six: A Decade of Social Science Research* (Chicago: University of Chicago Press, 1940); Martin Bulmer, "The Early Institutional Establishment of Social Science Research: The Local Community Research Committee at the University of Chicago, 1923–30," *Minerva* 18 (1980): 51–110.

5. See, for example, the following in the *International Journal of Ethics* 47 (1936–37): Charles E. Clark, "The Higher Learning in a Democracy," 317–35; W. Preston Warren, "Philosophy, Politics, and Education: Our Basic Dilemma," 336–

45; Charner Perry, "Education: Ideas or Knowledge?" 346–59; Benjamin F. Wright, Jr., "History as a Central Study," 360–64; Talcott Parsons, "Remarks on Education and the Professions," 365–69; Richard McKeon, "Education and the Disciplines," 370–81. John Dewey, "Rationality in Education," *Social Frontier* 3 (1936–37): 72, agreed that "present education is disordered and confused" and in "President Hutchins' Proposals to Remake Higher Education" (in same), 103, found his criticisms "trenchant," though he did not agree with Hutchins' "remedy." Brian Alair Cole, "Hutchins and His Critics, 1936–1953" (Ph.D. thesis, University of Maryland, 1976), and Benjamin McArthur, "Revisiting Hutchins and *The Higher Learning in America,*" *History of Higher Education Annual* 7 (1987): 9–28, describe the wider debate; the response at the university raised all of the same issues.

6. RMH, *The Higher Learning,* 4.

7. RMH, *The Higher Learning,* 94, 95, 106.

8. Minutes of the University Senate, May 28, 1936, Box 87, Folder 7, PP, 1925–45, UC.

9. "Report of the Committee on Policy of the Division of the Humanities," 1938, Box 109, Folder 6, PP, 1925–45, UC.

10. McKeon to RMH, March 18, 1937, Box 109, Folder 6, PP, 1925–45, UC.

11. McKeon to RMH, March 19, 1937, Box 109, Folder 6, PP, 1925–45, UC.

12. Adler to RMH, March 26, 1937, Box 1, Folder 11, RMH(A)-UC.

13. RMH, "Reintegration of the University," *University of Chicago Magazine* 24 (April 1937): 5, 5–6, 6.

14. Adler to RMH, June 25, 1937, MJA-IPR.

15. George K. K. Link, Percy H. Boynton, and Ernst W. Puttkammer, American Association of University Professors, University of Chicago Chapter, "Report of the Committee on Academic Tenure" (February 1938), 20, Box 6, Folder 5, PP, 1925–45, UC (AAUP Report on Tenure).

16. RMH to Redfield, January 12, 1938, in response to Redfield to RMH, January 11, 1938, Box 110, Folder 1, PP, 1925–45, UC.

17. RMH, *Report of the President to the Board of Trustees, 1935–1936,* 4, UC.

18. AAUP Report on Tenure, 19. In 1926–27, 48.3% of the faculty were on permanent tenure, 19.3% were in two- to-five-year appointments, and 32.3% were in one-year appointments. By 1936–37 those percentages had changed to 32.6%, 7.8%, and 59.6%, respectively, according to the report (p. 19).

19. A. J. Dempster, H. Keniston, and B. Ullman, American Association of University Professors, University of Chicago Chapter, "Report of the Committee on the Organization of Departments" (February 1938), in *Report of the President, 1938,* 83–93, UC (AAUP Report on Departments).

20. "Conference with President Hutchins, July 18, 1939: President's Criticisms of the Tenure Report," Box 6, Folder 5, PP, 1925–45, UC.

21. RMH, *Report of the President, 1938,* 39.

22. RMH, *Report of the President, 1938,* 40, 41, 42.

23. RMH, *Report of the President, 1938,* 44.

24. RMH, *Report of the President, 1938,* 48, 47–48, 49.

25. RMH, "President Hutchins' Address to the Trustees [and faculty]," *University of Chicago Magazine* 31 (February 1939): 5, 6.

26. Senate Committee on University Policy, Report of the Subcommittee on Departmental Organization and Related Matters, November 13, 1939, Box 86, Folder 10, PP, 1925–45, UC. On faculty participation, approximately 56% favored greater participation in the appointment of chairs, 27.2% favored current practice, and 16.3% favored another method that was not clear on the survey. Almost 60% favored greater participation in the appointment of deans, 31% favored current practice, and 9% another (not described) method. On deans' powers, 78% favored more clearly delineated and limited powers, and 22% favored current practices. In contrast, only 40% favored greater participation in making faculty appointments, 43% favored current practice, and 16.5% another (not described) method. While a clear majority favored increased advisory power of divisional committees in determining ideals and aims, the development of instruction and research, interrelations between departments, and budgetary problems in the area of instruction and research, a clear majority opposed greater committee advisory powers in the appointments of chairs and faculty and in promotions within ranks.

27. "At Its meeting on Friday, June 7, 1949," Box 86, Folder 11, PP, 1925–45, UC.

28. "Recommendations of the University Senate concerning Academic Tenure," Box 18, Folder 10, PP, 1940–46, UC.

29. RMH, "The University at War," *University of Chicago Magazine* 34 (January 1942): 3–6, 22–24.

30. RMH, "To the Members of the Senate," December 31, 1942, Box 86, Folder 11, PP, 1925–45, UC.

31. Some of his revisions were made reluctantly, particularly when the deans suggested limitations on administrative power for the president and deans; see, for example, RMH to the Deans, July 2, 1942, Box 87, Folder 8, PP, 1925–45, UC.

32. RMH to Harold Swift, July 3, 1942, with July 2, 1942, confidential document, Box 49, Folder 13, HHS-UC.

33. Bell to RMH, July 7, 1942, Box 49, Folder 13, HHS-UC.

34. RMH, *Education for Freedom* (Baton Rouge: Louisiana State University Press, 1943), 91, 93, 100–101, 101, 104–5.

35. RMH, "The Next Fifteen Years," *University of Chicago Magazine* 36 (April 1944): 10, 9.

36. Viner et al. to RMH, February 28, 1944 (copy), Box 49, Folder 15, HHS-UC.

37. RMH to Viner et al., March 2, 1944 (copy), Box 49, Folder 15, HHS-UC.

38. Viner et al. to Hutchins, March 18, 1944 (copy), Box 49, Folder 15, HHS-UC.

39. RMH to Viner et al., March 25, 1944 (copy), Box 49, Folder 15, HHS-UC.

40. RMH, "At the request . . . ," May 12, 1944, Box 86, Folder 12, PP, 1925–45, UC.

41. "Memorial to the Board of Trustees on the State of the University," n.d. (ca. May 6, 1944), Box 16, Folder 7, RMH-UC.

42. Minutes of the University Senate, May 22, 1944, Box 87, Folder 9, PP, 1925–45, UC.

43. Katz and Nef to the President and Board, June 7, 1944, Box 71, Folder 7, RMH(A)-UC.

44. The Board of Trustees to the Senate of the University of Chicago, June 8, 1944, Box 16, Folder 7, RMH-UC.

45. RMH, *The Organization and Purpose of the University* (Chicago: University of Chicago, July 1944).

46. RMH to Bell, August 3, 1944, Box 41, Folder 2, PP, 1945–50, UC, and RMH to Bell, December 1, 1944, Box 196, Folder 6, HHS-UC.

47. Outlined in Edward Shils, "Presidents and Professors in American University Government," *Minerva* 8 (1970): 440–47.

48. "The background and motives of the Senate action . . . ," June 9, 1944, Box 41, Folder 2, PP, 1945–50, UC, and Joseph J. Schwab to Ernest E. Quantrell, June 6, 1944, Box 196, Folder 13, HHS-UC.

49. Interview with Ralph Tyler, October 20, 1985.

50. Joseph H. Willets to Raymond B. Fosdick, April 14, 1944, RFA, RG 1.1, 216, Box 1, Folder 7, RAC.

51. "The recent public pronouncements . . . ," n.d. (ca. 1944), Box 5, Folder 4, LW-UC. The essay is not signed but is almost certainly Wirth's. See Edwin R. Embree, "In Order of Their Eminence: An Appraisal of American Universities," *Atlantic Monthly* 155 (1935): 652–64, and John Chamberlain, "The University of Chicago," *Fortune* 16 (December 1937): 141–50, 152, 154, 157, on the university's preeminence.

52. RMH to Ernest C. Colwell, August 10, 1944, Box 8, Folder 9, PP, 1945–50, UC.

53. RMH to McKeon, August 14, 1944, Box 8, Folder 9, PP, 1945–50, UC.

54. Clarence H. Faust Oral History, 1973, p. 2, FFA.

55. Ronald S. Crane, Avery O. Craven, L. M. Graves, and H. I. Schlesinger were the members from the divisions; Minutes of the Faculty Senate, November 17, 1944, Box 41, Folder 2, PP, 1945–50, UC.

56. Minutes of the University Senate, July 2, 1945, Box 18, Folder 9, PP, 1940–46, UC.

57. Walter Gellhorn, ed., *The States and Subversion* (Ithaca: Cornell University Press, 1952), and Ellen W. Schrecker, *No Ivory Tower: McCarthyism and the Universities* (New York: Oxford University Press, 1986).

58. E. Houston Harsha, "Illinois: The Broyles Commission," in *The States and Subversion,* ed. Walter Gellhorn, 54–139, is my principal source. Others will be so noted.

59. *The Great Investigation* (All-Campus Committee Opposing the Broyles Bills and the Broyles Investigation, 1949).

60. Ibid., 2, 3.

61. Ibid., 11.

62. Ibid., 29.

63. Robert M. MacIver, *Academic Freedom in Our Time* (New York: Columbia University Press, 1955), 186.

64. Schrecker, *No Ivory Tower,* 337.

65. T. V. Smith, *A Non-existent Man: An Autobiography* (Austin: University of Texas Press, 1962), 233–34; Shils, "Presidents and Professors," 440.

66. RMH, "The Administrator," in *The Works of the Mind,* ed. Robert B. Heywood (Chicago: University of Chicago Press, 1947), 141, 137, 142, 150, 151.

67. Linn to RMH, June 3, 1938, Box 85, Folder 13, RMH(A)-UC.

68. "Agenda of Conference with President Hutchins," June 23, 1938, Box 6, Folder 5, PP, 1925–45, UC.

69. William T. Hutchinson (WTH) journal, April 14, 1944, April 12, 1948, and April 9, 1953, Box 2, WTH-UC.

70. Smith, *A Non-existent Man,* 232, 233. He excepted Thornton Wilder from this assessment.

71. RMH to Marshall Field, September 16, 1943, Box 55, Folder 12, RMH(A)-UC, and Interview with John Nef, July 22, 1986.

72. Interview with Elizabeth Paepcke, February 16, 1989. A collection of Maude's Christmas cards is in Box 49, Folder 4, HHS-UC.

73. Interview with Elizabeth Paepcke, February 16, 1989.

74. William J. Hutchins to Francis S. Hutchins, September 25, 1946; Francis S. Hutchins to W. J. Hutchins, September 27, 1946; WJH-BCA.

75. Harry S. Ashmore, *Unseasonable Truths: The Life of Robert Maynard Hutchins* (Boston: Little, Brown & Company, 1989), 78–79, 93–94, 173–75, describes the problems more fully.

76. Carolyn G. Heilbron, *Writing a Woman's Life* (New York: Ballantine Books, 1989 [1988]), explores this conflict between the "marriage plot" and the "quest plot" in women's lives, a conflict particularly notable in the lives of artists and other professionals.

77. Interview with Elizabeth Paepcke, February 16, 1989. His avoidance of her is described in Ashmore, *Unseasonable Truths,* 290.

78. RMH to Mother and Father, n.d. (ca. April 1947), WJH-BCA.

79. Ashmore, *Unseasonable Truths,* 287–93.

80. Russell to RMH, February 7, 1939, Box 102, Folder 8, PP, 1925–45, UC.

81. Shils, "Presidents and Professors," 440.

82. WTH journal, February 3, 1949.

83. WTH journal, January 11, 1951.

CHAPTER TEN

1. RMH, *Annual Confidential Statement to the Board of Trustees, August 31, 1939,* 7, UC.

2. RMH to Raymond Fosdick, November 7, 1940, and Fosdick to RMH, November 20, 1940, RFA, RG 1.1, 216, Box 1, Folder 5, RAC, for the request and the refusal of the foundation to "come to the rescue of the situation in Chicago."

3. RMH, *Annual Confidential Statement, 1939,* 8.

4. Harry S. Ashmore, *Unseasonable Truths: A Life of Robert Maynard Hutchins* (Boston: Little, Brown & Company, 1989), 200–202.

5. John Gunther, *Inside U.S.A.* (New York: Harper & Brothers, 1947), 372. See letters in Box 48, Folder 12, Box 49, Folder 4, and Box 190, HHS-UC, for example; and Lloyd Everett Stein, "Hutchins of Chicago: Philosopher-Administrator" (Ed.D. thesis, University of Massachusetts, 1971), 132–45.

6. "The Reminiscences of Robert M. Hutchins," COHC, 87–89; RMH, "Dedication of the Laird Bell Quadrangles," October 12, 1966, Box 168, Folder 3, WB-UC; and Mary Ann Dzuback, "Robert M. Hutchins, 1899–1977: Portrait of an Educator" (Ph.D. thesis, Columbia University, 1987), 220–22, on the Medical School debate.

7. Abraham Flexner, *Medical Education in the United States and Canada* (Carnegie Foundation for the Advancement of Teaching, bulletin 4, 1910).

8. Charles B. Huggins, "Medicine," *University of Chicago Magazine* 43 (June 1951): 10.

9. Ashmore, *Unseasonable Truths,* 203.

10. Interview with Edward H. Levi, October 26, 1988.

11. Faculty minutes, Division of the Social Sciences, March 8, 1949, Box 34, Folder 8, PP, 1945–50, UC.

12. RMH to William James Hutchins, March 30, 1938, WJH-BCA; RMH to Adler, July 27, 1938, MJA-IPR.

13. William James Hutchins to RMH, April 6, 1939, WJH-BCA.

14. RMH to Adler, July 27, 1938, MJA-IPR.

15. William J. Hutchins to RMH, November 28, 1934, Box 72, Folder 2, RMH(A)-UC. See Dzuback, "Robert M. Hutchins," 242–49; Ashmore, *Unseasonable Truths,* 191–99.

16. Leland DeVinney et al., "The statement signed . . ." and "Statement by Members of the Faculty of the University of Chicago," January 23, 1941, Box 5, Folder 4, LW-UC.

17. RMH, "The Path to War: We Are Drifting into Suicide," *Vital Speeches of the Day* 7 (1941): 258–61; Ashmore, *Unseasonable Truths,* 205–20.

18. Bigelow to RMH, May 19, 1930, Box 112, Folder 5, PP, 1925–45, UC.

19. Frederic Woodward to Bigelow, December 10, 1930, Box 112, Folder 5, PP, 1925–45, UC.

20. Irving Eisenstein et al. to RMH, April 10, 1931, Box 112, Folder 5; Emery T. Filbey to Bigelow, April 18, 1933, Box 112, Folder 6; PP, 1925–45, UC.

21. William O. Douglas to RMH, April 15, 1932, Box 49, Folder 1; Felix Frankfurter to RMH, March 5, 1930, Box 58, Folder 3; RMH to Charles E. Clark, January 20, 1932, Box 35, Folder 6; RMH(A)-UC.

22. "Pre-Legal Course of Study," n.d. (ca. February 25, 1934), Box 112, Folder 6, PP, 1925–45, UC; Adler, *Philosopher,* 154–55; Amy Apfel Kass, "Radical Conservatives for a Liberal Education" (Ph.D. thesis, Johns Hopkins University, 1973), 124–29.

23. Crosskey to RMH, n.d. (ca. 1936), and RMH to Crosskey, November 2, 1936, Box 112, Folder 7, PP, 1925–45, UC.

24. *Announcements: The University of Chicago, the Law School, for the Sessions of 1934–1935* (hereinafter *Announcements*) (Chicago: University of Chicago, 1934), 2.

25. *Announcements, 1937–1938,* 3.

26. Interview with Edward H. Levi, October 26, 1988; Wilber G. Katz, "A Four-Year Program for Legal Education," *University of Chicago Law Review* 4 (1937): 527–36; Alfred Harsch, "The Four-Year Law Course in American Universities," *North Carolina Law Review* 17 (1939): 263–66.

27. Interview with Edward H. Levi, October 26, 1988.

28. Interview with Ralph Tyler, October 25, 1985, for all information on the committee.

29. See, for example, Robert J. Havighurst et al., *Adolescent Character and Personality* (New York: John Wiley & Sons, 1949).

30. Interview with John U. Nef, July 22, 1986. See also John U. Nef, *Search for Meaning: The Autobiography of a Nonconformist* (Washington, D.C.: Public Affairs Press, 1973).

31. RMH to Knight, Nef, and Redfield, March 23, 1942, Box 59, Folder 6, FHK-UC.

32. The following letters contain the discussion: Knight to RMH, Redfield, and Nef, February 12, 1942; Redfield to RMH, Nef, and Knight, February 23, 1942; RMH to Knight, Redfield, and Nef, February 26, 1942; Knight to RMH, Nef, and Redfield, February 27, 1942; Redfield to RMH, March 2, 1942; RMH to Knight, Nef, and Redfield, March 6, 1942; Box 59, Folder 5; and RMH to Knight, Nef, and Redfield, March 10, 1942; Knight to RMH, Redfield, and Nef, March 11 and 25, 1942; Box 59, Folder 6; Nef to Executive Committee on Social Thought, December 4, 1943, with Redfield memorandum, "Anthropology and Sociology," Box 59, Folder 8; all in FHK-UC.

33. Interview with John U. Nef, July 22, 1986, and with Ralph Tyler, October 20, 1985; Ashmore, *Unseasonable Truths,* 229–32.

34. RMH, "The University at War," *University of Chicago Magazine* 34 (January 1942): 3.

35. William Benton to the Board of Trustees, November 14, 1941, Box 21, Folder 5, OVP-UC.

36. Richard Rhodes, *The Making of the Atomic Bomb* (New York: Simon & Schuster, 1986); Arthur Holly Compton, *Atomic Quest: A Personal Narrative* (New York: Oxford University Press, 1956); Henry DeWolf Smyth, *Atomic Energy for Military Purposes: The Official Report on the Development of the Atomic Bomb under the Auspices of the United States Government, 1940–1945* (Princeton: Princeton University Press, 1948 [1945]).

37. Alice Kimball Smith, *A Peril and a Hope: The Scientists' Movement in America, 1945–1947* (Chicago: University of Chicago Press, 1965); Dzuback, "Robert M. Hutchins," 342–49; Ashmore, *Unseasonable Truths,* 251–53.

38. U.S. Senate, *Atomic Energy Act of 1946: Hearings before the Special Committee on Atomic Energy on S. 1717,* 79th Congress, 2d sess., 1946, Pt. 2, 101–34.

39. RMH, "The Reminiscences of Robert M. Hutchins," 81, COHC.

40. Edward Shils, "Robert Maynard Hutchins," *American Scholar* 59 (1990): 221.

41. Ashmore, *Unseasonable Truths,* 265–66.

42. Harrison Brown, "The Atomic Sciences," *University of Chicago Magazine* 43 (June 1951): 12.

43. Dzuback, "Robert M. Hutchins," 293–303, 326–42, 350–57; Ashmore, *Unseasonable Truths,* 255–86, 293–98.

44. Herman Kogan, *The Great EB: The Story of the Encyclopaedia Britannica* (Chicago: University of Chicago Press, 1958), and Sidney Hyman, *The Lives of William Benton* (Chicago: University of Chicago Press, 1969).

45. Mortimer J. Adler, *Philosopher at Large: An Intellectual Autobiography* (New York: Macmillan, 1977), 237–39.

46. Adler to Buchanan, December 26, 1943, complained about Hutchins' "silly" prejudices against certain authors, no. 3, Folder 33, and Adler to Buchanan, June 26, 1944, complained about Hutchins' frequent absences (due to marital problems and other commitments), no. 3, Folder 35; SB-HU; Buchanan to Adler, May 3, 1944, no. 528, Folder 6, SB-HU, noted that Hutchins thought Adler was neglecting his teaching duties for the great books groups and Syntopicon.

47. See, for example, Adler to Buchanan, May 12 and June 14, 1944, no. 3, Folder 34, SB-HU. Interviews with the following people confirmed this perception: Milton Mayer, August 19, 1984; Joseph Schwab, August 10, 1984; Florence Mischel, October 1, 1984; Elizabeth Paepcke, February 16, 1989.

48. RMH to Barr, Buchanan, and Adler, September 8, 1944, Box 11, Folder 20, RMH(A)-UC.

49. RMH to Benton, October 4, 1946, Box 70, Folder 13, RMH(A)-UC.

50. "Book Group Seeks to Reach 15,000,000," *New York Times,* June 10, 1947, 25.

51. George E. Arnstein, "The Great Books Program and Its Educational Philosophy" (Ph.D. thesis, University of California at Berkeley, 1953), 46–47. James A. Davis, *Great Books and Small Groups* (Glencoe, Ill.: Free Press of Glencoe, 1961), describes the retention problems of the groups.

52. James Sloan Allen, *The Romance of Commerce and Culture: Capitalism, Modernism, and the Chicago-Apen Crusade for Cultural Reform* (Chicago: University of Chicago Press, 1983).

53. Ashmore, *Unseasonable Truths,* 337.

54. Adler, *Philosopher,* 258.

55. RMH, *The Great Conversation: The Substance of a Liberal Education* (Chicago: Encyclopaedia Britannica, 1952), 5.

56. Dwight Macdonald, "The Book-of-the-Millenium Club," *New Yorker* 25 (November 29, 1952): 187.

57. Gilbert Highet, "Ideas That Shape the Minds of Men," *New York Times Book Review,* September 14, 1952, 34.

58. Jacques Barzun, "The Great Books," *Atlantic Monthly* 190 (December 1952): 82, 84.

59. RMH to William Benton, February 25, 1939, Box 13, Folder 16, RMH(A)-UC.

60. Commissioners included Charles E. Merriam and Robert Redfield from the University of Chicago; William E. Hocking, philosopher, Zechariah Chafee, professor of law, and Arthur M. Schlesinger, historian, from Harvard; Archibald MacLeish of the Library of Congress; Harold D. Lasswell of the Library of Congress and then Yale; Reinhold Niebuhr of Union Theological Seminary; John Dickinson, professor of law, of the University of Pennsylvania; George N. Shuster, president of Hunter College; and Beardsley Ruml, the one nonacademic member, of R. H. Macy Company and the Federal Reserve Bank of New York.

61. RMH, "The Commission on the Freedom of the Press," n.d., Box 8, Folder 5, RMH-UC.

62. Adler to RMH, n.d. (ca. November 30, 1943), Box 7, Folder 6, RMH-UC.

63. RMH to Henry Luce and Eric Hodgins, December 12, 1943, Box 7, Folder 8, RMH-UC.

64. For more detailed accounts of the workings of the commission, see Margaret A. Blanchard, "The Hutchins Commission, the Press and the Responsibility Concept," *Journalism Monographs* 47 (May 1977); Dzuback, "Robert M. Hutchins," 326–42; and Ashmore, *Unseasonable Truths,* 272, 293–98.

65. They all were published by the University of Chicago Press: Robert D. Leigh and Llewellyn White, *Peoples Speaking to Peoples* (1946); Llewellyn White, *The American Radio* (1947); William E. Hocking, *Freedom of the Press: A Framework of Principle* (1947); Zechariah Chafee, *Government and Mass Communications,* 2 vols. (1947); and Ruth A. Inglis, *Freedom of the Movies* (1947).

66. Commission on the Freedom of the Press, *A Free and Responsible Press: A General Report on Mass Communications: Newspapers, Radio, Motion Pictures, Magazines, and Books* (Chicago: University Chicago Press, 1947).

67. Lippmann to RMH, November 2, 1946, Box 8, Folder 2, RMH-UC; A. J. Liebling, "Some Reflections on the American Press, *Nation* 164 (1947): 427; Louis

M. Lyons, "Press Reaction to the Free Press Report," *Nieman Reports* 1 (July 1947): 14–19.

68. Luce to RMH, November 29, 1946, Box 8, Folder 2, RMH-UC; "Dangers to Press Freedom," *Fortune* 35 (April 1947): 2–5.

69. Norman E. Isaacs, "Why We Lack a Press Council," *Columbia Journalism Review* 9 (fall 1970): 17; *Proceedings of the Twenty-fifth Anniversary Convention of the American Society of Newspaper Editors* (April 1947): 212–29.

70. He did participate in a radio discussion with George Shuster and Wilbur Forrest, president of the American Association of Newspaper Editors: *A Free and Responsible Press* (University of Chicago Round Table Pamphlet [UCRT], no. 472, April 6, 1947).

71. William L. Rivers, Wilbur Schramm, and Clifford G. Christians, *Responsibility in Mass Communications* (3d ed., New York: Harper & Row, 1980), 44. See also Karl E. Meyer, "A Message for the Media," *New York Times,* May 10, 1972, 47, and Garth Jowett, *Film: The Democratic Art* (Boston: Little, Brown & Company, 1976), 135, on Inglis' study.

72. Members included Richard McKeon, Antonio Borgese, professor of Italian language and literature, Wilber Katz of the Law School, Robert Redfield, Rexford G. Tugwell, and Adler, all from the University of Chicago; James M. Landis and Charles H. McIlwain of Harvard; Reinhold Niebuhr; and Albert Leon Guerard of Stanford. Beardsley Ruml and William E. Hocking withdrew for personal reasons, Niebuhr for political reasons. They were replaced by Erich Kahler of the New School for Social Research, Stringfellow Barr, and Harold A. Innes of the University of Toronto. Borgese, Guerard, and Kahler were immigrants to the U.S.

73. Dzuback, "Robert M. Hutchins," 350–57, and Ashmore, *Unseasonable Truths,* 262–63, 269–70, 275–82, for more detailed accounts of the committee.

74. Also published as *Preliminary Draft of a World Constitution* (Chicago: University of Chicago Press, 1948).

75. This perception is evident in the following speeches on world peace: *Peace and the Atomic Bomb* (UCRT, no. 399, November 11, 1945); "Atomic Energy: Peace or War with Soviet Russia?" (UCRT, no. 416, March 10, 1946); *What Should Be Our Policy toward Soviet Russia?* (Town Meeting of the Air, 11, April 25, 1946); and *The Third Year of the Atomic Age: What Should We Do Now?* (UCRT, no. 492, August 24, 1947).

76. See, for example, RMH, *The Constitutional Foundation for World Order* (Denver: University of Denver Press, 1947), and RMH, *St. Thomas and the World State* (Milwaukee: Marquette University Press, 1949), on justice and world peace.

77. Gerald J. Mangone, *The Idea and Practice of World Government* (New York: Columbia University Press, 1951); Martin Bernard Dworkis, *An Analytical*

Survey of Concepts and Plans of World Government (New York: New York University, 1952); and Leonard S. Cottrell and Sylvia Eberhart, *American Opinion on World Affairs in the Atomic Age* (Princeton: Princeton University Press, 1948).

78. Ellen Condliffe Lagemann, *The Politics of Knowledge: The Carnegie Corporation, Philanthropy, and Public Policy* (Middletown: Wesleyan University Press, 1989).

79. Susan M. Kingsbury et al., *Newspapers and the News: An Objective Measurement of the Ethical and Unethical Behavior by Representative Newspapers* (New York: G. P. Putnam's Sons, 1937), represents an early attempt to use empirical research to examine press abuse of responsibility.

80. RMH to Clarence Faust, February 15, 1954 (copy), Box 100, Folder 4, WB-UC.

81. RMH to William James Hutchins, n.d. (ca. October 1950), WJH-BCA.

82. Interview with Ralph Tyler, October 20, 1985, and Daniel Boorstin to RMH, April 9, 1951, Box 71, Folder 1, RMH(A)-UC, for example.

83. Robert Redfield, "A Social Scientist," Edward H. Levi, "The Law School," Charles E. Merriam, "Academic Freedom," and Lawrence A. Kimpton, "An Administrator," *University of Chicago Magazine* 43 (June 1951): 9, 12–15; Ashmore, *Unseasonable Truths,* 304–6.

84. RMH, "A Farewell Address to Students," *Tower Topics* 17 (March 1951): 1, 2.

85. Shils, "Robert Maynard Hutchins," 214.

PART THREE

1. Edward Shils, "Robert Maynard Hutchins," *The American Scholar* 59 (1990): 234.

CHAPTER ELEVEN

1. On the Ford Foundation, see Dwight Macdonald, *The Ford Foundation: The Men and the Millions* (New York: Reynal & Campany, 1956); Thomas C. Reeves, *Freedom and the Foundation: The Fund for the Republic in the Era of McCarthyism* (New York: Alfred A. Knopf, 1969); Waldemar A. Nielsen, *The Big Foundations* (New York: Columbia University Press, 1972); and Francis X. Sutton, "The Ford Foundation: The Early Years," *Daedalus* 116 (1987): 41–91.

2. H. Rowan Gaither, Jr., ed., *Report of the Study of the Ford Foundation on Policy and Program* (Detroit: Ford Foundation, 1949).

3. RMH to Paul Hoffman, December 23, 1949, Box 6, Folder 16, PP, 1945–50, UC.

4. Merle Curti and Roderick Nash, *Philanthropy in the Shaping of American Higher Education* (New Brunswick: Rutgers University Press, 1965), 228–33.

5. RMH to Father, Tuesday, n.d. (ca. October 1950), WJH-BCA.

6. RMH, *The Democratic Dilemma* (Uppsala, Sweden: Almquist & Wiksells, Boktyckeri, 1952), 9, 11.

7. RMH, *The Conflict in Education in a Democratic Society* (New York: Harper & Brothers, 1953), 75.

8. Harry S. Ashmore, *Unseasonable Truths: The Life of Robert Maynard Hutchins* (Boston: Little, Brown & Company, 1989), 315, on his family's adjustment.

9. Ashmore, *Unseasonable Truths,* 314.

10. Ashmore, *Unseasonable Truths,* 312–39, on the foundation and Hutchins' activities. See also Macdonald, *The Ford Foundation,* and Reeves, *Freedom and the Foundation.*

11. RMH to Mother and Father, January 19, n.d. (ca. 1951), WJH-BCA.

12. John Walker Powell, *Channels of Learning: The Story of Educational Television* (Washington, D.C.: Public Affairs Press, 1962); Robert J. Blakeley, *To Serve the Public Interest: Educational Broadcasting in the United States* (Syracuse: Syracuse University Press, 1979), 81–114.

13. RMH memorandum to Rowan Gaither, September 29, 1952, p. 5, FFA, Report 010520.

14. Paul Woodring, *Investment in Innovation: An Historical Appraisal of the Fund for the Advancement of Education* (Boston: Little, Brown & Company, 1970), on the fund. Other sources will be so noted.

15. RMH, *The University of Utopia* (Chicago: University of Chicago Press, 1953), 7, 56.

16. Chester C. Davis, Monthly Letter to the Trustees, June 30, 1952, Box 19, FR-PUL.

17. Clarence H. Faust Oral History, 1973, pp. 11, 83–88, FFA, on the board's reaction.

18. Faust Oral History, 1973, pp. 32–34, FFA. See also Macdonald, *The Ford Foundation,* 51–54.

19. Dennis C. Buss, "The Ford Foundation and Public Education: Emergent Patterns," in *Philanthropy and Cultural Imperialism: The Foundations at Home and Abroad,* ed. Robert F. Arnove (Bloomington: Indiana University Press, 1980), 331–62.

20. Woodring, *Investment in Innovation,* 125–30.

21. Woodring, *Investment in Innovation,* 211, 215–16.

22. Faust Oral History, 1973, p. 10, and W. H. Ferry Oral History, 1972, p. 46, FFA.

23. Robert M. Hutchins Oral History, 1972, p. 9, and W. H. Ferry Oral History, 1972, p. 46, FFA.

24. Redfield to RMH, September 20, 1952, Box 18, FR-PUL; memorandum to Rowan Gaither and Dyke Brown from RMH, April 13, 1953, FFA, PA53–227.

25. Chester C. Davis, Monthly Letter to the Trustees, June 30, 1952, Box 19, FR-PUL.

26. See Kathleen D. McCarthy, "From Cold War to Cultural Development: The International Cultural Activities of the Ford Foundation, 1950–1980," *Daedalus* 116 (1987): 93–101.

27. Ashmore, *Unseasonable Truths,* 323–28, details some of the problems.

28. Faust Oral History, 1973, pp. 7–8, and Bernard L. Gladieux Oral History, 1972, p. 21; FFA.

29. Macdonald, *The Ford Foundation,* 153.

30. Report to the Board of Trustees, July 15, 1952, pp. 6–8, Box 17, FR-PUL.

31. Ferry to RMH, September 11, 1951, Box 15, and RMH, "Fund for Democratic Freedoms," n.d. (ca. August 1951), Box 18, FR-PUL.

32. Ashmore, *Unseasonable Truths,* 325–26.

33. RMH, "The Fund for the Republic: History," n.d. (Ca. 1952), FFA, Report 010612.

34. Reeves, *Freedom and the Foundation;* Frank K. Kelly, *Court of Reason: Robert M. Hutchins and the Fund for the Republic* (New York: Free Press, 1981); Ashmore, *Unseasonable Truths;* and Mary Ann Dzuback, "Robert M. Hutchins, 1899–1977: Portrait of an Educator" (Ph.D. thesis, Columbia University, 1987). Other sources will be so noted.

35. RMH to Paul G. Hoffman, September 19, 1952, Box 16, FR-PUL.

36. Henry Ford II to RMH, May 12, 1952, Box 15, FR-PUL.

37. Hutchins Oral History, 1972, p. 15, FFA; Ford to RMH, September 30, October 2 and 14, 1952, RMH to Ford, October 1 and 3, 1952, Box 15, FR-PUL. Board members included businessmen James Brownlee of J. H. Whitney & Company, New York; William H. Joyce of Joyce, Inc., Pasadena; Meyer Kestnbaum of Hart Schaffner & Marx, Chicago; M. Albert Linton of Provident Mutual Life Insurance Company, Philadelphia; Jubal R. Parten of Woodley Petroleum Company, Houston; James D. Zellerbach of Crown Zellerbach Corporation, San Francisco; Malcolm Bryan, president of the Federal Reserve Bank of Atlanta; law-

yers Huntington Cairns of Washington, D.C., and Russell L. Dearmont of St. Louis; market analyst Elmo Roper of New York; editor Richard Finnegan of the *Chicago Sun-Times;* educators Charles W. Cole, president of Amherst College; Erwin N. Griswold, dean of Harvard Law School; George N. Shuster, president of Hunter College; and Eleanor Bumstead Stevenson, civil liberties activist and wife of the president of Oberlin College.

38. RMH to Paul G. Hoffman, September 19, 1952, Box 19, FR-PUL.

39. Ford Foundation board minutes, February 23–26, 1953, Box 19, FR-PUL.

40. William Benton to RMH, July 15, 1953, Box 100, Folder 3, WB-UC.

41. RMH to Gentlemen (the board members), July 6, 1953; William Benton to RMH, July 15, 1953; RMH to Benton, July 18, 1953; in Box 100, Folder 3, WB-UC.

42. *Congressional Record,* 83d Congress, 1st sess., 1953, vol. 99, Pt. 8, 10023.

43. RMH to Hoffman et al., n.d. (ca. 1951), Box 15, FR-PUL.

44. Clarence H. Faust memorandum to H. Rowan Gaither, April 9, 1953, FFA, Report 010605, and Robert M. Hutchins, "The Academy Idea," August 10, 1953, FFA, Report 010611. The participants included Etienne Gilson, Jacques Maritain, Robert Oppenheimer, Robert Redfield, Mortimer Adler, Paul Tillich, Neils Bohr, Jose Ortega y Gasset, Michel Polanyi, and R. H. Tawney, as well as members of fund's board.

45. RMH to Benton, June 1, 1953, Box 100, Folder 3, WB-UC.

46. RMH to Benton, September 22, 1953, Box 100, Folder 3, WB-UC.

47. RMH to Clarence Faust, February 15, 1954, Box 100, Folder 4, WB-UC.

48. RMH, *Freedom, Education, and the Fund: Essays and Addresses, 1946–1956* (New York: Meridian Books, 1956), 20–21.

49. Ashmore, *Unseasonable Truths,* 329; U.S. Congress, House, *Hearings before the Select Committee to Investigate Tax-exempt Foundations and Comparable Organizations on H. Res. 561,* 82d Congress, 2d sess., 1952, 263–99.

50. Ferry Oral History, 1972, pp. 93–97, FFA. Victor S. Navasky, "The Happy Heretic," *Atlantic Monthly* 218 (July 1966): 53–57, on Ferry's personality and beliefs.

51. Interview with David Freeman, June 30, 1986.

52. RMH to William Benton, n.d. (ca. March 1956), Box 100, Folder 6, WB-UC.

53. U.S. Congress, House, *Hearings before the Special Committee to Investigate Tax-exempt Foundations and Comparable Organizations on H. Res. 217,* 83d Congress, 2d sess., 1954, Pt. 2, 1016–55; Reece Committee Report, December 20, 1954, Box 20, FR-PUL.

54. RMH, "Remarks of Robert M. Hutchins," January 26, 1955, Box 2, FR-PUL.

55. Interview with W. H. Ferry, May 6, 1986.

56. Peter Kihss, "Hutchins Condemns Red Party but Would Give a Job to Member," *New York Times,* November 8, 1955, 34.

57. Ferry Oral History, pp. 100–101, FFA. See also Henry Ford II to Paul Hoffman, October 27, 1955, and Hoffman to Ford, November 17, 1955, Box 1, FR-PUL.

58. RMH, Memorandum to the Board of Directors, November 3, 1955, Box 82, FR-PUL.

59. Reeves, *Freedom and the Foundation,* 183, and Kelly, *Court of Reason,* 63–67. The trustees were Erwin N. Griswold, John Lord O'Brian, James Zellerbach, and M. Albert Linton.

60. Griswold, quoted in Reeves, *Freedom and the Foundation,* 183.

61. F. Emerson Andrews, *Philanthropic Foundations* (New York: Russell Sage Foundation, 1956), 67–79, on the composition of boards of trustees. The fund's board differed only in its inclusion of a woman and its geographical diversity.

62. RMH to Paul G. Hoffman, December 13, 1955, Box 1, Folder 62, WHF(A,3)-DCA.

63. Interview with W. H. Ferry, July 26, 1986.

64. Fund for the Republic, Board Minutes, January 6–7, 1956, Box 83, FR-PUL.

65. Ashmore, *Unseasonable Truths,* 366–67. Transcript of series, CSDI-UCSB.

66. John Cogley, *Report on Blacklisting,* 2 vols. (New York: Fund for the Republic, 1956).

67. *The Fund for the Republic: A Report on Three Years' Work* (May 31, 1956). Andrews, *Philanthropic Foundations,* 142, on percentage of total expenditures devoted to administration, usually between 7 and 12 percent, depending on total assets.

68. Harold Ravitch, "Robert Maynard Hutchins: Philosopher of Education" (Ph.D. thesis, University of Southern California, 1980), explores the transition from metaphysics to politics in Hutchins' thinking from 1936 to the 1950s.

69. Roger D. Lapham to Linton and Shuster, April 10, 1956, Box 2, FR-PUL.

70. RMH to the Board of Trustees, May 4, 1956, Box 65, FR-PUL.

71. RMH, *Freedom, Education, and the Fund,* 231.

72. RMH to the Board of Directors, September 6, 1956, Box 65, FR-PUL.

73. RMH to the Board of Directors, October 15, 1956, Box 65, FR-PUL.

74. O'Brian, Zellerbach, and Chester Bowles. Bowles had other responsibilities that demanded his time.

75. Interview with David Freeman, June 30, 1986; Adam Yarmolinsky, unpublished draft of autobiography, chap. 7; Ashmore, *Unseasonable Truths,* 383–84.

76. Board Minutes, November 15, 1956, Box 84, FR-PUL.

77. Board Minutes, February 20 and November 20, 1957, Box 64, FR-PUL.

78. RMH to Mother and Father, May 1, 1956, WJH-BCA; and RMH to William Benton, June 8, 1961, Box 167, Folder 5, WB-UC, on Griswold.

79. Unpublished Yarmolinsky autobiography, chap. 7, explores these ideas.

80. Harry Kalven, Review of *Freedom, Education, and the Fund, Journal of Legal Education* 10 (1957): 141.

81. RMH, "Recommendations on the Basic Issues," February 6, 1957, Box 60, FR-PUL, on biographies.

82. Leonard W. Levy, *Emergence of a Free Press* (New York: Oxford University Press, 1985), vii.

83. Mortimer Adler to RMH, October 9, 1957, Box 60, FR-PUL, with an analysis of discussions.

84. Hallock Hoffman to RMH, October 15, 1957, Box 60, FR-PUL.

85. Buchanan to RMH, January 2, 1958, Box 64, FR-PUL.

86. RMH, Report and Recommendations to the Board, May 6, 1958, Box 64, FR-PUL.

87. Board Minutes, May 21, 1958, Box 64, FR-PUL.

88. RMH to Douglas, December 2, 1958, Box 64, FR-PUL.

89. Reeves, *Freedom and the Foundation,* 275.

90. Board Minutes, May 20, 1959, Box 12, FR-PUL. See also Ashmore, *Unseasonable Truths,* 390–92.

91. RMH, Memorandum on Basic Ideas in Civil Liberties, May 23, 1956, Box 65, FR-PUL.

92. Andrews, *Philanthropic Foundations,* 297, on foundation activity in this field.

CHAPTER TWELVE

1. Scott Buchanan to Stringfellow Barr, August 2, 1959, no. 540, Folder 2, SB-HU.

2. Buchanan to Barr, August 2, 1959.

3. W. H. Ferry Oral History, 1972, pp. 105–7, FFA.

4. Harry S. Ashmore, *Unseasonable Truths: The Life of Robert Maynard Hutchins* (Boston: Little, Brown & Company, 1989), is a well researched account by a center participant. See also Frank K. Kelly, *Court of Reason: Robert Hutchins and the Fund for the Republic* (New York: Free Press, 1981), for an extensively detailed

but different perspective, also by a center participant. Finally, see Mary Ann Dzuback, "Robert M. Hutchins, 1899–1977: Portrait of an Educator" (Ph.D. thesis, Columbia University, 1987), for a less detailed but more analytical examination of Hutchins and the center. Other sources will be so noted.

5. Ashmore, *Unseasonable Truths,* 407, 406.

6. Hutchins' desire in his last months to create a memorial to Douglas resulted in Harry S. Ashmore, ed., *The William O. Douglas Inquiry into the State of Individual Freedom* (Boulder, Colo.: Westview Press, 1979).

7. Letter to John J. McCloy and Henry T. Heald from Elmo Roper et al., September 5, 1961; letter to John J. McCloy from same, December 12, 1961; letter from Henry T. Heald to Elmo Roper, February 21, 1962; letter from RMH to Henry T. Heald, October 25, 1962; all in Office of the President, Henry T. Heald Papers, Box 5, Folder 60, FFA.

8. Ashmore, *Unseasonable Truths,* 420–22.

9. The thirty-seventh draft with Tugwell's commentary was published in *Center Magazine (CM)* 3 (September/October 1970): 10–49.

10. Elisabeth Mann Borgese, "A Ten-Year Struggle for a Law of the Sea," *CM* 10 (May/June 1977): 52–62.

11. RMH, *The Two Faces of Federalism: An Outline of an Argument about Pluralism, Unity, and Law* (Santa Barbara, Calif.: Center for the Study of Democratic Institutions [CSDI], 1961).

12. Buchanan to Stringfellow Barr, August 15, 1964, no. 540, Folder 6, SB-HU (by permission of the Houghton Library).

13. RMH, "Dissenting Opinion as a Creative Art," *Saturday Review* 44 (August 12, 1961): 12, 35–36; "Center Symposium: Limits of Dissent," *CM* 1 (November/December 1968): 3.

14. RMH, "Emerging Problems in the Law: Jurisprudence," March 24, 1961, pp. 4, 8, 9, CSDI-UCSB.

15. RMH, "The Limits of Law and Order," *CM* 3 (May/June 1971): 3.

16. RMH, "The New Supreme Court," *CM* 5 (September/October 1972): 13, 14, 22. See also "The Constitution under Strain," *CM* 7 (March/April 1974): 43–52, for a center discussion of the Court's recent decisions.

17. RMH, "The Issues," in *The University in America* (Santa Barbara, Calif.: CSDI Occasional Paper, 1967), 7.

18. These drafts are in the center files. See, for example, RMH, "The Issues in Education," March 2, 1964, and "A Study of a National Policy For Education," March 3, 1964, CSDI-UCSB.

19. RMH, *The Learning Society* (New York: Frederick A. Praeger, 1968).

20. Kennedy was U.S. attorney general in the early 1960s, Clark's psychology research influenced the *Brown* decision, Lewis had conducted ethnographic research in minority communities, and Sullivan was superintendent of the Berkeley Unified School District, responsible for its successful desegregation plan; "Ghetto Education," *CM,* Special Supplement, November 1968.

21. RMH, "Permanence and Change," *CM* 1 (January/February 1968): 3, 4.

22. RMH, "The Constitution of Public Education," *CM* 2 (July/August 1969): 8–14; "The Constitution for Public Education II," August 25, 1969; and "A Constitution for Public Education," November 24, 1969; CSDI-UCSB.

23. RMH, "The Schools Must Stay," *CM* 6 (January/February 1973): 16, 19.

24. RMH, background paper for the conference "The Public Interest in Education: Toward a Policy for the United States," March 7, 1973, p. 10, CSDI-UCSB.

25. Kelly, *Court of Reason,* 198–201, 225–36, describes these in detail.

26. Kelly, *Court of Reason,* 307–26; *Students and Society: Report on a Conference* (Santa Barbara, Calif.: CSDI Occasional Paper, December 1967).

27. Ashmore, *Unseasonable Truths,* 444–45, on Hutchins' discomfort and skepticism.

28. Interview with Harry S. Ashmore, August 14, 1984.

29. Ashmore, *Unseasonable Truths,* 439.

30. Donald McDonald, "The Liberation of Women," *CM* 5 (May/June 1972): 25–43.

31. "Follow Up: The Liberation of Women," *CM* 5 (July/August 1972): 13–20.

32. Interview with W. H. Ferry, July 26, 1986.

33. RMH to Staff, November 21, 1960, Box 137, FR-PUL.

34. Scott Buchanan to Stringfellow Barr, August 29, 1962, no. 540, Folder 5, SB-HU.

35. PR (Philip Rieff) to RMH, April 8, 1964, Box 8, RMH(AU)-UC.

36. W. H. Ferry Oral history, 1972, pp. 105–7, FFA.

37. Frank Kelly to RMH, February 3, 1966, Box 5; (PF) Ferry to RMH, August 18, 1966, and August 28, 1967, Box 3; JRS (John R. Seeley) to RMH, October 3, 1966 (and note from Ashmore to RMH on same), and August 25, 1967, Box 8; all in RMH(AU)-UC.

38. Ashmore, *Unseasonable Truths,* 461–63.

39. RMH to John R. Seeley, August 13, 1968, CSDI-UCSB, and Seeley to Fellows, October 28, 1968, Box 8, RMH(AU)-UC, for example.

40. Ferry to RMH, March 7, n.d. (ca. 1968), Box 9, Folder 14, WHF-DCA.

41. Harvey Wheeler, "The 1969 Reorganization," pp. 15, 16, Box 9, RMH-(AU)-UC.

42. RMH to Ferry, June 6, 1969, and June 4, 1969, Box 3, RMH(AU)-UC.

43. RMH to James H. Douglas, September 17, 1969, Box 3, RMH(AU)-UC.

44. Ferry to Seeley, November 22, 1967; Ferry to Seeley, August 15, 1968; Box 9, Folder 1; Ashmore to Staff, December 13, 1967, Box 9, Folder 3; WHF-DCA, on fellows' responses and Ferry's and Seeley's concerns.

45. RMH to Southern California Founding Members, July 21, 1969, CSDI-UCSB.

46. In addition to Comfort and Ritchie-Calder, these associates included Bertrand de Jouvenale, French economist; Mircea Eliade, historian of religion from the University of Chicago; Alexander King, president of the Federation of Institutes of Advanced Study in Stockholm; and Sir Arthur Lewis, vice-chancellor of the University of the West Indies. Neil Jacoby, dean of the UCLA Graduate School of Business; Stanley K. Sheinbaum, economist from the University of California at Santa Barbara; Fred Warner Neal, former journalist; Richard Bellman, mathematician from the University of Southern California; Paul Erlich, biologist from Stanford; and Karl Pribham, professor of psychiatry at Stanford, were locals who also became associate fellows. See Ashmore, *Unseasonable Truths,* 475–76.

47. Harvey Wheeler, "The 1969 Reorganization," 24–25.

48. Tugwell to RMH, March 9, 1970, Ashmore to RMH and Fellows, March 24, 1970, Cogley to RMH and Fellows, March 25, 1970, RMH to the Joint Committee on Organization, April 4, 1970, Box 31; Ashmore to RMH, December 10, 1973, and Ashmore to Senior Fellows, April 4, 1974, Box 2; RMH(AU)-UC.

49. Wheeler, "The 1969 Reorganization," 14.

50. Ashmore, *Unseasonable Truths,* 486–87.

51. This account of Moos' brief presidency is from Kelly, *Court of Reason,* 503–603, and Ashmore, *Unseasonable Truths,* 503–14.

52. Kelly, *Court of Reason,* 532–33.

53. Letter from Ralph Tyler, June 27, 1986.

54. Otis L. Graham, "Striking Up for a New World," *Reviews in American History* 11 (1983): 156, 155.

55. Ashmore, *Unseasonable Truths,* 520.

56. RMH, "The Intellectual Community," *CM* 10 (January/February 1977): 3, 7, 9.

57. Graham, "Striking Up for a New World," 155.

58. Interview with W. H. Ferry, July 26, 1986. See also Ferry, "Robert

Hutchins's Platonic Grove," *Nation* 246 (January 30, 1988): 119–22. Interview with Ralph Tyler, October 20, 1985, on Hutchins' poor personnel choices.

59. Interview with Donald McDonald, August 9, 1984; Scott Buchanan, "The Nature of the Dialogue in a Democratic Society: A Conversation," in *The Civilization of the Dialogue* (Santa Barbara, Calif.: CSDI Occasional Paper, December 1968), 32.

60. Paul Dickson, *Think Tanks* (New York: Atheneum, 1971), provides descriptions of many of these in existence in the early 1970s.

61. My principal source on the institute is Sydney Hyman, *The Aspen Idea* (Norman: University of Oklahoma Press, 1975). See also James Sloan Allen, *The Romance of Commerce and Culture: Capitalism, Modernism, and the Chicago-Aspen Crusade for Cultural Reform* (Chicago: University of Chicago Press, 1983), for its founding.

62. Interview with Preston Cutler, March 30, 1989. Our conversation helped me understand these basic differences in conceptions of scholarship as they applied to the two institutions.

63. Interview with Ralph Tyler, October 20, 1985.

64. Interview with Frank Kelly, August 15, 1984.

65. Graham, "Striking Up for a New World," 158.

66. Stanley K. Sheinbaum, "Robert Hutchins's Platonic Grove," 122–23; Harry Ashmore, in same, 123–24; Harvey Wheeler, "The Center Dialogue," in *The Civilization of the Dialogue,* 25.

67. Michael Harrington, "Robert Hutchins's Platonic Grove," 124.

68. Kelly, *Court of Reason;* Ashmore, *Unseasonable Truths.*

69. Michael Harrington, "Robert Hutchins's Platonic Grove," 124.

EPILOGUE

1. Ralph W. Tyler Oral History, p. 154, interviewed by Malca Chall, University of California at Berkeley, Regional Oral History Office, the Bancroft Office, 1987, copy in UC.

2. Will Hutchins to RMH, October 25, 1937, Box 72, Folder 2, RMH(A)-UC.

3. RMH to Bill Benton, January 4, 1966, Box 168, Folder 3, WB-UC.

4. Thanks to Scott Fletcher for this insight in a different context.

5. Edward Shils, "Robert Maynard Hutchins," *American Scholar* 59 (1990): 235.

6. RMH, "The Administrator," in *The Works of the Mind,* ed. Robert B. Heywood (Chicago: University of Chicago Press, 1947), 151.

7. Will Hutchins to RMH, February 9, 1943, WJH-BCA.

8. *General Education in a Free Society: Report of the Harvard Committee* (Cambridge, Mass.: Harvard University Press, 1945), 4.

9. *General Education in a Free Society,* 9, 12.

10. Interview with Preston Cutler, March 30, 1989.

11. Harry S. Ashmore, *Unseasonable Truths: The Life of Robert Maynard Hutchins* (Boston: Little, Brown & Company, 1989), 304–5.

12. Leon Botstein, "The Liberal Learning," *Center Magazine* 10 (March/April 1977): 22; and "Wisdom Reconsidered: Robert Maynard Hutchins' *The Higher Learning in America* Revisited," in *Philosophy for Education,* ed. Seymour Fox (Jerusalem: Van Leer Jerusalem Foundation, 1983), 17–38.

13. Interview with Ralph W. Nicholas, September 19, 1990, and recent catalogs from the University of Chicago.

14. Clark Kerr, *The Uses of the University* (New York: Harper & Row, 1966 [1964]), 33.

15. Shils, "Robert Maynard Hutchins," 235.

16. Maxine Greene, "Wanted: A Philosophy of American Education," *School and Society* 83 (1956): 165.

S O U R C E S

MANUSCRIPT COLLECTIONS AND UNPUBLISHED MATERIALS

Berea College Archives. Berea College, Berea, Kentucky.
  Francis S. Hutchins Papers.
  William James Hutchins Papers.

Butler Library. Columbia University, New York, New York.
  Oral History Collection.

Dartmouth College Archives. Dartmouth College, Hanover, New Hampshire.
  Wilbur H. Ferry Papers.

Ford Foundation Archives. Ford Foundation, New York, New York.
  General Correspondence.
  Grant Files.
  Office of the President, Papers of H. Rowan Gaither.
  Office of the President, Papers of Henry T. Heald.
  Oral History Transcripts: Bernard Berelson, Philip N. Coombs, Chester C. Davis, Alvin C. Eurich, Clarence H. Faust, W. H. Ferry, Bernard L. Gadieux, Robert M. Hutchins, Milton Katz, George F. Kennan.
  Unpublished Staff and Consultant Reports.

Houghton Library. Harvard University, Cambridge, Massachusetts.
  Scott Buchanan Papers.

Institute for Philosophical Research. Chicago, Illinois.
  Mortimer J. Adler Files.

Joseph Regenstein Library, Special Collections. University of Chicago, Chicago, Illinois.
  Archival Biographical Files.
  William Benton Papers.
  Dean of the College Records.
  Louis Gottschalk Papers.
  Robert M. Hutchins Papers, Addenda, Unprocessed Addenda.
  William T. Hutchinson Papers.
  Charles Hubbard Judd Papers.
  Frank H. Knight Papers.
  Charles E. Merriam Papers.
  John U. Nef Papers.
  Office of the Vice-President Papers.

Presidents' Papers, 1925–50.
Robert Redfield Papers.
Harold H. Swift Papers.
Louis Wirth Papers.

Mudd Library. Princeton University, Princeton, New Jersey.
Fund for the Republic Papers.

Oberlin College Archives. Oberlin College Library, Oberlin, Ohio.
Walter K. Bailey Papers.
Faculty Records.
Kemper Fullerton Papers.
Presidents' Papers, Henry Churchill King.
Logan Omer Osborn Papers.
Student Life Memorabilia (Scrapbooks, Albums, Diaries).
Student Records.

Rockefeller Archive Center. Pocantico Hills, New York.
General Education Board Files.
Laura Spelman Rockefeller Memorial Files.
Rockefeller Foundation Archives.

Yale University Library, Manuscripts and Archives. New Haven, Connecticut.
James Rowland Angell, Presidential Records.
Chester Bowles Papers.
Charles E. Clark Papers.
Jerome N. Frank Papers.
Institute of Human Relations Files.
Secretarial Records.
Yale Corporation Records.
Yale University Law School, Faculty, Governing Board and Board of Permanent Officers' Minutes.

University of California at Santa Barbara Library, Special Collections. Santa Barbara, California.
Robert M. Hutchins Center for the Study of Democratic Institutions Papers: Audiotapes, Files, and Videotapes.

INTERVIEWS

Mortimer J. Adler, May 25, 1985, Chicago, Illinois.

Mark Ashin, February 17, 1989, Chicago, Illinois.

Harry S. Ashmore, August 14, 1984, Santa Barbara, California.

Preston Cutler, March 30, 1989, Palo Alto, California.

Thomas I. Emerson, June 21, 1988, by telephone.

Wilbur H. Ferry, May 6, 1986, New York, New York, and July 26, 1986, Scarsdale, New York.

David Freeman, June 30, 1986, New York, New York.

Francis S. Hutchins, January 8, 1985, Berea, Kentucky.

Barry D. Karl, November 30, 1988, Chicago, Illinois.

Frank K. Kelly, August 15, 1984, Santa Barbara, California.

Edward H. Levi, October 26, 1988, Chicago, Illinois.

Milton Mayer, August 19, 1984, Carmel, California.

Donald McDonald, August 9, 1984, Santa Barbara, California.

Florence Mischel, October 1, 1984, New York, New York.

John U. Nef, July 22, 1986, Washington, D.C.

Ralph W. Nicholas, September 19, 1990, by telephone.

Elizabeth N. Paepcke, February 16, 1989, Chicago, Illinois.

John Henry Schlegel, July 7, 1989, by telephone.

Joseph Schwab, August 10, 1984, Santa Barbara, California.

Ralph W. Tyler, October 20, 1985, New York, New York.

MAJOR PUBLICATIONS BY ROBERT M. HUTCHINS

The Conflict in Education in a Democratic Society. New York: Harper & Brothers, 1953.

The Democratic Dilemma. Uppsala, Sweden: Almquist & Wiksells Boktyckeri, 1951.

Education for Freedom. Baton Rouge: Louisiana State University Press, 1943.

Freedom, Education, and the Fund: Essays and Addresses, 1946–1956. New York: Meridian Books, 1956.

The Great Conversation: The Substance of a Liberal Education. Chicago: Encyclopaedia Britannica, 1952.

The Higher Learning in America. New Haven: Yale University Press, 1936.

The Learning Society. New York: Frederick A. Praeger, 1968.

No Friendly Voice. Chicago: University of Chicago Press, 1936.

St. Thomas and the World State. Milwaukee: Marquette University Press, 1949.

Some Observations on American Education. Cambridge: At the University Press, 1956.

The University of Utopia. Chicago: University of Chicago Press, 1953.
Zuckerlandl! New York: Grove Press, 1968.

A NOTE ON SOURCES

Initially, this study was to be an intellectual biography. After reading all of Hutchins' published work and many of his speeches, after talking with people who knew him, reading recollections about him, comparing him with other university leaders, and spending months reading his and others' papers, I concluded that an intellectual biography of Hutchins would be a short, and probably not very interesting, book. Hutchins was a man with a few ideas. One can track them easily through his major books and his numerous essays, most of them based on speeches he delivered over the course of fifty-six years as an educator. Beyond the list and notes in this study, Reuben Frodin, "Bibliography of Robert M. Hutchins, 1925–1950," *Journal of General Education* 4 (1950); 303–24, and Mary Ann Dzuback, "Robert M. Hutchins, 1899–1977: Portrait of an Educator" (Ph.D. dissertation, Columbia University, 1987), 494–530, are the most complete bibliographies of his work, short of the list possessed by the University of Chicago, Joseph Regenstein Library, Special Collections.

When I began work on the dissertation, there was no other biography of Hutchins. When I finished three years later, there still was no published biography. Unsatisfied with the dissertation, I decided to pursue a complete revision, using some of the framework of the thesis but shifting the focus, specifically to Hutchins' leadership of the University of Chicago. Searching for models of how to reorient the work, I turned to a number of biographies.

Geraldine Jonçich's *The Sane Positivist: A Biography of Edward L. Thorndike* (Middletown: Wesleyan University Press, 1968) combines intellectual and social biography in an exhaustive exploration of the development of Thorndike's ideas in a period of social change. She describes his initiation into the study of psychology at a time when psychology as a discipline was becoming distinct from philosophy and analyzes how he applied his ideas to curriculum and pedagogy to develop a science of education. Although I found Hutchins' intellectual work less richly complex and influential than Thorndike's, Jonçich's study emphasized the importance of locating ideas in a larger context and the role of the modern university in shaping twentieth-century scholarship. Ellen Condliffe Lagemann's *A Generation of Women: Education in the Lives of Progressive Reformers*

(Cambridge: Harvard University Press, 1979) makes a strong case for examining closely the ways family, community, other institutions, and particular individuals contribute to the shaping of the self. Her work was invaluable for my exploration of Hutchins' early life and career.

Jonçich's and Lagemann's studies oriented me in particular ways to Hutchins' life and experiences, but two other works served as strong models for framing the biography. The simplicity of Edmund S. Morgan's *The Puritan Dilemma: The Story of John Winthrop* (Boston: Little, Brown & Company, 1958) was not only appealing but also indicative of how to reconstruct the life of a man who was at the center of his community, who had clear and definite ideas about leadership, and who was vested with a mission. Hugh Hawkins' *Between Harvard and America: The Educational Leadership of Charles W. Eliot* (New York: Oxford University Press, 1972) is a sensitive portrayal of Eliot's administration of Harvard University throughout the latter half of the nineteenth century. My portrait of Hutchins is quite different from Hawkins' of Eliot. But when I decided to change the focus of my study of Hutchins, I found enlightening Hawkins' attention to the difficulties Eliot faced with faculty, trustees, and the public in his efforts to make Harvard into a modern university.

Continuing interest in Robert Hutchins has produced a variety of studies. The most notable is Harry S. Ashmore's *Unseasonable Truths: The Life of Robert Maynard Hutchins* (Boston: Little, Brown & Company, 1989), a detailed, chronological account of Hutchins' life and career by an associate. Frank K. Kelly's *Court of Reason: Robert Hutchins and the Fund for the Republic* (New York: Free Press, 1981), also by an associate, focuses on Hutchins' work at the fund and the Center for the Study of Democratic Institutions.

In addition, there are numerous dissertations. The most useful for my understanding of Hutchins include Brian Alair Cole, "Hutchins and His Critics, 1936–1953" (Ph.D. thesis, University of Maryland, 1976), an examination of the critical response to Hutchins' *Higher Learning in America* and later lectures; Amy Apfel Kass, "Radical Conservatives for a Liberal Education" (Ph.D. thesis, Johns Hopkins University, 1973), an exploration of the group of educators, including Mortimer Adler, Stringfellow Barr, Scott Buchanan, Hutchins, and Richard McKeon, advocating a liberal arts curriculum in the great books and how their ideas shaped various programs in institutions; Harold Ravitch, "Robert Maynard Hutchins: Philosopher of Education" (Ph.D. thesis, University of Southern California, 1980), an analysis of subtle changes in Hutchins' writings after he left the University of Chicago; and Lloyd Everett Stein, "Hutchins of Chicago: Philosopher-Administrator" (Ed.D. thesis, University of Massachusetts, 1971), a description of Hutchins' presidency of the University of Chicago.

Autobiographies and biographies of Hutchins' friends and colleagues are illuminating. Keeping in mind James Olney's theoretical essay in *Metaphors of Self: The Meaning of Autobiography* (Princeton: Princeton University Press, 1972), which suggests that autobiography is a means of imposing order on the past in the process of reconstructing the self, written from a particular point of view that can be both limiting and enlightening, I have found many of the autobiographies quite revealing. Mortimer J. Adler's *Philosopher at Large: An Intellectual Autobiography* (New York: Macmillan, 1977) has probably been the most useful for its scope and detail, as Hutchins and Adler were colleagues and friends for fifty years, and Adler's influence on Hutchins' thinking about higher education and culture is undisputed. In addition, William O. Douglas, *Go East, Young Man: The Early Years* (New York: Dell Publishing Company, 1974); David E. Lilienthal, *The Atomic Energy Years, 1945–1950,* vol. 2 of *The Journals of David E. Lilienthal,* 7 vols. (New York: Harper & Row, 1964–83); John U. Nef, *Search for Meaning: The Autobiography of a Nonconformist* (Washington, D.C.: Public Affairs Press, 1973); and T. V. Smith, *A Nonexistent Man: An Autobiography* (Austin: University of Texas Press, 1962), all offer fascinating cameos of Hutchins. Taken together, they provide a multidimensional picture of a man of great strengths and significant weaknesses.

Biographies of Hutchins' contemporaries have been important sources for understanding his relationships and times. Gilbert A. Harrison, *The Enthusiast: A Life of Thornton Wilder* (New Haven: Ticknor & Fields, 1983); Linda Simon, *Thornton Wilder: His World* (New York: Doubleday & Company, 1979); Sidney Hyman, *The Lives of William Benton* (Chicago: University of Chicago Press, 1969); and W. A. Swanberg, *Luce and His Empire* (New York: Charles Scribner's Sons, 1972), are studies of men who shared collegiate experiences with Hutchins and with whom he had lifelong connections.

The biographies, memoirs, and essays of university leaders who introduced innovations in the same period Hutchins was active at the University of Chicago offer useful comparisons. Reuben A. Holden's portrait of James Rowland Angell in *Profiles and Portraits of Yale University Presidents* (Freeport, Me.: Bond Wheelright Company, 1968), George

Wilson Pierson's description in *Yale: The University College,* vol. 2 of *Yale: College and University, 1871–1937,* 2 vols. (New Haven: Yale University Press, 1952 and 1955), and James Rowland Angell, *American Education: Addresses and Articles* (New Haven: Yale University Press, 1937); Cynthia Stokes Brown, ed., *Alexander Meiklejohn: Teacher of Freedom* (Berkeley, Calif.: Meiklejohn Civil Liberties Institute, 1981), G. C. Sellery, *Some Ferments at Wisconsin, 1901–1947: Memories and Reflections* (Madison: University of Wisconsin Press, 1960), and Alexander Meiklejohn, *The Experimental College* (New York: Harper & Brothers, 1932); James Bryant Conant, *My Several Lives: Memoirs of a Social Inventor* (New York: Harper & Row, 1970), and *Education in a Divided World* (Cambridge: Harvard University Press, 1948); James Gray, *The University of Minnesota* (Minneapolis: University of Minnesota Press, 1951), Lotus Delta Coffman, *The State University, Its Work and Problems: A Selection from Addresses Delivered between 1921 and 1933* (Minneapolis: University of Minnesota Press, 1934), and *Freedom through Education* (Minneapolis: University of Minnesota Press, 1939), are such works.

One of the challenges in reconstructing Hutchins' life has been to articulate the role his family and community played in shaping his predilections, his thinking about education, and his leadership qualities. The literature on the relationship between evangelical Protestantism and progressivism that was generally helpful included Henry May, *Protestant Churchs and Industrial America* (New York: Octagon Books, 1963); William R. Hutchison, *The Modernist Impulse in American Protestantism* (Cambridge: Harvard University Press, 1976); Bruce Kuklick, *Churchmen and Philosophers: From Jonathan Edwards to John Dewey* (New Haven: Yale University Press, 1985); Louise L. Stevenson, *Scholarly Means to Evangelical Ends: The New Haven Scholars and the Transformation of Higher Learning in America, 1830–1890* (Baltimore: Johns Hopkins University Press, 1986); and Robert M. Crunden, *Ministers of Reform: The Progressives' Achievement in American Civilization, 1889–1920* (Urbana: University of Illinois Press, 1984 [1982]). Lawrence A. Cremin, *American Education: The Metropolitan Experience, 1876–1980* (New York: Harper & Row, 1988), is an invaluable work that helped me to place Hutchins' family background and his life in the broader context of education in the twentieth century.

The work on the transition in colleges from nineteenth-century piety to twentieth-century progressivism, including Thomas Le Duc, *Piety and Intellect at Amherst College, 1865–1912* (New York: Arno Press, 1969

[1946]), and George E. Peterson, *The New England College in the Age of the University* (Amherst: Amherst College Press, 1964), indicate that change at Oberlin was not an isolated occurrence. For understanding Oberlin College, I found most helpful Robert Samuel Fletcher, *A History of Oberlin College: From Its Founding through the Civil War,* 2 vols. (Oberlin: Oberlin College, 1943); John Barnard, *From Evangelicalism to Progressivism at Oberlin College, 1866–1917* (Columbus: Ohio State University Press, 1969); and Donald M. Love, *Henry Churchill King of Oberlin* (New Haven: Yale University Press, 1956).

The work on Yale College and University continues to grow. George Wilson Pierson's *Yale: College and University, 1871–1937* has been augmented by his study *The Education of American Leaders: Contributions of U.S. Colleges and Universities* (New York: Frederick A. Praeger, 1969), with comparisons between Yale and other institutions, and *A Yale Book of Numbers: Historical Statistics of the College and University, 1701–1976* (New Haven: Yale University Press, 1983). Brooks Mather Kelley, *Yale: A History* (New Haven: Yale University Press, 1974), is the standard single-volume history of Yale. Henry Seidel Canby's *American Memoir* (Boston: Houghton Mifflin Company, 1947) is a colorful account of college life at Yale. Marcia Graham Synnott, *The Half-Opened Door: Discrimination in Admissions at Harvard, Yale, and Princeton* (Westport, Ct.: Greenwood Press, 1979), and Dan A. Oren, *Joining the Club: A History of Jews and Yale* (New Haven: Yale University Press, 1985), provide useful analyses of the ways Yale dealt with an increasingly diverse group of students in the same period in which Hutchins was a student and an administrator.

For exploring legal realism as an intellectual, educational, and professional movement in academic law, I found to be generally informative Lawrence M. Friedman, *A History of American Law* (rev. ed.; New York: Simon & Schuster, 1985); Robert Stevens, *Law School: Legal Education in America from the 1850s to the 1980s* (Chapel Hill: University of North Carolina Press, 1983); Gerald L. Fetner, "Counsel to the Situation: The Lawyer as Social Engineer, 1900–1945" (Ph.D. thesis, Brown University, 1973); David E. Ingersoll, "American Legal Realism and Sociological Jurisprudence: The Methodological Roots of a Science of Law," *Journal of the History of the Behavioral Sciences* 17 (1981): 490–503; and John W. Johnson, *American Legal Culture, 1908–1940* (Westport, Ct.: Greenwood Press, 1981). More specifically, William Twining, *Karl Llewellyn and the Legal Realist Movement* (Norman: University of Oklahoma Press, 1985 [1973]), provides a rich biography of one of Hutchins' early law teachers.

John Henry Schlegel, "American Legal Realism and Empirical Social Science: From the Yale Experience," *Buffalo Law Review* 28 (1979): 459–586, and "American Legal Realism and Empirical Social Science: The Singular Case of Underhill Moore," *Buffalo Law Review* 29 (1980): 195–323, and Laura Kalman, *Legal Realism at Yale, 1927–1960* (Chapel Hill: University of North Carolina Press, 1986), are most useful for the perspectives the authors bring to bear (both have legal training) and for their differing interpretations of Hutchins' brief leadership of the Yale Law School.

The general historical frameworks provided by Frederick Rudolph, *The American College and University: A History* (New York: Vintage Books, 1962), Laurence R. Veysey, *The Emergence of the American University* (Chicago: University of Chicago Press, 1965), Richard Hofstadter and Walter P. Metzger, *The Development of Academic Freedom in the United States* (New York: Columbia University Press, 1955), and Konrad Jarausch, ed., *The Transformation of Higher Learning, 1860–1930: Expansion, Diversification, Social Opening, and Professionalization in England, Germany, Russia, and the United States* (Chicago: University of Chicago Press, 1983), helped me to view what was occurring at the University of Chicago in light of larger changes in higher educational institutions.

Similarly, the development of the academic disciplines in universities in the late nineteenth and the twentieth century is explored in such works as Alexandra Oleson and John Voss, eds., *The Organization of Knowledge in Modern America, 1860–1920* (Baltimore: Johns Hopkins University Press, 1979), Edward A. Purcell, Jr., *The Crisis of Democratic Theory: Scientific Naturalism and the Problem of Value* (Lexington: University Press of Kentucky, 1973), and Roger L. Geiger, *To Advance Knowledge: The Growth of American Research Universities, 1900–1940* (New York: Oxford University Press, 1986), which examine how conceptions of scholarship changed within the modern university.

Institutional histories of the University of Chicago, particularly up to the Burton years, include Thomas W. Goodspeed, *The Story of the University of Chicago, 1890–1925* (Chicago: University of Chicago Press, 1925), and Richard J. Storr, *Harper's University: The Beginnings* (Chicago: University of Chicago Press, 1966); both are useful accounts, but neither is a critical study. Thorsten Veblen's *The Higher Learning in America: A Memorandum on the Conduct of Universities by Businessmen* (New York: Sagamore Press, 1957 [1918] is not a history but is quite critical of the management of the university. William Michael Murphy and D. J. R.

Bruckner, eds., *The Idea of the University of Chicago: Selections from the Papers of the First Eight Chief Executives of the University of Chicago from 1891 to 1975* (Chicago: University of Chicago Press, 1976), offers its presidents' perceptions of the university and its mission. And Floyd W. Reeves et al., *The University of Chicago Survey,* 12 vols. (Chicago: University of Chicago Press, 1933), provides an invaluable examination of much of the university's activities, of students, faculty, and administration in its first four decades. More critical histories of the University of Chicago are forthcoming in several dissertations and will be important additions to the scholarship.

The first essay I encountered that raised the issue of an urban university's relationship to the city in the development of scholarly resources is Douglas Sloan's "Science in New York City, 1867–1907," *Isis* 71 (1980): 35–76. There is a small, but rich, body of work exploring the University of Chicago's relationship to the city of Chicago, including Helen Lefkowitz Horowitz, *Culture & the City: Cultural Philanthropy in Chicago from the 1880s to 1917* (Lexington: University Press of Kentucky, 1976); Kathleen D. McCarthy, *Noblesse Oblige: Charity & Cultural Philanthropy in Chicago, 1849–1929* (Chicago: University of Chicago Press, 1982); and Steven J. Diner, *A City and Its Universities: Public Policy in Chicago, 1892–1919* (Chapel Hill: University of North Carolina Press, 1980).

Clifford Geertz's conception of "thick description," proffered in *The Interpretation of Cultures* (New York: Basic Books, 1973), has influenced scholars in a number of disciplines, including history. I have found it a particularly useful orientation for examining academic culture as perceived by faculty members across the university and within particular departments. A number of specific works figured in my thinking about the University of Chicago's academic culture prior to and under Hutchins' leadership. Walter Metzger, "The Academic Profession in the United States," in *The Academic Profession: National, Disciplinary, and Institutional Settings,* ed. Burton R. Clark (Berkeley: University of California Press, 1987), 123–208; Bruce Kuklick, *The Rise of American Philosophy: Cambridge, Massachusetts, 1860–1930* (New Haven: Yale University Press, 1977), and Charles Morris, *The Pragmatic Movement in American Philosophy* (New York: George Braziller, 1970), belong in this group.

More specifically, Darnell Rucker, *The Chicago Pragmatists* (Minneapolis: University of Minnesota Press, 1969); Melvin W. Reder, "Chicago Economics: Permanence and Change," *Journal of Economic Literature* 20 (1982): 1–38; Martin Bulmer, *The Chicago School of Sociology:*

Institutionalization, Diversity, and the Rise of Sociological Research (Chicago: University of Chicago Press, 1984); and Barry D. Karl, *Charles E. Merriam and the Study of Politics* (Chicago: University of Chicago Press, 1974), have been important for understanding the developments in different departments. Edward S. Shils, "Robert Maynard Hutchins," *American Scholar* 59 (1990): 211–35, is a telling portrait that reveals as much about Shils as about Hutchins and the university.

The literature on college students has enabled me to view more critically Hutchins' vision of undergraduate education. Burton J. Bledstein, *The Culture of Professionalism: The Middle Class and the Development of Higher Education in America* (New York: W. W. Norton & Company, 1976); David O. Levine, *The American College and the Culture of Aspiration* (Ithaca: Cornell University Press, 1986); Colin B. Burke, "The Expansion of American Higher Education," in *The Transformation of Higher Learning,* ed. Konrad Jarausch, 108–30; and, particularly, Harold S. Wechsler, *The Qualified Student: A History of Selective College Admission in America* (New York: John Wiley & Sons, 1977), explore the growth of middle-class college enrollment and, in Wechsler's work, how institutions responded. Lynn D. Gordon, *Gender and Higher Education in the Progressive Era* (New Haven: Yale University Press, 1990), is an insightful and illuminating analysis of the experiences of women students and the culture they created at a number of colleges, including the University of Chicago.

General examinations of the philosophical basis of a liberal arts curriculum provide an intellectual context for viewing Hutchins' ideas. Bruce A. Kimball's *Orators & Philosophers: A History of the Idea of Liberal Education* (New York: Teachers College Press, 1986) is a fascinating account of the transformation of the idea. Leon Botstein's "Wisdom Reconsidered: Robert Maynard Hutchins' *The Higher Learning in America* Revisited," in *Philosophy for Education,* ed. Seymour Fox (Jerusalem: Van Leer Jerusalem Foundation, 1983), 17–38, makes an argument for the importance of providing a liberal education, though Botstein's idea of liberal learning is more comprehensive than Hutchins'.

A number of works explore the incorporation of liberal education or of general education in various collegiate experiments. These include R. Freeman Butts, *The College Charts Its Course: Historical Conceptions and Current Proposals* (New York: McGraw-Hill, 1939); Russell Thomas, *The Search for a Common Learning: General Education, 1800–1960* (New York: McGraw-Hill, 1962); Daniel Bell, *The Reforming of General Educa-*

tion: The Columbia College Experience in Its National Setting (New York: Columbia University Press, 1966); and Frederick Rudolph, *Curriculum: A History of the American Undergraduate Course of Study since 1636* (San Francisco: Jossey-Bass, 1977). Studies that describe the University of Chicago's undergraduate program have been very useful. Chauncey Samuel Boucher, *The Chicago College Plan* (Chicago: University of Chicago Press, 1935), and F. Champion Ward, ed., *The Idea and Practice of General Education: An Account of the College of the University of Chicago* (Chicago: University of Chicago Press, 1950), particularly the essay by Reuben Frodin, "Very Simple, but Thoroughgoing," pp. 25–99, are carefully detailed accounts.

In his last decade at the University of Chicago and in the remaining years of his life, Hutchins translated his vision of democratic culture, education, and politics into a variety of activities. Margaret A. Blanchard, "The Hutchins Commission, the Press, and the Responsibility Concept," *Journalism Monographs* 49 (May 1977), is the most detailed study of the Commission on the Freedom of the Press. William L. Rivers, Wilbur Schramm, and Clifford G. Christians, in *Responsibility in Mass Communication* (3d ed.; New York: Harper & Row, 1980), explore its implications.

Books describing some aspects of Hutchins' work with the atomic scientists include Arthur Holly Compton, *Atomic Quest: A Personal Narrative* (New York: Oxford University Press, 1956); Alice Kimball Smith, *A Peril and a Hope: The Scientists' Movement in America, 1945–1947* (Chicago: University of Chicago Press, 1965); and Richard Rhodes, *The Making of the Atomic Bomb* (New York: Simon & Schuster, 1986).

George E. Arnstein, "The Great Books Program and Its Educational Philosophy" (Ph.D. thesis, University of California, 1953), and Herman Kogan, *The Great EB: The Story of the Encyclopaedia Britannica* (Chicago: University of Chicago Press, 1958), describe the EB and the great books program. By far, the most critical analysis of Hutchins' involvement in both organizations is James Sloan Allen's *The Romance of Commerce and Culture: Capitalism, Modernism, and the Chicago-Apen Crusade for Cultural Reform* (Chicago: University of Chicago Press, 1983).

Histories of philanthropic foundations have provided some context for Hutchins' efforts to shape American culture through his work in the foundation world after he left the University of Chicago. Standard histories of foundations include F. Emerson Andrews, *Philanthropic Foundations* (New York: Russell Sage Foundation, 1956); Raymond B. Fosdick, *Adventure in Giving: The Story of the General Education Board* (New York:

Harper & Row, 1962); Waldemar A. Nielsen, *The Big Foundations* (New York: Columbia University Press, 1972); and the more critical work of Ben Whitaker, *The Foundations: An Anatomy of Philanthropy and Society* (London: Eyre Methuen, 1974), and Robert F. Arnove, ed., *Philanthropy and Cultural Imperialism: The Foundations at Home and Abroad* (Boston: G. K. Hall, 1980).

Ellen Condliffe Lagemann's studies of the Carnegie Foundation and the Carnegie Corporation, *Private Power for the Public Good: A History of the Carnegie Foundation for the Advancement of Teaching* (Middletown: Wesleyan University Press, 1983), and particularly, *The Politics of Knowledge: The Carnegie Corporation, Philanthropy, and Public Policy* (Middletown: Wesleyan University Press, 1989), present marked contrasts to the ways Hutchins dispensed foundation funds and pursued cultural, educational, and policy problems through the Ford Foundation and the Fund for the Republic. Both studies raise critical questions about the agenda of foundations, particularly when their activities influence public policymaking.

Books that focus more specifically on Hutchins' activities include Dwight Macdonald, *The Ford Foundation: The Men and the Millions* (New York: Reynal & Company, 1956); Paul Woodring, *Investment in Innovation: An Historical Appraisal of the Fund for the Advancement of Education* (Boston: Little, Brown & Company, 1970); Dennis C. Buss, "The Ford Foundation in Public Education: Emergent Patterns," in *Philanthropy and Cultural Imperialism,* ed. Robert F. Arnove, 331–62; and John Walker Powell, *Channels of Learning: The Story of Educational Television* (Washington, D.C.: Public Affairs Press, 1962).

Thomas C. Reeves, *Freedom and the Foundation: The Fund for the Republic in the Era of McCarthyism* (New York: Alfred A. Knopf, 1969), provides a critical but sympathetic portrayal of Hutchins' support of the fund programs in civil liberties and civil rights as well as his shift to discussion of the basic issues. Frank Kelly, *Court of Reason,* explores in great detail similar territory but with less analysis; Kelly covers the remaining eight years of the fund's and Hutchins' life. Harry S. Ashmore, *Unseasonable Truths,* devotes nearly half of the biography to the last twenty-seven years of Hutchins' career. It is by far the most comprehensive account of Hutchins' leadership of the fund and the Center for the Study of Democratic Institutions.

I N D E X